W9-CGT-352

AFRICAN AMERICAN PIONEERS OF SOCIOLOGY: A CRITICAL HISTORY

In *African American Pioneers of Sociology*, Pierre Saint-Arnaud examines the lasting contributions that African Americans have made to the field of sociology. Arguing that social science is anything but a neutral construct, he defends the radical stances taken by early African American sociologists from unfair criticism by considering the racist historical context of the time in which these influential works were produced.

Examining key figures such as W.E.B. Du Bois, Edward Franklin Frazier, Charles Spurgeon Johnson, Horace Roscoe Cayton, J.G. St Clair Drake, and Oliver Cromwell Cox, Saint-Arnaud reveals the ways in which these authors' radical views on race, gender, religion, and class shaped the emerging academic discipline of sociology. Faithfully and elegantly translated from the original French, *African American Pioneers of Sociology* is an extraordinary study of the influence of African American intellectuals and an essential work for understanding the origins and development of modern sociology.

PIERRE SAINT-ARNAUD is a professor in the Department of Sociology at Université Laval.

PETER FELDSTEIN is a Montreal-based freelance translator who specializes in literature, politics, and the sciences.

PIERRE SAINT-ARNAUD

African American Pioneers of Sociology

A Critical History

Translated by Peter Feldstein

UNIVERSITY OF TORONTO PRESS
Toronto Buffalo London

This work is a translation of *L'invention de la sociologie noire aux États-Unis d'Amérique: Essai en sociologie de la connaissance scientifique*, by Pierre Saint-Arnaud, published in 2003 by les Presses de l'Université Laval
Toronto Buffalo London
www.utppublishing.com
Printed in Canada

ISBN 978-0-8020-9122-2 (cloth)
ISBN 978-0-8020-9405-6 (paper)

Printed on acid-free paper

Library and Archives Canada Cataloguing in Publication

Saint-Arnaud, Pierre
African American pioneers of sociology : a critical history / Pierre Saint-Arnaud ; translated by Peter Feldstein.

Translation of: L'invention de la sociologie noire aux États-Unis d'Amérique.
Includes bibliographical references and index.
ISBN 978-0-8020-9122-2 (bound). ISBN 978-0-8020-9405-6 (pbk.)

1. Sociology – United States – History. 2. African American sociologists – History. 3. United States – Race relations – History. I. Feldstein, Peter, 1962– II. Title.

HM477.U6S2513 2009 301′.08996073 C2008-905030-4

University of Toronto Press acknowledges the financial assistance to its publishing program of the Canada Council for the Arts and the Ontario Arts Council.

University of Toronto Press acknowledges the financial support for its publishing activities of the Government of Canada through the Book Publishing Industry Development Program (BPIDP).

This book is dedicated to three people whom I had the good fortune to meet during my stay in Chicago – Bradley, a clerk at the University of Chicago's Joseph Regenstein Library; Jacob, a vendor of the alternative weekly StreetWise, *and Sally, a housekeeper at the establishment on East Delaware Street where I stayed – as well as to the millions of other African Americans whose individual and collective struggle for equality throughout modern history will remain an inspiration to me.*

[O]ne can and must acknowledge that science is a thoroughly historical social fact without concluding that its productions are relative to the historical and social conditions of their emergence ...

Pierre Bourdieu, *Science of Science and Reflexivity*

Your country? How came it yours? Before the Pilgrims landed we were here. Our song, our toil, our cheer, and warning have been given to this nation in blood-brotherhood. Are not these gifts worth the giving? Is not this work and striving? Would America have been America without her Negro People?

W.E.B. Du Bois, *The Souls of Black Folk*

Contents

Preface

My fundamental epistemological stance in this book is that science is anything but a neutral construct, comfortably ensconced in the realm of pure ideas, ignored and hence spared by ideology. I can therefore assume at the outset that the sociology produced by the African American pioneers is an undeniable historical social fact without thereby conceding that its content was socially determined.

When considering the two American sociological visions of race that competed for legitimacy in the twentieth century, it is essential to remember that this confrontation was structured by a racist context that extended into the academic setting. The situation was complicated, however, by the singular fact that the main scientific players, white and black, for the most part entertained personal and professional relations built upon mutual esteem and respect even as they confronted one another across the color line. Nevertheless, the most intrepid of the early African American sociologists adopted a radical stance in their effort to occupy a discursive space too long monopolized by their Anglo-American counterparts. It would be a serious mistake to represent this radicalism as an unfortunate intellectual infirmity. In fact it was one of the tools with which these sociologists laid the foundations of a different science of power relationships in the United States, one that held out hope that the social utopia of a world without oppression could one day be realized.

I wish to thank the University of Toronto Press, and in particular Virgil Duff, Executive Editor, Social Sciences, for publishing the English translation of my book and ensuring that it sees distribution to an English-speaking public. As well, I am grateful to my translator, Peter Feldstein, who rendered my prose into English with clarity, erudition, and intelligence from the first sentence to the last. My thanks to him for his exceptional artistry and professionalism. Finally, I wish to thank the Société québécoise de développement des entreprises culturelles (SODEC) for its invaluable financial assistance with the English translation of this book.

AFRICAN AMERICAN PIONEERS OF SOCIOLOGY: A CRITICAL HISTORY

Introduction

'Who now reads Spencer?' For my purposes, that opening sentence from Talcott Parsons's foundational work *The Structure of Social Action*[1] can be paraphrased as follows: Who now reads William Edward Burghardt Du Bois, who was 'not only the founder of the field [of sociology] in its modern, empirical, and theoretically sophisticated form but also arguably the founder of modern American sociology tout court'?[2] Who has even heard the names Edward Franklin Frazier, Charles Spurgeon Johnson, Horace Roscoe Cayton, or Oliver Cromwell Cox – thinkers who in the first sixty years of the twentieth century forged an authentic African American sociology and a new American approach to race relations in reaction to and on the margins of what mainstream Anglo-American sociology was concurrently putting forward? In truth, not enough of us. Our ignorance, if not indifference, furnishes an initial goal for my book: to rescue these first American sociologists of color from obscurity and reemphasize their contribution to the collective store of knowledge.

Consider Du Bois's accomplishment: far from lagging behind the social science of his time, he anticipated methods and practices still two decades in the future with his detailed 1899 empirical study *The Philadelphia Negro*; it would not be until 1918 that a similar approach would be taken by William Thomas and Florian Znaniecki in *The Polish Peasant in Europe and America*, the first great work of Anglo-American empirical sociology. Yet he faced implacable institutional ostracism from his earliest publications onward, while the sociology of race 'took shape almost as a conversation among whites.'[3] Why was he marginalized? Steven Seidman propounds a plausible sociological explanation:

> American sociology was institutionalized with control in the hands of white Anglo-Saxon middle class men. This speaks to the dominant characteristics of the profession. It describes the points of view and values that shaped sociological theory and research. Blacks or women may have been topics of sociological thinking. However, the perspectives of sociology – its basic premises, concepts, and explanations – articulated the experience, social interests, and values of predominantly White, middle class men.[4]

Du Bois's exclusion, then, obeyed the dictates of a physical system of academic control and segregation just as discriminatory as the society in which it evolved. And it was equally well the product of the deeply racist ethos that pervaded scientific thinking about race in the late nineteenth century, an ethos rooted in naturalism (among other antecedents) and integral to the normative core of Anglo-American sociology as taught and written by its 'founding fathers.' Its unbroken throughline or narrative held that black Americans were inferior to whites and that this was part of the natural – biological and/or cultural – order of things. Given the pervasiveness of this oppressive belief both in and outside of academe, it was surely inevitable that the sociology of race would bifurcate into two distinct variants, an Anglo-American one occupying the institutional center and an African American one confined to the periphery. Being disallowed from contributing to mainstream sociology and demeaned for the color of his skin, what choice did Du Bois have but to innovate in isolation? Yet it should not be imagined that the result was some sort of epistemic hermeticity between the two resulting sociologies of race, as if African American sociology arrived from another planet governed by intrinsically different norms of scientific objectivity. On the contrary, Du Bois's work, as well as that of his followers, was an attempt to bring objectivity to the field of sociology using the formal rigor and many of the same concepts as their white contemporaries.

At the same time it was an emancipatory enterprise in the strongest sense of the term. If black sociology was able to persist alongside Anglo-American sociology and challenge its scientificity, it is because its protagonists refused to internalize the image of inferiority projected on them by white intellectuals. Instead of foundering into the reflex of what the philosopher Charles Taylor calls 'self-depreciation' before the dominant group, they worked tirelessly to create an authentic emancipatory alternative, an antidote to their oppression: '[W]hite society has for generations projected a demeaning image of [blacks], which some of them have been unable to resist adopting. Their own self-depreciation, on this view, becomes one of the most potent instruments of their own oppression. Their first task ought to be to purge themselves of this imposed and destructive identity.'[5]

It would take most of the twentieth century for black American sociologists to forge a positive identity for themselves and their people and to assert their academic equality. This book covers that founding period of African American sociology, bracketed between two years that represent milestones in the process: 1896, when Du Bois commenced work on *The Philadelphia Negro*, and 1964, when Cox published his last theoretical work – the last, also, in a series of distinctive original works produced by the second generation of African American sociologists using the tools provided by Du Bois and a range of other materials. After 1964, three trends combined to usher in a new era for these scholars and their intellectual heirs: (1) ideological currents in society (the civil rights struggle, affirmative action, black power, etc.) were breaking down the walls of institutional segregation; (2) the body of African American sociological writing had, willy-nilly, acquired undeniable scientific authority; and (3) blacks' academic status was enriched accordingly, pointing the way toward equality with their white counterparts.

My purpose here is not to write a history of sociology as such, although many elements of that history will be brought into the discussion, but to make a contribution to the sociology of scientific knowledge, an approach whose legitimacy in the field of knowledge and epistemology is uncontroversial. The sociology of scientific knowledge begins by positing that science is socially inscribed within a universe of diverse and possibly mutually contradictory social imperatives. It is an eminently social and historical activity and must be comprehended with careful reference to the context from which it emerges. Imagistically, the work of the discipline can be described as that of building an arc between two poles, scientific knowledge *stricto sensu* on the one hand and sociohistorical context on the other, and of analyzing and explaining what happens along this arc. Scientific knowledge, for this purpose, is usefully described by Matalon as being 'not reducible to a collection of mutually independent laws, theories, or empirical data,' but rather 'constituting a *structure* composed of more or less consistent elements depending on the discipline.'[6] Thus, my primary task in each chapter is to elucidate, so as to better compare, the complex structures of Anglo-American and African American sociological thinking on race and race relations with reference to methods, empirical data, and above all theory; for theory, when articulated as a system, embodies the content of science par excellence, the hard core of rational knowledge.

The other pole of the arc, the context, is a multidimensional framework for the practice of science that influences it in various ways. A context may be composed, for example, of a set of economic imperatives, a given community of scientists, and/or one or more ideological representations. There is no principle that prevents the various dimensions of a context from playing off against or even contradicting each other, nor are nonlogical considerations ruled out a priori as playing an affirmative role in the scientist's interpretive act:

> It is obviously important to know the logical conditions under which an argument should, in principle, be acknowledged as a convincing proof. But it is equally necessary to know whether the effective practices of researchers and the operation of the community allow these conditions to be satisfied and, even more important, to know what is accepted as a convincing argument by certain researchers at a given point in time, which acceptance may not depend solely on logical considerations.[7]

Clarifying the fundamental stance of the sociology of scientific knowledge in this way helps to distinguish it from its close cousin, epistemology. But there is a further (and controversial) question on which a position must be taken at the outset: the question of causality. Is there a special class of factors ultimately responsible for the directions taken by science (without ignoring the specific content that distinguishes it from other ways of knowing)? Positions taken on this issue in the last thirty years have fallen along an interpretive spectrum between two extremes, termed internalism and externalism.[8] The older of these two, internalism, maintains in its purest form that science, while taking place within a multidimensional social context, remains a strictly rational process in which ideas engender other ideas independently of that context.[9] Pure externalism (regarded by many as a form of postmodernism) argues that not only the organization of science but also its content (explanatory theories) are socially determined or depend directly and intimately on social factors.[10] Along the spectrum between these two positions are scholars who, by and large, support the idea that the development of scientific knowledge is indeed influenced by a variety of social factors (private interests, circumstances of time and place, political or religious movements, ideological convictions, beliefs, prejudices) without going so far as to claim that its theoretical content (the concepts by which knowledge is structured) is necessarily and obligatorily socially determined. The proponents of this view, which I shall adopt in this book, wed openness to social explanations with unequivocal epistemological objectivism in their explanations of science.[11] Thus, I shall attempt to shed light on the genesis of the sociology of race relations with reference to both social and cognitive factors, giving precedence to the latter in attempting to account for its substantive content, its theoretical constructs as such,[12] but not ignoring the influence of the former in setting the direction of research or theorization. Among the social factors at play, I will pay special attention to ideological schemas, for an examination of ideology is indispensable to an in-depth analysis of societies:

> We must integrate the concept of ideology, but to relate it to some of the less negative functions of ideology. Unless social life has a symbolic structure, there is no way to understand how we live, do things, and project these activities in ideas, no way to understand how reality can become an idea or how real life can produce illusions; these would all be simply mystical and incomprehensible events.[13]

Ideology distorts or deforms reality, undoubtedly because it is the collective counterpart of individual consciousness, yet it is critical to an understanding of the content of cultures and the genesis of knowledge, as Fernand Dumont explains:

> Ideology is central to the study of culture. Culture is a relatively consistent set of behavioral models comprising language, norms, ideals, roles, and social statuses; ideologies differ from the rest in taking a more systematic form. As discourses on the situations of groups preparing for action, they represent the counterpart of a consciousness.
>
> ...
>
> Ideology both clarifies and dissimulates, as does the growth of the individual. It is, in its way, an attempt at making the world intelligible. And, by both drawing on and challenging it, one uses ideology as a device for the understanding of cultures ... Science itself cannot escape such an analysis, for if culture produces ideologies, surely science begins with them.[14]

At the dawn of Anglo-American sociology in the mid-nineteenth century, the distinct ideologies of progress and reformist humanitarianism played a decisive role in shaping the new discipline. By century's end, the white pioneers' enthusiasm for general sociological theories had become bound up with positivism and biological evolutionism, two scientific ideologies compatible with the grand idea of progress. Meanwhile black sociology, as one quickly discovers, derived a rejoinder to this dogma from the ideology of democratic egalitarianism. This brings us to another reason for giving special importance to ideology; namely, it was by and through this means – and here is a central thesis of this book – that the first black sociologists attempted to gain scientific credibility for theories they put forward as part of an emancipatory agenda for blacks in American society in general, and academia in particular. To avoid melting into the stigmatizing image of blacks disseminated by nearly all the Anglo-American founders of sociology, the first black social scientists – or at any rate the boldest among them – adopted an ideology that denounced the established social order and pointed the way for their community to take its rightful place in America's past and future. Here ideology appears not as a factor in the genesis of science but as a necessary instrument for converting the tragic historical episode of slavery into a rational striving for collective self-affirmation – in a phrase, the conquest of freedom through knowledge. Ideology, then, played two roles, first upstream as a wellspring of science, and second downstream where, as Ricoeur might put it, it allowed black intellectuals to symbolically inflect the course of events and help members of their group project their action into new ideas, such that the plural nature of reality itself could be made self-evident: from emancipation to disalienation and freedom. Thus, we have here two dimensions of a particular type of consciousness (referring again to Dumont's analogy) that serve as the cornerstone of this book.

Let it be clear that there is no reason at the outset to postulate anything but strict epistemological parity between the two rival sociologies, in the absence of any evidence to the contrary. If the Anglo-American variety was considered superior, one should not assume that this was on intrinsically scientific grounds; it may well have been – and we shall see that it was – simply the result of biased rhetoric produced by the Anglo-American establishment in its own interests. Du Bois's methodical objectivization was a priori just as valid as that of William Sumner or Robert Park according to the accepted canons of mid-twentieth-century social science.[15] A related principle to which I shall adhere strictly is Weber's value neutrality as presented in his *Gesammelte Aufsätze zur Wissenschaftslehre*. I shall reconstruct the structural components of the two sociologies within their historical context and without value judgments at any stage of the analysis. One advantage of this approach is that it helps to avoid the temptation to distort the study object by viewing or judging it through the lens of contemporary concerns. This has made it necessary for me to set aside much recent literature, such as Seymour Martin Lipset's *American Exceptionalism* (1997), which contains a chapter about the African American experience,[16] and Andrew Hacker's *Two Nations: Black and White, Separate, Hostile, Unequal* (1992). The contemporary works that I have cited are all either histories of ideas or essays in the sociology of knowledge; from these I have derived valuable analytical perspectives (e.g., Bourdieu) or taken advantage of contemporary developments in the historical study of American social science.

To summarize the outline of this book: in parts one and two I examine the work of the two groups of sociologists squaring off around the complex 'race question' between 1896 and 1964, comparing and contrasting their discourses. Part one focuses on the Anglo-American cohort, who possessed the strategic advantage of having 'gotten there first' – the first race-oriented works of sociology date from 1854 (see pp. 23–4). Until Du Bois's appearance on the scene they held a discursive monopoly on race and race relations in the United States, presenting an amalgam of science and ideology as the standard of reference on the subject. In the absence of a countervailing force, the dogma of blacks' intrinsic inferiority was rapidly accepted and assimilated into the broader society, persisting for more than a century across generations and through internal crises in mainstream sociology, the two world wars, the Great Depression, and many other events. It is this redoubtable dogma that I shall meticulously examine, using mainly primary but also secondary sources (a method I shall follow for the entire book). Clearly, the fashioners of an authentic black sociology, Du Bois leading the way, would have no choice but to challenge the hegemony of this through-line in American culture.

In part two I consider the small cohort of black sociologists, beginning with an exposition of their guiding ideas in terms of theory and methodology. As I have indicated, one would err in thinking that black sociology structured itself as a mere rejection of the normative content of Anglo-American race relations theory. On the contrary, during the first half of the twentieth century, all manner of reinterpretation and commentary upon that theory filtered into the discourse and practice of black social scientists, making the analysis of their work that much more subtle and captivating. One must constantly keep in mind, moreover, that this face-off took place in a decidedly asymmetrical situation. For example, not one of the significant early black sociologists was allowed to pursue an academic career at a prestigious American university. Possession of formal academic qualifications – doctorate, research experience, publication list – none of it was to any avail. They had to content themselves with horizontal mobility through various 'inferior' universities serving a black clientele, in the Deep South (Mississippi, Tennessee), the Outer South (North Carolina, South Carolina), and Washington, D.C. None of them earned an honorary doctorate or other academic distinction from Princeton, Harvard, Chicago, Stanford, or the like. The only chink in this segregationist armor occurred when Edward Franklin Frazier was elected president of the American Sociological Association in 1948.

In part three I take critical distance from these matters, using the tools offered by the sociology of scientific knowledge to conduct a meticulous comparison of the conceptual cores of the two sociologies, seeking to identify their significant similarities and differences. I dwell on black sociology's compulsory relationship to the biggest source of resistance it encountered between 1896 and 1964 – the deeply racist culture of Anglo-American academia – and conclude with some hypotheses to explain the persistence of these African American scholars in their attempts to overcome this institutional obstacle.

The reader is forewarned: quite a few of the passages that I cite in chapters one to three are startling in their crude racism, plunging us into a social universe in which discrimination and segregation were central to all institutions and racist oppression was a fixture of ordinary life. One is inevitably led to ponder one of the great paradoxes of modern history: that a solemnly self-professed democratic republic could overtly practice two forms of racism against its oldest cultural minorities: genocide against the native Americans and ethnocide against the African Americans. The intensity of the oppression in the case of blacks – from the brutal slave system of the seventeenth to mid-nineteenth centuries to the 'economic quasi-slavery'[17] of sharecropping, a system enforced by the ever-present threat of lynching, and on to the urban ghettos that provided cheap labor for burgeoning industry – gives their case a kind of universal resonance. It is no stretch to assert that all these systems of social and economic control greatly assisted the United States in becoming the uncontested economic power of the twentieth century. The methods of social science must suffice to conduct an impartial, dispassionate, sociological analysis thereof, even if the reality was so abusive it frequently spilled over into horror. It is my hope that this book will make a useful contribution to the universal store of knowledge that serves as a bulwark against injustice, unfairness, and oppression around the world. While it is true that the essays of Du Bois, Cayton, Frazier, and others discussed in this book are, as Jean-Michel Chapoulie recently wrote, 'to some extent obsolete,'[18] there can be no doubt that these scholars accomplished a Herculean task in their day: namely, that of restoring scientific objectivity to a discipline fraught with unchallenged ideological assumptions.

PART ONE

Anglo-American Sociology and the Race Question

The century of Anglo-American sociology of race relations from 1865 to 1965 can be conveniently divided into three phases: from the Civil War to the First World War, between the two world wars, and from the Second World War to 1965. The first phase saw the emergence of the discipline with its characteristic scientific and ideological approach. In the second, the discipline asserted its difference from its European sources and moved toward a putatively scientific definition of race relations as a societal phenomenon. The final phase, from the vibrancy of postwar America to the agitation of the 1960s, was marked by a degree of intellectual pluralism in a context of far-reaching change and passionate debate about race relations. In this first part of the book, I will trace the progress of Anglo-American theories of race through these three periods to discover how they became entrenched in the dominant sociological tradition.

Before proceeding, it is helpful to provide widely accepted modern definitions of three key terms that will recur constantly throughout this book, bearing in mind that their use by the historical figures whom I discuss diverged radically from these definitions in many cases. 'Race,' as is now acknowledged by a wide range of social scientists, is properly defined as a social construct, not a natural or biological fact, as for example in this definition by Herbert Blumer: 'A race has come to mean simply a group of people who are regarded and treated in actual life as a race. The membership of the race simply consists of those individuals who are identified and classified as belonging to it.'[1] I shall complement this definition with another that explicitly identifies racial designations as being rooted in social fact: 'Race is a socially constructed process that produces subordinate and superordinate groups. Racial stratification is the key social process behind racial classifications. The meaning of race depends on the social conditions in which it exists.'[2]

For 'racism,' the renowned U.S. scholar of the phenomenon William Julius Wilson provides the needed definition, here again stressing its socially constructed nature:

> Racism – a term frequently used imprecisely in discussions of the conditions of racial minorities in the United States, especially the conditions of African Americans – should be understood as an ideology of racial domination. This ideology features two things: (1) beliefs that a designated racial group is either biologically or culturally inferior to the dominant group, and (2) the use of such beliefs to rationalize or prescribe the racial group's treatment in society and to explain its social position and accomplishments.[3]

The third term, 'black,' refers to Americans of African descent. The term 'Negro' was universally used by both Anglo-American and black sociologists from 1865 to 1950 but, as everyone knows, has fallen into disuse and taken on pejorative connotations. I have let the word stand where it appears in original quotations, preserving the lower-case form typical of the period (although this usage was often decried by Du Bois). I shall also use the term 'African American,' since this is now a widely accepted term for the population in question.

1 From the Civil War to the First World War

The first English-speaking intellectuals to present themselves as sociologists in the United States came onto the scene during the last three decades of the nineteenth century. Of practically equal importance, these northern and Midwestern 'founding fathers' – Franklin Giddings, Edward Ross, Lester Ward, William Sumner, Albion Small, and Charles Cooley – were keenly interested in developing a new science of society as well as promoting a broad range of social reforms.[1] As clergymen or descendents of clergymen they had made a clear choice to transfer their moral concerns and careers from the church pulpit to the university lectern. In terms of their scientific approach, these men propounded grand social theories with the avowed objective of resolving the social problems arising from the accelerated industrialization and urbanization that followed the Civil War. Social reformism, Protestantism, and intellectual ambition were the strands of the close-knit fabric from which these first university sociologists were woven:

> The social reform movements of the day thus provided the subject matter and ideological *problemata* to which the academic courses were oriented. And the movement and literature of reformism far outstripped academic forms of sociology ... Each of these founders developed his distinctive views in an intellectual world formed largely by the set of interrelated reform movements that developed after the Civil War ... These movements provided opportunities to write, edit, lecture, engage in practical politics and philanthropy, and, on occasion, perform empirical research.[2]

Thus there was a close relationship between the new scientific exuberance and the socioeconomic context in which it evolved. The Industrial Revolution had resumed after the Civil War. At the behest of industrialists and financiers, job specialization and automation were pervading the labor market. At the same time, structural transformations in the economy were producing a mass migration of labor from agriculture to urban industry and manufacturing.[3] The economist Harold Faulkner indicates the magnitude of industrial, hence economic, acceleration in the wake of the War of Secession: 'the census figures of 1870 ... place the increase in the number of industrial establishments for the decade at 252,148, an advance of 79.6 per cent and the greatest for any decade in our history. The number of wage earners in industrial establishments advanced from 1,1311,246 to 2,053,996, an increase of 56.6 per cent which was not equaled even during the decade of the First World War.'[4]

As spectacular as this socioeconomic development was, it essentially represented the continuation of a trend begun well before the 1860s. The two or three decades preceding the Civil War had seen large numbers of immigrants arrive in the United States, packing into urban areas and leading to lowered living standards and wages for the majority: 'In actual practice few immigrant wage earners escaped to the [Western] frontier ... That grim poverty existed, particularly in the cities and notably in the 'forties and 'fifties, we have ample evidence.'[5] In short, immigration and urbanization, closely correlated before the war of 1860, were major drivers of structural change at mid-century.[6]

While internal migration patterns – from the countryside to the cities – also contributed to this urban growth, the wave of immigration taking place from 1840 to 1880 was remarkable for its magnitude, leading to a tenfold increase in the number of immigrants living in the United States:

> During the 1840s crop failures in Europe set off a surge of emigration from Ireland, southwestern Germany, and Scandinavia. In the 1850s some 2,750,000 immigrants landed in the United States. The pace increased after the Civil War and peaked in 1873, when 400,000 newcomers landed in American ports. Following a lull during the depression years of the middle and late 1870s, the movement resumed and reached unprecedented volume in the 1880s.[7]

The synergistic effects of these economic, demographic, and migrational forces of change inevitably exacerbated already severe inequalities in income, health and hygiene, and general well-being between the capitalist elites and entrepreneurs on the one hand and the middle and (increasingly industrial and multiethnic) working classes on the other: 'In the 1880s and 1890s, immigrants were pouring in from Europe at a faster rate than before. They all went through the harrowing ocean voyage of the poor. Now there were not so many Irish and German immigrants as Italians, Russians, Jews, Greeks – people from Southern and Eastern Europe, even more alien to native-born Anglo-Saxons than the earlier newcomers.'[8]

Numerous problems festered in the divide between rich and poor. Educational opportunities for poor people were extremely limited, while illiteracy, systematic exploitation (particularly of women and children), crime, delinquency, and prostitution flourished in the new, rapidly expanding urban ghettos. These problems met with a working-class response in the form of protest movements – most often reformist, but at times revolutionary – coalescing out of pre-Civil War labor currents. Initial organizing revolved around guilds of shoemakers, typesetters, milliners, and others who sought to improve their harsh working conditions through collective bargaining, at times locally, at times on a wider scale. After mid-century the labor movement became more visible and active with the formation of national organizations (National Labor Union [1866], Knights of Labor [1869], American Federation of Labor [1886]). As the problems became more acute and the numbers of those in society facing the indifference of the governing elites continued to increase, the movement spilled over into the general population. It became an authentic ideological and political force whose influence would henceforth be felt throughout American society, as Howard Zinn notes:

> It seemed that despite the strenuous efforts of government, business, the church, the schools, to control their thinking, millions of Americans were ready to consider harsh criticism of the existing system, to contemplate other possible ways of living. They were helped in this by the great movements of workers and farmers that swept the country in the 1880s and 1890s. These movements went beyond the scattered strikes and tenants' struggles of the period 1830–1877. They were nationwide movements, more threatening than before to the ruling elite, more dangerously suggestive. It was a time when revolutionary organizations existed in major American cities, and revolutionary talk was in the air.[9]

The nascent academic sociology took many of its cues from this protest movement but did not fully identify with it. The founding fathers were striving for science, not ideology. Their challenge, in carving out a position as critics of the existing social order, was to strike a balance between the aforementioned societal demands, on the one hand, and two perceived intellectual imperatives: the need to close the gap with European social science, and the desire to avoid duplicating the journalistic essays gaining in popularity after 1870 (e.g., Henry George's *Progress and Poverty* or Edward Bellamy's *Looking Backward*), with their eccentric or utopian scenarios for America's future.

Another strong influence on the nascent Anglo-American sociology was the ongoing transformation of higher education into the modern university system. Sociology derived significant benefits from this institutional shift, as did other disciplines:

> The founding years of sociology coincided with the phenomenal expansion of the American university system. By the turn of the century, sociology courses were taught routinely. The first department of sociology was established by the University of Kansas in 1889, followed closely by the University of Chicago in 1892. By World War I, sociology was a recognized academic discipline, with its own departments, doctoral programs, professional associations, conferences, and journals.[10]

Also an influential part of the environment in which the new sociology grew up was the 'liberal credo,' a pervasive idea in the middle-class background from which all the founding fathers emerged:

> The successful institutionalization of sociology was facilitated by the relatively broad-based liberal ideological consensus that characterized middle America at the time ... For the new middle classes, sociology was embraced as a vehicle to manage the myriad social problems of an urban, industrial liberal society. Advocacy for sociology was a way for the new middle classes to prove their superiority over older elites by showing their competency to solve social problems and to maintain America on the path of social progress. Animated by the spirit of liberal reform and social progress, sociology functioned as a secular expression of the Christian faith in the manifest destiny of America that was at the core of the American civil religion.[11]

If the most progressive of these academic sociologists limited themselves to moderate reformism, avoiding overt association with the more radical positions holding sway in the Socialist Party of America, for example, or among the anarchists, it was because their 'American civil religion' was bound up with the fundamentally individualistic and melioristic ideology of liberalism. Adherence to this ideology meant that the nascent sociology had to keep its bourgeois origins pure and free from radical associations.

Another group of social scientists, much lower profile than the academic sociologists, had appeared on the scene in the decade following the War of Secession. The 'social surveyors' were nonacademic government employees who learned their rather crude science on the job. Most of what they did consisted of taking head counts and compiling census data that could serve to assess the status of social problems such as unemployment. The Massachusetts Bureau of Statistics of Labor, founded in 1869, was a typical initiative of this kind. As rudimentary as their work was, the social surveyors could be credited with striving for objectivity and methodological correctness at a time when no community of statisticians or official standards existed by which such work could be evaluated. Such was the infancy, alongside the much more prestigious academic sociology, of a kind of grassroots sociological knowledge based on practical intervention that would take on greater sophistication as time went on. Looking back decades later with undeniable admiration and respect, Robert Park termed it a genuine American 'protosociology.'

The formal structure of the earliest American academic sociology took the form of so-called general theory, which, as Roscoe Hinkle notes,

> was believed to confer academic respectability on the discipline and to prevent the field from 'degenerating' into mere practical amelioration of social problems. General theory or general sociology sought to discover the first principles, causes, and laws of the origin, structure, and change of human association, human society, or social phenomena generically and irrespective of variant, particular, idiosyncratic, or unique forms. Irrespective of what they might be or become, all special (or specialized) sociology (or sociologies) were assumed to begin from, contribute, and eventually return to general sociology or general theory.[12]

To put it in a nutshell, sociologists 'really believed that sociology could emulate the natural sciences.'[13] This initial configuration of the discipline answered a number of other needs from the founding fathers' standpoint as well. Because of its abstractness, general theory would allow academic sociologists to keep their distance from reformism and its insistent demands; in so doing, they could avoid converting the numerous melioristic desiderata of the time into scientific premises. Moreover, general theory seemed to them the best substitute for the commonsense philosophy of the Civil War era, a philosophy they saw as outdated and retrograde in the new secular, urban, industrial context. Finally, it allowed the new Anglo-American academic elite to narrow the theory gap with their more advanced and imaginative European counterparts.

So much for the aims of general theory – what of its substantive content? The founding fathers instinctively gravitated toward those European liberal thinkers whose ideological assumptions matched their own: following a quintessentially American recipe, they melded the positivism of Auguste Comte with the organicism and individualism of Herbert Spencer. Most central to the new sociology was an evolutionary system of thought known as evolutionary naturalism:

> The term 'evolutionary naturalism' is an appropriate designation for the general theoretical orientation of early American sociology by virtue of the primacy and centrality of the problem of social origins in relation to the more usual problems of social structure and by virtue of the particular set of accompanying assumptions and tenets about social phenomena and sociology. As the term suggests, evolutionary naturalism is fundamentally preoccupied with the explanation of the genesis of and orderly change within social phenomena.[14]

The considerable allure of this theoretical foundation for the earliest American sociologists deserves to be dwelled upon. One of its attractions was certainly its positivist core, the possibility it held out of theorizing society scientifically by analogy to the natural science model. Society, like physical nature, could be methodically reduced by this means to a more or less complex set of specific, describable, classifiable, natural forces – *social* as opposed to physical or biological forces. Evolutionary naturalism thus served the founding fathers' agenda of freeing sociological thought from its moralistic strictures. A second virtue of evolutionism in the eyes of its proponents was its vision of social forces as operating within an overarching mechanism of gradual change. Such a dynamic – even grandiose – representation of the world found motivation in the wider American society of the late nineteenth century. All American intellectuals, for example, believed that their country, above all others, possessed a manifest destiny. Seen from this angle, the aura of scientificity provided by grand evolutionary theories was reassuring. Moreover, the lay public shared their orientation, being

> receptive to grand, cosmic-sounding theories, perhaps as a substitute for the religious-reformist world views with which they had been raised. Indeed, the enormous popularity of Herbert Spencer in America at the turn of the century signals the extent to which early 'theory' in sociology filled a need in the lay public for grand theorizing that seemed scientific and capable of directing reform and progress.[15]

The word 'progress' suggests a third reason for the uptake of evolutionism, one again rooted in the wider society. A firm belief in social progress was de rigueur at the time, largely because of the permeation of Spencer's ideas, but also because of a scientific theory that had become an uncontested dogma by the end of the century after surmounting fierce resistance between 1860 and 1880: the evolutionary biology of Charles Darwin. Darwinism held that the progress of living species on earth was due to natural selection of the fittest individuals. As such it gave anyone who, like the early academic sociologists, believed in progress as a driving force in American society, the means with which to draw all manner of biological analogies. Thus industrialization and urbanization, massive foreign immigration, and demographic processes were interpreted by scholars as convincing evidence of selection pressure at work within the human groups of their society. The fierce competition among ethnic groups and subgroups for integration into the majority culture and gradual improvement of their condition was also decoded with the help of Darwinian theory, whose claims to universality made it the reigning scientific instrument of the day. Given such fertile ground, it is no surprise to discover that evolutionary naturalism rapidly acquired the status of an epistemological matrix for the emerging Anglo-American sociology and provided the basis for a far-reaching scientific program:

> early American sociology in its commitment to evolutionary naturalism is basically indebted to and dependent upon Darwinian (and Spencerian) views of organic evolution ... In its simplest terms, evolutionary theorization in sociology proposes that human association in general and human society in particular originated and persisted because they facilitated man's survival under the typical conditions of human existence ... Early

American 'evolutionary naturalism' endeavored to explain the origins of social phenomena and human societies, structure (i.e., maintenance or persistence), and change (i.e., variation, modification, and transformation) both naturalistically and evolutionarily in accordance with a substantially Darwinian-Spencerian stance.[16]

Sociological Theories of Race

Concurrent with the implantation of these grand explanatory schemes in the emerging academic sociology, American society was profoundly wracked by racial conflict, a phenomenon to which we now turn. At the outbreak of the Civil War, the total population of the United States was 31,443,321, including 4,441,830 blacks, the largest minority group.[17] An overwhelming majority of these, though by no means all, had experienced institutionalized slavery. The war, of course, resulted in abolition, though this was not its initial motivation:

> For Negroes the Civil War was, from its beginning, inextricably bound up with their future and their freedom. They saw it first of all as a war for the emancipation of the slaves ... Neither the Administration at Washington nor white public opinion generally regarded the war in this light at the start. To them it was emphatically a war to preserve the Union, not to end slavery, much less to obtain for Negroes the rights of citizens.[18]

The fifteen years following the conflict saw the etiolation of the immediate civil rights gains made by blacks after the Civil War. Slavery gave way to a substitute system of southern racial segregation in which blacks occupied the job ghettos of plantation work and domestic service, were legally prohibited from entering into mixed marriages, and were increasingly denied suffrage and other political rights through mob violence. Segregation crystallized into a caste-based society that governed public interracial contact according to a vertical schema of white 'superiority' and black 'inferiority.' These ugly trends in society were publicly sanctioned by the Compromise of 1877, in which the federal government withdrew its troops from the former Confederate states in return for Republican control of the White House, leaving blacks to fend for themselves against their terrorizers and paving the way for the wholesale adoption of a racist system. By now it was obvious that emancipation had been ephemeral:

> Negroes throughout the country found themselves increasingly the victims of discrimination, proscription, and mob violence ... the acceptance of white and Democratic hegemony in the South by the officials at Washington left Southern Negroes without any effective defense, permitting the unimpeded development of a race system that supplanted the old institution of slavery as a mechanism of social control.[19]

The overwhelming majority of the people subjected to this new regime of segregation, a more damaging one than slavery in many respects, were southern country dwellers, also known as 'folk Negroes.' However, the rapidly growing black population (from 4,888,000 in 1870 to 6,580,793 in 1880, 7,488,676 in 1890, and 9,194,000 in 1900)[20] would soon experience successive waves of outmigration to the North, swelling the ghettos of the large industrial cities. Most contemporary observers viewed this as an immense social problem, not least the founding fathers of Anglo-American sociology, almost all of whom advanced theories to account for the racial conflict that had begun in the social microcosm of the South and was gradually becoming prevalent in the whole country. It is notable, though, that their race theories were not set out in treatises on this specific subject, but rather piecemeal, within the context of their general sociological theories. Another important fact is that they were not the first American scholars to evince an intellectual interest in the race question, or even to use the word 'sociology'; the latter distinction belonged to two white southerners, Henry Hughes and George Fitzhugh, for whom race had been a burning issue:

> the very term, 'sociology,' was introduced into the American lexicon of social science in 1854 by Henry Hughes, an obscure Mississippi lawyer. His *Treatise on Sociology, Theoretical and Practical* is the first book-length work to employ that term in its title ... Despite the availability of his *Treatise*, Hughes, a southerner, a slavocrat, and the first self-designated American sociologist, remains an elusive and protean figure in the lyceum of American life and letters.[21]

> The discipline's connection with the region [the South] goes way back, back to 1854 in fact, when George Fitzhugh of Virginia and Henry Hughes of Mississippi almost simultaneously published books with the newfangled Greco-Latin hybrid word *sociology* in their titles. These were the first American titles to use the word, which had been coined a few decades

earlier by the French philosopher Auguste Comte (with whom, as a matter of fact, Henry Hughes had studied in Paris).[22]

Dissimulated behind the noble new word 'sociology' was an apology, in both these books, for slavery. Hughes maintained that slavery was morally and civilly good and should be preserved. For his part, Fitzhugh contended that only Christianity and slavery could guarantee order and morality in society, a view attested more provocatively by the title of his later work *Cannibals All! Or Slaves without Masters* (1857). So anachronistic is the representation of blacks found in these books – more characteristic of late-seventeenth-century than pre-Civil War era views[23] – that one must conclude that Hughes and Fitzhugh were not merely reflecting the conventional wisdom of their day but were actively engaged in a racist enterprise. What is perhaps more surprising, and will shortly become clear, is that the founding fathers of Anglo-American academic sociology could all trace some part of their lineage back to these forerunners.

The Founding Fathers

Franklin Giddings (1855–1931), the first full-time professor of sociology at Columbia University, set down his profession of evolutionist faith in two books, *The Principles of Sociology* (1896) and *The Elements of Sociology* (1898). The human race, he held, descended from a species that had become social before it exhibited the anatomical and physiological traits of humans per se: 'society originated ages before man appeared on the Earth ... [therefore] the earliest human beings lived in rather large bands or communities ...'[24] Humans were fundamentally social animals. Evolution, a process different from social change, involved the totality of a society and could be conceptualized as a change from 'ethnogenesis' to 'demogenesis' over time; that is, from a societal state composed of small, relatively homogeneous or undifferentiated units structured around bloodlines and kinship to another societal state made up of larger, more heterogeneous or differentiated units structured around territory and polity. In short, it was a change from primitive to modern or civilized society, a society in which reason represented a victory over the purely physical struggle to survive: 'through the supremacy of intellectual over physical strife can the higher and finer results of social evolution be attained ... Intellectual strife makes for rational, and ultimately for ethical, like-mindedness; it makes for peace, prosperity, and happiness.'[25]

Elsewhere in Giddings's writings, though, is clear evidence that he did not consider all human races to be equal – far from it – nor eligible for the social evolution he considered so salutary:

> When higher and lower races come in contact, it is necessary for the higher in many ways to sustain the lower; otherwise it would be impossible for two very different races to live together ... Though intellectually superior to the negro, the Indian has shown less ability than the negro to adapt himself to new conditions. The negro is plastic. He yields easily to environing influences. Deprived of the support of stronger races, he still relapses into savagery, but kept in contact with the whites, he readily takes the external impress of civilization, and there is reason to hope that he will yet acquire a measure of its spirit.[26]

Lester Ward (1841–1913) was the first person to author a systematic treatise of general sociology (*Dynamic Sociology* [1883]). Society, he argued, was not viable without structures to reinforce its permanence and guarantee its functioning. The most important of these structures were institutions, 'a moving equilibrium ... which makes possible their adaptation to both internal and external modification, to changes in both individual character and the environment.'[27] Institutions were essentially obligatory because of their effectiveness in meeting the requirements arising from the social conditions of existence. Societal evolution could be represented as a vast unilinear process taking place in three stages: the protosocial – a primitive, savage, aboriginal, ahistorical state; the metasocial – an intermediate phase of transformed primitivism close to the emergence of writing and history; and finally, the social, which marked the shift to a culture of writing and history among the entire community aware of having entered a stage of 'evolved' civilization.[28] A strict Darwinist[29] in his conception of the early stages of evolution, Ward was more ecumenical in his views on the subsequent stages. Education, for him, was pivotal as a deliberate effort to attenuate inequalities caused by natural differences. He coined the term 'conation' to express this desirable, nondetermined social change. His ideas about race are astonishingly forward-looking for the time, challenging the then-prevalent idea of nonwhite inferiority: 'It is not therefore proved that intellectual equality, which can be safely predicated of all classes in the white race, in the yellow race, or in the black race, each taken by itself, cannot also be predicated of all races taken together, and it is still more clear that there is no race and no class of human beings who are incapable of assimilating the social achievement of mankind and of profitably employing the social heritage.'[30] Racial conflict remained inevitable but was not to be feared; rather, it was the engine of step-by-step social assimilation. Looking to the future, Ward envisioned an evolutionary stage at which races would disappear and hereditary marks would be subsumed: 'if we could but peer far enough into the great future, we should see this planet of ours ultimately peopled with a single homogeneous and completely assimilated race of men – the human race – in the composition of which could be detected all the great commanding qualities of every one of its racial components.'[31]

William Sumner (1840–1910) was the first American professor of sociology (1872, Yale College). His most original sociological ideas are found in his magnum opus, *Folkways* (1906). Like Ward a Social Darwinist,[32] Sumner differed in regarding human beings as largely passive spectators to the action of natural laws. The first humans, he believed, had been caught up in a process of conflict, a struggle for existence, involving all living species. The conflict intensified as increasing numbers of individuals competed within an environment of limited resources, though cooperation may have allowed them to 'raise their efforts against nature to a higher power.'[33] Over time, a heritage composed of folkways and mores came into being. Some of these were simple structures, while others – laws, institutions, an ethos, morality – were more complex. Folkways and mores, which Sumner saw as the kernel of any human society, were subject to very slow change, if any. Skeptical of social progress, he openly espoused laissez-faire, rejecting the idea that sociologists should support social reforms or that any organization could engage in purposive social change. The race 'problem' took up an insignificant amount of space in his work; just a few paragraphs in *Folkways* referring essentially to the South; the problem could be explained, he believed, by the severance of white-black relations with the abolition of slavery: 'In our southern states, before the civil war, whites and blacks had formed habits of action and feeling towards each other. They lived in peace and concord, and each one grew up in the ways which were traditional and customary. The civil war abolished legal rights and left the two races to learn how to live together under other relations than before.' For Sumner, learning to live 'under other relations' meant adopting other mores, yet this was a formidable stumbling block: 'The whites have never been converted from the old mores ... The two races have not yet made new mores.'[34] By every indication the gap between whites and blacks was widening. Humanists might want to intervene by making laws or imposing other means of control, but this was in vain: 'Some are anxious to interfere and try to control. They take their stand on ethical views of what is going on. It is evidently impossible for any one to interfere. We are like spectators at a great natural convulsion. The results will be such as the facts and forces call for.'[35]

The Civil War, Sumner thought, had been caused by differing mores between North and South and between blacks and whites; this led him to favor the status quo as the best possible situation for the time being and to shun assimilationism, which had no place in his worldview:

> Under slavery the blacks were forced to conform to white ways, as indeed they are now if they are servants. In the North, also, where they are in a small minority, they conform to white ways. It is when they are free and form a large community that they live by their own mores. The civil war in the United States was due to a great divergence in the mores of the North and the South, produced by the presence or absence of slavery.[36]

Edward Ross (1866–1951), the youngest of the founding fathers, dedicated his most important work, *Social Control* (1901), to his teacher and brother-in-law, Lester Ward. Like Ward, he argued the case for an optimistic, even progressive evolutionism. While the primitive social universe had been a world of rough competition – survival of the fittest – 'the more peaceable elements of the population gain[ed] a steadily increasing preponderance' through social selection.[37] Individuals driven by social sentiments such as sympathy and sociability, a sense of justice, and a distrust of hostility and contempt had prospered and proliferated. Each of these sentiments facilitated human association in a specific way; for example, sociability 'foster[ed] friendly interest, spontaneous helpfulness, and a sense of solidarity, all of which conduce to the maintenance of order.'[38] At the highest level of generality, the social structure could be conceived of as a community-society dichotomy (an idea that Ross advanced without defining it anywhere explicitly).[39] Community consisted of groups in which primary, natural, spontaneous social relations predominated. Social cohesion was strong enough that social control was not necessary. These conditions prevailed 'when the rural neighborhood or the village community was the type of aggregation ...'[40] Society, by contrast, referred to a collective living context marked by voluntary associations, economic specialization, elaborate stratification and differentiation, and organizational complexity. In a society, planned social control in the form of sanctions was essential to the maintenance of the social order. As everywhere in the existing universe, societies were subject to change, defined by Ross as 'any qualitative variation' or as 'adaptation – at first, perhaps, very imperfect – to new conditions.'[41] His race theory followed directly from his vision of continuous social transformation. Since different races are empirically observable and their differences threaten the social order, society must evolve toward their assimilation, which begins with the acculturation of minorities: 'Unless the all-inclusive group finds means to assimilate and reconcile its members and weaken the ties that bind men into minor groups, the social order will be disrupted.'[42] The social values of the majority could prevent such a disruption while favoring the improvement of minorities, blacks in particular:

> The uplifting of the American negro is another field for the method of control by social valuations. It is now recognized that not churches alone will lift the black race; not schools; not contact with the whites; not even industry. But all of these cooperating can do it. The growth of new and higher wants, coupled with the training to new skill, is the best lever for raising the idle, quarrelling, sensual Afro-American. Certainly it is necessary to infect the backward portion of the race with a high estimate of cleanliness, neatness, family privacy, domestic comfort, and literacy ...[43]

One might assume that Ross would draw the obvious conclusion from his emphasis on 'lifting the black race' – that African Americans could and should enjoy social and political equality with whites – but the idea appears nowhere in his writings.

Albion Small (1854–1926), who founded the Department of Sociology at the University of Chicago in 1892, was the least interested of all the founding fathers in the race question, at least insofar as his writing and teaching attest; his published work contains practically nothing on the subject. Small's indirect contribution was to vet publication, as founding editor of the *American Journal of Sociology* for many years, of articles on race relations by academics, reformers, amateur sociologists, and teachers.

Charles Cooley (1864–1929), one of the first and most influential U.S. social psychologists, spent most of his career at the University of Michigan. In his 'soft' version of Darwinian evolutionism, the first humans were not blindly given to brute force in the struggle for subsistence: 'then as now, the man fit to survive was a moral man, a "good" man in his relation to the life of the group.'[44] Articulate language, ideas, even thought itself had appeared through the gradual effect of association: 'In this way man, if he was human when speech began to be used, rapidly became more so, and went on accumulating a social heritage.'[45] Organization was a necessity of societal evolution, 'a system of co-ordinated activities fitted to the conditions.'[46] Integral to societal organization (including modern society) were what he referred to as primary and secondary groups, the first consisting of social groups whose members share close, enduring personal bonds (e.g., family), the second consisting of more temporary groups established to serve specific functions, their specific members therefore being largely interchangeable. Also found in modern society were different social classes, some hereditary, relatively fixed, the equivalent of castes, others allowing for more individual mobility.[47] The increasingly formal and impersonal social relations of the modern world had inevitably given rise to social disorganization, a reduction in 'general order and discipline'; 'society as a whole want[ed] unity and rationality.'[48] This was worrying, since it implied a severe breakdown in standards, traditions, and moral codes.

It was important, for Cooley, to differentiate social evolution from change, and he preferred the term 'development': 'Development, I should say, can be proved. That is, history reveals, beyond question, a process of enlargement, diversification, and organization, personal and social, that seems vaguely analogous to the growth of plant and animal organisms ...'[49] He did believe in progress as a complex concept, a moral category,[50] describing it as 'a tendency to humanize the collective life, to make institutions express the higher impulses of human nature, instead of brutal or mechanical conditions.'[51] It was up to society, not sociologists, to do what was necessary to reinforce its progressive tendencies. However, specialists could help society by developing criteria for use by the voluntary associations so important to its fabric. Cooley believed that sociology could best prove its practical value by disseminating a kind of social knowledge that he called 'public intelligence';[52] meaning, the cumulative store of knowledge held by society and its institutions, as opposed to the knowledge held by individuals.

Cooley's characteristic open-mindedness on the race question was evident early in his career. In 1897 he challenged the bullish theory of hereditary transmission of racial character traits by insisting on the importance of environment in explaining the diversity of human attributes and abilities.[53] But he was ambivalent about the South and its profoundly entrenched caste system and did not rule out the possibility of innate racial differences: 'Two races of different temperament and capacity, distinct to the eye and living side by side in the same community, tend strongly to become castes, no matter how equal the social system may otherwise be ... The race caste existing in the Southern United States illustrates the impotence of democratic traditions to overcome the caste spirit when fostered by obvious physical and psychical differences.'[54] As a proponent of the 'brotherhood of races' and, consequently, an opponent of 'that caste arrogance which does not recognize in the Negro a spiritual brotherhood underlying all race difference and possible "inferiority,"'[55] he regarded southern caste relations as intolerable and contemptible. Such an attitude 'belonged with slavery and [was] incongruous with the newer world.' Despite this, Cooley could see no alternative to the caste system and ultimately defended what was impossible to reconcile: 'The practical question here is not that of abolishing castes but of securing just and kindly relations between them, of reconciling the fact of caste with ideals of freedom and right.'[56]

The Southerners[57]

The canonical sociologists discussed above were not alone in propounding and disseminating race theories between 1860 and 1915. They were joined by a number of southern white essayists, most of them amateurs, who had earned history, political economy, or sociology degrees from northern universities. As might be expected, the views of these writers were the most extreme in all of early Anglo-American sociology.

Joseph Tillinghast was a graduate of Cornell University and the son of South Carolina slave owners. In *The Negro in Africa and America* (1902) he argued that the 'precarious position' of southern blacks at the turn of the century had more to do with their African heritage than their recent history of servitude.[58] Since the West Africans had 'no great industrial system, no science, and art,' American blacks were at a disadvantage in developing the abilities responsible for the success of civilized humanity: 'The consideration of the general laws of biological evolution would lead us, aside from the evidence above adduced, to believe the mind of a lower tropical race is unfitted to assimilate the advanced civilization of a strenuous and able northern race.'[59] Slavery had been a 'vast school' that had enabled blacks to advance, particularly in terms of work, by comparison with West African standards. Without it, he claimed, they would have regressed.

The two-volume *The Negro Races* by Jerome Dowd, who studied at

Duke University and interned in 1903–4 in the University of Chicago sociology department, employed similar biological arguments to justify the stigmatization of West African ancestry: '[The West African's] brain is so constituted that its sensorimotor activities predominate over his idio-motor activities; i.e., his passions and natural impulses are exceptionally potent and his inhibiting power exceptionally feeble.' Slavery compared favorably with European colonialism as an institution for educating blacks: 'The Negroes of America, especially in the Southern United States, were put through a course of training which corresponded more nearly to the natural evolution of things than the training which the black people have received in any part of the world.'[60] Ignoring the fact that nearly all enslaved American blacks had been used as field hands,[61] Dowd asserted that they had acquired the habits of constant effort and learned various trades: 'When the time came for them to enter schools and colleges they had already gone through a period of training which gave them an industrial and moral foundation ...[!]'[62]

H.E. Belin, a South Carolina Confederate Civil War veteran, was one of those social science amateurs who had the privilege of publishing in the *American Journal of Sociology* under the reign of Albion Small. In a 1908 article he asserted that the institution of slavery had been justified by its effect of uplifting blacks 'industrially, mentally, and even morally ... to a higher level than that ever accomplished by [their] kinsmen in Africa.' Slaves had not been 'generally ill-treated' by their owners, judging by the 'wonderful increase in their numbers [through] natural growth.'[63] Slavery had essentially been used by whites to uplift the inferior Africans so that harmonious coexistence between the races could ensue: 'What the theory of evolution is to the scientist, that the institution of slavery was to the southern man. It might not be absolutely the true and perfect solution to the Negro problem, but it was at least the best "working hypothesis" known to him for harmonizing the conflicting elements brought into compulsory contact in the South.'[64]

Walter Fleming, a Columbia University-educated historian, claimed that the postbellum southern plantation system was 'probably the most efficient plantation system the world ever saw.' Slavery could not be condemned since it had taught blacks to be reliable, efficient workers: 'Clothes were cut out in the "big house" and made by the Negro under the direction of the mistress. There was much need for skilled labor, and this was done by blacks ... They often earned money at odd jobs, and church records show they contributed regularly. Negro children were trained in the arts of industry and sobriety by elderly Negroes of good judgment and firm character, usually women.'[65] During and after Radical Reconstruction, the objective status of blacks had deteriorated, but this, he said, was due to their inability to survive without whites' help. Many, he claimed, had regressed to a state of barbarism analogous to that of their African ancestors: 'The Negroes deteriorated much in personal appearance and dress ... religion nearly died out ... there was a tendency to return to the barbarous customs of their African forefathers; witchcraft and voodoo were practiced, and in some cases human sacrifices were made.'[66] No credible documentation for this explanation of southern blacks' terrible postwar experience was forthcoming. Fleming's work would be vehemently denounced by his contemporary, W.E.B. Du Bois.

It should be noted in passing that there were northern adherents to the arbitrary claim of these white southerners that slavery had been beneficial to blacks by teaching them the habits and customs of white society. Carl Kelsey, a sociology professor at the University of Pennsylvania and a Congregationalist minister, proclaimed precisely this 'truth' in his teaching and writing.[67] Perhaps more surprisingly, Robert Park (whose work and legacy are discussed below, pp. 49–76) flirted with the argument that the institution of slavery had been an effective way of assimilating blacks in the United States.

Southern white professional sociologists – that is, those engaged in ongoing university research – were far outnumbered by the amateurs. Howard Odum (1884–1954) obtained his doctorate under Giddings at Columbia University; he also did doctoral-level work in psychology and took an anthropology course with Franz Boas (1858–1942). His *Social and Mental Traits of the Negro* (1910) was based on first-hand observations of two black communities in Mississippi and Georgia as well as a survey of black living standards in the South-east. He claimed that blacks were much inferior to whites in their ability to engage in viable economic, political, and social relations with the other race. They had progressed beyond their African ancestry but still lacked the cultural traits that would enable them to improve their current status because of the following 'natural traits':

> First, the Negro easily responds to stimuli, that is, he is controlled by present impulses. This results in almost complete lack of restraint, including both yielding to impulses and inertia. Second, this free response tends always to pleasure ... The Negro is therefore inactive. Third, the Negro

> tends to carry all responses to an extreme. He loves plenty of stimuli. This exhausts and degenerates his vital powers. Fourth, the Negro has little capacity for sustained control. This applies to sustained efforts, conduct in general, morality, convictions and thought. He is, therefore, weak in social and self-control and lacking in self-direction. Fifth, he does not, therefore, lend himself to the development of permanent qualities through the working out of essential processes. Sixth, he is, therefore, superficial and irresponsible.[68]

Odum added some positive inherent traits to this nomenclature: flexibility, adaptability, and 'plasticity of ... consciousness[!].'[69] He claimed that the negative traits of blacks would disappear once their economic condition changed; however, this would only occur 'through the help and cooperation of the whites.'[70] The economic problem was 'the only important problem in the Negro's environment.' Since the races were politically and socially unequal because of their 'different abilities and potentialities,' blacks should not be given the vote and should be segregated to prevent intermarriage. Theorizing what Robert Park would later describe as a biracial structure for society, he optimistically declared that blacks would eventually hold positions parallel to those of whites: 'The Negro has an unlimited field before him in the higher work of teaching, preaching, and professional work among his own people. There will be no competition there outside of his own.'[71] These pseudoscientific considerations – in perfect harmony with the bourgeois southern credo – legitimated the status quo by suggesting that blacks should reconcile themselves to their inferior social condition.

The first decade of the twentieth century saw a plethora of radical tracts concocted and disseminated under the pious veil of social science. One Alfred Holt Stone (1870–1955) gave a controversial paper on race relations at the annual congress of the American Sociological Association in 1907 and returned to the theme in a 1908 article for the *American Journal of Sociology*. With his law degree from the University of Mississippi, Stone had managed to secure teaching positions in history, economics – even race relations – at several southern universities, and presented himself as an authority on the subject. According to his theory of white/nonwhite relations, white racial prejudice – he called it 'racial antipathy' – was not a fiction but a natural phenomenon. What mattered to him, though, was 'the question of differences – the fundamental differences of physical appearances, of mental habit and thought, of social customs and religious belief, of the thousand and one things keenly and clearly appreciable ... these are the things that at once create and find expression in what we call race problems and race prejudices.'[72] In order to keep racial antipathy in check, it was necessary for whites and non-whites to obey natural laws founded on notions of 'superior' and 'inferior': 'open manifestations of antipathy will be aggravated if each group feels its superiority over the other,' while relations would be 'milder when one race accepts the position of inferiority outwardly, or really feels the superiority of the other.' As to racial friction, it resulted from the self-assurance tinted with arrogance that newly emancipated blacks displayed: '*post-bellum* racial difficulties are largely the manifestations of friction growing out of the novel claim to equality made by the Negro after emancipation, either by specific declaration and assertion, or by conduct which was equivalent to an open claim, with the refusal of the white man to recognize this claim.'[73] Slavery, he contended, had had nothing to do with this friction; quite the contrary, it had formerly helped to rein it in, to the extent that blacks had reconciled themselves to white superiority and had accepted their own inferior status.

What did the future hold? If blacks remained arrogant and failed to adapt by accepting their inferiority, racial friction would be exacerbated. If, on the contrary, they somehow regained the 'marvelous power of adaptation to conditions' that they had exhibited during slavery – if, in other words, they agreed to be inferior – they could coexist with whites and keep friction to a minimum, since in any case white superiority was a universal reality.[74] Stone was well aware of the efforts of both southern and northern blacks to build what he called 'a consciousness of [their] own racial solidarity,' but for him this was pointless. Racial solidarity would inevitably lead to social equality, and this to intermarriage, a practice that whites would never condone. In that event, racial friction would increase throughout the country.

An examination of the controversy surrounding this paper is useful in gaining a fuller understanding of the prevailing ideological climate in which it was written. Whereas most of Stone's listeners approved of his decree of black inferiority, some challenged both his causal explanation and his prognosis. The northern demographer Walter Willcox (1861–1964) did not foresee more intense racial friction but, rather, a mutual effort by both races to replace slavery with a caste system. Although contrary to the political and moral ideals of the United States, such a system did not 'menace the perpetuity of the country.'[75] The northern historian Ulysses Weatherly (1865–1946) argued that blacks had not largely been responsible for racial conflict during slavery or after emancipation.

Rather, they had suffered the ill effects of a profound difference of opinion and sentiment between southern and northern whites. This had been caused by the latter's militant abolitionism, which had whipped up southern white resentment and lit the powder keg. The disastrous historical episode of Reconstruction and its aftermath had not represented a direct attack on blacks but, rather, on the idea of their being granted social rights and privileges from outside the South. As blacks migrated northward, Weatherly prophesied, their purportedly unseemly behavior would exacerbate the intolerance of whites, who would come to recognize 'the essential justice of the South's attitude on the Negro problem.'[76] Two southerners, the political scientist James Garner (1871–1936) and the historian John Bassett (1867–1928), while accepting the postulate of innate white superiority, blamed southern politicians for having altered black-white relations. This alteration, they argued, had led to the Civil War and to the chaos of Reconstruction. Under these conditions, a truly integrated society remained highly improbable; the most likely model was that of two parallel social worlds.[77]

Summary

The obvious remark that applies to all, or nearly all, of the first generation of Anglo-American sociologists is that they were scientific racists.[78] Their 'science' rationalized, without much care or subtlety, the mental image then cherished by the Protestant middle and upper classes of belonging to a biologically pure, superior race. And biological superiority implied psychological, social, cultural, even spiritual superiority. It also implied the normality of the exercise of privileges and powers to keep weaker or inferior groups in a subordinate position, to maintain the 'natural' state of affairs. Southern sociologists in particular, as we have seen, explicitly agreed with the southern credo crudely but lucidly set down by T.P. Bailey:

> 1. Blood will tell. 2. The white race must dominate. 3. The Teutonic peoples stand for race purity. 4. The negro is inferior and will remain so. 5. 'This is a white man's country.' 6. No social equality. 7. No political equality. 8. In matters of civil rights and legal adjustments give the white man, as opposed to the colored man, the benefit of the doubt; and under no circumstances interfere with the prestige of the white race. 9. In educational policy let the negro have the crumbs that fall from the white man's table.

> 10. Let there be such industrial education of the negro as will best fit him to serve the white man. 11. Only Southerners understand the negro question. 12. Let the South settle the negro question. 13. The status of peasantry is all the negro may hope for, if the races are to live together in peace. 14. Let the lowest white man count for more than the highest negro. 15. The above statements indicate the leadings of Providence.[79]

From Biological Racism to Cultural Racism

Anglo-Saxon academic sociology emerged during a time when belief in the innate inequality of the races was not only all-pervasive but enjoyed the backing of contemporary natural science. As such, this belief was readily endorsed by a large majority of sociologists. To grasp the fervor with which the natural sciences were invoked in this racist enterprise, it is necessary to understand the social climate in which these sociologists lived.

When the smoke cleared from the battlefields in 1865, half a million men had died in the fighting and approximately four million slaves could now look to emancipation as a real possibility. Three objectives thus became urgent for the southern white majority: to put these former plantation workers to economic use; to resolve the political question of racial harmony; and to maintain social control over a group of human beings they deemed biologically inferior or even retarded, hence difficult to educate. These objectives were attained with the implementation of a caste system that structurally restored antebellum white domination, along with sharecropping, leaseholding, and debt arrangements that provided economic control over black workers. Segregation was legalized, and blacks were deprived of the franchise that they had formally been granted by the Fifteenth Amendment to the Constitution.

In this context, the natural sciences provided an ideal foundation for sociologists seeking to explain racial conflict. The era's natural scientists wanted to adduce a scientific justification for the grand nineteenth-century idea of a hierarchical ordering of the human races. In this effort they drew correlations between physical features – face, skull, brain volume, genitals – and psychology, behavior, intellect, or other observable human attributes. The newly emancipated blacks would serve as guinea pigs for this agenda; with their alleged inferiority in all these areas, blacks would provide the proof that a hierarchical ordering of the races could be determined. The naturalist agenda became especially prominent after 1870 when Darwin's theory of evolution made its appearance in the United States: 'In time the hypothesis of evolution and the factors of variation and survival of the fittest gave added scientific sophistication to the heritage of the naturalist's racial characterizations.'[80]

With these racial characterizations shored up by Darwinism, the natural scientists could fashion an even more derogatory representation of blacks. They did not hesitate to consecrate the openly racist dogma – biological 'evidence' at the ready – of the innate inferiority of nonwhites and their modest place in the hierarchical ordering of the races. The sociologists followed suit, this being the best imaginable justification for their deep-seated beliefs: 'It is probable that most scientists did not envision the extinction of black people as the working out of the evolutionary process. But almost without exception they agreed that the scientific evidence demonstrated the superiority of the white population to the black and, in fact, to all the nonwhite races.'[81]

This biological racism – rather harshly stated by the southern sociologists, couched in more subtle terms by the northerners – was reinforced by the fact that everyone's model, Herbert Spencer, the prototypical Social Darwinist, wrote forthrightly of a natural hierarchy of the human races.[82] Late-nineteenth-century biologists added further grist to the mill with experiments aiming to discover the mechanism of heredity and demonstrate the predominance of biology over environment in the evolutionary process. One result of the naturalist offensive was to provide scientific backing for the nascent eugenics movement, which, in the first three decades of the twentieth century, would incessantly call for immigration restrictions and sterilization of the 'unfit.'

The biological racism common to all the founding fathers appeared in various guises depending on each one's version of evolutionism. The ultra-Darwinists, including Sumner and the southerners, found the idea of black assimilation utterly abhorrent; the only solution to the 'race problem' was to maintain the status quo, buttress inequality, and prevent miscegenation with this 'naturally' inferior group. The more progressive Darwinists – Giddings, Ross, Cooley, Ward – were open-minded (liberal?) racists who did not oppose assimilation in principle, even though they accepted black biological inferiority as a fact. Ward was exceptional among this cohort in preaching social interventionism as a means of accelerating black assimilation into U.S. society, the idea being to help along the 'natural' process predicted by evolutionary theory.

It is worth dwelling for a moment on Ward's atypical stance. The

1890s had seen the rise to prominence of a young anthropologist who sought to move the social sciences in a direction different from biological racism. In his first paper in 1894, the German-born Franz Boas (who had immigrated to the United States in 1887) sharply criticized biological determinism as an explanation of blacks' different temperament and attitudes.[83] Instead, he stressed the power of cultural factors in explaining the achievements of various human races, blacks included. He continued along these lines in subsequent years and into the new century with a series of empirical papers, courses, conferences, and papers focusing largely on the American Indians. The culmination of this trajectory was a major work, *The Mind of Primitive Man* (1911). Initially trained as a physical anthropologist, Boas would remain reticent throughout his life to renounce the idea of significant correlations between biological traits (e.g., cranial capacity) and qualitative differences in aptitudes among races. But ultimately, culture – favorable circumstances or environment – won out as his chief explanatory variable:

> historical events appear to be much more potent in leading races to civilization than their faculty, and it follows that achievements of races do not warrant us in assuming that one race is more highly gifted than the others ... Thus all attempts to correlate racial types and cultural stages failed us, and we concluded that cultural stage is essentially a phenomenon dependent upon historical causes, regardless of race.[84]

Of blacks, Boas wrote, 'there is every reason to believe that the negro, when given facility and opportunity, will be perfectly able to fulfill the duties of citizenship as well as his white neighbor ... It may be that he will not produce as many great men as the white race, and his average achievement will not quite reach the level of the average achievement of the white race; but there will be countless numbers who will be able to outrun their white competitors.'[85]

It may be safely assumed that a progressive like Ward drew inspiration from Boasian culturalism, and in this he was followed by another liberal, William Thomas (1862–1947), whose career bridged the first two generations of Chicago sociologists.[86] In 'The Mind of Woman and the Lower Races,' Thomas questioned the widespread belief in white superiority: 'we shall have to reduce very much our usual estimate of the difference in mental capacity between ourselves and the lower races, if we do not eliminate it altogether; and we shall perhaps have to abandon altogether the view that there has been an increase in the mental capacity of the white race since prehistoric times.'[87] In an era when anatomical measurements greatly influenced the race debate, Thomas departed from the norm: 'In respect, then, to brain structure and the more important mental faculties we find that no race is radically unlike the others ... it may well be that failure to progress equally is not due to essential unlikeness of mind, but to conditions lying outside the mind.'[88]

However, others of his writings indicate that Thomas never fully renounced his belief in heredity as a factor in racial aptitudes. In 1904, introducing the concept of race prejudice into the sociological vocabulary, he maintained that it was tantamount to 'an instinct originating in the tribal stage of society, when solidarity of feeling and action was essential to the preservation of the group'; an 'intense and immediate' instinct evoked 'primarily by the physical aspects of an unfamiliar people' and only secondarily by 'their activities and habits.'[89] Like Boas, he oscillated between environment and biology, culture and nature. It was a subtle position in that it emphasized the possibility of dispelling or demolishing racial prejudice, whatever its organic basis, through human association. People of different racial backgrounds were not condemned to live in a system of segregation or caste-governed interaction. Having been raised in Tennessee, Thomas had firsthand familiarity with the reality of caste and its stifling effect on blacks, and he eloquently described the relationship between that system and the genesis of prejudice:

> Psychologically speaking, race-prejudice and caste-feeling are at bottom the same thing, both being phases of the instinct of hate ... Of the relation of black to white in this country it is perhaps true that the antipathy of the southerner for the negro is rather caste-feeling than race-prejudice, while the feeling of the northerner is race-prejudice proper. In the North, where there has been no contact with the negro and no activity connections, there is no caste-feeling, but there exists a sort of *skin*-prejudice – a horror of the external aspect of the negro – and many northerners report that they have a feeling against eating from a dish handled by a negro. The association of master and slave in the South was, however, close, even if not intimate, and much of the feeling of physical repulsion for a black skin disappeared.[90]

To sum up – the spectrum of Anglo-American sociological positions on the race question ranged from the brutal biological racism of the postbellum southern amateurs – the direct heirs of the pro-slavery writers Hughes and Fitzhugh – to the more nuanced but nonetheless explicit biological racism of most northerners, to a mixture of biology and culture in more open-minded individuals like Ward and Thomas, who were directly influenced by Boas.

From Race Problem to Race Relations

Boas's work heralded a conceptual shift in the Anglo-American race relations episteme that would be complete by the end of the First World War. Some sociohistorical background to this turbulent period in American life is useful in understanding this development.

In demographic terms, the population had grown by 50 percent, from 62.9 million in 1890 to 96 million on the eve of the war, the result not only of an excess of births over deaths but also of a spectacularly high rate of immigration: 'Between 1900 and 1909 alone some 8.2 million people landed on American shores, and the total for the forty-year span from 1880 to 1920, when the great era of foreign immigration closed, came to almost 23.5 million, while the average number of arrivals per decade amounted to about 6 million individuals.'[91] In economic terms, the late nineteenth century saw the country enter an era of unprecedented change driven by industrial expansion and the rise of new forms of monopoly capitalism. The result: 'In the mid-1890s, the United States became the leading industrial power, and by 1910 its factories poured forth goods of nearly twice the value of those of its nearest rival, Germany. In 1913, the United States accounted for more than one-third of the world's industrial production.'[92]

As a direct reaction to these trends, the intermediate social formations (local communities, organizations, etc.) became deeply involved in political struggle, often taking the form of violent labor strikes, striving to make maximum gains on behalf of the poor.[93] The tenor of the times, along with the abusive practices of the elites, led the masses to redouble their resistance and organizing efforts. Meanwhile big cities, a new entity in the U.S. social fabric, represented the crux of a transformation toward greater societal complexity.[94]

Blacks, for their part, were largely omitted from this great leap forward. While the great majority of them lived in the South under abject segregation, many were moving northward, especially to the cities. The figures indicate an uneven but continuous exodus: 'Rural southern blacks envisioned northern cities as a kind of "promised land"' in the post-Civil War years. Over the entire period from 1870 to 1920, about 1,100,000 southern blacks became northern urban dwellers. The movement was especially strong after 1900 because of the promise of economic opportunity.'[95] For many, this promise remained unfulfilled. Blacks arriving in northern cities met with fierce competition for jobs and housing from a white population that had become much more multiethnic as a result of immigration since 1880. From pitiless segregation in the South to violence, discrimination, and racism in the northern cities: such was the social fate of black people (who numbered more than 10 million) just before the First World War. The war itself helped to alleviate the situation:

> Although the migration of blacks from the South to the North had increased steadily from 1870 through 1910, by 1915, when the World War began to impede the flow of cheap labor from Europe, and when many immigrants returned to their homelands to take part in the conflict, larger numbers of blacks were recruited to take the places left vacant in Northern industries. Even more blacks came North after 1917 when industries began expanding as the United States entered the conflict.[96]

American social scientists' representation of blacks at this time was in perfect keeping with the prevailing view held by whites in general; just as blacks' inferiority in the social order was taken for granted by the man on the street, it was axiomatic in the ivory tower, though a new dialectic had been introduced between the biological and the cultural (symbolic) referents of race. The 1910s were a transitional period auguring a shift – particularly evident after 1920 – to a new episteme of race:

> During the 1910s, the rise of a naturalistic [i.e. empiricist as opposed to dogmatic or doctrinaire] worldview in the social sciences coincided historically with internal conceptual stresses [nature versus culture] and social structural changes. These conditions stimulated reassessments of the capabilities of blacks, the analysis of prejudice, and the nature of race relations ... The emphasis on the use of empirical data as a basis for authoritative statements on the capabilities of blacks was liberating, insofar as it provided sociologists with a factual basis for their ethical beliefs.[97]

This shift to empiricism was extremely significant. With the continued exodus of blacks from the South, northern social scientists had an opportunity to observe living conditions in the urban ghettos directly.

They could see and measure for themselves the severity of the conflicts experienced by blacks in their day-to-day relations with other races. Direct observation was a major methodological innovation for its time, relegating the practices of nineteenth-century pioneers such as Giddings and Sumner to another age. As we have seen, these academics' discourse on racial conflict was never based on valid data for, with the exception of Odum, who conducted a few small surveys in his native South, they did not have any. Yet their geographic distance from and general unfamiliarity with the South never deterred them from holding arbitrary, dogmatic opinions and using their cloistered university positions as platforms from which to express them.

But although the principle of empiricism was in the air, it was not yet fully incorporated into social science practice. The discourse of writers on the race question straddled the old and the new methodologies. The key research problem, as they saw it, was to compare aptitudes and capacities across the races. But on the psychological and intellectual capacities of black people, psychology – or what passed for it – actually had very little to say. A great many crude tests of unproven scientific merit were administered and, invariably, 'found' that blacks possessed meager psychological and intellectual aptitudes; naturally, this was put down to their innate inferiority.

In a stinging rejoinder to this brand of psychology (whose most ambitious and least scrupulous representative was George O. Ferguson), William Thomas further revealed his culturalist bias. Adducing empirical data, he maintained that both immigrants and blacks were essentially bearing the brunt of a problem created by whites; namely, the forced social and intellectual isolation that had impeded their progress. Their race was not intrinsically inferior to any other: 'race-prejudice may be regarded as a form of isolation. And in the case of the American Negro this situation is aggravated by the fact that the white man has developed a determination to keep him in isolation – "in his place." Now, when the isolation is willed and has at the same time the emotional nature of a tabu, the handicap is very grave indeed.'[98]

Remarkable, indeed unique for their time, were Thomas's dozen citations of W.E.B. Du Bois's *The Philadelphia Negro* (1899) in support of his argument. As well, the following passage finds him diminishing the importance of race and emphasizing that of contextual or cultural factors: 'individual variation is of more importance than racial difference ... the main factors in social change are attention, interest, stimulation, imitation, occupational differentiation, mental attitude, and accessibility to opportunity and copies. In other words, I have emphasized the social rather than the biological and economic aspects of the problem.'[99] To further buttress his argument, Thomas invoked Boas's anthropology: 'Present-day anthropology does not pretend that any of the characteristic mental powers, such as memory, inhibition, abstraction, logical ability, are feeble or lacking in any race.'[100]

Another sociologist whose writings exhibit tension and ambivalence as to the relative importance of nature and culture in explanations of race was Ellsworth Faris (1874–1953), a white southerner who spent most of his career in the North, particularly at the University of Chicago where he was the second chairman of the sociology department. Faris was well acquainted with equatorial Africa from having spent several years there as a missionary. In a 1918 article on his empirical research among Congolese tribes, Faris accepted Boas's theory that a 'primitive' child was 'on the average, about the same in capacity as the child of civilized races.' He continued: 'Instead of the concept of different stages or degrees of mentality, we find it easier to think of the human mind as being, in its capacity, about the same everywhere, the difference in culture to be explained in terms of the physical geography, or the stimuli from other groups ...'[101] But he also displayed a penchant for cross-racial correlations of brain weight with intellectual aptitude, with particular reference to blacks.

Similarly, in Charles Cooley's mature work on the race question, particularly his *Social Process* (1918), progressive views coexist with reactionary vestiges. The reactionary in him came out in sentences such as, 'why should races be presumed equal in mental and moral capacity when family stocks in the same race are so evidently unequal in these respects?'[102] and in his certainty that the races were divided by 'spiritual differences' generated by sociohistorical forces. In contrast, the open-minded progressive gave greater weight to environmental factors than to biological attributes: 'a race problem [is] one in which biological and social factors, working together, produce lasting differences sufficient to keep the groups apart ... the ruling factor is not the precise amount of strictly racial difference, as distinct from social, but the actual attitude of the groups toward each other.'[103]

But of all the Anglo-American sociological figures who assisted at the birth of the discipline of race relations theory, the most important was unquestionably Robert Ezra Park (1864–1944), whose first essays on race relations were published in 1913. Since his scientific trajectory fits more naturally into the period between the two world wars, it is covered in the next chapter.

CONCLUSION

Within the web of events, practices, and disputes making up the American social order between 1865 and 1914, American blacks were codified as inferior human beings by virtue of their race. The emerging Anglo-American sociology, devised by intellectuals of petty-bourgeois Protestant background, took up this ambient codification of inferiority and transmuted it into a problematic of *inferiorization*, a social process that could be interpreted according to the logic of probable causes and foreseeable consequences. From this common foundation, two continua of argument diverged across the decades. One continuum sought to inscribe the theorization process between two referents – biology and culture – neither reducible to the other, both dialectically opposable, to produce the more sophisticated conceptualizations of Thomas and others on the eve of the First World War. The other continuum shifted the characterization of the study object to a more scientifically valid and modern one: from race as a social problem to race relations as a social phenomenon. These differences accounted for, the explanatory work of the first sociologists remained trapped within the framework of evolutionism, the episteme that, for late-nineteenth-century intellectuals, represented the very essence of rigor. Evolutionary theory was still the epistemological foundation for causal and functional explanations of society, as it had been since the beginnings of the discipline.

2 The Rise of the Chicago School

The most important change that occurred in the Anglo-American sociological corpus after the First World War was the gravitation from grand theoretical speculation – general theory – to a much more empirically focused approach.[1] This, it must be emphasized, was a gradual rather than an abrupt change of direction; while the prestige of general theory diminished from its nineteenth-century heyday, prominent sociologists continued to cultivate it.[2] As for the substantive premises of the discipline, they remained unaltered. Evolutionary naturalism in particular retained its pivotal role as an explanatory principle.

Among the founding fathers, Sumner and Ward had died before the First World War (in 1910 and 1913, respectively), while Small would pass away in 1926. He and the three other remaining founding fathers pursued their work on general theory, a nuance here or there indicating their awareness of the new empiricist currents. Meanwhile, the idea of social process enshrined by Cooley's eponymous 1918 book greatly influenced the course of Anglo-American sociology. While Cooley's later work *Sociological Theory and Social Research* (published in 1930, shortly before his death) as well as Ross's *Principles of Sociology* (1920) and Giddings's *Studies in the Theory of Human Society* (1922) carried on the general theory tradition, works by their contemporaries attested to a new vision of scientific objectivity and of sociology as a discipline: the five-volume *The Polish Peasant in Europe and America* (1918–20), by William Thomas and Florian Znaniecki (1882–1958); Park and Burgess's contribution to the increasingly competitive textbook market, *Introduction to the Science of Sociology* (1921), and *Social Change,* by William Ogburn (1886–1959). Stephen and Jonathan Turner show how the differences between Giddings's and Ogburn's works signaled the arrival of a new sociological generation:

> Giddings's last theory book (1922), a collection of essays, and Ogburn's major work (1922) represented the passing of the generational torch in the Columbia [University] tradition. The differences in these last two texts typify the change. Franklin Giddings was centrally concerned with the lag between material conditions and collectively shared ideas, but he theorized about this lag as a part of a general conception of the selective processes behind social evolution. In contrast, Ogburn made 'cultural lag' into a much narrower problem to be addressed 'empirically' and independently of any grand cosmic scheme.[3]

This phenomenon of generational difference between sociologists at Columbia is readily generalizable to the entire discipline in the years after 1918. Two major transformations took place. Concerning the conceptual underpinnings of the discipline, the macrosocial dimension of evolutionary naturalism dear to the pioneers gradually gave way to a microsocial focus. The 1920s saw the last specimens of Spencerian grand theories about society, which were diminished to the status of introductory considerations or prolegomena. Only theories propounded in the spirit of what has undoubtedly come to constitute the hallmark of Anglo-American thinking – empiricist pragmatism – would henceforth be considered acceptable.[4] The cognitive value of any theory would largely be gauged by its instrumentality within an empirical research strategy.

The other transformation concerned the relationship between social reform as an objective and sociology as a science. We have seen that reform was a fundamental goal of the first academic sociologists. The new century saw a new generation, still legitimately motivated by a desire to heal society's ills and aided by substantial research funding from new philanthropic foundations (e.g., the Rockefeller Foundation), rapidly relinquish reformist sentimentality for putatively scientific curiosity and detached observation of facts. One by one, all the academic sociology departments endorsed this sweeping transformation. Leading it were the members of the sociology department at the University of Chicago, which fashioned the paradigmatic construction of a different Anglo-American sociological corpus. On the race question per se, the Chicago School of sociology's remarkable reign of influence would extend to the eve of the Second World War; hence its importance to the issues discussed in this book. To understand the genesis of the American sociological avant-garde between the two world wars and the internal culture of the Chicago School, it is useful to trace its development from its beginnings. I shall describe in general terms the new approach it represented, then go on to discuss the theories of race developed by scholars associated with it.[5]

Origins of a Scientific Hothouse: 1892–1914

The department of sociology at the University of Chicago was founded in 1892, as was the university itself, thanks to a multimillion dollar Rockefeller grant. It was understood that the new institution was to position itself at the forefront of knowledge in every field, regardless of the cost and the necessary infrastructure. Its first president, William Rayney Harper, a Baptist minister (Rockefeller, too, was a Baptist) and former professor of Greek and Hebrew at Yale, aggressively recruited department heads and exhibited the entrepreneurial spirit that would characterize the institution.[6]

Albion Small chaired the new sociology department, which consisted of George Vincent (1864–1941), William Thomas, and Charles Henderson (1848–1915). As president of Colby College since 1889, Small had acquired considerable administrative experience, and he enjoyed a good reputation as a sociologist versed in German sociology, which was to become a major source of inspiration for the new university. He was also, as a Protestant minister, of like mind with Harper and with Rockefeller, the university's benefactor. The year 1895 saw the inception of the *American Journal of Sociology*, the first U.S. journal of its kind, which Small would edit until his death in 1926.

Small was, however, a pivotal figure in the evolution of sociology. While his biography and intellectual background placed him squarely in the first generation of sociologists, his acceptance of the position at the University of Chicago clearly indicated his belief that sociology had to partake of the institution's founding ideology of resolute pragmatism. In short, he straddled the two generations and, as the key sociological figure in late-nineteenth-century Chicago, set the tone for the department. One of his key intellectual goals was to secure sociology's independence from socioreligious movements and interest groups that sought to usurp the discipline for various political and ethical purposes. In *The Methodology of the Social Problem*, a set of seminar notes published in 1898 by the University of Chicago Press, he dealt with the sensitive issue of the link between sociology and social reform. From the outset he showed his antireformist colors, which would become those of his entire department: 'Radical error and persistent confusion would be forestalled, if students could be familiar from the start with the fact that sociology is not, first and foremost, a set of schemes to reform the world.'[7] On the contrary, it was the University of Chicago's role to establish the scientificity of the young discipline of sociology and thus to place it on an equal footing with history, economics, and philosophy.

The foundational work best expressing the new department's conceptual cast was Small's *General Sociology: An Exposition of the Main Development in Sociological Theory from Spencer to Ratzenhofer.* As the subtitle indicates, this work presented sociology as an arc between the poles of general theory and applied research, but also as a discipline firmly guided by more compact and modest, less all-encompassing conceptual ambitions than it had possessed just after the Civil War: 'Our thesis is that *the central line in the path of methodological progress, from Spencer to Ratzenhofer, is marked by gradual shifting of effort from analogical representation of social structures to real analysis of social processes.*'[8] This quotation underscores a European movement, then in full swing, that would form the nucleus of American standard sociology from the 1920s onward; Georg Simmel, the German sociologist who was one of its architects, would profoundly influence the theories of the Parkian generation of Anglo-American sociologists (see p. 50). In a 1916 article that represented the first critical history of the discipline of sociology, then fifty years old, Small argued that this period fell cleanly into two segments lying on either side of the year 1892. The founding of the University of Chicago had, he claimed, propelled sociology into a sort of intellectual middle age:

> there need be little hesitation about selecting the date 1892 as memorable, not merely for American university work in general, but for sociology in particular ... After 1892 sociology came out into the open as an accredited university subject, but I very strongly doubt if this consummation would have been reached at that time – I am not sure that it would have occurred at all – if the University of Chicago had not been founded.[9]

As biased as this opinion might seem, given the author's relationship to the university, it was a fairly good summation of the situation at the turn of the century, in which sociology was becoming more independent from other disciplines in terms of both its theories and its administrative structures. And this was just a foretaste of what would occur under the leadership of Robert Park after the First World War.[10]

Before we move on, a word should be said about William Thomas, who was, of the first four Chicago School sociologists, scientifically at least the equal of Albion Small. Thomas published two works of interest to this topic before the First World War: *Source Book for Social Origins* (1909), an ethnological reader on primitive societies that still showed traces of his early biologistic and psychologizing bias; and 'Race Psychology' (1912), which I have already discussed. While preparing these two works, Thomas pursued research that would lead to his mammoth study of Polish immigrants several years later.

The Parkian Era

Park came to Chicago for a short stay at Thomas's invitation in 1913 on the fiftieth anniversary of the Emancipation Proclamation, and remained in the city for most of the rest of his professional life.[11] His innovativeness was evident from the outset in his articles on race and other subjects (e.g., urban studies, in his famous *American Journal of Sociology* article 'The City: Suggestions for the Investigation of Human Behavior in the Urban Environment'). After a few years as a lecturer, he was promoted to a professorship in 1919 in an aging department whose numbers were declining as a result of death, forced resignation (Thomas in 1918),[12] retirement, and transfer to administrative positions. It so happened that an interdisciplinary committee called the Local Community Research Committee (LCRC) had recently been struck to administer a huge social science research endowment from the Rockefeller family – a lucky coincidence for both Park and his department:

> Park was a distinctive intellect, but it was something of an accident that his ideas became as important as they did. The department might have gone in a quite different direction in the early 1920s, but the LCRC was established at a time when the sociology department was in a plastic state ... The sociology department was virtually a blank slate at the time Park became a full member of the faculty, and the LCRC grant enabled Park to create a new kind of sociology at Chicago.[13]

If Park found himself in this strategic position in 1920, it was in part because he was perceived as the man of the situation by the university authorities and in part because his personal charisma gave him considerable influence over the LCRC, allowing him to raise the money necessary to advance specifically sociological research. Park's 'new kind of sociology' was, as we shall now discover, a departure in terms of both conceptual approach and research organization.

By virtue of his education, Park was heir to the German conception of sociology and particularly that of Georg Simmel, whom he regarded as 'the greatest of all sociologists'[14] and whose concepts he transposed to the U.S. context more or less wholesale. For both men, society arose from the intertwining of various relationships between individuals in an uninterrupted flow of mutual interaction.[15] If so, then sociology could be conceived of as the science whose role is to describe and analyze this vast process of human interaction and formation of specific groups; in short, the science of social processes and collective behavior. Quite naturally, this science also appeared as a method for analyzing the singular processes whereby individuals are led to cooperate, and to encourage others to cooperate, in the constitution of a set of community groups – society. This was the conceptual kernel of Parkian sociology after 1920, the pivotal theoretical concept being that of the social process.

On the institutional level, Park and his acolytes sought to perfect a framework that could balance theoretical work with the empirical research that their funders demanded. One of their innovations in this regard was the research program model (about which Imre Lakatos has theorized at length).[16] These research programs were incorporated – another first at Chicago – into the very structure of the department: 'Sociological research at the University of Chicago between 1915 and 1930 was the first successful example of the integration of extensive research into a university department of sociology ... not only was there an integrated pattern of research, but an infrastructure and simple research organization to support it were created, coupled with outside financial support ...'[17] The hard core of Park's research program involved no systematic theories, since these were at odds with his intellectual temperament; at base he was an essayist.[18] However, he was open to theorizing in relation to what he saw as a fundamental goal of sociology: expanding the rigorous knowledge of U.S. society in its most concentrated form, the metropolis:

> The theory developed at Chicago sought to explain the changing behaviour of the various ethnic groups living in the metropolis. It was a theoret-

> ical model that rested on circumstantiated analysis of urban (and also rural) communities, of the processes of immigration and assimilation, of the structure of the family, and of long-term social trends whose indubitably most salient aspects were immigration and urbanization. It was this convergence of 'ideas in common,' of an 'accepted way of working,' that fashioned the Chicago sociologists into a School.[19]

The 'accepted ways of working' in question were bounded by human ecology on the one hand and interactionism on the other. It was a highly instrumentalist approach, largely because of the research program itself, whose role was to guide empirical research: 'The choice of the term "program" is important, for it indicates that the research activity was oriented, that the researchers had intentions, that they pursued goals. For example, the goal might be to explain a certain phenomenon, to develop a theory, or to prove it superior to others. Any new result would be evaluated with respect to these goals.'[20]

By contrast with the pioneering generation, the Chicago School's mark of distinction was thus to build a sociological corpus through oriented research conducted by teams. The word 'team' is rather grand, for at first the team consisted of only Park and Thomas. Ernest Burgess joined the department in 1916 and, after Thomas's dismissal, became Park's main collaborator. Ellsworth Faris replaced Thomas as a professor of social psychology but did not join the team, while the human ecologist Roderick McKenzie (1887–1937) joined in the mid-1920s. The field work was done by graduate students working under individual supervision, while the funding came from the LCRC.

Three early works served as the flagships of the Chicago School's scientific credo or orthodoxy: Thomas and Znaniecki's *The Polish Peasant in Europe and America* (1918–20), and Park and Burgess's *Introduction to the Science of Sociology* (1921) and *The City* (1925). The basic conceptualization of sociology as both theory and method laid out in these works served as a guidepost to empirical research and formed the 'protective layer' (*sensu* Lakatos) for their sociology, enabling them to reach out into the broader social environment, meet the LCRC's requirements for 'realistic' social research, pinpoint the needs of the ethnic communities making up Chicago's social fabric, and, in short, implement the 'social laboratory' portion of an ambitious theoretical and applied research program:

> The main instrument which Park and Burgess fashioned to stimulate

> empirical research was their graduate seminar on field studies, given every year from 1918 onwards until Park's retirement in 1934. Park considered, as he set out in his 1915 article on the city, that the city could be treated as a social laboratory or clinic in which human nature and social processes might be conveniently studied.[21]

The result was an impressive series of case study-based monographs,[22] each an embodiment of the combination of theory and methodology that characterized the new Chicago sociology. In fact, titles such as Charles Johnson's *The Negro in Chicago* (1922; published under the institutional authorship of the Chicago Commission on Race Relations), Nels Anderson's *The Hobo* (1923), Frederic Thrasher's *The Gang* (1927), Louis Wirth's *The Ghetto* (1927), Harvey Zorbaugh's *Gold Coast and Slum* (1929), John Landesco's *Organized Crime in Chicago* (1929), Clifford Shaw's *The Jack-Roller* (1930), and Paul Cressey's *The Taxi-Dance Hall* (1932) also followed in the tradition of the turn-of-the-century research conducted by empirical-minded amateurs – the social surveyors briefly discussed in the previous chapter, who were particularly active after 1905. By that time their numbers were mainly composed of social workers closely associated with the settlement-house movement[23] and reformers motivated by what Park sardonically termed 'do-gooderism.' According to Jennifer Platt, the continuity between these monographs and the nonacademic tradition after 1900 was marked by borrowing and revisitation:

> Work done by such non-sociologists often contained empirical data at least as thorough and systematic as that of the sociologists ... If we look simply at the substantive topics on which the famous university monographs were written, we find that most of these had been the subject of earlier work by non-sociologists (or at any rate by people who either did not at the time hold that job title, or have not been accorded it by posterity).[24]

Nevertheless, two features of the Chicago School's works constituted clear scientific advances: their thoroughgoing commitment to detachment or a-reformism, evident in their pervasive positivistic conception of rigor; and their explicit resort to theory for purposes of generalization. In these respects, the influence of Park and Burgess was decisive. Burgess was, of the two, the more skilled research methodologist. To the qualitative tools carefully developed by the Chicago School from the outset he added elaborate and sophisticated statistical compilations, charts, and diagrams based on the best mathematical methods of the time. The qualitative and quantitative skill that he imparted to his students is noticeable in each of the above-mentioned monographs. As for Park, he put his talent and experience into the job of dissuading his students from do-gooderism and inculcating in them a detachment or distance from the emotional dimensions of social problems. He saw this stance as a sine qua non for any social scientist attempting to discern the real causes of problems and plan objective interventions with an eye to improvement. His personal manner, though often gruff or abrupt, was generally appreciated by his students and colleagues.

Concerning the necessity of combining detachment with abstraction and theorization in the interests of true science, Park and Burgess made it a fundamental precept of their *Introduction to the Science of Sociology*: 'The attempt to describe ... the historical, cultural, political, and economic processes, is justified in so far as it enables us to recognize that the aspects of social life, which are the subject-matter of the special social sciences ... are involved in specific forms of change that can be viewed abstractly, formulated, compared, and related.'[25]

To set the stage for a discussion of Park's theory of race relations – which, as we shall see, was something of a departure from the basic Chicago corpus – I shall summarize the distinctive features of that corpus, the standard-bearer of the new Anglo-American sociology. Briefly, it wedded German theory (Simmel, Wundt, Tönnies) with social psychology (Cooley, Mead) and typically Anglo-Saxon pragmatism (Dewey and James, under whom Park had worked at Harvard at the turn of the century). Because of the particular academic conditions of its genesis, it was rather hermetic in its scientific and institutional standards: 'Chicago's model of sociology – an academic culture in a department with many students and a vital *gemeinschaftliche* ambiance – was not readily generalizable to the broader discipline or to other departmental situations.'[26] The Chicago hothouse fascinated the first generation of black American sociologists who went to study there, and it would stand in the forefront of mainstream sociology while Park taught and published at the university.

It was not until 1934, with Park's retirement, that the way would be opened for the Chicago School's theoretical conception to be challenged on fundamental points of epistemology. As seductive as it might have been, it was actually quite a fragile position; the claims of explanatory power adduced for social realism were exaggerated, while an abstract system of thought – the alpha and omega of any authentic scientific theory – was mainly notable for its absence: 'Neither does it appear that the Park and Burgess text or any of the subsequent three Park volumes offers, or sought to offer, a rigorous, systematic, integrated, and unified conception of the field such that it could warrant the characterization of being a macro- or general theory.'[27] But surprisingly, this sociology met with no serious critical assault before the Second World War; it remained the standard throughout Park's life. Aside from a few innocuous critiques appearing between 1935 and 1940, the first event that posed a serious challenge to Park's theory of race relations was the publication of Gunnar Myrdal's voluminous *An American Dilemma* (1944), to which we return in chapter 3.

Park's Theory of Race Relations

Park's sociology of race relations is imbued with the spirit of the Chicago School's golden years.[28] As background to this theory, it is useful to review the racial and ethnic situation of the country after 1918. Demographic growth had, of course, continued,[29] and immigration, interrupted during the conflict, resumed at a tremendous rate, producing a backlash that culminated in the Immigration Acts of 1921 and 1924, targeting Asian immigrants especially. The economic prosperity reigning between 1918 and 1929 was paralleled only by the appetite for consumption exhibited by all social classes, from the most opulent to the most destitute. Black migrants fleeing poverty on the southern plantations flocked to the industrialized areas of the country.[30] This phenomenal migration brought its share of difficulties, even for those blacks who managed to find work, often taking the place of unskilled immigrant laborers who had left in search of better prospects (or had been fired). Little by little, blacks integrated into nearly all basic industries (automotive, metallurgy, packing, etc.), but they remained relegated to the lowest socioeconomic status, subjected to endless varieties of discrimination by employers, and forced to live isolated in urban ghettos. Many whites reacted with hostility, or even fanaticism, in the face of the immigration of blacks and other ethnic groups: 'The increasing migration of large numbers of blacks from the South into Northern urban-industrial areas after 1920 coincided historically with the rise of anti-black, anti-Semitic, and anti-Catholic feelings among Americans of British ancestry. Furthermore, nativism was being reinforced by some intellectuals.'[31]

The twentieth century was young when the first black advocacy organizations, dedicated to the improvement of blacks' living standards (employment, housing) and to fending off nativism and other antagonistic currents in American society, made their appearance. The National Association for the Advancement of Colored People (NAACP) was founded in May 1910 at the initiative of a group of liberal whites and radical blacks (including Du Bois) in response to violent and discriminatory practices.[32] The Universal Negro Improvement Association (UNIA) was a pan-Africanist movement (founded in 1916) that was headed by the charismatic Jamaican immigrant Marcus Garvey and led by him until his imprisonment and deportation in 1925.[33] And the Urban League (founded in 1911) grew out of the work of Booker T. Washington (1856–1915) and his belief that black Americans should cooperate with white-sponsored initiatives to improve their socio-economic status and, in general, 'accommodate' to their inferior and segregated social status. Park helped to found the Chicago section of the Urban League and served as its president for a time. A moderate association, it met with little success. On the one hand, it was eclipsed by the more assertive positions of the NAACP; on the other, it was shunted out of the limelight in the 1920s by the 'Harlem Renaissance,' a brief but exceptional explosion of creativity among a group of New York-based black artists and writers who glorified a 'new Negro' and, in stark opposition to accommodationism, assertively demanded recognition of black equality.

Park's first articles on race relations appeared in 1913, and he showed a sustained level of scientific interest in the subject for the rest of his life, more than any other Anglo-American scholar of his generation. His educational background gives insight into this peculiarity. After doctoral studies in Strasbourg and Heidelberg with Windelband, followed by a year of teaching at Harvard (1904–5), Park became affiliated with the Congo Reform Association and its attempts to publicize atrocities committed by the Belgian colonial regime in that country. It was while planning a trip to Africa to study the issue that he met the activist Washington, who persuaded him instead to go to his Tuskegee Institute in Alabama and begin his study of Africa in the South. He spent from 1905 to 1913 in daily contact with the colorful Virginia-born figure known to all Americans for his philosophy of accommodationism, serving as his publicist, writing most of his speeches, finding time to conduct personal research, and taking every opportunity to disseminate his mentor's philosophy. It is generally agreed that he wrote most of Washington's *The Story of the Negro* (1909) and *The Man Farthest Down* (1912). Here is Park describing the role Washington played in kindling his interest in race relations:

> I had grown tired of books, and while I was looking about for something more thrilling than a logical formula, I discovered a new interest in the study of the Negro and the race problem.
>
> This new interest grew out of meeting Booker Washington. The result of that meeting was that I spent seven winters, partly at Tuskegee but partly roaming about the South, getting acquainted with the life, the customs, and the condition of the Negro people ... I think I probably learned more about human nature and society, in the South under Booker Washington, than I had learned elsewhere in all my previous studies ... I was interested in the Negro in the South and in the curious and intricate system which had grown up to define his relations with white folk. I was interested, most of all, in studying the details of the process by which the Negro was making and has made his slow but steady advance. I became convinced, finally, that I was observing the historical process by which civilization, not merely here but elsewhere, has evolved, drawing into the circle of its influence an ever widening circle of races and peoples.[34]

Was Park conscious, during his time with Washington, of all that he discusses in this account, in particular the last two sentences, or did this clear awareness of his true interests only come to him with thirty years of hindsight? Ultimately, it matters little. What is important are the choices that he made as he began to write about interracial contact in the second decade of the century; in particular, his firm alignment with evolutionism, the era's great scientific dogma. The history of Park's ideas on race relations may be divided into two chronological periods, the first corresponding to his twenty-one years at the University of Chicago, and the second to what came afterward.

1913–1932

Park established a conceptual framework for his race relations theory in three early papers, the first two dating from 1913. 'Negro Home Life and Standards of Living' was intended as a blow to the stereotype that blacks formed a homogeneous population that was excluded from progress by virtue of its innate degeneracy. He noted an improvement in the living conditions of rural southern blacks – the fact that a sizable number of farmers had attained a decent standard of living despite thirty years of legal segregation.[35] In 'Racial Assimilation in Secondary Groups with Particular Reference to the Negro,' he focused for the first time – it would not be the last – on the ambiguous concept of assimilation as applied to both blacks and 'non-whites' (Asians) living in the United States.[36] His definition of assimilation here gives an early indication that his interest in the coming years would be focused more on relations between groups generally thought of as races than on innate racial characteristics: 'It is the process of assimilation by which groups of individuals, originally indifferent or perhaps hostile, achieve this corporate character, rather than the process by which they acquire a formal like-mindedness, with which this paper is mainly concerned.'[37] He nuanced the concept with a biological analogy: 'Assimilation, as the word is here used, brings with it a certain borrowed significance which it carried over from physiology where it is employed to describe the process of nutrition. By a process of nutrition, somewhat similar to the physiological one, we may conceive alien peoples to be incorporated with, and made part of, the community or state.'[38]

Allusions to physiology notwithstanding, Park had little patience for the allegedly innate biological differences that most of his contemporaries put forward as arguments for blacks' natural inferiority. Rather, it was their outward features that constituted the greatest obstacle to an assimilation considered impossible by nearly everyone around him:

> the chief obstacle to the assimilation of the Negro and the Oriental are not mental but physical traits. It is not because the Negro and the Japanese are so differently constituted that they do not assimilate ... The fact that the Japanese bears in his features a distinctive racial hallmark, that he wears, so to speak, a racial uniform, classifies him ... It puts between the races the invisible but very real gulf of self-consciousness ... Where races are distinguished by certain external marks these furnish a permanent physical substratum upon which and around which the irritations and animosities, incidental to all human intercourse, tend to accumulate and so gain strength and volume.[39]

Yet there was, thought Park, a historical time in which blacks had been able to assimilate – the time of slavery:

> The most striking illustration of this is the fact of domestic slavery. Slavery has been, historically, the usual method by which peoples have been incor-

> porated into alien groups. When a member of an alien race is adopted into the family as a servant, or as a slave, and particularly when that status is made hereditary, as it was in the case of the Negro after his importation to America, assimilation followed rapidly and as a matter of course.[40]

Slavery had rapidly instilled in blacks the customs, family patterns, and 'civilization' of their masters, but, Park believed, such movement toward assimilation had ended with emancipation:

> When the Negro moved off the plantation upon which he was reared he severed the personal relations which bound him to his master's people. It was just at this point that the two races began to lose touch with each other. From this time on the relations of the black man and the white, which in slavery had been direct and personal, became every year, as the old associations were broken, more and more indirect and secondary.[41]

Meanwhile, the postbellum context of segregation favored the development of closer ties within a black community cut off from its heritage and left to its own devices. On this point, Park would agree with his contemporaries until the end of his career. The segregation that followed emancipation had progressively isolated blacks from the surrounding society, leading to the formation of race consciousness, a distinctive sociocultural development:

> It is hard to estimate the ultimate effect of this isolation of the black man. One of the most important effects has been to establish a common interest among all the different colors and classes of the race. This sense of solidarity has grown up gradually with the organization of the Negro people ... The sentiment of racial loyalty, which is a comparatively recent manifestation of the growing self-consciousness of the race, must be regarded as a response and 'accommodation' to changing internal and external relations of the race.[42]

The specific case of blacks could be likened to the development of nationalities in Europe: 'The progress of race adjustment in the southern states since the emancipation has, on the whole, run parallel with the nationalist movement in Europe.'[43] Feelings of belonging and solidarity had gradually affirmed this race consciousness. In both America and Europe, such consciousness had grown in direct reaction to attempts to suppress national languages or cultures, intensifying with the development of nationalistic art and literature: 'Literature and art, when they are employed to give expression to racial sentiment and form to racial ideals, serve, along with other agencies, to mobilize the group and put the masses *en rapport* with their leaders and with each other. In such case art and literature are like silent drummers which summon into action the latent instincts and energies of the race.'[44] Park approved unhesitatingly of such movements ('it seems as if it were through conflicts of this kind, rather than through war, that the minor peoples were destined to gain the moral concentration and discipline that fit them to share, on anything like equal terms, in the conscious life of the civilized world')[45] but refrained from putting too fine a point on the analogy between American blacks and European nationalities: 'This sketch of the racial situation in Europe is, of course, the barest abstraction and should not be accepted realistically. It is intended merely as an indication of similarities, in the broader outlines, of the motives that have produced nationalities in Europe and are making the Negro in America, as Booker Washington says, "a nation within a nation."'[46] He concluded his paper with some prudent speculation on the model of social evolution toward which the South was headed: 'In the South ... the races seem to be tending in the direction of a bi-racial organization of society, in which the Negro is gradually gaining a limited autonomy. What the ultimate outcome of this movement may be is not safe to predict.'[47]

The third paper, 'Race Prejudice and Japanese-American Relations,' published as the introduction to Jesse F. Steiner's *The Japanese Invasion* (1917), includes Park's first reflections on racial prejudice. Like his colleague Thomas, he viewed prejudice as a form of instinct, but where Thomas set it down to a reaction to the Other's physical appearance, Park saw in it a manifestation of competition:

> Race prejudice may be regarded as a spontaneous, more or less instinctive defense-reaction, the practical effect of which is to restrict free competition between races. Its importance as a social function is due to the fact that free competition, particularly between people with different standards of living, seems to be, if not the original source, at least the stimulus to which race prejudice is the response.[48]

Park's reference to free competition hinted at the strains being placed on society in a postwar context in which massive foreign (and particularly Asian) immigration had resumed. He argued that where fundamental racial interests are not yet controlled by law, custom, or other arrangement between the groups in question, racial prejudice will inexorably develop. It may, however, be deflected by 'the extension of the machinery of cooperation and social control' – in the U.S. case, the caste system and slavery:

> we may regard caste, or even slavery, as one of those accommodations through which the race problem found a natural solution. Caste, by relegating the subject race to an inferior status, gives to each race at any rate a monopoly of its own tasks. When this status is accepted by the subject people, as in the case where the caste or slavery systems become fully established, racial competition ceases and racial animosity tends to disappear ... Each race being in its place, no obstacle to racial cooperation exists.[49]

This paper shows that Park's thought in 1917 was not free of obfuscation and bias. One finds him maintaining that while 'caste and the limitation of free competition is economically unsound,' it is nonetheless 'politically desirable'[50] because of the racial harmony it creates. He had very little to say about the forms of racial 'cooperation' (his term) that might arise in a democratic system free of prejudice. Nevertheless, he concluded the piece by describing the harm done by prejudice to people exhibiting 'external marks':

> When a race bears an external mark by which every individual member of it can infallibly be identified, that race is by that fact set apart and segregated. Japanese, Chinese, and Negroes cannot move among us with the same freedom as the members of other races because they bear marks which identify them as the members of their race. This fact isolates them. In the end, the effect of this isolation, both in its effects upon the Japanese themselves, and upon the human environment in which they live, is profound. Isolation is at once a cause and an effect of race prejudice. It is a vicious circle – isolation, prejudice; prejudice, isolation.[51]

Park would revisit the important concept of race prejudice several times over the next twenty years. A final paper from 1918, 'Education in Its Relation to the Conflict and Fusion of Cultures,' is noteworthy for two lines of argument, the first establishing his doubts as to the persistence of African heritage among American blacks:

> It has been generally taken for granted that the Negro brought a considerable fund of African tradition and African superstition from Africa to America ... My own impression is that the amount of African tradition which the Negro brought to the United States was very small. In fact there is every reason to believe, it seems to me, that the Negro, when he landed in the United States, left behind him almost everything but his dark complexion and his tropical temperament. It is very difficult to find in the South today anything that can be traced directly back to Africa.[52]

The second line of argument concerns the delicate subject of black intellectual aptitude and general culture. Park comes at this from a social rather than a biological perspective when he writes that the question of alleged black intellectual inferiority 'remains where Boas left it when he said that the black man was little, if any, inferior to the white man in intellectual capacity and, in any case, racial as compared with individual differences were small and relatively unimportant.'[53] But only a few pages later the reader finds Park juggling with the biologistic concept of 'racial temperament.' The following sentences in particular would return to haunt him in the coming years:

> Everywhere and always [blacks have] been interested rather in expression than in action; interested in life itself rather than in its reconstruction or reformation. The Negro is, by natural disposition, neither an intellectual nor an idealist, like the Jew; nor a brooding introspective, like the East African; nor a pioneer and frontiersman, like the Anglo-Saxon. He is primarily an artist, loving life for its own sake. His *métier* is expression rather than action. He is, so to speak, the lady among the races.[54]

One strains to find anything other than a racist interpretation for these lines, yet the same paper predicted that the putative black racial temperament would erode through gradual assimilation to the white population:

> When the physical unity of a group is perpetuated by the succession of parents and children, the racial temperament, including fundamental attitudes and values which rest in it, is preserved intact. When, however, society grows and is perpetuated by immigration and adaptation, there ensues, as a result of miscegenation, of breaking up or [sic] the complex of the biologically inherited qualities which constitute the temperament of the race.[55]

Park's assessment of black culture at this phase of his career carried other biases as well. For example, he identified a cultural hierarchy among blacks as a function of their ability to reproduce models of white middle-class behavior; that is, he used a white benchmark to evaluate black progress. This construct predicated the equality of black people on their ability to accomplish the same things as whites under appropriate circumstances. It departed significantly from Boas's relativistic prescription whereby any observer of a culture other than his own must strive to shed the opinions and sentiments entrenched in the social environment in which he was formed.

Such difficulties aside, Park was able to develop a respectable scientific arsenal with these writings, most prominently his second 1913 paper. To quote Chapoulie: 'The conceptual framework defined by this essay comprises ... a conception of race, an outline of a definition of assimilation, and the central hypothesis of Park's sociology of racial and cultural interaction: namely, that face-to-face personal contact is the path that may lead to assimilation.'[56] As mentioned above, this paper concludes with an outline of biracialism as a possible model for the future, and includes discussion of the concept of race prejudice and the much more tenuous concept of racial temperament.

The 1920s and early 1930s saw Park add new elements to his framework and produce a number of variations on his themes. Most important and influential was his introduction of a universal interpretive schema for the evolution of contact between human races. The kernel of the idea, whose earliest avatar appeared in *Introduction to the Science of Sociology,* is that such contact obeys a sequence of four stages: competition, conflict, accommodation, and assimilation. The migration of different population groups around the globe inevitably leads them into contact with one another along a 'racial frontier,' resulting in competition and then conflict over valuable resources. Conflict is eventually resolved through accommodation, a relatively stable if unequal social order in which one race dominates and controls while the other is subordinated, exploited, or even enslaved. But accommodation in turn gives way to assimilation, a cultural and ultimately physical fusion of the two races whose outcome is a homogeneous social whole:

> Assimilation is a process of interpenetration and fusion in which persons and groups acquire the memories, sentiments, and attitudes of other persons or groups, and, by sharing their experience and history, are incorporated with them in a common cultural life ... As social contact initiates

> interaction, assimilation is its final perfect product. The nature of the social contacts is decisive in the process. Assimilation naturally takes place most rapidly where contacts are primary, that is, where they are the most intimate and intense, as in the area of touch relationship, in the family circle and in intimate congenial groups. Secondary contacts facilitate accommodations, but do not greatly promote assimilation. The contacts here are external and too remote.[57]

Somewhat later, Park redefined the key stage of assimilation by putting the emphasis on its cultural dimension, thus stressing its polysemic character: 'It is the name given to the process or processes by which peoples of diverse racial origins and different cultural heritages, occupying a common territory, achieve a cultural solidarity sufficient at least to sustain a national existence.'[58] And in 1926, Park introduced the concept of a race relations cycle to encapsulate his four-stage hypothesis. The following passage clearly shows that he viewed this cycle as a great inexorable law of societal evolution: 'The race relations cycle ... is apparently progressive and irreversible. Customs regulations, immigration restrictions and racial barriers may slacken the tempo of the movement; may perhaps halt it altogether for a time; but cannot change its direction; cannot at any rate, reverse it.'[59]

Park also refined certain concepts brought to the fore by his interest in race relations, often drawing inspiration from the historical moment in doing so. Take the concept of race consciousness, for example: he enthusiastically heralded what he saw as an instance of it in the emergence of the Harlem Renaissance movement in the early 1920s:

> The new literacy movement ... is the natural expression of the Negro temperament under all the conditions of modern life. The Negro has learned to write; and as he feels life keenly, he expresses it emotionally ... The new poetry, the poetry of the Negro renaissance, is distinctly of this world. It is characteristically the poetry of rebellion and self-assertion ... The new poetry is not irreligious. No poetry that seeks to express, define and justify the deepest emotions of men can be called irreligious. It is, however, radical.[60]

From 1920 to 1924, Park formed close associations with immigration research teams around the country (including New York) in the capacity of scientific adviser, one result being his contribution to William Thomas's *Old World Traits Transplanted*. Since the data collected for this work contradicted some of the predictions of his cycle theory, he devoted considerable attention to the factors hindering assimilation, and this led him to revisit his concept of race prejudice. A 1924 essay found him introducing the new concept of social distance: 'What we ordinarily called prejudice seems then to be more or less instinctive and spontaneous disposition to maintain social distances.'[61] If so, then prejudice answered a specific need: 'Prejudice and race prejudice are by no means to be identified by social distance, but arise when our personal and racial reserves are, or seem to be, invaded. Prejudice is on the whole not an aggressive but a conservative force; a sort of spontaneous conservation which tends to preserve the social order and the social distances upon which that order rests.'[62] He stressed that democracy was not to be blamed for maintaining social distance, provided that it was strictly individual, not collective: 'Democracy abhors social distinctions but it maintains them. The difference between democracy and other forms of society is that it refuses to make class or race, i.e., group distinctions. Distinctions and distances must be of a purely individual and personal nature.'[63]

In two 1926 articles, Park touted interracial relations and friendships as perhaps the best means of overcoming the race barrier. In 'Behind Our Masks' he wrote: 'Personal relations and personal friendships are the great moral solvents. Under their influence all distinctions of class, of caste, and even of race, are dissolved into the general flux which we sometimes call democracy.'[64] In 'Our Racial Frontier on the Pacific,' he argued that the case of slavery was instructive in showing how close ties of interracial friendship could cause the breakdown of the system from within: 'It was the intimate and personal relations which grew up between the Negro slave and his white master that undermined and weakened the system of slavery from within, long before it was attacked from without. Evidence of this was the steady increase, in spite of public opinion and legislation to the contrary, of the number of free Negroes and emancipated slaves in the South.'[65]

According to Park, the Civil War had put an end to slavery but had also reinitiated the race relations cycle. What blacks had won in their close association with whites, they had rapidly lost with emancipation and the dwindling of assimilation. Moreover, prejudice against blacks had resumed with a vengeance and was still taking its toll in the twentieth century. In a 1928 paper, he elaborated on the subject of prejudice as a general concept, though he made specific reference to blacks for historical proof of his case. Race prejudice, he began, is a profoundly human phenomenon but does not develop in all societies. As a precondition, different races have to come into direct contact. Prejudice then appears, if at all, as an outgrowth of competition for vital resources. It persists until a modus vivendi, a system of coexistence, puts an end to competition and establishes a moral order among the antagonistic groups. Prejudice then gives way to accommodation, expressed in the form of 'racial etiquette.' In any human society, the intensity of race prejudice is inversely related to the society's capacity to effect change and adjustment. This was the key to blacks' difficulties, even though as individuals they were legally free: 'Prejudice – that is caste, class and race prejudice – in its more naive and innocent manifestations, is merely the resistance of the social order to change. Every effort of the Negro – to take the most striking example – to move, to rise and improve his status, rather than his condition, has invariably met with opposition, aroused prejudice and stimulated racial animosities.' The fact was that since emancipation blacks had been confronting constant racial prejudice and its manifestations, ranging from lynching at worst to all manner of subtle discrimination at best. Nevertheless, wrote Park, blacks had neither given up nor regressed; they were making their way along a difficult path: 'There is probably less racial prejudice in America than elsewhere, but there is more racial conflict and more racial antagonism ... The Negro is rising in America and the measure of the antagonism he encounters is, in some very real sense, the measure of his progress.'[66]

Race hybrids – mulattoes – had a real advantage over blacks, Park believed, in the face of deadly white prejudice. They were well-placed, as a group more than as individuals, to identify with the cause of all blacks and play a leadership role in the struggle for emancipation. He elaborated on this theme two years later in a paper devoted to 'racial hybrids':

> More and more in the course of his struggle for position and status in the white's man world the brown man has chosen to throw in his fortunes with the black and make the Negro's cause his own. He has made himself not merely the leader but the teacher, the interpreter, and in some sense the emancipator of the race. In this struggle the black man, as education has been more widely diffused, has begun to play a more important role. However, the mulatto, in spite of his smaller numbers, still largely repre-

> sents the intellectual class of the race. This struggle, gathering in breadth and intensity ... has been at once an inspiration and a discipline to the mulatto. What is more, it has given him a cause and a career.[67]

Finally, Park's semantic inventions of the 1920s included the concept of 'bi-racial organization,' which he first articulated in 1917. His 1928 essay 'The Bases of Race Prejudice' ends with a direct reference to this type of organization. It was, he felt, an especially viable model in the context of the great southern upheavals in race relations:

> Originally race relations in the South could be rather accurately represented by a horizontal line, with all the white folk above, and all the Negro folk below. But at present these relations are assuming new forms, and in consequence changing in character and meaning. With the development of industrial and professional classes within the Negro race, the distinction between the races tends to assume the form of a vertical line. On one side of this line the Negro is represented in most of the occupational and professional classes; on the other side of the line the white man is similarly represented ... The result is to develop in every occupational class professional and industrial bi-racial organizations. Bi-racial organizations preserve race distinctions, but change their content. The distances which separate the races are maintained, but the attitudes involved are different. The races no longer look up and down; they look across. These bi-racial organizations, so far as I know, are a unique product of the racial struggle in this country; they do not exist outside the United States.[68]

Park was notable among his white American colleagues for the scientific ambition that he brought to the race question. Using a diversified arsenal of concepts, he rebuilt mainstream sociology, pulling it out of the biological racialism in which it was mired – a major advance. Pervasive in his writings is the postulate that the cultural differences between human races are of greater importance than biological differences. Still, Park never broke the Social Darwinist mold in which he and the rest of his generation had been formed. Free (unregulated) competition between the races remained central to his thinking. Any form of intervention in the race relations cycle (whether by the state or a social group) was harmful, since it interfered with the self-regulating thrust of the whole process toward assimilation or, if that proved temporarily unworkable, some substitute. Park had little to say on 'white-organized actions – in the South or elsewhere – to reinforce blacks' inferior status or buttress segregation in housing and employment.' His universalizing vision of the evolution of race relations was deeply colored by his membership in the dominant Anglo-Saxon Protestant group, which 'saw assimilation to this group (in a sense that cannot be stated with precision) as the only conceivable future for other population groups.'[69] In short, Park's reasoning partook not of biological but of a form of cultural determinism in which 'inferior' groups would conveniently melt into the 'superior' Anglo-Saxon group. This brand of sociology was in perfect keeping with the prevailing early-twentieth-century conception of relations between whites and other races – particularly blacks, the most numerous and 'worrisome' minority.

In deriving his examples almost exclusively from the South during an era of massive black emigration from that region, Park appeared to be somewhat behind the times. Two factors account for this omission. Since he was not a field researcher, Park had no other direct point of reference for race relations than his own personal experience in the South, whence his natural tendency to draw upon it. Furthermore, prior to 1930, no sociologist had yet conducted an in-depth scientific survey of black migration or its major structural impact, the rapid formation of urban ghettos. Consequently, Park had no reliable expertise about the phenomenon. The first rigorous sociological study of blacks' living conditions in the urban north only appeared in 1932: E. Franklin Frazier's *The Negro Family in Chicago*. But as we shall see, Park's mature writings show him correcting his aim under pressure from the tumultuous social and intellectual developments to come.

1932–1944

Apart from the economic debacle of 1929 and its aftermath, the development that polarized the nation at the start of this period was the implementation of the New Deal under the administration of President Franklin D. Roosevelt, elected in 1932. This interventionist regime proved itself accommodating and tolerant to the different cultures and ethnic groups coming to the United States. The flux of immigration had slowed considerably over the preceding decade as a result of a ban on Asian immigration (1924) and various checks on other immigration, but Roosevelt's administration still opted for affirmative recognition of the undeniable cultural heterogeneity existing in the United States. In parallel, the idea had been making headway in public discourse that total assimilation of immigrants to the Anglo-American majority was not necessarily the only possible or desirable option; that 'ethnic pluralism' was perhaps not so much threatening to the country's future as simply reflective of an increasingly undeniable historical trend.

The case of blacks was, however, socially coded as an exception to this pattern of increasing interracial tolerance. The influx of southern rural blacks into northern cities frightened many people already living there, and segregation, discrimination, and violent exclusion were the daily lot of these migrants in their interactions with members of other groups in the urban North. Like other social observers of his time, Park was a careful observer of this pattern of conflict. In the political arena, by contrast, the New Deal encouraged an openness to all racial and ethnic minorities, blacks included, a situation capitalized on by left-wing organizations. The Communist Party (founded just after the First World War) was resurgent in 1932 after a number of lean years and was intent on recruiting black workers and intellectuals. Likewise, the NAACP's protests against job discrimination and other injustices were becoming more radical. A new trade union federation, the Congress of Industrial Organizations, hived off from the American Federation of Labor (founded in 1886) between 1936 and 1938 and began to recruit industrial workers throughout the country, and the NAACP successfully lobbied for blacks' admission to the union. Meanwhile, union leaders were becoming convinced of the necessity of blacks' participating in labor organizations in all the industries where the new unionism was gaining a foothold.

In academia, cultural approaches to long-standing research problems had the wind in their sails. Culturalism had arisen as an attempt to resolve two problems afflicting sociological theory: (1) the lack of general or systematic theorization, and (2) the fact that theory had been reduced to a minimal formalism; the term 'theory' had been stretched thin to cover a sterile methodological debate between 'objectivists' and 'subjectivists.'[70]

Pitirim Sorokin of Harvard University was the first social researcher to suggest that theoretical systematization should become a normal and necessary part of the construction of sociological objects, regardless of the choice of methodology. His paradigm replaced biologism with sociological cycle theory, in which he argued that societies could be classified according to their 'cultural mentality.' He began to develop these ideas in the late 1920s (*Contemporary Sociological Theories*, 1928), while a definitive synthesis had to wait until the 1937–41 publication of his massive four-volume *Social and Cultural Dynamics*.

A second culturalist scenario was taking shape as well, different from Sorokin's in its goals but not necessarily incompatible with it. This second approach concerned itself with the increasingly fragmented nature of sociology's objects and operational procedures and took as its challenge that of finding a way to study human society as a whole. Earle Edward Eubank, a University of Cincinnati sociologist, was the first to put forward this holistic strategy in a 1932 work titled *A Treatise Presenting a Suggested Organization of Sociological Theory in Terms of Its Major Concepts*. He argued that sociology, as a recently developed discipline, had to emerge from the 'conceptual disorder'[71] by which it had come to be characterized, or else it would regress on all fronts. This could be achieved through systematization of the great many sociological concepts then in circulation. Conceptual systematization would replace the unified theory promised but never delivered by Spencerian biologism, this unity being essential to fully apprehend the social totality. Eubank's work 'became one of the most widely cited texts of the era'[72] but never fulfilled its promise of organizing sociology's central concepts within a general, systematic theory. He merely succeeded in enumerating the more fashionable Anglo-American sociology concepts of the time – nothing more original or substantial. Still, the conclusion to his work included a statement that pointed the way forward: 'Sociology is concerned with *human beings associated in activity*. By re-stating our major points of attention in terms of *action* a basis of synthesis of the entire body of material becomes at once apparent.'[73]

Eubank had opened an extremely promising door that another sociologist would rewardingly pass through only a few years later. The synthesis toward which he unsuccessfully strove was achieved by Talcott Parsons in *The Structure of Social Action* (1937), which contained an utterly novel definition of sociology as 'the science which attempts to develop an *analytical theory of social action systems* in so far as these systems can be understood in terms of the property of common-value integration.'[74] Edward Shils, a keen-eyed observer of U.S. and world sociology, explains how a new epistemological era was being ushered in:

> It was [*The Structure of Social Action*] which brought the greatest of the partial traditions into a measure of unity. It precipitated the sociological outlook which had been implicit in the most interesting of the empirical inquiries; it made explicit the affinities and complementarity of the sociological traditions which had arisen out of utilitarianism, idealism, and

positivism. It redirected sociology into its classical path, and, in doing so, it began the slow process of bringing into the open the latent dispositions which had underlain the growth of sociological curiosity.[75]

Parsons was not the only person responsible for this decisive leap in terms of theory. Robert Merton displayed an equally creative imagination while working in a less abstract conceptual register, one closer to empirical interventionism. The result of the two men's work was two distinct, complementary versions of what came to be called functionalism. What was the relationship to Park's sociology of race relations? These developments did much to speed the disappearance of Darwinism from the Anglo-American sociological paradigm in the 1930s. In so doing, they created the conducive and necessary conditions for scientific acceptance of the idea of assimilation as part of a far-reaching *cultural* process; namely, the modernization of the United States. There was a great deal of common ground between these trends and Park's concerns, and he drew upon it for his work on race. However, one would be wrong to conclude that by shedding their belief in blacks' innate biological inferiority, mainstream sociologists (Park included) necessarily gave up their racialist bias; at worst they merely formulated it in new language.

Culturalism gave weight to an ideological shift in the 1930s whose direct effect on the sociology of race relations would be felt over the next decade. It represented a profound break with the quasi-sacred dictum of detachment from activism that Park transmitted to all his disciples, the idea that personal passions should be set aside so that the facts can be examined impartially. Spearheaded by Robert Lynd, coauthor (with his wife Helen) of the important *Middletown* (1929) and *Middletown in Transition* (1937), culturalism restored Anglo-American sociology to the humanitarian, reformist aims of its inception, presenting sociologists as intellectuals deeply involved with their society. This program was Lynd's explicit subject in *Knowledge for What? The Place of Social Science in American Culture* (1939). A responsible sociologist, he wrote, must never cultivate value-neutrality. Her primary task is to gain a comprehensive understanding of her society and especially its culture, defined as 'all the things that a group of people inhabiting a common geographical area do, the ways they do things and the ways they think and feel about things, their material tools and their values and symbols.'[76] However, this must not be done in a vacuum but, rather, with a view to fulfilling every sociologist's moral responsibility of putting her knowledge to work for desirable social change:

> social science is confined neither to practical politics ... Nor is its role merely to stand by, describe, and generalize, like a seismologist watching a volcano ... The responsibility is to keep everlastingly challenging the present with the question: But what is it that we human beings want, and what things would have to be done, in what ways and in what sequence, in order to change the present so as to achieve it?[77]

Although mainstream sociologists still perceived it but dimly, the ideological table was set for Myrdal's monumental survey of the next decade.

Returning to Park with the foregoing discussion as a backdrop, we find him, in the years after his retirement from the University of Chicago, retreading the paths he had followed previously, adding some new concepts or considerations in response to the political times or other motivating factors. In 1934 he agreed to write an introduction for *Shadow of the Plantation*, a work about southern black plantation workers by his first black student, Charles S. Johnson. In this paper Park revisited the concept of marginal peoples that he had introduced in a general paper of six years earlier,[78] applying it specifically to black people: '[Blacks live] on the margins of our culture [and] occupy a place somewhere between the more primitive and tribally organized and the urban populations of our modern cities.'[79] Park was well aware of southern black emigration patterns and the uprooting of the more rudimentary, static southern folk culture that they were causing. He remained highly respectful of southern rural blacks, with whom he had close personal experience:

> It is very curious that anyone in America should still think of the Negro, even the Negro peasant of the 'black belts,' as in any sense an alien or stranger, since he has lived here longer than most of us, has interbred to a greater extent than the white man with the native Indian, and is more completely a product than anyone of European origin is likely to be of the local conditions under which he was born and bred.[80]

In 1937, Park wrote another introduction, this time for *The Etiquette of Race Relations in the South* by Bertram Doyle, a southern black pastor and professor at Tennessee's Fisk University (where Park himself would end his academic career). After defining etiquette as an arrangement designed to preserve social distances ('Etiquette, so far as it can be conceived to be a form of government, or control, functions only in so far as it defines and maintains "social distances"'),[81] Park distanced himself from his early ideas about the caste system. He reasoned that the race and color-based caste system that had arisen during slavery was under attack:

> Although caste still persists and serves in a way to regulate race relations, many things – education, the rise within the Negro community of a professional class (teachers, ministers, and physicians) and of an intelligentsia, seeking to organize and direct the Negro's rising race consciousness – have conspired not merely to undermine the traditional caste system but to render it obsolete.[82]

Furthermore, blacks were progressing in such a way as to diminish the distance between them and whites within any given occupational class. It was clear to Park that black Americans throughout the country were going through a decisive transformation: they were becoming a racial or national minority, marking a new phase in race relations:

> the slow but steady advance of the Negro, as a result of competition within and without the group, and the gradual rise of a Negro society within the limits of the white man's world have changed the whole structure of race relations in the United States, both in the North and in the South. The restrictions on intermarriage still persist and continue to make of the Negro an endogamous social group, in much the same sense that the Jews, the Mennonites, and any of the more primitive religious sects are endogamous. On the other hand, in view of the fact that he has developed a society in which all the professions and many, if not most, occupations are represented, the Negro has an opportunity now, which he did not have earlier, to rise within the limits of the Negro world. Under those circumstances the Negro group has gradually ceased to exhibit the characteristics of a caste and has assumed rather the character of a racial or national minority.[83]

Park authored a third introduction, again in 1937, to a work about intermarriage in the Hawaiian islands between aboriginal Polynesians and immigrants of Japanese, Chinese, Portuguese, Philippine, or Anglo-

Saxon descent. This was an opportunity for him to make a prudent adjustment to the cycle theory to which he had been attached for twenty years: 'race relations ... can best be interpreted if what they seem to be at any time and place is regarded merely as a phase in a cycle of change which, once initiated, inevitably continues until it terminates in some predestined racial configuration, and one consistent with an established social order of which it is a part.'[84] In other words, he no longer regarded assimilation as the 'perfect final product' of the race relations cycle. Why did Park recant on its inexorability? As he compared the status of American blacks with other historical cases of interracial contact (in Africa, China, Hawaii, and Brazil), he had come to believe that their full and effective assimilation with the dominant white majority, whether through interaction or miscegenation, was nearly impossible. The case of American blacks appeared to constitute an exception to what he had read and experienced elsewhere; it was unique, and his theory had to be rectified accordingly. Thus Park's renewed emphasis on the concept of biracial organization, which in turn led to the hypothesis of accommodation rather than assimilation between races, at least for the foreseeable future. It also led to the idea of a permanent struggle for individual and group promotion within a context of underlying inequality in every area of life.

> Park believed that 'bi-racial organization,' which he thought contributed to the emergence of a black middle-class, was the 'unique' outcome of racial conflict in the USA. Bi-racial organization meant that blacks would not be relegated strictly to menial occupations, but would work at jobs in trades, businesses and the professions, which although not integrated, were the same as those in which whites worked.[85]

His final works find Park emphasizing more than ever, often on a general or worldwide comparative scale, concepts such as hierarchization or structural differentiation, social class, class struggle, and conflict. Illustrative of this tone was the conclusion to a late-1930s essay:

> Looking at race relations in the long historical perspective, this modern world which seems destined to bring presently all the diverse and distant peoples of the earth together within the limits of a common culture and a common social order, strikes one as something not merely unique but millennial! Nevertheless, this new civilization is the product of essentially the same historical processes as those that preceded it. The same forces which

> brought about the diversity of races will inevitably bring about, in the long run, a diversity in the peoples in the modern world corresponding to that which we have seen in the old. It is likely, however, that these diversities will be based in the future less on inheritance and race and rather more on culture and occupation. That means that race conflicts in the modern world, which is already or presently will be a single great society, will be more and more in the future confused with, and eventually superseded by, the conflicts of classes.[86]

A 1942 paper devoted not to the race question but to the general characteristics of modern society finds Park predicating emancipation as being contingent upon an awareness of subjugation and the need for struggle: 'only those are free who are conscious of their slavery ... there are a great many people in the world today who are conscious of their slavery and are rebellious against it. Modern society is, or seems to be, very largely made up of the emancipated. The 19th century witnessed the emancipation of the slaves in the United States ...'[87] He implied that this emancipatory struggle, in the case of American blacks, had to be pursued in a new, modern context. In a paper published in Ogburn's *American Society in Wartime* (1943), he advanced a sociological explanation for what he saw as the continuing improvement of black-white relations since the end of slavery:

> changes began when the freedmen first realized that they were free to change masters, so to speak, and to move from one plantation to the next. It changed profoundly when Negroes began to leave the plantation altogether and make their home in the slums of the cities, where they had a freedom that exists nowhere else except on the frontiers of settlement and civilization. It has continued to change with the progress of Negro education in the South and with the migration of the Negro population to the North, where they have in the public schools the same opportunities to get an education as the immigrant and all the other national and racial groups of which the American population is made up. The most profound changes in race relations, if not in racial ideology, have come about with the rise of a hierarchy of occupational classes within the limits of the Negro race, so that Negroes can and do rise to some sort of occupational and professional equality with other races and peoples who have not been handicapped by the segregations and institutions of a caste system. The class system, as it exists in the United States at least, does permit individuals and eventually races to rise. At present, at least in the northern cities,

to which the Negroes in recent years have migrated in such large numbers, the status of the Negro population is no longer that of a caste. It is rather that of a racial and cultural minority ...[88]

He presented a prescient prediction of the necessity of conflict in what he saw as an 'emerging world society':

One thing ... seems certain: the races and peoples which fate has brought together in America and within the limits of the larger world economy will continue, in the emerging world society, their struggle for a political and a racial equality that was denied them in the world that is passing. As far as this prediction turns out to be true, it will be, perhaps, because the historical process, as it operates among human beings, is determined finally not merely by biological but by ideological forces, and not by what men have or are merely but what they hope for and believe.[89]

Two professions of faith pervade this paragraph: faith in the sovereignty of evolutionism as a general explanatory framework, and faith in the primacy of culture (ideology) over nature (biology) within this framework. Undoubtedly, as Chapoulie maintains with specific reference to the substantial essay 'The Nature of Race Relations' (1939), the importance that Park assigned to conflict toward the end of his career reflected 'the watershed events of the period since 1913, particularly the periodic urban riots of which blacks were first the victims and, from the 1930s on, at times the active agents.' But in my view, a more profound influence was also at play. As I shall show in chapter 6 (see pp. 247–8), Park's new insistence on 'seeing the development of conflict and black action as one of the essential drivers of evolution'[90] reflected the direct influence on his thought of the methodical research carried out by his more radical black disciples in Chicago – Johnson and especially Frazier. For most of his career, Park had presented himself as a liberal on the race relations question, a proponent of gradual qualitative change rather than revolution. But in a letter to his former student Horace Cayton in 1943, he was at pains to declare that his views were the polar opposite of liberalism:

I think the liberals realize now that the Negro's cause must in the long run win. The only thing is, they don't want it to win too soon and they don't want the change to be so rapid as to result in the disorders that we have had. Personally I don't agree with these liberals. In fact I've never been a

> liberal. If conflicts arise as a result of the efforts to get their place it will be because the white people started them. These conflicts will probably occur and are more or less inevitable but conditions will be better after they are over.[91]

If Park expressed such thoughts in 1943, as he was right to do, it was because the ideas of Frazier in particular – the leading sociological expert on American black living conditions – had filtered into his own from 1935 on and had nudged his views on the present and future of black-white relations in a more radical direction. Frazier was a radical sociologist throughout his career, and one hears his voice speaking through Park's words in the above quotation.

Alternative Positions in the Interwar Period

Park's construction was certainly highly influential on Anglo-American race relations theory, but it did not hold a monopoly. The 1930s produced a competing theory: W. Lloyd Warner's theory of caste and class. Warner (1898–1970) was a Harvard University social and cultural anthropologist working on the topic of race relations in the South. In 1936 he moved to the anthropology department of the University of Chicago and published a theoretical article in the *American Journal of Sociology* that laid the foundations of his theory. In the deep South, he argued, whites and blacks formed separate castes, one superior, the other inferior. He defined a caste as 'a theoretical arrangement of the people of the given group in an order in which the privileges, duties, obligations, opportunities, etc., are unequally distributed between the groups which are considered to be higher and lower. There are social sanctions which tend to maintain this unequal distribution.' Within each of these castes, a class structure could be discerned. Caste and class were antithetical social systems in that while one prohibited movement and intermarriage across race boundaries, the other allowed for 'inter-group movement and at least certain kinds of marriage between higher and lower classes.' Over time, the caste and class systems had 'accommodated themselves to each other in the southern community ...'[92] Due to black economic, educational, and social initiatives, this dual hierarchical structure was in the process of changing; blacks were steadily moving into higher social positions within their own caste, although any hope of crossing the caste line was dim, whence the high probability of enduring biracial organization.

It is worth dwelling on two case studies performed by members of Warner's team to provide an empirical demonstration of the arguments he adduced in a quite conscious effort to unseat Park's theory. John Dollard's *Caste and Class in a Southern Town* combined psychological considerations with Warner's caste theory. The work concerns a small deep South locality, 'Southerntown' (actually Indianola, Mississippi), with a population of about 2,500. Dollard, a white northerner, expressed his purpose as being 'to reveal the main structure of white-Negro adjustment in Southerntown from the standpoint of emotional factors.'[93] The term 'adjustment' betrays Park's influence to some degree; Dollard is asserting that the logic of accommodation is necessary to understand caste as a social structure. Caste was a specific type of accommodation between two races, but, being irreconcilable with American democratic values, it was bound to constitute a conflict-ridden structure, a rigid social order in which opposing mores faced off in an asymmetry mostly favorable to whites. Employing the life history method that he learned from members of Warner's team, Dollard examined the multiple consequences of this situation, largely from a psychological standpoint. There were, as he saw it, 'gains' and/or 'losses' for each group. Whites, he argued, derived economic and sexual gains as well as heightened prestige. Blacks, even though they were in a captive social situation, gained 'the compensations of the slave who has become a caste man ... The Negro makes the best of his situation and exploits his freedom from onerous responsibility and renunciation; as a realist there is nothing else he can do.'[94] However, only blacks took the losses: sexual losses, especially for the men, who unlike black women were not permitted to be intimate with or marry members of the other race; economic losses, as they were confined to the most degrading jobs and unable to shake off their financial dependency on whites (as exemplified in the tenantry system, white-owned stores for blacks, etc.); political losses – that is, disenfranchisement; and social losses in the broad sense of the term, in that blacks were trapped within a structure of relations requiring them to bow to the 'superior' whites. In this context, according to Dollard, blacks developed a double identity: a social mask composed of deference to whites, a convenient facade behind which to hide their hostile feelings; and a second, more 'authentic' identity visible only when with other blacks.

Dollard's generously detailed book contains much material that is beyond the scope of this analysis. What is important is his emphasis on the psychological dimension of the caste structure in Indianola. He devoted several pages to explaining and describing the prevalent black-on-black aggression, stressing the important role played by this violence in the maintenance of the caste system: 'One cannot help wondering if it does not serve the ends of the white caste to have a high level of violence in the Negro group, since disunity in the Negro caste tends to make it less resistant to the white domination.'[95]

Toward the end of the book he made reference to the romantic image of blacks as a happy people despite their objective status as a subordinated caste: 'The matter of gains is often summed up in a single statement: Negroes are a happy people. This belief has indeed become part of the romantic image of the Negro.'[96] While the foregoing sentence sounds intended as irony, Dollard in fact tried to demonstrate the merits of this belief by drawing on Freudian concepts. Blacks had allegedly been spared the sexual repression of whites, whose western European background had placed taboos on their primal drives. Since blacks could give free rein to their inner nature, they could be 'happy' despite their structural inferiority within the caste system. Undoubtedly because of its original analytical approach to southern race relations, *Caste and Class in a Southern Town* became widely read and influential, going through three editions.

The second book, *Deep South,* was the collaborative work of a biracial research team composed of Allison Davis (black), Burleigh and Mary Gardner (white), and Warner, who wrote the introductory chapter. In this voluminous, meticulously researched work, the authors immersed themselves in the life of 'Old City' (actually Natchez, Mississippi), with a population of about 10,000, half of them black. The city was a commercial hub serving cotton plantation owners in the neighbouring counties, where the population was 80 per cent black. The first part of the book discusses the dual system of social stratification in Old City and Old Country, the rural area surrounding it. The terms 'caste' and 'class' are defined, the first as:

> a theoretical arrangement of the people of a given group in an order in which the privileges, duties, obligations, opportunities, etc., are unequally distributed between the groups which are considered to be higher and lower ... The 'caste line' defines a social gulf across which Negroes may not pass either through marriage or those other intimacies which Old City calls 'social equality.' A ritual reminder is omnipresent in all relationships that there are two separate castes – a superordinate white group and a subordinate Negro group. Within each of these separate social worlds there

are other divisions: families, religious groups, associations, and a system of social classes. The most fundamental of these divisions within each caste is that of social class ...[97]

The concept of class is given an even more formal definition:

> As here used, a 'social class' is to be thought of as the largest group of people whose members have intimate access to one another. A class is composed of families and social cliques. The interrelationships between these families and cliques, in such informal activities as visiting, dances, receptions, teas, and larger informal affairs, constitute the structure of a social class. A person is a member of that social class with which most of his participations, of this intimate kind, occur.[98]

The authors describe the ways in which the dual caste/class stratification affected all aspects of daily life for the residents of Old City. For example, it was impossible to abolish the deep-seated inequality between the two groups:

> Both Negroes and whites recognize the fact that the white group is superordinate in power and prestige, and they exemplify this awareness in both their behavior and thought. Furthermore, each of the groups is endogamous; that is, marriage between them is absolutely forbidden, and any children of extralegal sex relations are automatically relegated to the subordinate Negro group. Each individual is born into the Negro or white group and must remain in it for life.[99]

Physical relations between blacks and whites in the city were controlled not by biological or genetic factors but by traditions taking the form of an organized social system in which certain things were permitted and others prohibited. Thus, for example, white men, but not white women, were allowed to engage in sexual activity for pleasure; but if ever a white man were to display the sense of responsibility normally expected of American fathers by acknowledging a child born of a cross-caste relationship, he would face the condemnation of his own caste.

The authors meticulously describe the specific distribution of social classes within each caste in Old City as well as different caste members' perceptions or images of them. The white caste was divided into three 'objective' classes – upper, middle, and lower – and each of these was subdivided into upper and lower, for a total of six subclasses. There were also subjective class perceptions on the part of each class. The 'upper-upper' class tended to divide whites into 'old aristocracy,' 'aristocracy, but not old,' 'nice, respectable people,' 'good people, but "nobody,"' and 'po' whites,' while the lower-lower-class saw whites as being divided into 'Society, or the folks with money,' 'way-high-ups, but not Society,' 'snobs trying to push up,' and 'people just as good as anybody.'[100]

Blacks, too, had a complete system of social classes, though 'it is more fully developed within the upper caste.'[101] It exhibited the same general configuration as for the whites; namely, an upper class, a middle class, and a lower class, though no subclasses were distinguished. Antagonisms were the best indicator of black perceptions of the existence of classes within their caste:

> Upper-class colored persons, when angered by the behavior of lower-class individuals, accused them of being black, boisterous, murderous, stupid, or sexually promiscuous, as a class. Middle-class persons were generally even more severe in their criticisms of the lowest social group, regarding shiftlessness, dirtiness, laziness, and religious infidelity as their chief characteristics. In the same fashion, lower-class people accused upper-class persons (the 'big shots,' the 'Big Negroes') of snobbishness, color preference, extreme selfishness, disloyalty in caste leadership ('sellin' out to white folks'), and economic exploitation of their patients and customers.[102]

Upward and downward mobility were observable in both castes, though the two phenomena operated differently: 'The adoption by a person of the behavior of a higher class than that into which he was born is frequently evidence of an attempt at upward mobility. Adoption of the behavior of a lower class is often symptomatic of extreme maladjustment both to one's own class and to the whole society.'[103]

The first part of *Deep South* also contains a wealth of examples of caste and class attitudes. The authors adduce family, social cliques, and all sorts of organizations and associations as examples of how caste and class are omnipresent and constantly impinge on everyone's lives, white and black. They also present careful descriptions of political and legal arrangements as proof that although the law itself provides no evidence of discrimination in Natchez, effective practices were replete with discrimination against blacks, even as the moral code described in the legal documents of the municipality and environs was 'officially' taken into account.

Part two of *Deep South*, consisting of twelve chapters, describes economic activities in the context of this dual social stratification. Landholding, financing, and accounting arrangements are scrutinized along with the division of labor on the cotton plantations. Labor recruitment and retention are discussed in detail. For the majority of blacks, but not for all, the economic system of Natchez entailed abject subordination to the white caste. Subordination could be lessened by making good within the class system; after all, some blacks were better off than many whites. This phenomenon, the authors suggest, indicated that changes had gradually been introduced into the social system of Natchez and its environment:

> The Negro group has gradually changed its character, and new groups have formed within it. Its social life has become more like that of the larger white community of the rest of the country. All the pleasant and profitable jobs are no longer controlled entirely by the whites, and all the poorly paid and unpleasant jobs are not now done entirely by the Negro. The more desirable activities are now shared, although unequally in proportion, by both Negroes and whites.[104]

But effective economic mobility for a small proportion of blacks put the conflictive nature of the caste/class stratification into relief. Blacks who reached for or were born into the upper class found themselves in the difficult position of being much wealthier than lower-class whites yet still subordinate to them. Their personality was inevitably marked by the outward conflict between the two groups. Warner commented trenchantly on the disruptive effect of the caste/class conflict on the black inhabitant of Natchez:

> He is known to be superior to the 'poor white' (he is a doctor, say); but he is still a 'nigger' or 'Negro,' according to the social context in which the words are used. Metaphorically speaking, he is constantly butting his head against the caste line. He knows himself to be superior to the poor white; yet to the poor white, the upper-class Negro is still a 'nigger,' which is a way of saying that the Negro is in a lower caste than himself.[105]

The book ends with the evocation of a dramatic event: the hanging of one black man for the killing of another. Such an event, the authors argued, is only fully intelligible within the interpretive framework of caste/class stratification:

> To the whites the execution ceremony is much more than the punishment of a Negro by a group of whites. It is a ritual sanctioned by God, that is, by the most important power of the total society, whereby the complete subordination of the individual to the society is upheld. The proper role of the victim is one of complete subordination to the caste society and to God ... With the Negro group the situation is somewhat different. To them the courts and the law are primarily an expression of the authority of the white group rather than that of the total society ...[106]

And, in a most revealing remark, 'The hanging of a Negro ... is the most dramatic method which the white community has of reaffirming its title to power – its superordinate caste position. It is a reaffirmation of the fact that caste is a reality and that any variations from the pattern will be severely punished.'[107]

The one-page conclusion of *Deep South*, titled 'Caste and Class: The Social Matrix,' reiterates the basic research findings; primarily, that life in Natchez follows an ordered pattern:

> The inhabitants live in a social world clearly divided into two ranks, the white caste and the Negro caste. These color-castes share disproportionately in the privileges and obligations of labor, school, and government, and participate in separate families, associations, cliques, and churches. Only in the economic sphere do the caste sanctions relax, and then but for a few persons and in limited relationships. Within the castes are social classes, not so rigidly defined as the castes, but serving to organize individuals and groups upon the basis of 'higher' and 'lower' status, and thus to restrict intimate social access. Both the caste system and the class system are changing through time; both are responsive to shifts in the economy, in the social dogmas, and in other areas of the social organization. Both are persisting, observable systems, however, recognized by the people who live in the communities; they form Deep South's mold of existence.[108]

Park versus Warner: The Outcome of a Dispute

As the 1940s began, race relations researchers were faced with a clear conceptual choice between Warner's model, which stressed the stability and persistence of the caste system despite ongoing change in the black community, and Park's model, which took account of new patterns emerging between blacks and whites as a result of the inherent instability of northern cities and the normality of conflict in these vibrant social spaces. It seems clear that different researchers fell into these camps more as a function of their ideological convictions than because they were swayed by learned arguments. The conservatives among them (southern whites for the most part), who were not in the minority, opted for the caste theory, which was compatible with their belief that blacks were neither fit nor ready to emerge from the traditional racial order. Still, they agreed with Park that gradual assimilation could eventually – at some far-off time – take place. The liberals and radicals differed from the conservatives in their awareness of structural obstacles to black socioeconomic mobility as well as the likely consequences of forces that were in the process of irreversibly transforming the traditional structure of race relations. The second group took their distance from Warner and aligned themselves with Park, whom they saw as having adequately accounted for the conflictive social reality of the times:

> liberal and radical sociologists, both black and white, who were aware of the swift changes (and progress) in American race relations tended to argue that Warner's concept of caste was static. It ignored the dynamic forces that were altering traditional patterns of race relations, it mistakenly assumed that blacks approved of the restrictions against intermarriage and segregation, and it ignored the use of violence by whites in their attempt to maintain the status quo.[109]

As the radicals saw it, Warner and his disciples were not defending falsehoods so much as overly partial, hence scientifically unacceptable, truths. In a 1941 paper in the *American Journal of Sociology,* black Chicago School adherents Elaine Ogden McNeil and Horace Cayton maintained that, despite the validity of the 'structural approach' taken by researchers in the Deep South, it could not fully account for the changing situation in the North: 'In the North, the social structure does not depend on the subordination of the Negro, and rapid changes in his status have occurred within a relatively short period of time. Therefore, in addition to a structural analysis, it is necessary to study the processes and the sentiments sanctioning the processes which allow the Negro to change his position in the structure.'[110]

In part two of this book I shall examine the views of the small cohort of black sociologists on the two leading race relations models of the day. For the time being, it suffices to note that most of them kept a prudent distance from Warner's theory of class and caste. By and large they gravitated toward Park's theory but also criticized it, at times severely. Thus, Park lived to see his ideas debated on both the right and the left of the ideological spectrum.

To conclude: the impetus for scientific race relations theory between the two world wars undoubtedly came from the University of Chicago, particularly Park's theory in sociology and Warner's theory in social and cultural anthropology. The hard core of Anglo-American race relations theory was expanded during these fifteen years as a result of the confrontation between these two irreconcilable models. But this crisis of content in no way lessened the vogue of the assimilationist thesis emerging from Park's thinking since 1921. It continued to hold its considerable force of attraction for mainstream researchers.

Although central to the social science of the early twentieth century, the concept of assimilation was always rather hazily defined, and I have considered above how this definitional haziness affected Park's work. Where blacks were concerned, the concept was tainted with ideological bias, hence the near impossibility of neutral or objective treatment.[111] The next chapter concerns itself with the debate among Anglo-American sociologists after Park on this delicate question. It should be noted in passing that Warner's caste theory waned as an object of scientific interest throughout the 1940s, and he himself, probably under the influence of Myrdal's *An American Dilemma*, appeared to back away from it: 'At [the] present time there are indications ... that the present system may reform into something quite different which will give Negroes many – if not all – [of] the opportunities now denied them.'[112]

3 From the Second World War to the 1960s

True to the approach taken in the rest of this book, I shall begin by reconstructing the sociopolitical landscape of this period – both the general background and the current events more specifically relevant to race relations – then go on to examine the sociological approaches to race relations developed contemporaneously, sometimes in direct response to the social context, at times as an outgrowth of entirely different factors.

The Sociopolitical Landscape

The 1940s began with another mass mobilization for world war. The population was increasing,[1] making available an abundant pool of labor supported by fabulous economic resources.[2] A return to full employment in such a short time, accompanied by unheard-of technological productivity in strategic industries such as steel, warships, aircraft, and automobile manufacturing, can only be understood as a result of the exceptional transitory economy created by the country's joining the war. This technological vibrancy would lead the United States to victory with the use of the atomic bomb in 1945, an event whose details are too well known to dwell on.

After 1945 the economy leveled off, but it was clear to all that the nation had definitively regained its former prosperity. Its leaders, both elected officials and industrialists, would henceforth strive to spread their conception of a neoliberal political and economic order around the globe. The unions, only recently staunch opponents of the existing economic system, became one by one incorporated into that system; by 1950, they all presented themselves as partners rather than adversaries of big business. In international affairs, the end of the decade saw the collapse of the alliance with the Soviet Union and the onset of the dark extended period known as the Cold War, another extremely well-documented period in U.S. foreign policy. Of note in this connection was the ensuing national anticommunist hysteria of which certain black intellectuals would be the unfortunate victims.[3]

Nothing could hold back the spectacular progress of the U.S. economic, technological, and industrial powerhouse at mid-century. With the help of the newly founded Central Intelligence Agency (1947), the country's large corporations were systematically organizing their operations on an international basis.[4] The country was so immensely rich that it could afford to invest millions in a European reconstruction program, the Marshall Plan, with a view to building long-term foreign markets for U.S. products as Europe recovered from the ravages of the Second World War. Elsewhere, overseas U.S. military operations resumed as the nation became involved in the Korean War (1950–3), which Democratic president Harry Truman perceived as an attack on the noncommunist world and a threat to American security. The conduct of the war, and especially Truman's decision to fire Douglas MacArthur, commander of the UN/U.S. forces in Korea, was a major factor in his precipitous decline in popularity through the early 1950s. He was not even a contender for the 1952 elections, won in a landslide by the Republican Dwight D. Eisenhower. The new president reinforced the power of the U.S. elite, created the conditions for the implementation of a gigantic military-industrial complex, and presided over the spread of material comfort and wealth to the middle class. Rampant economic prosperity and smiling, satisfied political conservatism: these were the salient features of triumphant 1950s America, the glory days of the 'American way of life.' But behind this image lay numerous contradictions.

While advertising held out the illusion of a society of wealth for all, socioeconomic inequalities widened inexorably. The rich became richer, the poor poorer, and the unequal distribution of wealth went hand in hand with unequal access to education, culture, social assistance, and health care.[5] Inequality also continued to characterize race relations in a country vaunted as the most democratic on the planet. In particular, blacks and other minority groups were subjected to many forms of segregation, a matter to which we return shortly.

The economic optimism of the period was troubled by social turbulence among the poorest in society, but President Eisenhower did little to find constructive solutions. His attention was distracted by other matters, such as the successful launch of the first two Soviet satellites (4 October and 3 November 1957). He and the Congress turned their attention to allaying public fears about American technological backwardness on long-range missiles, a matter regarded as vital to the Cold War nuclear equilibrium. In 1958, Eisenhower made special funding available for scientific education, then went on a nineteen-day 'peace mission' to eleven countries on three continents. This was largely spoiled by an embarrassing incident, the Soviet Union's capture of an American U-2 spy plane in its airspace on 5 May 1960. By the elections of that year, a sizable portion of the electorate was discontented with the Republican administration. In one of the closest races in the country's history, the Democrat John F. Kennedy beat the Republican Richard Nixon, Eisenhower's vice-president.

Kennedy's 'New Frontier,' at first a slogan used in his inaugural speech, became the umbrella name for a program involving a wide range of domestic and foreign-policy components. It would have little time to prove its worth – just three years until the president's assassination in November 1963. Domestically, Kennedy and his cabinet worked to alleviate certain social problems. They increased the federal minimum wage, provided federal assistance to poorer states and communities, instituted a housing program, and introduced a Medicare bill for coverage of the elderly (8 million of whom then lived in poverty). On racial discrimination, however, Kennedy's measures were rather timid. The enforcement of existing laws was beefed up and more powers were granted to the existing agencies. Unfortunately, very little of the New Frontier program was passed into law; most of Kennedy's proposed reforms (such as a civil rights bill) never came to a vote in Congress, while the Senate rejected his Medicare plan. At his death his domestic record was surprisingly poor.

Internationally, he used the financial, technological, and military assets at his disposal to oversee the economic development of the neocapitalist world under the banner of spreading freedom and democracy. During his term the defense budget ballooned to support a panoply of programs (Polaris rockets, nuclear submarines, Apollo), but Kennedy's strategy was not solely military; he stepped up aid to the Third World, oversaw a number of development studies, reorganized aid under the newly created Agency for International Development (AID), and created the Peace Corps. Fearing the rise to power of a new Fidel Castro in the Western Hemisphere, his administration put special emphasis on aid to Latin America. In 1961 it implemented the Alliance for Progress, a vast economic cooperation and development program involving $80 billion in investment by the Latin American countries themselves, with an additional $20 billion to be supplied or guaranteed by the United States within a decade. However, the credibility of the commitment to democracy that the Alliance for Progress nominally represented was severely compromised by the administration's inconsistent response to the six military coups that took place during the first two years of the program. While temporary diplomatic sanctions were applied in some cases, most of the juntas were recognized in short order.[6] The program's democratic focus was further compromised by a 1962 White House decision to direct U.S. cooperation efforts in the region toward internal policing, giving rise to an official 'death squad' culture that claimed many thousands of civilian lives.[7]

Another infamous chapter in the Kennedy administration's Latin American involvement was the abortive 1961 invasion at the Bay of Pigs in Cuba, culminating in the Cuban Missile Crisis of the following year, which brought humanity to the brink of nuclear war. In southeast Asia, the U.S. government was keeping close watch on major American economic interests as Vietnam and Laos moved toward communism in China's wake. Seeking to reassure his allies and prove that he was in control, Kennedy sent the U.S. military into what would become a notable quagmire, paving the way for the murderous escalation of 1965. All things considered, on both the foreign and domestic fronts, Kennedy delivered on few of the promises of the New Frontier program that had brought him to power. His successor, Lyndon Johnson, was left to deal with complex and unresolved issues, an important one being omnipresent racial discrimination.

Race Relations after the War

Race relations after the Second World War were in turmoil all over the country. Flagrant housing and employment disparities continued to be a big source of discontent and unrest during and after the Roosevelt administration. In June 1941, President Roosevelt had set up the Fair Employment Practices Commission to promote black employment, which led to some gains for blacks in the war industries. But blacks remained greatly disadvantaged as compared with the many whites getting rich off the war economy. The result was not only a deep racial divide but also a recrudescence of the urban rioting that had left such a bitter memory (in Chicago in 1919 and Harlem in 1935). The 1943 race riot in Detroit left thirty-four dead.

The more liberal elements of the Anglo-American elite, disturbed by these trends, decided they needed new tools with which to act. A new job classification had sprung up – the intergroup relations specialist, who addressed race relations as a social problem that could be solved rationally through gradual social change. Local committees on interracial conflict were struck, and a new group, the National Association of Intergroup Relations Officials, was formed.

The postwar status of blacks was influenced by two major phenomena: the rise of black ghettos in the cities of the North, East, and Midwest, and efforts by progressives to defeat the most shocking forms of racial discrimination, which led to some encouraging gains. The 1950s saw the NAACP successfully sue to put an end to school segregation in the South and make some progress on civil rights. The organization's biggest triumph was the *Brown* v. *Board of Education* decision of 17 May 1954, a historic reversal of the 'separate but equal' interpretation of the Fourteenth Amendment that had long made de facto segregation a reality in American society. Following this decision, many more blacks became involved in nonviolent mass action. In 1955–6, a months-long bus boycott in Montgomery, Alabama, led by Martin Luther King, Jr, spurred that city's desegregation of its mass transit system. On the strength of these peacefully won victories, blacks believed that their dream of a nation free of racial discrimination was now within reach. This hope was embodied in the creation of a new organization, the Congress of Racial Equality (CORE), which took direct action as one of its guiding principles and made fighting poverty one of its chief goals.

The optimism proved short-lived. The situation changed abruptly after 1955, with positions hardening on both sides. On 24 September 1957, an angry mob of whites summarily expelled nine black children from a public school in Little Rock, Arkansas, and President Eisenhower had to send in the National Guard to enforce the law. In northern cities, the economic situation was deteriorating after notable improvements since the 1930s, mainly as a result of a decline in the number of unskilled jobs. As tensions rose, riots broke out again, while the leaders attempted to channel protest into nonviolent direct action (symbolic gatherings, sit-ins in front of companies with discriminatory hiring policies, mass marches, etc.). Kennedy's election in 1960 and his immediate attempts to reduce discrimination through several new housing and employment measures raised many people's hopes (he also increased federal hiring of blacks). But these initiatives remained unequal to the complexity of the problems, particularly the poverty experienced by increasing numbers of blacks in the urban ghettos and their sordid exploitation by whites.

In closing this discussion, several important dates should be mentioned. In 1963, a massive march on Washington took place calling for a more aggressive federal civil rights legislation; the result was the passage, on 2 July 1964, of the Civil Rights Act, which officially banned segregation. That same year, riots broke out in poor neighborhoods of several cities, evidencing an unquestionable radicalization of certain black advocacy organizations, the most extreme being the one founded by Malcolm X. He was assassinated the following year in Harlem, while Martin Luther King, the most illustrious proponent of nonviolent mass protest, lost his life to a fanatic's bullets on 4 April 1968.

Moving now to the social science versions of race relations – and especially black-white relations – produced during this period, the general profile of Anglo-American race relations theory shifted noticeably away from the Parkian model in the early 1940s, largely because of a prestigious research project commissioned by the Carnegie Foundation from the Swedish economist Karl Gunnar Myrdal (1898–1987). The resulting work, the monumental *An American Dilemma: The Negro Problem and Modern Democracy* (1944), had an immediate impact on American social science. Although not produced by a member of the indigenous scientific 'tribe,' Myrdal's contribution was such that it could not leave American race relations specialists indifferent. As we shall see, Park's disciples had kept the master's works alive, and to varying degrees kept their distance from Myrdal's conclusions. Other Anglo-American academics attracted by the phenomenon of race relations for various reasons fell somewhere along the continuum between old and new. The result was a series of works between 1944 and 1960 that, while differing in many respects, coincided in their basic representation of African Americans as deserving of equality yet in some sense culturally inferior to whites.

An American Dilemma

In the summer of 1937, the president of the Carnegie Corporation, Frederick Keppel, invited Myrdal to head up a 'comprehensive study of the Negro in the United States, to be undertaken in a wholly objective and dispassionate way as a social phenomenon.'[8] Why a non-American? As Keppel explained in a foreword to the work, it was hoped that Myrdal could provide not only the necessary scientific expertise but also the open-mindedness of someone who had not grown up as a participant in the U.S. race relations problem:

> There was no lack of competent scholars in the United States who were deeply interested in the problem and had already devoted themselves to its study, but the whole question had been for nearly a hundred years so charged with emotion that it appeared wise to seek as the responsible head of the undertaking someone who could approach his task with a fresh mind, uninfluenced by traditional attitudes or by earlier conclusions ...[9]

Myrdal began work in the fall of 1938 with a two-month tour of the South. In January 1939 he submitted a draft research plan, which was peer-reviewed by a group of eminent social scientists and race relations experts: Ruth Benedict, Franz Boas, Allison Davis, W.E.B. Du Bois, E. Franklin Frazier, Charles Johnson, Melville Herskovits, Robert Park, William Thomas, and Louis Wirth. Backed by the corporation's financial muscle, Myrdal could afford to think big. He wrote, 'Upon the basis of the reactions I had received, I reworked my plans and gradually gave them a more definite form in terms of feasible approaches and the manner of actually handling the problems.'[10] In the spring he submitted a revised and detailed version of his plan, whose general terms of reference read as follows:

> The study, thus conceived, should aim at determining the social, political, educational, and economic status of the Negro in the United States as well as defining opinions held by different groups of Negroes and whites as to his 'right' status. It must, further, be concerned with both recent changes and current trends with respect to the Negro's position in American society. Attention must also be given to the total American picture with particular emphasis on relations between the two races. Finally, it must consider what changes are being or can be induced by education, legislation, interracial efforts, concerted action by Negro groups, etc.[11]

The plan, fully in keeping with the Carnegie Corporation's focus on educational projects, was accepted. Myrdal formed a research team comprising an inner circle of full-time researchers and a group of advisers commissioned to prepare research papers on specific topics. The second group included many distinguished scholars, white and black, including Frazier, Herskovits, Davis, Wirth, Johnson, J.G. St Clair Drake, Otto Klinneberg, and Edward Shils (for the more distant relationship of Du Bois to the project, see pp. 283–4). The team, filled out by some thirty research assistants, embarked on the largest American research enterprise carried out up to that time.

Myrdal meticulously apportioned the work to his assistants, and the research got underway in the fall. But the Second World War intervened. The following spring, with the Germans occupying Denmark and Norway, Myrdal decided to return to Sweden, hiring Samuel Stouffer to oversee the work in his absence. Several of the commissioned papers were ready by September 1940. Uncertain as to the date of Myrdal's return or when it could expect a final report, the corporation authorized the publication of several of these papers with a preface by Myrdal.[12]

By the spring of 1941 he was back in the United States, and the second phase of research – the one that would be capped by the publication of *An American Dilemma* – could begin. In the preface to the book, Myrdal mentioned the use he had made of unpublished manuscripts from the first phase, and went on to acknowledge the help of two academics, one black and one Jewish:

> Before making my final revision of the manuscript I have had the invaluable help of having it read critically and carefully by two friends who are at the same time outstanding social scientists with a great familiarity with the problems treated in the book: Professors E. Franklin Frazier of Howard University and Louis Wirth of the University of Chicago. They have not spared any effort, and as a result I have had their criticisms and suggestions often from page to page, referring to everything from the syntax and the arrangement of chapters and appendices to fundamental problems of approach and to conclusions. In my revision nearly every point raised by them has caused omissions, additions, rearrangements, clarifications or other alterations.[13]

Content of the Work

An American Dilemma is a massive work divided into eleven sections and forty-five chapters plus ten appendices, the first two ('A Methodological Note on Valuation of Beliefs,' and 'A Methodological Note on Facts and Valuations in Social Science') discussing the main concepts entering into the book's definitions as well as the theories of human behavior, attitudes, and motivations underlying them. The introduction begins with a resounding statement: 'There is a "Negro problem" in the United States and most Americans are aware of it.'[14] This problem, wrote Myrdal, was first and foremost a moral problem related to individual values: 'The American Negro problem is a problem in the heart of the American. It is there that the interracial tension has its focus. It is there that the decisive struggle goes on.' He elaborated:

> Though our study includes economic, social, and political race relations, at bottom our problem is the moral dilemma of the American – the conflict between his moral valuations on various levels of consciousness and generality. The 'American Dilemma,' referred to in the title of this book, is the ever-raging conflict between, on the one hand, the valuations preserved on the general plane which we shall call the 'American Creed,' where the American thinks, talks, and acts under the influence of high national and Christian precepts, and, on the other hand, the valuations on specific planes of individual and group living, where personal and local interests; economic, social, and sexual jealousies; considerations of community prestige and conformity; group prejudice against particular persons or types of people; and all sorts of miscellaneous wants, impulses, and habits dominate his outlook.[15]

This moral problem, for Myrdal, was primarily a problem created by white Americans: 'Although the Negro problem is a moral issue both to Negroes and to whites in America, we shall in this book have to give *primary* attention to what goes on in the minds of white Americans.'[16] It is unclear at the outset, however, whether this statement is meant as an assumption or a provable hypothesis. As to the 'American Creed,' Myrdal described it as emanating from three ideological sources. The first was 'a humanistic liberalism developing out of the epoch of Enlightenment when America received its national consciousness and its political structure ... For practical purposes the main norms of the American Creed as usually pronounced are centered in the belief in equality and in the rights to liberty. In the Declaration of Independence ... equality was given the supreme rank and the rights to liberty are posited as derived from equality.'[17] The second source was Christianity, 'particularly as it took the form in the colonies of various lower class Protestant sects, split off from the Anglican Church.'[18] The third source was that of British law, from which America derived its democratic conception of law and order and its fundamental conservatism. It was all laudable in theory, but in the case of its black citizens the country was far from living up to the American Creed:

> In principle the Negro problem was settled long ago; in practice the solution is not effectuated. The Negro in America has not yet been given the elemental civil and political rights of formal democracy, including a fair opportunity to earn his living, upon which a general accord was already won when the American Creed was first taking form. And this anachronism constitutes the contemporary 'problem' both to Negroes and to whites.[19]

The problem, unsurprisingly, was perceived differently by whites and blacks:

> The difference between the two groups, with respect to the recognition of the Negro problem, corresponds, of course, to the fundamental fact that the white group is above and the Negro group is below, that the one is intent upon preserving the *status quo,* while the other wants change and relief from the pressure of the dominant group. The one group is tempted to convince itself and others that there is 'no problem.' The other group has a contrary interest to see clearly and even make visible to others the existence of a real problem.[20]

Similarly, northerners and southerners had different views of the problem:

> In the North the observer finds a different mental situation in regard to the Negro problem. The South is divergent from the rest of the country not only in having the bulk of the Negro population within its region but also in a number of other traits and circumstances ... There has been less social change in the South ... The South is more agricultural and rural. Parts of it are isolated ... The South is poorer on the average: it is true both that there are more poor people in the South and that they are poorer than in the North ... The Negro problem has nowhere in the North the importance it has in the South.[21]

All of the foregoing remarks concerning the American Creed and the 'Negro problem' are found in the first part of the book, 'The Approach.' The remaining ten parts described different spheres of American life in which the Negro problem manifests itself. It would be a Herculean task to review all of this material, but, for example, on the issue of racial beliefs, Myrdal contended that it is unsurprising for whites to believe in blacks' innate inferiority,[22] even though this was antithetical to the value of equality at the center of the American Creed that everyone claimed to share. When this belief was enacted in the economic sphere, it inevitably had stigmatizing consequences:

> The most important intellectual bridge between the American Creed and actual practices in the economic sphere is, of course, the complex of racial beliefs ... Their import in the economic sphere is that the Negro is looked upon as inherently inferior as a worker and as a consumer. God himself has made the Negro to be only a servant or a laborer employed for menial, dirty, heavy and disagreeable work. And, since practically all such work is badly paid, it is God's will that the Negro should have a low income.[23]

The prejudice of racial inferiority came into conflict here with the value of equality, and more specifically that of equal opportunity, with the result being de facto discrimination. Another flagrant example of discrimination, this one in the political sphere, was southern black disenfranchisement:

> A Negro in the South expecting to vote knows that he is up to something extraordinary. In order to register and to appear at the polls, he will have to leave the protective anonymity of being just another Negro. He will become a specific Negro who is 'out of his place,' trying to attack the caste barriers. He knows further that the primary – which is the main election in the South – is closed to Negroes by formal and express rule in the major part of the South. There is a whole barrage of *formal* devices to keep him from voting in other elections ... There is another barrage of *informal* devices to keep Negroes from voting – ranging all the way from the insults and threats presented to the prospective Negro voter as he enters the polling place to the violence administered to his person and property by the Klan.[24]

Equality in 'social' (meaning interpersonal) relations was 'commonly denied American Negroes,'[25] yet the American Creed loftily prohibited discrimination on the grounds of race and color. Whether or not blacks accepted or accommodated to them, social segregation and discrimination formed 'a system of deprivations forced upon the Negro group by the white group.' This was best illustrated by the one-sidedness of the system: 'Negroes are ordinarily never admitted to white churches in the South, but if a strange white man enters a Negro church the visit is received as a great honor ... Likewise, a white stranger will be received with utmost respect and cordiality in any Negro school, and everything will be done to satisfy his every wish, whereas a Negro under similar circumstances would be pushed off the grounds of a white school.'[26]

As attractive as it might be in the abstract, the concept of class struggle was of no use to Myrdal in explaining American, and particularly southern, social stratification:

> The Marxian concept of 'class struggle' ... is in all Western countries a superficial and erroneous notion. It minimizes the distinctions that exist within each of the two main groups; it exaggerates the cleft between them, and, especially, the consciousness of it; and it misrepresents the role and the development of the middle classes ... In America it is made still more inapplicable by the traversing systems of color caste.[27]

The concept of 'caste struggle' was much more relevant. The caste line, popularly known as the color line, was 'not only an expression of caste differences and caste conflicts, but [had] come itself to be a catalyst to widen differences and engender conflicts.'[28] Caste solidarity among southern whites was ostensibly sacred. The situation was different in the North, yet even there a color line was evident: 'the color line in the North is not a part of the law or of the structure of buildings and so does not have the concreteness that it has in the South. But still ... most white individuals and groups discriminate in one way if not in another; all feel a difference between themselves and Negroes ...'[29]

The black counterpart of white caste solidarity, though not identical to it, could be thought of as a 'protective community' that provided solidarity in times of crisis and helped people with the many problems in their daily lives. Myrdal claimed to descry a 'sensitiveness' in blacks because of the constant humiliation they suffered at the hands of whites: 'Much of the Negro sensitiveness is centered around the word "Negro" and its several synonyms. Even the lower class Negro in the rural South feels insulted when he is called a "nigger" by a white man. The word is hated because it symbolizes what prejudiced white people think of Negroes.'[30]

Such sensitiveness, Myrdal maintained, had developed in some southern blacks to an atypically high degree but was much less acute in the North. It was a short step from humiliation, constantly exacerbated sensitiveness, to open aggression: 'some Negroes will openly tell the interviewer that: "I just get mad when I think about it all." Some really "get mad" occasionally and hit at the whites in the fury of frustration.'[31]

Education was, for Myrdal, a vital institution for the promotion of black Americans: 'Education means an assimilation of white American culture. It decreases the dissimilarity of the Negroes from other Americans.'[32] In practice, the situation in the North was relatively encouraging, while the situation in the South was lamentable:

> [In the North] Negroes have practically the entire educational system flung open to them without much discrimination. They are often taught in mixed schools and by white teachers; some of the Negro teachers have white pupils. Little attempt is made to adjust the teaching specifically to the Negroes' existing status and future possibilities. The American Creed permeates instruction, and the Negro as well as the white youths are inculcated with the traditional American virtues of efficiency, thrift and ambition ... [In the South] the Negro schools are segregated and the Negro school system is controlled by different groups with different interests and opinions concerning the desirability of preserving or changing the caste status of Negroes.[33]

In rural areas particularly, the situation was frankly appalling: 'The educational facilities for Negroes [there] are scandalously poor. The white community often blinds itself to the entire matter.'[34] Still, Myrdal saw hope that the situation could gradually be improved.

The concluding chapter, 'America Again at the Crossroads in the Negro Problem,' reveals that the initial proposition – whites face a moral dilemma in the form of the 'Negro problem' – was indeed a hypothesis not an axiom: 'We started by stating the hypothesis that the Negro problem has its existence in the American's mind.'[35] The chapter oscillates between discussion of the lessons to be derived from the research and description of observable trends that augur a better future. For example, concerning occupational and employment status during the 1940s, a period of mass wartime industrial production, the figures indicated a worrying situation for blacks:

> Negro unemployment mounted in all cities, particularly in the North, and the Negro workers increasingly became a relief burden. The whole country, and particularly the North, was much more generous toward the Negro in doling out relief to him than in allowing him to work and earn

his bread by his own labor ... Up to the time when this is being written (August, 1942), the Negro has been almost excluded from the great bulk of the war industries. Discrimination is the rule practically everywhere.[36]

The North is described as a long-standing, blatant 'social paradox':

> The social paradox in the North is exactly this, that almost everybody is against discrimination in general but, at the same time, almost everybody practices discrimination in his own personal affairs.
>
> It is the cumulation of all these personal discriminations which creates the color bar in the North and for the Negro causes unusually severe unemployment, crowded housing conditions, crime and vice.[37]

As a counterpoint to these observations, Myrdal suggested that improvement and the hope of a brighter future were on the horizon: 'We have become convinced in the course of this inquiry that the North is getting prepared for a fundamental redefinition for the Negro's status in America. The North will accept it if the change is pushed by courageous leadership. And the North has much more power than the South.'[38] In the South as well, where race relations were much more tense, there was hope: 'Even if there are going to be serious clashes and even if their short-run effects will be devastating to the Negroes involved and, perhaps, to Negroes in the whole region, we believe that the long-run effect of the present opinion crisis in the South, because it is a catharsis for the whites, will be a change toward increased equality for the Negro.'[39]

Myrdal closed the work with a self-consciously prophetic paragraph:

> the Negro problem is not only America's greatest failure but also America's incomparably great opportunity for the future ... If America in actual practice could show the world a progressive trend by which the Negro became finally integrated into modern democracy, all mankind would be given faith again – it would have reason to believe that peace, progress and order are feasible. And America would have a spiritual power many times stronger than all her financial and military resources – the power of the trust and support of all good people on earth.[40]

The Work in Intellectual and Social Context

An American Dilemma appeared at a time in American history when a generational divide between sociologists interested in race relations was in evidence. The Parkian era, which had done much to stimulate that interest, was drawing to a close. Many young scholars of the 1940s readily accepted and identified with a new analytical model, which, without rejecting the central themes of the Parkian tradition, especially assimilation, made room for New Deal-style social engineering. Myrdal sensed this paradigm shift in the making and reflected it in his book, combining generational continuity with a change of perspective. Thus, while adopting a decisively culturalist approach (race as a moral problem; American culture united around a set of common, dearly held values; a democratic creed as the cornerstone of the national consciousness), he explicitly supported the thesis of assimilationism and the integrationist model on which it was based.[41] But he severely criticized what he saw as the intolerable founding conservatism of Anglo-American social science, too deeply influenced as it was by philosophies of natural rights, positivism, and utilitarianism. He argued that white social scientists, like whites generally, reproduced the prevailing societal prejudices each time they judged blacks, an inevitable reflex in practice: 'Full objectivity ... is an ideal toward which we are constantly striving, but which we can never reach. The social scientist, too, is part of the culture in which he lives, and he never succeeds in freeing himself entirely from dependence on the dominant preconceptions and biases of his environment.'[42]

Was this serious difficulty surmountable? What should the country's sociologists and other scientists have done from the outset, and what ought they to do now? Recognize their values as such, was Myrdal's answer. They should assign their own values a specific status within their scientific constructions: 'There is no other device for excluding biases in social sciences than to face the valuations and to introduce them as explicitly stated, specific, and sufficiently concretized value premises. If this is done, it will be possible to determine in a rational way, and openly to account for, the direction of theoretical research.'[43] To rigorously identify the appropriate values on which to base a race relations theory, a selection process would be necessary: 'Values do not emerge automatically from the attempt to establish and collect the facts. Neither can we allow the individual investigator to choose his value premises arbitrarily. *The value premises should be selected by the criterion of relevance and significance to the culture under study.*'[44]

Because white American social science had systematically ignored all this, it was now mired in a profound, unacceptable conservatism.

Myrdal explicitly blamed Sumner, Park, and Ogburn for this state of affairs. It was these three canonical authors who had contributed the most broadly to the construction of the sociological corpus, and it was their profound influence that loomed over the numerous scholars looking for models to follow. In hewing to an overly pure ideal of science, they had made the logical error of 'inferring from the facts that men can and should make no effort to change the "natural" outcome of the specific forces observed. This is the old do-nothing (*laissez-faire*) bias of "realistic" social science.'[45]

As a social democrat committed to rational planning and social engineering, Myrdal could see that such a bias was ruinous. He called on the social sciences to embrace reformist interventionism and to demand that the federal government and other authorities do the same, and it is in this spirit that Myrdal's many recommendations should be taken. But it is important to emphasize that he offered nothing resembling a revolutionary program for systematic transformation of race relations, limiting his policy recommendations to those that might find acceptance among liberals in key sectors such as education and employment. The most ambitious of these recommendations involved the creation of new federal agencies to raise the employment rate in the black community.

Myrdal's fundamentally interventionist scientific model represented a sharp break with that of Park and his collaborators, not only in terms of its ideological assumptions but also in terms of its key themes. To Myrdal, Park's exclusion of the possibility of intervention in race relations and his embrace of evolutionism were obvious indications of his conservative bias. This critique was all the more interesting and suggestive in that, by the 1930s, Park's social science teaching and practice were coming into conflict with new Anglo-American approaches to race. Moreover, Myrdal sensed the shifts in the political landscape and the urgency of lessening racial tensions in American society. Indeed, he was only one of many scholars then advocating intervention as a way of realizing a situation of shared ideals and curtailing prejudice and discrimination. Park, in contrast, remained silent on the subject.[46]

Although it laid the 'Negro problem' largely at the door of whites, Myrdal's book devoted considerable attention to black Americans. Central to this discussion was a burning question: What does it mean to be black; what is the American black identity? The author's reasoning on this issue was peculiar in that he hovered between two logically incompatible positions, never really choosing between them. While he was at pains to describe how black Americans were in the process of assimilating with the majority culture and becoming full-fledged actors in the shared national experience, he dwelled on cultural differences that might suggest the contrary (roots in slavery, inability to achieve equality, persistent social and political subordination, isolation from mainstream culture). He mentioned three main factors distinguishing black culture from white: the existence of protest movements, an ingrained defensiveness in the face of negative white opinions and attitudes, and the presence of 'pathologies,' whose origins Myrdal situated in the majority culture: 'In practically all its divergences, American Negro culture is not something independent of general American culture. It is a distorted development, or a pathological condition, of the general American culture.'[47] Such pathologies – observed by Myrdal in the chronic instability of the American black family, the unsuitability of the educational infrastructure provided for blacks, the high crime rate in the black community, and many others[48] – did not materialize out of the void; they were the result of cultural conditions imposed by the white majority: 'Here the interest is in the fact that American Negro culture is somewhat different from the general American culture, that this difference is *generally created* by American conditions even if some of the *specific forms* are African in origin ...'[49]

At first sight Myrdal appears to be caught in a contradiction in his espousal of both assimilationism and differentialism, but this contradiction dissolves on close scrutiny. In his use of the then generally accepted explanatory model for interracial cultural dynamics, Myrdal showed himself to be much more of an assimilationist than a differentialist. Where he emphasized difference it was to explain blacks' transitory cultural inferiority; but he believed that the arrow of change pointed toward assimilation and that the process could be expedited by appropriate intervention. In other words, blacks formed an inferior cultural community with respect to whites, but, as the number of educated, urbanized blacks increased, they could be expected to shed their distinctive cultural traits in favor of those characteristic of the dominant Anglo-American culture. This process could be catalyzed by new government-induced employment opportunities and, most importantly, by public education, which, by acting on the ingrained but malleable white belief structure, could pave the way for behavioral change:

> A legitimate task of education is to attempt to correct popular beliefs by subjecting them to rigorous examination in the light of the factual evi-

> dence. This educational objective must be achieved in the face of the psychic resistance mobilized by the people who feel an urgent need to retain their biased beliefs in order to justify their way of life ... When supporting beliefs are drawn away, people will have to readjust their value hierarchies and, eventually, their behavior.[50]

It is clear enough that for Myrdal, a change in the nature of race relations had to follow and not precede the elimination of prejudice, which in turn would require reformed, enlightened education.

A third important driver of qualitative change would be to grant blacks the right to vote once and for all. Black disenfranchisement was a particularly severe problem in the South ('In the North, for the most part, Negroes enjoy equitable justice'),[51] so Myrdal's analysis and recommendations were largely directed at the South: '*the Southern conservative position on Negro franchise is politically untenable for any length of time ... changes should, if possible, not be made by sudden upheavals but in gradual steps* ... it is an urgent interest and, actually, a truly conservative one, for the South *to start enfranchising its Negro citizens as soon as possible.*'[52] He apparently regarded the franchise for southern blacks as a bellwether of emancipation; if they were granted this right, and thereby full citizenship, then major progress on race relations was possible. He proposed that the franchise be phased in by first granting it to the most educated strata of the black population, while enhancing the civic education offered to all blacks. However, he cautioned against harboring any illusions as to the outcome of such efforts, given the great many individuals lacking sufficient education to participate.

Myrdal considered two other issues of special relevance to the southern black population: their high poverty rate and their poor health status. He offered no miracle solution to these problems, but believed that even the most radical social policy could not effect any rapid change. Change could occur in the longer term, provided that blacks were involved in bringing it about. He suggested a strategy consisting of two parts: a black offensive led by not one organization (the NAACP, for example) but several, for maximum effectiveness; and a search for white allies, whose cooperation was necessitated by blacks' material poverty, lack of political culture, and exclusion from power. History's lesson for the black movements could not be clearer: 'When we look over the field of Negro protests and betterment organizations, we find that *only when Negroes have collaborated with whites have organizations been built up which have had any strength and which have been able to do some-*

thing practical.'[53] This strategy of alliance was a controversial position among black intellectuals of the 1940s, many of whom held that not only their own race but all American minorities should gain their freedom and cultural independence by their own efforts, not by relying on others. This position, it might also be mentioned, was yet another difference between Myrdal and Park on the subject of race relations.

Scholarly Reactions to Myrdal

Though it did not become the canonical work on the 'Negro problem,' and though not all academics agreed on its merits, *An American Dilemma* was a powerful and authoritative contribution to Anglo-American social science, as McKee notes: 'For probably two decades after its publication, Myrdal's *An American Dilemma* continued to be a force within the social sciences and the discipline of history; it was both praised and made use of in scholarly work, as well as criticized and rejected ... Yet it was not in encouraging specific forms of research but in sustaining a basic perspective that *An American Dilemma*'s influence on the new generation can be found.'[54] If so, I would add, then it is because Myrdal had the skill to construct his perspective in harmony, not in conflict, with at least two powerful forces in U.S. society. First, by promoting interventionism instead of laissez-faire in black-white relations, Myrdal fulfilled the expectations of his sponsor, the liberal-leaning Carnegie Foundation, which believed in resolving the race crisis through specific reforms, primarily in education. Myrdal's voluminous study set a course in precisely this direction: not stopping at academic debate, he put forward a set of tangible (educational and other) measures that he saw as providing for real social progress. At the heart of the American-liberal temperament is a deep pragmatic strain, and Myrdal astutely played to it.

Second, he willingly adopted the assimilationism that was still a central part of Anglo-American race relations theory and, as he had savvily grasped, a deep-seated conviction of nearly all of his white colleagues. His assertion of assimilation as the ultimate goal of evolving white-black relations – a principle that had survived across several generations of American sociologists – served to avert unproductive conflict with most sociologists of race. But he went further, presenting assimilation and cultural or national unity as mutually reinforcing principles central to the American experience from the very first. This was a more controversial position among sociologists, but it struck a chord with a broad segment of the white population who liked to think of the American polity as cohesive and unified in its racial and ethnic diversity, not to mention its often intense interracial conflict. Myrdal's affinity with this group undoubtedly enhanced his influence.

Myrdal's Supporters

A number of emerging scholars adopted several of Myrdal's principles as working hypotheses; namely, that the American 'Negro problem' was rooted in white attitudes, that the problem could only be solved by removing irrational white prejudices, and that reasoned or planned intervention would be necessary to achieve this. These social scientists applauded the postwar creation of various local organizations dedicated to lessening interracial tensions. They also welcomed the appearance on the scene of the intergroup relations specialists, whose work they saw as a rational response to these tensions. Their task as academics, as they conceived it, was to cultivate intellectual synergies with this pragmatic societal improvement movement, believing that both theoreticians and practitioners could benefit from such synergies. In this section I discuss some of the works published in this spirit of heightened interaction between theory and practice.

In 1947, the newly created American Council on Race Relations commissioned Arnold Rose, a close collaborator on the preliminary research for *An American Dilemma,* to produce a critical review of the abundant American psychosociological literature on racial prejudice, the number one problem identified by Myrdal. The result, *Studies in Reduction of Prejudice,* found that although a great many themes had been addressed (the effectiveness of public education in reducing racial prejudice, attitude measurement techniques, the appearance of prejudice in children, the psychology of prejudice as such, and so forth), little of practical value had been produced because of the contradictions and vaguenesses of the work. Rose recommended that new research be undertaken using a more suitable conceptual apparatus. That same year, the sociologist Robin Williams published his theoretical and practical essay *The Reduction of Intergroup Tensions* at the behest of the Committee on Techniques for Reducing Group Hostility, a body of the Social Science Research Council. In part one of his book, he hewed to Myrdal's path, reiterating that high tension between whites and blacks was understandable in a country with a history such as that of the United States, and that these tensions were caused by profound conflicts of interest between the two races as well as differences in terms of representations, values, and objectives. In part two, he presented 102 suggestions for lessening interracial hostilities founded on the premise that such hostilities can be reduced, or at least controlled, by nonviolent strategies that construe conflict as a natural, beneficial process strengthening the democratic character of the nation. A few, though not many, of his working hypotheses offered useful guidelines for practitioners. For example, he stressed the need to distinguish between prejudice as an attitude and discrimination as a behavior and noted the significance of the inverse correlation between prejudice and social class, an aid in discerning the social causes of prejudice and intervening intelligently to curtail it.

Another work bearing Myrdal's imprimatur was Robert MacIver's *The More Perfect Union* (1948). MacIver, an older academic who had never specialized in race and ethnicity, structured the work around his theoretical concern for the nature and progressive evolution of modern society out of traditional community structures. He was concerned to preserve societal or national unity throughout this process and regarded interracial tensions as a serious threat to it. For MacIver, the existence of such a threat stemmed from the existence of a 'multiplicity of compartmented groups' in society. Such compartmentation inevitably strengthened 'the natural tendency to group-bound thinking, the gravest peril in the social orientation of modern man.' Neither assimilation nor its opposite, cultural pluralism, could provide the solution to this problem, since 'they alike, though in different degrees, reject the spontaneous processes that from the beginning have built up community life.'[55]

These remarks indicate a significant divergence from Myrdal's normative standard of assimilation. Rejecting any suggestion that racial and ethnic groups should be homogenized, MacIver viewed the acceptance of a modicum of cultural pluralism as a necessity. The solution, he proposed, was for race relations specialists to work to remodel racial interaction with respect and tolerance for differing allegiances; that is, to minimize intercultural discrimination, which he defined as 'the denial of equal access to public opportunity.'[56] In short, MacIver's view was that national unity in a country like the United States did not necessitate the dissolution of its racial and ethnic groups into a melting pot, as had always been believed. Such unity could instead be conceived of as minimal recognition of cultural pluralism combined with a sustained effort by reformers to reduce discriminatory behavior. The premise of necessary assimilation was the only point on which MacIver departed from Myrdal's model; otherwise, he observed it to the letter, calling for a new type of social science that could nurture the interface between abstract research and planned intervention (social policy) to combat racial and ethnic discrimination. Such reform would have to be carried out on the institutional, political, and educational fronts, and the relevant strategies would largely come from white experts, since the problems stemmed from white attitudes. However, it would be desirable, he thought, to have the collaboration of more liberal-minded nonwhites.

Several other works dealing with the many manifestations of prejudice during the 1940s and 1950s were driven by a new sense of urgency in light of the recent European experience with fascism. As the victor in the war, the United States was expected by many to present itself as a model of democracy. A new generation of sociologists saw the country's interracial conflict as more than an embarrassing and flagrant contradiction of this image: it augured the potential for racial intolerance to shade into authoritarianism in the United States.[57] The year 1950 saw the culmination of an ambitious project, 'Studies in Prejudice,' begun in 1944 under the auspices of the American Jewish Committee, with the appearance of five separate studies of anti-Semitism. Notable among them was *The Authoritarian Personality*, a psychological study by the celebrated German exile Theodore Adorno and his colleagues. The authoritarian personality, for the authors, was built on a foundation of ethnocentrism, a 'general state of mind' that could be scored numerically and correlated with psychological and social variables including age, class, political ideology, religion, intelligence (IQ), and education. The work was perceived as breaking new ground in the study of racial prejudice generally, and prejudice between Jews and other groups (including blacks) specifically. In addition, since the authoritarian personality was perceived as a fascistic, socially dangerous phenomenon to be rooted out of the polity, the authors took a stand similar to Myrdal's in favor of progressive social policy: 'the modification of the potentially fascist structure cannot be achieved by psychological means alone ... These are products of the total organization of society and are to be changed only as that society is changed.'[58]

The new sociologists of race were conscious that the conceptual, theoretical, and methodological limitations of their approaches to studying prejudice impaired the objectivity of their work and its applicability to social change. In 1949, another well-known sociologist who had never shown any particular interest in race relations joined the fray. In 'Discrimination and the American Creed,' Robert Merton sketched out what he viewed as the logical relationship between prejudice and discrimination, his goal being to help researchers and practitioners improve their chances of effecting behavioral change. Merton's key point was that prejudiced individuals do not necessarily commit discriminatory acts whenever they meet someone from another race, while unprejudiced individuals may do so under specific circumstances and rules of conduct. Instead, a spectrum existed between the extremes of pure prejudice and absence of prejudice. He agreed with Myrdal that whites, as the dominant group, were the only ones who could harbor harmful prejudices against others, and therefore constituted the sole target of any strategy for change. The obvious corollary was that minorities themselves had no role to play in transforming race relations.

Merton was not the only social scientist to take this position, and his paper was not an isolated instance of an exhortation to enrich the practice of reform by developing better instruments for analyzing prejudice as an attitude and discrimination as a behavior. George Simpson and J. Milton Yinger, in *Racial and Cultural Minorities: An Analysis of Prejudice and Discrimination*, conceptualized prejudice as an attitude that could derive not only from particular personality traits but also from the wider culture (inculcated through normal socialization) and from the economic and political structure of a given society. Once prejudice takes hold as a result of these factors, they argued, it will then give rise to discriminatory behavior. Practitioners must comprehend the whole process if they wish to intervene effectively in the structure of race relations.

Other Views

Interventionism was certainly the tenor of the times, but far from all the sociologists active from 1944 to 1964 rallied to Myrdal's camp. The tradition patiently constructed by Park over his thirty-year career was still being carried on at Chicago and elsewhere. Nevertheless, the golden years of Park's race relations sociology, like those of the Chicago School itself, were now in the past.[59] His epistemological and methodological postulates were falling out of fashion,[60] while forces internal to the University of Chicago sociology department (retirement, changes in intellectual orientation) were pushing in new directions. Given the historical importance of this topic, it has been central to several analyses of great critical value, and I shall not dwell on it further here.[61] Be that as it may, the postwar literature includes three authors – Louis Wirth (1897–1952), Everett C. Hughes (1897–1983), and Herbert Blumer (1900–87) – who sought to expand Park's heritage into the field of race relations, each with his own style and thematic preferences.

WIRTH

As we have seen, Park was the first Anglo-American sociologist to attempt – largely unsuccessfully – to introduce the concept of minority into race and culture studies (in 'The Nature of Race Relations'). Louis Wirth made a second attempt in a 1945 article containing conceptual considerations that aimed to broaden the discussion of the issue. He defined a minority as 'a group of people who, because of their physical or cultural characteristics, are singled out from the others in the society in which they live for differential and unequal treatment, and who therefore regard themselves as objects of collective discrimination. The existence of a minority in a society implies the existence of a corresponding dominant group enjoying higher social status and greater privileges.'[62] Exclusion ensues naturally from minority status: 'Minority status carries with it the exclusion from full participation in the life of the society. Though not necessarily an alien group the minority is treated and regards itself as a people apart.'[63] Prejudice inevitably arises – in the dominant group, of course: 'The members of minority groups are held in lower esteem and may even be objects of contempt, hatred, ridicule, and violence.' The tangible experience of minority status is bound to generate 'a sense of isolation and of persecution ... a conception of themselves as more different from others than in fact they are.'[64] This state of affairs may have any number of outcomes. A minority may resign itself to its lot in frustration or may rebel and demand emancipation or equality, thus becoming 'a political force to be reckoned with.'[65]

Prior to Wirth's paper, Anglo-American sociology had invariably put the emphasis on parameters of origin such as race and culture and had rarely dwelled on the experience of subordination itself, as experienced by a minority group in its unequal relations with members of the majority culture. Wirth's contribution thus added color to the explanatory palette, as well as finally gaining acceptance for the concept of minority in the postwar psychological arsenal. The twin concepts of minority and majority provided the academic apparatus with which to make comparisons between, for example, blacks and other racial groups sharing the same devalued minority status – Indians, Japanese, Chinese, and others. The addition of the concept of minority did not, however, erase the dearly held mainstream sociological distinction between 'assimilable' ethnic groups and 'unassimilable' racial groups, which would persist until the 1960s.

Wirth's paper offered the following typology of minorities according to the objectives they seek to attain: '(1) pluralistic; (2) assimilationist; (3) secessionist; and (4) militant.' The first of these seeks only 'toleration for its differences on the part of the dominant group';[66] the second 'craves the fullest opportunity for participation in the life of the larger society with a view to uncoerced incorporation in that society';[67] the third has as its objective 'to achieve political as well as cultural independence from the dominant group';[68] while the fourth 'has set domination over others as its goal.'[69] He contended that this typology puts sociologists 'in a better position to analyze the empirical problems of minority situations and to evaluate the proposed programs for their solution.'[70] It was, indeed, a powerful tool for comparative analysis of American and other societies, and Wirth followed Park's example in presenting a set of comparative case studies with other minorities around the globe. Moreover, it marked a significant departure from orthodox Parkian tradition in two respects: its suggestion that assimilation was only one of several possible trajectories for a minority such as African Americans, and its evident incompatibility with the idea of a race relations cycle.[71]

HUGHES

Another product of Chicago was Everett Hughes, who adhered rather more strictly than Wirth to the Parkian corpus. Where Wirth became an activist to the detriment of his research productivity, Hughes remained faithful to the master's model throughout his career, resolutely detached from political ends and engagements. In the realm of ideas, he was willing to entertain variations on the Parkian theme while retaining its most durable elements.

After obtaining his doctorate with Park in 1928, Hughes taught sociology at McGill University in Montreal for a little more than ten years (1927–38), whereupon he returned to the University of Chicago sociology department as a full professor. From 1938 to 1961 he conducted original research on labor, occupations and professions, race relations, and institutions. He supervised the work of a large number of graduate students in ethnographic field work. He headed the department from 1952 to 1956 and edited the *American Journal of Sociology* from 1952 to 1960. As a result of intellectual disagreements and other issues, Hughes left Chicago in 1961 for Brandeis University, where he remained until 1968, ending his career at Boston College.

Although the study of occupations was his primary interest, Hughes devoted keen interest to interethnic relations, as witness several books and essays. He took advantage of his time at McGill in the 1930s to conduct research on the many effects of industrialization in Drummondville, Quebec, using comparative data from Germany. Begun in 1935, this research led to the publication of *French Canada in Transition* (1943), a study that exhibited the great strength of paying 'careful attention not only to interethnic contact but also to the class differences so often neglected by the University of Chicago community studies of the 1930s.'[72] Back in Chicago, he continued work on race relations in various settings (families, factories, government institutions, etc.), leading to the publication of several journal articles as well as *Where Peoples Meet: Racial and Ethnic Frontiers* (1952), written with his wife. Invoking Park's concept of racial frontiers, the authors proposed a more systematic conceptualization of interethnic relations within the context of macroprocesses such as industrialization, urbanization, migration, and the historical emergence of the United States. Their use of a wealth of historical examples from around the world, another feature that indicated the influence of Park on their work, further enriched their comparative approach and interpretation.

In the early 1960s, as president of the American Sociological Association (ASA), Hughes (like every other American) witnessed violent upheavals in race relations – indeed, a generalized situation of interracial crisis – that involved successful mass mobilizations, the proliferation of open conflict, and the radicalization of far-left forces who did not rule out violence as a means to racial justice and equality. These developments were especially disconcerting to Hughes in that they demonstrated how the Anglo-American sociology of race relations had overlooked the many postwar harbingers of an impending explosion along the color line. He reacted by devoting his presidential address of August 1963 (simultaneous with the March on Washington) to the subject of 'Race Relations and the Sociological Imagination.' Apart from a paper given to the 1967 ASA conference, it was the last substantial document he would produce on the subject.

Hughes's address illustrated his faithfulness to the Parkian tradition in many respects, while displaying some rather minor divergences. For both men, sociological analysis of the phenomenon of race meant the study of race relations, not racial or ethnic groups taken in isolation. Such relations tend to develop through a process characterized by conflict, which both saw as the proper object of analysis for sociologists of race relations. Conflict could best be analyzed through ethnography – field research involving observation and interviews with individuals or small groups. This approach could be complemented by historical perspective, making possible an instructive comparison between similar phenomena in different contexts or, contrariwise, different phenomena in similar contexts. Another likeness to Park illustrated here was Hughes's insistence on keeping his sociology free of immediate practical applications, although for neither man did this mean absolute indifference to such applications. Their comparable views on scientific objectivity demanded independence between knowledge on the one hand and practice or engagement on the other. (In Wirth's radically different vision, sociology had to support direct political action on race relations.)

The departures from the Parkian tradition that emerged from the address consisted of interest in class analysis and, like Wirth, lack of interest in the race relations cycle. These departures were rather predictable given the different scientific generation to which Hughes belonged and the changed society in which he lived. His Drummondville research had led him to a deeper analysis than Park of the ethnic division of labor as well as to an explanatory hypothesis entirely absent from Park's construction: namely, that a nation can exist even though not all its members share the same culture. Another difference from his mentor stands out as well: an acknowledgment of the existence of a non-negligible proportion of American blacks driven by the goal of separatism, to be attained by force if necessary; that is, a clear rejection on their part of any form of assimilation. Underlying this nuanced interpretation was Hughes's awareness of the renaissance of ethnic identities in the 1960s as well as his sensitivity – unlike the young Park if not the older one – to changes in American social class structure. This sensibility is one that he had derived in part from Frazier's penetrating analyses during the 1940s and 1950s (to which we return in chapter 6), in particular *Black Bourgeoisie* (1957) and *The Negro in the United States* (1949). All this said, his analysis of black cultural identity (which emerged in the course of a comparison with another North American minority, the French Canadians) largely stayed within the Parkian framework: 'The Negro Americans want to disappear as a defined group; they want to become invisible as a group, while each of them becomes fully visible as a human being ... They want to be seen, neither as Negroes nor as if they were not; but as if it did not matter.'[73] In short, he believed, most African Americans wanted unconditional assimilation.

BLUMER

Herbert Blumer, another Chicago School heir to the Parkian tradition, showed a great variety of research interests throughout his career.[74] His first essay on race relations appeared in the journal *Social Process in Hawaii* in 1939, but the bulk of his contribution would be made in the 1950s and 1960s. The principal elaboration on Park's work in Blumer was the concept of collective behavior, or social phenomena that arise spontaneously rather than as the predictable outcome of social structures. Racial segregation, in Blumer's view, was an example of such behavior. Departing from Park, he contended that it could best be challenged through policy and planned action. The intense 1950s struggle against public school segregation gave him a context in which to argue this point. In 'Social Science and the Desegregation Process,' he addressed educators and community leaders in a practical tone, offering to enlighten them on the social factors likely (or unlikely) to lead to successful desegregation. He argued that a successful strategy should not attempt to root out prejudiced attitudes in society, a Herculean task, but rather to prevail upon the individual agents or 'functionaries' of segregation, the persons who enforce the rules in practice, by capitalizing on the prestige and strength of organizations that call for the enforcement of a 'transcending moral standard.'[75]

Two years later, Blumer was invited by the United Nations Educational, Scientific, and Cultural Organization (UNESCO) to produce a critical review of American postwar race relations research. The resulting work analyzed some eight hundred published or unpublished studies, shedding much light on the state of the field at that time. One finds here, for example, one of the earliest acknowledgments by an Anglo-American of the value of black sociological research:

> A first-rate general treatment of the Negro in the United States is given by Frazier. The best of the intensive studies of the Negro in a given locality is presented in *Black Metropolis,* which deals with the Negro population in Chicago, Illinois. The best account, by far, of the life of any segment of American Negro society has been presented by Frazier in his award win-

ning book, *The Black Bourgeoisie*. This is a very incisive sociological analysis, showing the empty social forms of living developed by the upper classes of Negroes, largely as an adjustment to white discrimination.[76]

Blumer examined numerous studies of discrimination in all areas of public life: work, housing, education, trade unions, and so on. For him, the importance of these studies was that 'they often explored sites of interracial contact and revealed the complexity and variety of "situations" where relations were in process.'[77] He dealt harshly with research on discrimination and prejudice that focused only on attitudes to the exclusion of situations, calling it scientifically faulty. Stating that '[d]espite its vastness, research over the past decade has contributed little to solid theoretical knowledge of race relations,'[78] he attempted to assemble the elements of a new theoretical framework around the premise that behavior is effectively determined by the situational context. In his conclusion, he reiterated his conviction that organized action is necessary in order to achieve a desirable transformation of race relations, here again departing from Park:

> A final notion that will enter into a new theoretical perspective in the study of race relations refers to the efficacy of institutional decree and of organized action in bringing about deliberate changes in racial relationships. Until recent years the line of thinking that blanketed the racial field, for laymen and scholars alike, was that no deliberate changes of significance could be made in race relations until individuals changed their racial feelings and attitudes and until groups changed their mores. For laymen, this thought was largely a rationalization; for scholars, it was an academic illusion. Occurrences in recent years on the political scene, together with the findings of several research studies have led increasingly to a challenge of this thought.[79]

A final article by Blumer is relevant to the theme of this book: 'Industrialisation and Race Relations' (1965), a comparative study of the relationship between these two phenomena among four different regions of the globe (South Africa, the United States, Southeast Asia, and the new African states). He wrote, 'If we grant that industrialisation is a master agent of social transformation and if race relations in our contemporary world are in the throes of profound change, it is both timely and highly important to ask what effect the process of industrialisation exercises on the relations between racial groups.'[80]

After a brief review of the central features of industrialization, Blumer dwelled on the 'conventional wisdom' whereby it is expected to transform race relations by first undermining the established social order, then provoking the development of new social relations, and finally remodeling a new social order around the key features of industrialism. The reality, he noted, was considerably more complex. 'We are forced by empirical evidence to recognize ... that early industrialisation in these regions did not undermine the established racial system but merely came to fit inside it,' he wrote.[81] Likewise, the remainder of the cycle never manifested itself as the conventional wisdom predicted. The analytical framework had to be rectified to take account of these empirical facts:

> A realistic treatment of industrialisation and race relations must be based ... on an acceptance of the following points: (1) industrialisation and racial alignment act on each other; (2) their interaction is profoundly influenced by the character of the setting in which it occurs; and (3) the setting, in turn, changes under the play of social and political happenings ... the approach which I believe to be demanded by empirical happenings presupposes that racial alignment is shaped in major measure by non-industrial influences, that resulting patterns of racial alignment permeate the industrial structure, and that changes in such patterns are traceable mainly to movements in social and political happenings.[82]

His comparative historical analysis (never having done field work in the regions in question) led Blumer to exclude the idea of a simple, not to say simplistic, relationship between industrialization as a process and race relations as an entity in constant flux. The cautious nature of his conclusions is indicated by this final paragraph:

> Industrialisation will continue to be an incitant to change, without providing the definition of how the change is to be met. It will contribute to the reshuffling of people without determining the racial alignments into which people will fall. Its own racial ordering, to the extent that it has any, will be set by that in its milieu or that forced on it by the authority of a superior control. In general, it will move along with, respond to, and reflect the current of racial transformation in which it happens to be caught.[83]

In sum, the postwar Anglo-American sociology of race relations – an institutional and cognitive component of mainstream sociology – was divided into two interpretive schools, one a continuation of the Parkian tradition, the other a set of variations on *An American Dilemma*. While Park's heirs were theoretically recalcitrant to direct intervention in the existing racial 'order,' in practice Wirth, Blumer, and others countenanced departures from this norm without becoming professional reformers themselves; none of them gave up his academic career, and each kept a critical distance from collective action *stricto sensu*. One cannot avoid seeing the influence of the sociopolitical juncture in such departures. With racial tensions intensifying and well-meaning liberals urgently looking to mainstream sociology for direction, few sociologists could elude the pressure for social science to make suggestions to help reformers diminish these tensions.

In presenting this panorama of Anglo-American sociological views on race and race relations between 1865 and 1965, my purpose has been to meet the conventional scientific requirement of establishing the study object at the level of generality or conceptual abstraction necessary for theorization. The predominant case study, given the conflict-ridden history of the era, was of course that of race relations between blacks and whites, and the paradigmatic academic characterization of American blacks in this corpus was as *inferior* human beings. Up to 1918, biological, hence 'natural' or innate inferiority, was the predominant paradigm. After 1920, the paradigm became more complex, shading into cultural inferiority, although the biological referent never disappeared. Now, black Americans were doubly 'inferior': as individuals by nature, and as members of a distinct minority group by virtue of their culture. With the 1940s and in the wake of *An American Dilemma*, the biological stigma attached to blacks became a recessive trait in mainstream sociology, leaving the cultural paradigm to predominate. This was based on two postulates: first, that blacks were not, despite their efforts, ready to participate in modern white society – that is, not currently assimilable; and second, that unlike European immigrants, black Americans had no authentic culture of their own and did not therefore deserve to be treated as an ethnic group. They were merely a racial minority situated at the lowest level of the class structure.

To conclude this part, I shall situate our study object within the broader and more elucidating play of perspectives and ideological assumptions characteristic of the United States in the twentieth century, for it might be assumed that the deeply racist scientific construction I have examined was a quintessentially American phenomenon. It was not, as is easy to see by enlarging our interpretive framework. The Anglo-American sociological dominance considered in this chapter in fact partook ideologically of a broader asymmetry inscribed in the history of the European conquest of America, as the following passage clarifies:

> Europeanization began with the earliest colonial settlements. It entailed a Europeanized society in North America based in part on African slave labor and from which the native Indian population was largely if not wholly excluded ... Among the European settlers the Anglo-Americans by virtue of their numbers and control of the machinery of government emerged as the dominant ethnic element. In the course of time *American* for all practical purposes came to mean Anglo-American.[84]

The ideological corollary of placing a label of inferiority on another is to consider oneself superior, dominant, with respect to the people who have been kept subordinated through the structural and sociopolitical mechanism of conflict. Anglo-Americanism was an especially powerful construction precisely because it represented 'victory' in the conflict between races and ethnic groups on the new continent, a long-standing phenomenon in which blacks represented only one component. It would not be long before ideological rationalization would run away with this historical process and give it the imprimatur of inevitability. To maintain this conception, amalgamation and assimilation were necessary so that 'order' and 'harmony' could reign in the emerging new country:

> By stamping their ethnic traits on an amalgamated population the Anglo-Americans were forging a distinctive national character and bringing order and harmony to what would otherwise be a chaos of heterogeneous nationalities. The assimilating role performed in the name of nationality was to remain the self-assigned Anglo-American burden until well into the twentieth century. When American academic sociology arose in the 1890s this task was taken for granted, and assimilation was assigned a central place in Chicago ethnic theory.[85]

PART TWO

The Genesis of African American Sociology, 1896–1964

As everyone knows, it was as slaves that large numbers of Africans first came to the Americas at the start of the seventeenth century. The number of slaves living in the country by the early 1800s exceeded 330,000.[1] Jefferson's administration passed legislation to eliminate slavery, but it had no effect in practice, and so the system persisted. Blacks continued to be sold at auction like beasts of burden into lives of extreme harshness. One especially pernicious effect of the draconian social system put in place on the southern plantations was the destruction of ancestral African heritage. After the Civil War and emancipation, a rigid caste system was instituted on the southern plantations, while class stratification was increasingly observed among African Americans. Domestic servants formed a small privileged class while field hands made up a much larger underclass, enduring stricter social controls and having a more distant relationship with the white gentry. The class structure acquired further levels of complexity in the early twentieth century with the Great Migration to the large cities.[2]

Racism was rampant at all levels of white society, from the cultivated elites to the poor. In the South, blacks were unceasingly harassed by a culture of gross prejudice, exclusion, and multiform violence:

> As the nineteenth century drew to a close the Negro's position in American society was deteriorating steadily. Disfranchisement, lynchings, Jim Crow laws, farm tenancy, and peonage were the black man's lot in the South. Throughout the country, labor unions excluded him from the skilled trades. After 1900, race riots became commonplace in both North and South ... Southern propagandists held that not only were blacks an innately inferior, immoral, and criminal race, but that in fact freedom caused a reversion to barbarism ...[3]

In the North racism took more sophisticated but equally degrading forms, even when clothed in the majestic robes of science. As we saw in the preceding chapters, the ideological agenda of the early scientific racism was to reduce culture to nature: 'Although the racist theory which flourished briefly among intellectuals and academics at the turn of the century purported to be based on impersonal scientific principles it was clearly an effort to bring biology to the support of Anglo-Americanism.'[4] Mainstream social science in particular was pervaded with bias that clouded any attempt at impartial, objective analysis of interracial conflict.

The first sociologists of color appearing in the 1890s, four or five in total, were outsiders in that they belonged to a long-established minority community considered 'unassimilable' by the Anglo-Saxon elites who claimed to speak for the majority. Not coincidentally, these black sociologists all made social stratification a central focus of their research. If they were fervent about social science, and especially sociology, it is because they saw it as the road to a successful intellectual career as well as a great symbolic arena in which to prove their people's equality to any other – white Americans most pertinently. Historical circumstances after 1918 also made them the protagonists of a pivotal moment in their group's development; namely, the deruralization of the South, as thousands left for the northern cities and the promise of cultural emancipation that they held out. These sociologists could hardly fail to take positions on a phenomenon that was not just physical but symbolic, for this migratory pattern signified the entrance of African Americans into the spaces in their country where *modernity* was most obviously being forged.

The most important of these early black sociologists was W.E.B. Du Bois, who eclipsed his contemporaries in terms of conceptual originality. Du Bois unquestionably deserves to be known as the founding father of a distinct sociological tradition, and was the dominant figure of his intellectual generation until after the First World War, when others came on the scene: Charles S. Johnson (late 1910s), E. Franklin Frazier (early 1920s), Oliver C. Cox and Horace R. Cayton (early 1930s), and J.G. St Clair Drake (late 1930s). A half-dozen more – names such as Bertram Doyle, Edmund Haynes, and Ira de Augustine Reid – were of lesser importance since they did not make any substantial contribution to the theoretical core of the new black sociology, or at any rate nothing that could serve to counter the assertions of Anglo-American sociology.

I shall begin the next three chapters with brief intellectual portraits of these figures, continuing with detailed analyses of their most significant works. This procedure is necessary because of the unjust disregard in which these pioneers were long held. In the eyes of too many Anglo-American sociologists, Du Bois was little more than an inconvenient rival, Cox an unremarkable spouter of Marxist theory. Frazier, Johnson, Drake, and Cayton were noteworthy only as clones of either Park or Myrdal, the two most important contemporaneous white theorists of race relations. All were seen as having no effective originality or scientific authenticity. It is my purpose to demonstrate precisely the contrary.

4 W.E.B. Du Bois: Scientific Sociology and Exclusion

Du Bois was born in 1868 into a poor family in Great Barrington, Massachusetts, a small town relatively untouched by racial discrimination. A mulatto of French Huguenot, Dutch, and African descent, his education exposed him to the traditional values of Yankee Protestant culture. After initial schooling between 1885 and 1894, he hoped to continue his studies at Harvard, but this proved impossible because of inadequate finances. Instead, he accepted a scholarship to Fisk University in Nashville, a white-governed institution for black students that was affiliated with the Congregationalist church; he graduated in 1888. It was during this time in the Deep South that he discovered the handicap of his own skin color and the reality of discrimination and prejudice.

That same year Du Bois was given a scholarship to Harvard on the strength of his academic record at Fisk. Though he now held a bachelor's degree, Harvard rejected its equivalency, and he was forced to register as an undergraduate. In the next two years he continued his education in the social sciences and philosophy, earning a second bachelor's degree in 1890. He was immediately granted admission to a doctoral program in the social sciences, his project being to study the economic and social status of black Americans. In his posthumously published autobiography (1968) he described his studies as having been in the fields of 'history and political science and what would have been sociology if Harvard [had] yet recognized such a field.'[1]

At Harvard he was exposed to the work of the idealist philosopher George Santayana and, more influentially, that of the pragmatic philosopher and psychologist William James. In 1891 he obtained his master's degree and began writing his doctoral thesis while nurturing the project of a postgraduate stint at a European university. Supported by a loan, he registered for a one-year program at the University of Berlin with an option to renew for a second year, and thus in 1892 found himself in Germany studying history, economics, and sociology, absorbing the influence of Max Weber and Heinrich Treitschke, taking an interest in the work of Adolph Wagner and Rudolph von Gneist, and getting an introduction to Marxism.

Of all the German intellectuals with whom he came in contact, it was Gustav Schmoller whose work he found most captivating. Schmoller's methods provided a template of sorts for everything that Du Bois the sociologist would produce (see pp. 141–3). Back in the United States in 1894, he continued working on his doctoral thesis (published as *The Suppression of the African Slave Trade to the United States of America, 1638–1870* [1896], the first volume in the Harvard Historical Series) while accepting a job as a humanities professor teaching Latin, Greek, German, and English at Wilberforce University in Ohio, a Methodist-run institution for black students. He knew, of course, that he had no chance of being hired by a white university. He proposed to teach a sociology course, but the university administration saw no merit in the idea.

In 1896 the University of Pennsylvania made Du Bois the exceptional offer of a one-year appointment for the purpose of conducting a wide-ranging statistical study of the burgeoning black population of Philadelphia. The invitation came at the behest of Susan Wharton, the prominent leader of the Philadelphia settlement house movement.[2] Thus it was that he embarked on his first sociological field research project, and the result was the profoundly empirical monograph *The Philadelphia Negro* (1899). Based on both direct investigation and a variety of demographic data, this work constitutes not only one of the first American studies of racial or ethnic community but the magnum opus of Du Bois the sociologist (see pp. 131–40 for a detailed analysis of the work).[3]

The Philadelphia Negro was intended as the first volume in a grand research program that would study blacks in other large U.S. cities and in selected rural areas, but Du Bois never succeeded in eliciting interest or funding for this ambitious project. After completing the monograph he was hired by Atlanta University, the oldest black university in the country (founded 1865), as professor of social science (economics, history, sociology) and director of the sociological laboratory. He was given responsibility for organizing the annual Atlanta University Conferences, which dealt with the effects of urban life on the black population, and for editing the proceedings (published annually as Atlanta University Studies). Though a short period in his long life, Du Bois's decade-plus at Atlanta University (1897–1910) accounts for the bulk of his sociological writings, the most relevant for my purposes being 'A Program for a Sociological Society' (1897); 'The Study of the Negro Problems' (1898); 'The Laboratory in Sociology at Atlanta University' (1903); 'The Negro Farmer' (1904); 'Sociology Hesitant' (1904); 'Die Negerfrage in den Vereinigten Staaten' (1906), an article commissioned by Max Weber on his visit to the United States in 1904 and published the following year in *Archiv für Sozialwissenschaft und Sozialpolitik*; 'Race Friction between Black and White' (1908); and 'The Economic Aspects of Race Prejudice' (1910).

In 1900, Du Bois was invited by the publisher A.C. McClurg to compile several of his essays into a book. The third chapter of the resulting *The Souls of Black Folk* (1903), titled 'Of Mr Booker T. Washington and Others,' is unflinchingly severe in its criticism of Washington and his accommodationist program, arguing that it laid too much emphasis on compromise between blacks and whites and not enough on the need for the black community to take charge of its own affairs and acquire political power. In 1905 he furthered the insult and marked himself as a subversive among the black elite by cofounding the short-lived Niagara Movement (it folded in 1910) as a vehicle to promote civil rights and specifically oppose Washington's approach. He had thrown down the gauntlet to the era's most respected and redoubtable black reformer and would take the consequences by losing his professorship (see pp. 148–50).

It was more than a change of employment: the event marked the beginning of a new career – from academia to social action, or what Schmoller thought of as applied sociology. Du Bois's main role as a leader of the National Association for the Advancement of Colored People (NAACP), the successor to the Niagara Movement, was to publish the organization's journal, *Crisis*, which he did for a quarter-century (1910–34). His interests and activities were wide ranging, even as he focused on improving the socioeconomic status and civil rights of black Americans. He did not think that assimilationism, then the leading current of black thought, would serve to achieve this end,[4] and was at pains to disseminate a deeply segregationist doctrine in his editorials, lectures, and comments at various meetings and conferences; in fact, he was a lifelong promoter of pan-Africanism as a major identity alternative for African Americans, converging in this respect with Marcus Garvey and his 'back to Africa' doctrine. Simplifying his position somewhat, he held that equality for U.S. blacks could be achieved only through separate development, especially in the area of housing, as well as through the development of an authentic black culture within the broader American polity.[5] But this ideological position ran counter to the integrationist stance of the other NAACP leaders, and in 1934, at the age of sixty-six, Du Bois left the organization to return to Atlanta University, this time as head of the department of economics and sociology.

He was no longer the dedicated field researcher of three decades earlier but a man who had become deeply radicalized by his fight for the social promotion of men and women of color. He put his efforts into reviving and modernizing the Atlanta University Conferences and founding a new academic journal devoted to race and culture, *Phylon* (1940). Three years later, the twenty-sixth Atlanta University Conference was attended by thirty-four delegates from thirty different institutions, including important members of the new generation of black sociologists (Frazier, Johnson) and white sociologists such as Howard Odum.[6] It was a great moment for Du Bois in both political and academic terms, and the gathering tasked him with preparing a follow-up meeting for the next year. But some time after the event he was summarily fired and, at seventy-six, found himself a free agent again. His ideas and institutional initiatives had undoubtedly been too bold for the university administration.

After another short stint with the NAACP as 'director of special research projects' (essentially a ghost writer for the secretary), he was fired again in 1948 because of his ever-widening ideological differences with the association. By this time Du Bois was becoming increasingly active on international aspects of the race question. He accepted an honorary position as assistant director of the Council of African Affairs, an organization listed as subversive with the office of the U.S. attorney general, and also became director of the equally suspect Peace Information Center. Du Bois's positioning as a member of the American left had become unequivocal; he no longer hesitated to use words like 'communism' without the requisite pejorative connotations. With the onset of the Cold War, the elderly Du Bois became a world traveler, devoting all his efforts to the promotion of world peace and attending various conferences and gatherings on the subject.

On his return from one such conference in Prague, he and several colleagues were indicted as 'agents of a foreign principal.' The ensuing trial had contrasting legal and psychological outcomes: 'The trial began in November 1951, and after five days of prosecution testimony, the judge acquitted the defendants, ruling that the government had failed to support the allegations in the indictment. Even so, Du Bois was now more than ever a marked and tainted figure – acquitted of the alleged crime, but nevertheless deeply and irrevocably stigmatized; innocent, yet guilty of being accused.'[7] There is, perhaps, some melodrama in this account; be that as it may, from this incident until the end of his life, Du Bois was not to be left alone by the government.

Despite his advanced age, he continued to write and teach, giving courses on African American history at the New School for Social Research and the Thomas Jefferson School in New York. In 1957 he was invited to Ghana to attend its independence ceremonies but was denied a passport by the State Department and could not travel. Three years later he succeeded in obtaining a passport to attend the inauguration of the Republic of Ghana. During this visit, Du Bois, now aged ninety-three, accepted President Kwame Nkrumah's invitation to live in the country and work on the *Encyclopedia Africana*, knowing full well that it would probably be his last intellectual enterprise. A few months before leaving, he applied for membership in the U.S. Communist Party. He stated that his political thinking had shifted irreversibly from socialism to communism, and offered the party a ten-point program for restoring democracy to the nation. He would have only two years to spend on the encyclopedia, just long enough to conduct some preliminary research, before he died in 1963 and the project was shelved.

As we have seen, Du Bois left no one indifferent; while celebrated by many African Americans, he was hastily consigned to history by the Anglo-American elite along with the daunting shadow he had cast. It is an irony that after years of exclusion from the history of mainstream sociology, Du Bois is typically discussed today in laudatory tones (e.g., '*The Philadelphia Negro* is the first major empirical work in American sociology'[8] – quite a concession!). It is tempting, given the towering figure he became and the exceptional life he led, to analyze each phase of his life with reference to the upheavals taking place in U.S. society between 1868 and 1963, but this would be far beyond the scope of this book. Du Bois the creator of an authentically black sociology – which he regretfully left behind in a half-finished state – had moved on by 1910, and I will therefore focus on his writings prior to that year.

Early Works

Even before 1900, and especially in his doctoral thesis, his writings exuded enthusiasm not for current sociological fashions but for a different sociology, one whose outlines were already taking shape in his mind. His goals for this research were clear even before he applied to Harvard for a graduate fellowship in 1890, 'writing in his application that he desired to obtain a Ph.D. in social science, "with a view to the ultimate application of its principles to the social and economic rise of the Negro people."'[9] Since Harvard offered no formal sociology program, he was obliged to approach his subject through the departments of philosophy and history.

Then it was off to Europe and the pivotal encounter with Schmoller. Du Bois's thesis (like much of his sociological approach; see pp. 141–3) bore the older man's imprimatur. He pushed the inductive approach as far as it would go in terms of documentary sources, endeavoring to expand his explanatory perspective so as to avoid isolating the slave trade from the social context in which it had developed; more particularly, from the colonies taken as a socioeconomic system. His preface clearly adumbrates an approach that is as much sociological as it is historical: 'The question of the suppression of the slave-trade is so intimately connected with the questions as to its rise, the system of American slavery, and the whole colonial policy of the eighteenth century, that it is difficult to isolate it, and at the same time to avoid superficiality on the one hand, and unscientific narrowness of view on the other.'[10]

The other keys to understanding the genesis of Du Bois's sociology are found in a series of brief papers and lectures written between 1896 and 1899. His first description of his sociological objectives and approach appears in a paper published shortly after his appointment to Atlanta University. Here, he limns the discipline as a 'vast and fruitful field of inquiry into the mysterious phenomena of human action.'[11] Another 1897 speech, 'The Conservation of Races,' delivered before the newly created American Negro Academy, focused on the sensitive concept of race. As the title indicates, Du Bois was still under the powerful influence of evolutionism. After allowing the existence of racial divisions among human beings, he went on to say, 'The question we must seriously consider is this: What is the real meaning of Race; what has, in the past, been the law of race development, and what lessons has the past history of race development to teach the rising Negro people?'[12] His use of the word 'race' here appears to refer to both a verifiable fact of human existence and an analytical category. But within a paragraph he is at odds with the dominant scientific beliefs of his day, reining in the interpretation of the physical criteria used to determine race: 'The final word of science, so far, is that we have at least two, perhaps three, great families of human beings – the whites and Negroes, possibly the yellow race ... This broad division of the world's races ... is nothing more than an acknowledgment that, so far as purely physical characteristics are concerned, the differences between men do not explain all the differences of their history.'[13] And then he counterattacks:

> Although the wonderful developments of human history teach that the grosser physical differences of color, hair and bone go but a short way toward explaining the different roles which groups of men have played in Human Progress, yet there are differences – subtle, delicate and elusive, though they may be – which have silently but definitely separated men into groups ... these subtle forces ... have divided human beings into races, which, while they perhaps transcend scientific definition, nevertheless, are clearly defined to the eye of the Historian and Sociologist.[14]

He then returns to his starting question, refining the answer by excluding all reference to physical characteristics: 'What, then, is a race? It is a vast family of human beings, generally of common blood and language, always of common history, traditions and impulses, who are both voluntarily and involuntarily striving together for the accomplishment of certain more or less vividly conceived ideals of life.'[15] The key words here – family, history, tradition, striving, ideals of life – make clear that for Du Bois, race was in no way a fixed category, but was a *construct* arising from historical, social, and cultural processes. As such it was contingent and changeable, as is any property of human culture. This position may not seem earthshaking today, but it directly contradicted the essentialistic nineteenth-century idea of race as a fixed category in the great cosmic order, for better or worse determining the destiny of every individual. Since this view was couched in Darwinian terms, and Darwinism pervaded the scientific ethos, it was taken for an objective truth about the world. But in fact it was just scientific racism, an ideological *trompe l'oeil* fabricated by Anglo-American intellectuals to justify their people's superiority in the 'natural' hierarchy of the races. Du Bois's definition was not merely crucial but revolutionary; it laid the epistemological groundwork for *The Philadelphia Negro* by directly confronting the racial essentialism at the heart of mainstream American sociology: 'By conceiving of the Negro problem as a historical problem, contingent and ever changing, DuBois planted the seeds of a powerful critique of racial essentialism.'[16]

The rest of 'The Conservation of Races' found Du Bois fleshing out his central argument that races arise primarily out of historical, indeed materialistic processes. He stressed that he did not totally exclude physical differences as criteria of racial demarcation – 'Certainly we must all acknowledge that physical differences play a great part' – only to return to the idea that '[t]he deeper differences are spiritual, psychical, differences – undoubtedly based on the physical, but infinitely transcending them.'[17] He illustrated this point with reference to the 'Teuton nations,' considered the model of a well-differentiated race at the time: 'The forces that bind together the Teuton nations are, then, first, their race identity and common blood; secondly, and more important, a common history, common laws and religion, similar habits of thought and a conscious striving together for certain ideals of life.'[18]

Du Bois fundamentally conceived of the historical process of racial differentiation in time and space as a form of growth, and the influence of evolutionism is palpable here. The chief characteristic of this growth was, for him, 'the differentiation of spiritual and mental differences between great races of mankind and the integration of physical differences.'[19] This evolutionary process had occurred in a series of major phases:

> The age of nomadic tribes of closely related individuals represents the maximum of physical differences. They were practically vast families, and there were as many groups as families. As the families came together to form cities the physical differences lessened, purity of blood was replaced by the requirement of domicile, and all who lived within the city bounds became gradually to be regarded as members of the group; *i.e.*, there was a slight and slow breaking down of physical barriers. This, however, was accompanied by an increase of the spiritual and social differences between cities. This city became husbandmen, this, merchants, another warriors, and so on. The *ideals of life* for which the different cities struggled were different. When at last cities began to coalesce into nations there was another breaking down of barriers which separated groups of men. The larger and broader differences of color, hair and physical proportions were not by any means ignored, but myriads of minor differences disappeared, and the sociological and historical races of men began to approximate the present division of races as indicated by physical researches. At the same time the spiritual and physical differences of race groups which constituted the nations became deep and decisive. The English nation stood for constitutional liberty and commercial freedom; the German nation for science and philosophy; the Romance nations stood for literature and art,

> and the other race groups are striving, each in its own way, to develop for civilization its particular message ...[20]

This long quotation illustrates particularly well how Du Bois, with the help of evolutionism and, especially, his idea of the gradual selection of typical traits, devised an entirely different interpretation of the race phenomenon from the one offered by Anglo-American social science. As well, it reveals how thoroughly his thinking was rooted in nineteenth-century, not to say eighteenth-century, notions of race and nation.[21]

Toward the end of the paper he switched to a political analysis of race, one that became an exhortation to action – not surprising, given that the paper began as a lecture to blacks seeking enlightenment as to their shared destiny in the new century. He began by stating that black Americans had not yet given a 'full spiritual message' to civilization: 'Manifestly some of the great races of today – particularly the Negro race – have not as yet given to civilization the full spiritual message which they are capable of giving. I will not say that the Negro race has as yet given no message to the world ... however the fact still remains that the full, complete Negro message of the whole Negro race has not as yet been given to the world ...'[22] How was this message to be delivered? Through the development of racial groups, 'not as individuals, but as races.' He explained what he meant by 'development':

> For the development of Negro genius, of Negro literature and art, of Negro spirit, only Negroes bound and welded together, Negroes inspired by one vast ideal, can work out in its fullness the great message we have for humanity. We cannot reverse history; we are subject to the same natural laws as other races, and if the Negro is ever to be a factor in the world's history – if among the gaily-colored banners that deck the broad ramparts of civilization is to hang one uncompromising black, then it must be placed there by black hands, fashioned by black heads and hallowed by the travail of 200,000,000 black hearts beating in one glad song of jubilee.[23]

Here, in capsule, is the lyrical style of prose that would characterize nearly everything Du Bois wrote subsequently. He writes unequivocally that 'the Negro people... must not expect to have things done for them – they MUST DO FOR THEMSELVES.'[24] As is clear from this passage, he was already espousing in 'The Conservation of Races' what would set him apart from Washington the reformer, the proponent of accommodation to the white liberal program for black racial progress. The historicist epistemological template of *The Philadelphia Negro* was here for anyone to see. By the same token, he took distance from the standard critique of scientific racism by appeal to Christian monogenesis, which most of his black contemporaries since 1830 had maintained. Monogenesis was the doctrine that an acceptable scientific interpretation of racial origins had to be consistent with the Gospel, which offered no support for the idea of a separate, hierarchical origin of the races (or polygenesis). Therefore, the races must all have emerged at once, in nonhierarchical fashion: monogenesis. But Du Bois was no ordinary turn-of-the-century black intellectual. As one of a small number of blacks to have achieved significant academic stature, he understood full well that evolutionary science was moving away from religion and lending increasing credence to the notion of polygenesis. The racist Anglo-American doctrine of natural black inferiority had to be fought on its own turf, with religious rhetoric kept out of the discussion, and this is precisely what he attempted in 'The Conservation of Races.' In taking this original tack, he isolated himself not from the white intellectual tradition in which he had been schooled but from the black intellectual tradition – a matter that would prove a considerable nuisance to him.[25]

The year 1898 saw Du Bois produce several other papers in which he pursued his revamping of sociological science while working on his study of black Philadelphians. In 'The Study of the Negro Problems,' he returned to the need for the new sociology to ground its descriptions in accurate, well-documented history. The paper began with a description of the problems affecting black Americans in 1898:

> the particular Negro problems ... can be divided into two distinct but correlated parts, depending on two facts:
> First – Negroes do not share the full national life because as a mass they have not reached a sufficiently high grade of culture.
>
> Secondly – They do not share the full national life because there has always existed in America a conviction – varying in intensity, but always widespread – that people of Negro blood should not be admitted into the group life of the nation no matter what their condition might be.[26]

His solution consisted of rigorous historical research, an approach totally absent from the sociological methodology of his era:

> we should seek to know and measure carefully all the forces and conditions that go to make up these different problems, to trace the historical

> development of these conditions, and to discover as far as possible the probable trend of further development. Without doubt this would be difficult work, and it can with much truth be objected that we cannot ascertain, by the methods of sociological research known to us, all such facts thoroughly and accurately ... Scientific work must be subdivided, but conclusions which affect the whole subject must be based on a study of the whole. One cannot study the Negro in freedom and come to general conclusions about his destiny without knowing his history in slavery.[27]

Du Bois also stressed his view that rigorous scientific study of blacks as a social group must be multidisciplinary, combining historical, statistical, anthropological, and sociological approaches. During the same period he noted and decided to explore the phenomenon of northbound migration from Virginia, and so spent two months as a participant observer in the small commercial town of Farmville, Virginia (pop. 2,500), a black community of a very different sort from that of Philadelphia. The result, 'The Negroes of Farmville, Virginia' (1898), in its meticulous analysis of occupational structure and social stratification, offered a foretaste of his forthcoming monograph.

To conclude, Du Bois – as witness the publication of his doctoral thesis, his hiring by Atlanta University, and the publication of these important early papers – was coming into his own as a sociologist after his return from Europe. The culmination of this process was his great monograph of 1899.

The Philadelphia Negro

Philadelphia in 1896 was particularly conducive to an empirical sociological study in that it constituted the oldest and largest (pop. 9,675) of the northern black communities (the three cities with larger black populations – New Orleans, Washington, and Baltimore – were all in the South). Du Bois and his wife of three months took up lodgings in the black-dominated Seventh Ward, where they stayed for more than a year: '[we] settled in one room in the city over a cafeteria run by a College Settlement, in the worst part of the Seventh Ward ... Murder sat on our doorsteps, police were our government, and philanthropy dropped in with periodic advice.'[28] Du Bois commenced to study the geographical distribution of blacks in Philadelphia, their occupations, housing conditions, organizations, and, most important, their relations with whites. In addition to participant observation, Du Bois's methodology comprised house-to-house visits to every black family in the ward, yielding 5,000 copies of a questionnaire on a broad range of topics (migration, family composition, income, occupations, political activities, etc.) with an enormous amount of quantitative and qualitative data to be compiled and analyzed. The result was a rather somber portrait of black living conditions as well as a skillful description of the structure and workings of the black community, its institutions, its survival mechanisms, and its methods of improving race relations in a stultifying context of overt discrimination.

Three-fourths of black workers in the Seventh Ward, he found, were laborers or servants. Roughly equal proportions of women worked as day laborers and domestic servants. The race barrier was particularly high in manufacturing, in which only 8 percent of the ward's black residents held employment. A considerable majority of the black workforce was underpaid and had to make do with irregular employment. Barely a fourth of black men were skilled laborers or small businessmen – the local petty aristocracy, as Du Bois termed it. Even the most prosperous of these entrepreneurs, the barbers and caterers, worked under severe constraints. In the preceding decades, these two jobs had been held almost exclusively by blacks, but by 1900, fierce competition from whites had changed the situation dramatically: 'If the Negro caterers of Philadelphia had been white, some of them would have been put in charge of a large hotel, or would have become co-partners in some large restaurant business, for which capitalists furnished funds.'[29]

The difficult economic circumstances in which blacks lived engendered poverty, crime, illiteracy, family disruption, inadequate housing, and all manner of social problems, which were exacerbated by the influx of poor illiterate southern blacks:

> Without doubt there is not in Philadelphia enough work of the kind that the mass of Negroes can and may do, to employ at fair wages the laborers who at present desire work. The result of this must, of course, be disastrous, and give rise to many loafers, criminals, and casual laborers. The situation is further complicated by the fact that in seasons when work is more plentiful, temporary immigrations from the South swell the number of laborers abnormally ...[30]

This, of course, was precisely the social situation that had led the white philanthropists and social workers involved in the Philadelphia settlement-house movement to commission Du Bois's study.

The Family

Du Bois provided some trenchant insights into the relationship between economic status and family structure in the black community. The conventional lifestyle of 'well-to-do' families, he remarked, contrasted sharply with the transient cohabitation and common-law marriages of the poor. Du Bois was probably the first sociologist to note the disproportionate number of poor black households headed by women, a phenomenon he explained by invoking the heritage of slavery but also the harsh economic conditions of urban life. Black women played a major role as breadwinners even in families where the husband was present; according to his figures, 43 percent of black woman but only 16 percent of white women were breadwinners. Even in the large number of households headed by regularly employed men, their low wages and prohibitive housing costs created a difficult situation: 'The low wages of men make it necessary for mothers to work and in numbers of cases to work away from home several days in the week. This leaves the children without guidance or restraint for the better part of the day.'[31] Forced to rent out rooms in order to defray their rental costs, black families found their home life severely disrupted. In exploring the root causes of these social problems, Du Bois invoked the sombre heritage of slavery and Reconstruction, which had hindered blacks' effective integration into the larger Philadelphia population, as well as heightened competition and 'moral weakness' caused by migration from the South. Even more decisive, however, was the physical and social environment of white prejudice and discrimination in which black people were forced to live. Du Bois criticized this environment forthrightly while hewing to the general tone of academic detachment that characterizes the work:

> His strange social environment must have an immense effect on his thought and life, his work and crime, his wealth and pauperism. That this environment differs and differs broadly from the environment of his fellows, we all know, but we do not know just how it differs. The real foundation of the difference is the widespread feeling all over the land, in Philadelphia as well as in Boston and New Orleans, that the Negro is something less than an American and ought not be much more than what he is.[32]

Inequality of Opportunity

Du Bois commented in *The Philadelphia Negro* on what he saw as objective barriers to black economic promotion. Aptitude being equal, black workers did not enjoy the same opportunities for advancement as white workers. Inequality was observable in all fields and for all occupations. It was therefore no surprise for blacks to find themselves thrust into poverty, with the poorest of them becoming targets of philanthropy. In elucidating the impact of discrimination on black people's personalities and aspirations, Du Bois anticipated the 1940s work of Charles Johnson, E. Franklin Frazier, and Allison Davis.

Migration

Du Bois dwelled at length on the phenomenon of migration from the rural South to the urban North. By comparison with the Great Migration of the postwar era it was still a trickle, but nonetheless numerically significant.[33] For the most part young, poor, and illiterate, the new arrivals had been plunged into 'well-defined localities in or near the slums, and thus [got] the worst possible introduction to city life.'[34] He linked the problems of northern urban blacks to their southern rural origins. In discussing crime, for example, he observed that although arrests of black people had declined from 1865 until the mid-1870s, they had then increased in direct correlation with immigration: 'This migration explains much that is paradoxical about Negro slums ... Many people wonder that the mission and reformatory agencies at work there for so many years have so little to show by way of results. One answer is that this work has new material continually to work upon, while the best classes move to the west and leave the dregs behind.'[35]

Social Classes

A fundamental thesis of *The Philadelphia Negro* is that the marginal living conditions of Philadelphia's blacks were essentially social or environmental in origin. Describing his study methodology, Du Bois asserted that sociologists wishing to understand the social problems of an ethnic minority must look beyond the group as such to 'specially notice the environment; the physical environment of city, sections and houses, the far mightier social environment – the surrounding world of custom, wish, whim, and thought which envelops this group and powerfully influences its social development.'[36]

But perhaps the greatest conceptual coup of Du Bois's monograph, one that was integral to his proposals for racial advancement, was his detailed analysis of the social class structure of the Seventh Ward black community:

> There is always a strong tendency on the part of the community to consider the Negroes as composing one practically homogeneous mass. This view has of course a certain justification: the people of Negro descent in this land have had a common history, suffer to-day common disabilities, and contribute to one general set of social problems. And yet if the foregoing statistics have emphasized any one fact it is that wide variations in antecedents, wealth, intelligence and general efficiency have already been differentiated within this group.[37]

Du Bois's approach to stratification reflected the influence of late-nineteenth-century American social reformers as well as Weber and, in the background, Marx. He defined four classes or 'grades,' membership in which was determined as a function of rather coarse criteria by today's standards: income, occupation, property ownership, literacy, and lifestyle. About one-tenth of the black community fell into an upper or aristocratic class defined as '[f]amilies of undoubted respectability earning sufficient income to live well; not engaged in menial service of any kind; the wife engaged in no occupation save that of housewife. The children not compelled to be bread-winners, but found in school; the family living in a well-kept home.'[38] Most of these small businessmen and professionals had been born in Philadelphia and, together, made up the social class most identified with American middle-class culture.[39]

The second grade, the 'respectable working class,' accounted for nearly half the population. It consisted of economically and socially ambitious individuals such as domestic servants, porters, waiters, and skilled laborers who worked hard and managed to acquire property. Their prime concern, apart from economic advancement, was to secure access to good careers for their children, and the institution with which they were the most closely identified was the neighborhood church:[40] Du Bois wrote about this grade, 'The majority can read and write, many have a common school training, and all are anxious to rise in the world. Their wages are low compared with corresponding classes of white workmen, their rents are high, and the field of advancement opened to them is very limited.'[41]

The third class was that of the poor, defined as 'persons not earning enough to keep them at all times above want; honest, although not always energetic or thrifty, and with no touch of gross immorality or crime.'[42] This group, accounting for one-third of the population, was composed of persons without regular employment, including many immigrants, widows, and abandoned women, orphans (many of them very young), and psychologically unstable, unemployable, and/or transient persons. This class comprised the main clientele of the city's charitable institutions. The children's situation was particularly worrisome; too often out of school and neglected by their impoverished parents, they were prone to entering a life of crime.

At the bottom of the class structure was the 'lowest class of criminals, prostitutes and loafers; the "submerged tenth"';[43] few in number, but already too numerous for the whites of Philadelphia. Du Bois devoted considerable space to this group.[44]

The Church

The institutional structure of the Seventh Ward, and particularly its religious institutions, exhibited a stratification analogous to that of the population itself. Upper-class blacks attended the neighborhood Episcopal or Presbyterian church, where services were formal and reserved, while the 'respectable working class' attended African Methodist, Episcopal, or Baptist services. Most of the poorest citizens were not regular members of any church, but some of them went to 'a host of little noisy missions.'[45] The church had a wide range of social functions, some latent, others explicit, all of them powerful forces knitting together the black community:

> As a social group the Negro church may be said to have antedated the Negro family on American soil; as such it has preserved, on the one hand, many functions of tribal organization, and on the other hand, many of the family functions. Its tribal functions are shown in its religious activity, its social authority and general guiding and co-ordinating work; its family functions are shown by the fact that the church is a centre of social life and intercourse; acts as newspaper and intelligence bureau, is the centre of amusements – indeed, is the world in which the Negro moves and acts.[46]

Du Bois believed, but could not demonstrate, that the white churches exhibited similar phenomena. Since the black churches offered opportunities for advancement and greater social standing, their organization was 'almost political': 'all movements for social betterment are apt to centre in the churches. Beneficial societies in endless number are formed here; secret societies keep in touch ... the minister often acts as an employment agent ... The race problem in all its phases is continually being discussed, and, indeed, from this forum many a youth goes forth inspired to work.'[47]

Politics

The Philadelphia Negro contains an interesting functional analysis of black participation in municipal politics. In the late nineteenth century, Philadelphia's domination by the powerful Republican machine placed it among the most corrupt of American cities. Blacks were traditionally loyal to the Republican Party because of its role in Emancipation, and in Du Bois's eyes they were consenting instruments in the service of the machine. Nevertheless, he could see that the machine, in return for the black vote, played the role of protecting the community's petty criminals as well as its many new immigrants from police harassment. The machine was also the largest employer of blacks in white-collar positions.

In the concluding chapter, 'A Final Word,' Du Bois the man of science revealed the social reformer within him, presenting solutions to the problems he had elucidated. The platitudes and sermons proffered by Philadelphia's white establishment were of no use to blacks; what they needed were jobs and financial aid. It was the duty of whites to change their discriminatory attitudes and behaviors, particularly where the labor market was concerned.[48] However, this did not dispense blacks from primary responsibility for their community's advancement:

> Modern society ... can rightly demand that as far as possible and as rapidly as possible the Negro bend his energy to the solving of his own social problems – contributing to his poor, paying his share of the taxes and supporting the schools and public administration. For the accomplishment of this the Negro has a right to demand freedom for self-development ... the bulk of the work of raising the Negro must be done by the Negro himself ... Against prejudice, injustice and wrong the Negro ought to protest energetically and continuously, but he must never forget that he protests because those things hinder his own efforts, and that those efforts are the key to his future.[49]

To bring about this future, intensified social and economic cooperation and mutual assistance would be required among black people. In this regard the upper classes had to 'recognize their duty toward the masses.'[50] They would have to organize and deliver more social services, create more newspapers, and develop more trade unions based on mutual aid. In short, Du Bois was arguing the case for solidarity and self-determination under the guidance and leadership of an educated black elite.

Innovations of the Work

By today's scientific standards, *The Philadelphia Negro*, with its arid collection of facts and statistics, is a rather ordinary, commonsense work of empirical sociology, but in its original context there was nothing ordinary about empirical sociology. Straddling the boundary between history and sociology, Du Bois blazed the trail of empiricism in a time of great academic flux as well as in near total isolation from his peers. Mia Bay writes that the work 'has emerged as a classic across the disciplines precisely because it was written before the modern disciplines of sociology, anthropology, history, and economics were fully formed.'[51]

Its principal scientific merit was in documenting with meaningful empirical data the thesis that black Americans were facing a historically determined set of restrictive social conditions rather than an inviolable racial destiny, as the prevailing mainstream view held. Philadelphia's black community and its 'Negro problem' were in fact the product of historical forces – slavery, Emancipation, migration, racism – whose effects had been felt long before Du Bois came to that city. Whites could not claim to be extraneous to that historical process for, as social actors, they had played a crucial role in it. Du Bois brought the problem up to date with a barrage of facts, tables, and figures, trying (unsuccessfully, for reasons I shall discuss) not to accuse or blame anyone directly. His originality shines through in his resort to both history and statistics in support of his argument for the multiple social causation of the Seventh Ward's problems.

Another theoretical and analytical breakthrough in *The Philadelphia Negro* was its concept of class as the hierarchical organizing principle of the community. Du Bois acknowledged his debt to the Englishman Charles Booth in this connection but made no reference to Marx. (Such references would come later, in his maturity as an activist.) He laid out the proof for whites to see that there existed a black American elite with nothing, apart from money and power, to envy its white counterpart. His biographer David L. Lewis characterizes this breakthrough in the following terms:

> Before it was identified and described in *The Philadelphia Negro*, the class structure of Afro-America was mostly unknown, utterly mysterious, and even widely assumed as nonexistent. Most white people supposed that the periodic appearance of exceptional or 'representative' black people was due to providence, 'mixed blood,' or some mysterious current passing through a dark, undifferentiated mass. Otherwise, there were only good Negroes and bad ones.[52]

With his concept of class, Du Bois showed himself to be much more than an innovator: he was an iconoclast who sought to advance the cause of black people in American society, and that meant confounding whites by debunking their myths.

A third area in which Du Bois's monograph broke ground was that of urban studies. Philadelphia was a huge industrial city, the second most populous U.S. city after New York, when he moved there in 1896. Serious urban research was in its infancy; only *Hull House Maps and Papers* by the reformer Jane Addams (1895) and the Boston-focused *The City Wilderness* (1898) by an amateur named Robert Woods had preceded *The Philadelphia Negro*. Addams's book offered Du Bois a template, but he proceeded much more systematically, innovating with his deliberate melding of methodical fact-finding and theorization. Notably, his was also the first work of social science to focus on race in the 'urban' American setting. Moreover, as Zuberi astutely observes, it was the first community study in the United States to be performed by a scholar, here again showing the influence of Booth.[53]

The work was exceptional, in sum – nothing less than a landmark of social science – in that it anticipated by many years the moment when mainstream Anglo-American sociology would emerge from its amorphous state to become a less pompously declamatory science, one more rooted in social praxis and historical experience.[54] Du Bois's sociology was, in most respects, far ahead of its 'scientific time' – measured, it must always be remembered, on the clock of the Anglo-American intelligentsia. But in one respect – his mixing of the agendas of sociological science and social reform – Du Bois was very much of his time, cast in the same mold as Ward, Cooley, Giddings, or Ross. He presented himself as both a disinterested analyst of society and an enlightened contributor to the easing of racial friction. This combination of science and reform inevitably led him into ambiguities, exaggerations, and biases, a matter to which we return.

Sources of Du Bois's Innovation

I began this chapter by discussing Du Bois's major scientific objective of winning a place in the scientific pantheon for his authentically black American sociology. No doubt about it: he accomplished this objective with his writings of 1895 to 1899, *The Philadelphia Negro* chief among them, even if he had to stand as an utter heretic with respect to the conventional wisdom in order to do it. What choice did he have but to invent a countersociology, perhaps even an antisociology, in an intellectual context in which the Anglo-American founding fathers indulged in broad theoretical speculation on race relations, championing a theoretical model – Social Darwinism – that 'instinctively placed blacks at the primitive end of the evolutionary scale'?[55] When listening to the sages explain racial inequality as the inevitable result of grand natural laws, or invoke Spencer, their favorite prophet, Du Bois simply had no theoretical corpus on which to base a contrary position. He had to build a new science from the ground up, a science devoted to the advancement, as opposed to the near-term extinction, of black Americans.

His countersociology rested on two epistemological pillars – historicism and empiricist positivism – that are key to understanding his deconstruction of the reigning Anglo-American sociology. He opened *The Philadelphia Negro* by stating that 'the Negro problems are problems of human beings ... they cannot be explained away by fantastic theories, ungrounded assumptions or metaphysical subtleties.'[56] A ringing act of insubordination, this statement, one that represented a clean break with the dominant sociological tradition. If he could utter it with complete confidence, it was because he had been developing an epistemological counterpremise – the primacy of historical experience – since his 1897 lecture on the human races. He was deconstructing the sacrosanct Anglo-American idea of a preestablished social order obeying immutable natural laws by pitting it against the historical experience of slavery and racial oppression, from which an unbroken line led to the experience of contemporary black Americans. History had to be interpreted as both a heritage and an ongoing process of change that was fashioning the future for black Americans.

This postulate of historicism was the cornerstone of Du Bois's new theory, but it was not by itself a sufficient foundation for a revolutionary theory of sociological knowledge, as he knew full well. He needed positivism as a second epistemological postulate.[57] But not any sort of positivism would do; Du Bois's was poles apart from the doctrinaire positivism with which the Anglo-American pioneers had forged their high-flown discourse. Subtly combining theoretical considerations with inductivism, Du Bois's empiricist positivism was a logical complement to his historicism in the sense that it was the only approach that could provide factual, verifiable proof that the American Negro 'problem' arose fundamentally from contingent social conditions and that it was in no way predetermined by eternal laws.

As he confidently plied this bold intellectual course, Du Bois could look to some prestigious forebears. They could not have been American – no one in the country was practicing empiricist positivism. The following two quotations indicate the exact nature of these sources, one of which we have already seen:

> DuBois acknowledged the influence of both [Charles] Booth and Hull House [on his work for *The Philadelphia Negro*]. Like Booth, DuBois immersed himself in the life of the city ... conducting systematic observations, counting, tabulating, and integrating new data with historical records, vital statistics, and census data.[58]

> His scientific ambitions for *The Philadelphia Negro* unsupported by American models, white or black, DuBois based his study on European social theory and practice. He drew much of the structure and methodology for his study from Charles Booth's *Life and Labor of the People in London* (1889–1902) ... Great though DuBois's debt to Booth was, he took a still crucial inspiration for his empirical method from Gustav Schmoller, a German political economist whose seminars he had attended in Berlin.[59]

What explains Du Bois's interest in Booth? Since the Englishman's study population in London was relatively homogeneous, he had nothing to say about race. But both men were interested in the causes of social problems and, at any rate for Du Bois, the problems of African Americans were first and foremost human problems. Given the close kinship between their concerns and perspectives, it is safe to say that Du Bois essentially mimicked Booth's practical methodology: 'DuBois ... logg[ed] "some 835 hours interviewing approximately 2,500 households," using research schedules patterned after Booth's. Like Booth, he eschewed sampling, tabulating approximately fifteen thousand household schedules himself.'[60] He also borrowed certain promising theoretical avenues from Booth, notably his explicit reference to class for both scientific and reformist purposes. Booth's distinction between the 'poor,' the 'very poor,' and 'the lowest class of occasional loafers and semi-criminals,' was necessary in order to achieve his avowed goal of eradicating poverty. Likewise, with Du Bois, the concept of class served as both an analytical tool and a part of a strategy for inducing Anglo-Americans to see blacks as something other than a homogeneous and irresponsible human mass without a respectable elite to guide them.

As for Schmoller, he was one of a group of German economists (with Adolph Wagner [1835–1917] and Carl von Knies [1821–1898]) who broke with the deductivist methods of their predecessors. They argued that any generalizable economic theory must be based on empirical historical data. Schmoller in particular believed that rigorous empirical investigation and fact-finding were legitimate guides to social reform – indeed, to any effort to regulate human affairs. This amalgam of disinterested empiricism, devotion to historical fact, and science for social purposes was perfectly congruent with the positivist faith that had led Du Bois to social science, and he was understandably attracted to it. Schmoller's work provides the conceptual key to *The Philadelphia Negro.* From him Du Bois derived the method that enabled him to reason from carefully compiled data to general propositions. As well, the echo of Schmoller's caution against allowing the aims of social reform to dictate scientific findings is clearly audible in Du Bois's 1897 statement that '[w]e simply collect the facts; others may use them as they will.'[61] Similarly, in 1898 he wrote:

> Students must be careful to insist that science as such – be it physics, chemistry, psychology, or sociology – has but one simple aim: the discovery of truth. Its results lie open for the use of all men – merchants, physicians, men of letters, and philanthropists, but the aim of science itself is simple truth. Any attempt to give it a double aim, to make social reform the immediate instead of the mediate object of a search for truth, will inevitably tend to defeat both objects.[62]

Green and Driver argue that 'Schmoller ... probably more than any other teacher, influenced Du Bois's career as a sociologist ... Schmoller's methodological approach favored the use of induction to accumulate historical and descriptive material. He saw the goal of social science as the systematic, causal explanation of social phenomena, and he believed that social scientific facts, based on careful, inductive analysis, could be used as a guide to formulate social policy.'[63]

To summarize: given the enormous scope of the task Du Bois had assigned himself – that of rehistoricizing the Negro 'problem,' which the Anglo-American paradigm viewed through an ahistorical lens – he had to *invent* sociohistorical analysis as such. He had to revolutionize his field in order to make room for black sociology. His new theory of scientific knowledge was, in my view, structured by six postulates. First, race is a sociohistorical construct, a cultural fact rather than a natural, fixed, or innate category. Second, since race is spatiotemporally contingent, the origin of the races loses its scientific interest, becoming a matter of pure philosophical speculation rather than epistemology. Third, the essential phenomenon for the sociologist's purposes is that of the spatiotemporal plurality of races, a historical construct lending itself to empirical observation and analysis. Fourth, more than the inevitable physical or biological differences, the plurality of human races implies multiple *cultural* differences sometimes leading to racial conflict, and this must be the focal point of an authentic and specific American sociology of race relations. Fifth, racial conflict is a function of physical differences as well as the broader social environment in which they are inscribed; that is, the composite of demographic, economic, political, ideological, and symbolic features typical of a specific historical era. Sixth, black American sociology must use an inductive approach, the best way to avoid schematization of racial inequality based on eternal laws or fixed processes.

As Lewis notes, *The Philadelphia Negro* trenchantly embodies these six postulates, again illustrating its revolutionary character:

> *The Philadelphia Negro* was remarkable as an example of the new empiricism that was fundamentally transforming the social sciences at the beginning of the twentieth century. Although Du Bois's novel sociological insights would soon become conventional wisdom ... the Philadelphia study would be a breakthrough achievement, an important and virtually solitary departure from the hereditarian theorizing of the times. The armchair cerebrations of sociology's great nineteenth-century system builders – Auguste Comte, Karl Marx, and Herbert Spencer – would continue to inform, challenge, and inspire, but the watchword of the discipline was becoming *investigation*, followed by induction – facts before theory. More

than any other leading American sociologist during the decade after 1898, Du Bois undertook for a time the working out of an authentic objectivity in social science, 'to put science into sociology through a study of the conditions and problems of [his] own group.'[64]

The Institution Builder

The foregoing considerations all relate to Du Bois's cognitive contributions to social science, which were unquestionably of the utmost importance. Complementary to this and crucially important as well was his work to institutionally entrench the new sociology at Atlanta University and then disseminate it throughout North America. It was with some reluctance that he moved to Atlanta in 1897, for he had dearly hoped to be given a professorship at the University of Pennsylvania. That was impossible because of academic racism, and he had to content himself with a lower position despite his intellectual caliber.[65] Atlanta University was the best of the black institutions, and he knew full well that no better job offer would be forthcoming. From 1897 to 1910, Du Bois took sole responsibility for the annual sociological conferences, published an annual review of empirical studies, and taught economics, history, and sociology, this last to higher-level students. He dedicated himself to the colossal task of single-handedly improving southern black education, but it was not for want of attempts to interest the northern universities. At the forty-second annual convention of the American Academy of Political and Social Sciences held at the University of Pennsylvania in November 1897, Du Bois outlined a plan for cooperation with his northern colleagues:

> We hear much of higher Negro education, and yet all candid people know there does not exist today in the center of Negro population a single first-class fully equipped institution, devoted to the higher education of Negroes; not more than three Negro institutions in the South deserve the name of 'college' at all; and yet what is a Negro college but a vast college settlement for the study of a particular set of peculiarly baffling problems? What more effective or suitable agency could be found in which to focus the scientific efforts of the great universities of the North and East, than an institution situated in the very heart of these social problems, and made the center of careful historical and statistical research? Without doubt the first effective step toward the solving of the Negro question will be the endowment of a Negro college which is not merely a teaching body, but a

> center of sociological research, in close connection and co-operation with Harvard, Columbia, Johns Hopkins, and the University of Pennsylvania.[66]

All for naught; no intellectual cooperation – much less material or financial assistance – would come of this initiative. He was forced to accept that he was condemned, for ideological reasons, to work against the sociological current in a parallel universe, as he bitterly recalled years later: 'so far as the American world of science and letters was concerned, we never "belonged"; we remained unrecognized in learned societies and academic groups. We rated merely as Negroes studying Negroes, and after all, what had Negroes to do with America or science?'[67]

For an explanation of the disadvantageous situation in which Du Bois found himself, one need look no further than Pierre Bourdieu's sociological model of power dynamics in the field of scientific knowledge. He writes, 'Any field, the scientific field for example, is a force field and a field of struggle to preserve or transform that force field. A scientific arena or a religious arena may ... be described as a physical world comprising power dynamics or patterns of domination.'[68] Clearly, Du Bois was immersed in a force field in which he acted as a producing agent in competition with other producing agents:

> Under these conditions ... that which commands points of view, that which commands scientific interventions, sites of publication ... is the structure of objective relations between different agents ... it is the *structure of objective relations* between agents that determines what they can and cannot do. Or, more precisely, it is the position they occupy in this structure that determines or guides, at least negatively, the positions they take. This means that we can only truly understand what an agent involved in a field (an economist, writer, or artist, for example) says or does if we are able to refer to the position he occupies in that field, if we know the place from which he is speaking.[69]

The place from which Du Bois was speaking in the American sociological field was the periphery, and his words carried no symbolic weight because of pervasive scientific racism in Anglo-American sociology. Quite a paradox: from a strictly scientific standpoint, *The Philadelphia Negro* portended modern sociology while the vague Anglo-American doctrines were destined for oblivion; yet for social, ideological, and political reasons, Du Bois's work could make no headway with his peers. Bourdieu explains why: 'The chances of an individual agent bending the force field to his will are proportionate to his power over the field, i.e., his capital of scientific credit or, more precisely, his position within the structure of capital distribution.'[70]

In short, Du Bois was institutionally condemned to disseminate his knowledge within the southern university system since he was utterly invisible as a credible scientific agent in the more powerful northern system. Once he understood that none of this would change in the short term, he threw himself into the work of what he called 'race uplift' in the form of his scientific activities at Atlanta University. The institution had been founded just after the Civil War by northern Congregationalist missionaries who had gone south to teach the blacks of Georgia within the liberal arts college framework of New England. This philosophy largely still prevailed at the turn of the century, but the institution sought to modernize itself by incorporating the new social sciences, notably sociology, into its curriculum. Its objective was to develop the best possible expertise on the many problems experienced by blacks.

Although Atlanta University was part of this 'inferior' system, it nevertheless represented a producer of a particular kind of 'good' for the knowledge market. Du Bois felt that its physical location was particularly well suited to that enterprise: 'Atlanta University is situated within a few miles of the geographical centre of the negro population of the nation, and is, therefore, near the centre of that congeries of human problems which cluster round the black American.'[71] If he could not make productive inroads into mainstream academia, then he would work within the southern university system to reproduce, like a carbon copy, one of the best structural traits of the northern universities: a framework for systematic initiation to scientific knowledge.

He appears to have understood that this enterprise would require three separate types of involvement; together, these formed the backbone of his institutional innovations at Atlanta. The first of these was teaching – that is, everything relating to the socialization of young black recruits to a new body of knowledge, social science, as well as their controlled admission into the field through periodic testing and examination, the whole process culminating in a university degree. Du Bois worked tirelessly on this portion of the agenda throughout his association with Atlanta University. The second component was critical debate among scholars around the social problems affecting blacks. This task, too, was taken up by Du Bois with fervor and conviction in the form of the Atlanta University Conferences. No other black institution pursued similar activities in that era. The third component was research and its dissemination in the form of papers, reports, proceedings, and so forth. The annual conferences were explicitly paired with and nourished by applied research, of which Du Bois was a most rigorous advocate:

> The main significance of my work at Atlanta University, during the years 1897 to 1910, was the development at an American institution of learning, of a program of study on the problems affecting the American Negroes ... I sought to swing [this program] as on a pivot to one of scientific investigation into social conditions, primarily for scientific ends. I put no special emphasis on special reform effort, but increasing and widening emphasis on the collection of a basic body of fact concerning the social condition of American Negroes, endeavoring to reduce that condition to exact measurement whenever or wherever occasion permitted. As time passed, it happened that many uplift efforts were in fact based on our studies ... We came to be, however, as I had intended, increasingly, a source of general information and a basis for further study, rather than an organ of social reform.[72]

Du Bois's 'program of study' designated, among other things, a plan for the publication of sociological monographs at the rate of one per year. The Atlanta University archives show records of eighteen monographs published between 1896 and 1914, the first two completed before Du Bois joined the university, the last four after his departure. Each was an empirical study devoted to a carefully circumscribed topic and displaying the positivist faith with which the whole enterprise was imbued. The first ten-year cycle of studies reads as follows:

1896 Morality among Negroes in Cities
1897 Social and Physical Conditions of Negroes in Cities
1898 Some Efforts of Negroes for Social Betterment
1899 The Negro in Business
1900 The College-Bred Negro
1901 The Negro Common School
1902 The Negro Artisan
1903 The Negro Church
1904 Some Notes on Negro Crime, Particularly in Georgia
1905 A Select Bibliography on the American Negro.[73]

Not all of these studies were written by Du Bois himself: several were the work of graduate students and research assistants working under him. Nevertheless, he was a very active researcher who made great efforts to disseminate the results through any academic or other media willing to publish them. Not surprisingly, most such publications were written by and for blacks.

During his golden years as a sociologist, Du Bois went from one success to another, always, of course, within the isolated black university system. His *Philadelphia Negro* and other scholarly work, his transmission of social science to future generations, and his Atlanta University Conferences and Studies add up to a formidable achievement under severe constraints: the institutionalization of black American sociology as a new, autonomous discipline on the model of the best Anglo-American universities – though, as we have seen, this development was largely ignored by them.[74]

Controversy and Decline

As Du Bois was publishing the last in his initial series of monographs, threatening clouds were gathering over his head. They related to his funding sources. Atlanta University had been enthusiastic and generous at the launch of the Atlanta University Studies in 1895, but ten years later it was short of funds for the program. This difficulty, as I have indicated, was due to Du Bois's conflict with Booker Washington and his involvement in the Niagara Movement. In an era of colonial imperialism in Africa, South America, and the southern states, with big capital triumphant in its exploitation of the laboring masses, northern businessmen had designs on the South for reasons accurately summarized by Du Bois: 'The southern United States was one of the most promising fields for this development, with a fine climate, invaluable staple crops, with a mass of cheap and potentially efficient labor, with unlimited natural power and use of unequalled technique, and with a transportation system reaching all the markets of the world.'[75]

This state of affairs engendered two major ideological reactions among black intellectuals. The older and more widespread of these was represented by the charismatic orator Washington, director of the Tuskegee Institute in Alabama. His position essentially consisted of asking blacks to submit to Anglo-American capital, deny the devastating nature of racial inequality, and do their utmost, through 'industrial education,' to integrate into the white southern production system, which could benefit blacks if they took the trouble to acquire the necessary skills.[76] More than a rhetorical slogan, industrial education was a strategy carefully calculated by Washington to flatter powerful whites and thus to attract generous subsidies for his project of 'elevating the race.'[77] He did not, it should be noted, invent this strategy,[78] but he did have tremendous success with it. Tuskegee was awash in funding thanks to gifts from Carnegie and Rockefeller. When Du Bois was hired by Atlanta University to develop his original sociological research, Washington was already an iconic figure among northern and southern blacks, and he had the ear of the most powerful white politicians.[79]

The icon in question, on a visit to an international exhibition in Atlanta in 1895, had nothing but praise for the city's institutions, not least the university and its new social science programs. If the Atlanta University Studies program was so easily launched around this time, it was thanks to Carnegie's philanthropic contribution, subject to Washington's recommendation. And it was this system that Du Bois chose to defy in 1903 with *The Souls of Black Folk*, a paradigmatic statement of the second, more radical reaction to racial exploitation in the United States. While he had largely supported Washington over the previous decade, Du Bois had been intellectually transformed by the practice of sociology and his responsibilities at Atlanta. Without rejecting Washington's work outright, he now argued that the older man had, with his accommodationist bent, either underestimated or completely sidestepped the most crucial issues:

> The black men of America have a duty to perform, a duty stern and delicate, – a forward movement to oppose a part of the work of their greatest leader. So far as Mr Washington preaches Thrift, Patience, and Industrial Training for the masses, we must hold up his hands and strive with him ... But so far as Mr Washington apologizes for injustice, North or South, does not rightly value the privilege and duty of voting, belittles the emasculating effects of caste distinctions, and opposes the higher training and ambition of our brighter minds, – so far as he, the South, or the Nation, does this, – we must unceasingly and firmly oppose them.[80]

He was not fundamentally opposed to industrial education, but he was convinced that the future of the race was predicated on a vastly different model: a liberal arts education that would allow the 'Talented Tenth' of black students to make genuine economic, occupational, and cultural progress.[81] Since Washington's prestige in 1903 was nearly all-pervasive, Du Bois's radical remarks in effect signed the financial death warrant of Atlanta University, at least as far as its social science programs were concerned. The Tuskegee icon reacted promptly, and his philanthropist friends shut off the financial pipeline in the following months, as Du Bois recalls:

> the task of raising money for Atlanta University and my work became increasingly difficult. In the fall of 1904 the printing of our conference report was postponed by the trustees until special funds could be secured. I did not at the time see the handwriting on the wall. I did not realize how strong the forces were back of Tuskegee and how they might interfere with my scientific study of the Negro.[82]

This first imbroglio put Du Bois on a downward trajectory before the decade was out, seriously impairing his sociological projects at Atlanta. As if that were not enough, he exacerbated the situation by founding the Niagara Movement in 1905 with the goals of 'inaugurat[ing] an organized program of public agitation for the Negro's constitutional rights' and opposing Washington's initiatives.[83] Though Du Bois did not cease his research activities, he developed the alter ego of an increasingly committed, insubordinate activist. The Niagara Movement did not last long; only six meetings took place from 1905 to 1910 under Du Bois's vigorous leadership before the movement foundered, wracked by internal ideological differences. But it was long enough to enhance Du Bois's reputation as a subversive and exacerbate his differences with Washington. Ultimately, he was left with no choice but

> [to resign] from Atlanta University in 1910, after coming to the uneasy realization that the difficulties the university was having in obtaining general financial support, and particularly money for the Atlanta Studies, was in part a personal issue attributable to the controversy with Washington. As long as he remained on the faculty, he perceived, Atlanta, already under financial strain, would continue to have difficulties obtaining funds.[84]

The separation from academia was pragmatic, obviously, for if he had not resigned the university would probably have fired him. But it was also ideological in that (perhaps inevitably) he had lost his vibrant faith in pure knowledge. The sociologist in Du Bois had gradually given way to the polemicist, the militant advocate of racial equality, a category for which there was simply no room in turn-of-the-century academia.[85]

A Limited Scientific Legacy

Du Bois's sociological oeuvre was incontestably transgressive of turn-of-the-century cognitive norms, but it was not free of bias, ambiguity, and contradiction, because different sides of the same man were constantly coming into conflict. The reformer would prevail upon the scholar to take positions or denounce unacceptable facts. The idealist philosopher and poet would cast their shadow over the sordid realities brought to light by the cool-headed race relations researcher. As a result Du Bois's work – most notably, *The Philadelphia Negro* – is inevitably shot through with tension, tergiversation, and doubt.[86]

We have examined, with particular reference to 'The Conservation of Races,' Du Bois's approach to deconstructing the essentialism that undergirded the reigning scientific racism of his time. One is surprised to find examples of essentialism and stereotyping intruding into his own writing, thereby weakening and even contradicting the ideal of factual neutrality and objectivity to which he claimed to adhere. He opined, in reference to the factors conducive to the success of his interviews, that 'Only one fact was peculiarly favorable and that is the proverbial good nature and candor of the Negro.'[87] Similarly with Social Darwinism: even as he condemned the Anglo-American founding fathers' use of it to exalt 'natural' white superiority, he appeared to embrace it with utter detachment in his portrait of Philadelphia's blacks. He wrote that his study population formed 'a half-developed race,' 'a people comparatively low in the scale of civilization';[88] that the social evolution of blacks in large cities like Philadelphia was 'approaching a mediaeval stage.'[89]

His bias also poked through in his analysis of the class structure in the Seventh Ward as consisting of a small local elite, several middle strata, and an abject lower class of social rejects. Du Bois could not resist abandoning his oft-repeated standard of scientific neutrality and disinterestedness in order to blame the lower class for their customs, mores, and behaviors. More than once in the book, he held them largely responsible for the tenacity of white racial prejudice in Philadelphia, using reproving, moralistic, and elitist language. Evident in this departure from neutrality is a conscious strategy to maximize his credibility vis-à-vis whites, even if it meant leaving the scientifically revolutionary aspects of his work to be uncovered by the passage of time. The result, writes his biographer, was a 'great, schizoid monograph'[90] – a disconcerting phrase that he clarifies as follows:

> he obviously must have calculated that it would be necessary to write what amounted almost to two books in one – one that would not be immediately denounced or ridiculed by the arbiters of mainstream knowledge, influence, and order for its transparent heterodoxy; and a second one that would, over time, deeply penetrate the social sciences and gradually improve race-relations policy through its non-immediately apparent interpretive radicalism. He set about, then, to write a study affirming and modifying, yet also significantly subverting, the received sociological wisdom of the day.[91]

Here is an original and highly suggestive reading. Consciously or not, Du Bois mingled value judgments with empirical observations. The scientist and the reformer coexisted rather uneasily in the same man. In this he was no different from the others of his generation, regardless of race, who took up social science as a vehicle for the rational improvement of society. He frequently suspended his ideal of impartiality and let his bias filter through – hardly surprising in an era when what passed for social science was an undifferentiated mixture of 'positive' propositions and social moralizing pervaded with Protestant evangelism.

Du Bois's idealism and penchant for moralizing are particularly evident in the last chapter of *The Philadelphia Negro*, 'A Final Word,' where he set down five 'axiomatic propositions' to be derived from his research:

1. The Negro is here to stay.
2. It is to the advantage of all, both black and white, that every Negro should make the best of himself.
3. It is the duty of the Negro to raise himself by every effort to the standards of modern civilization and not to lower those standards in any degree.
4. It is the duty of the white people to guard their civilization against debauchment by themselves or others; but in order to do this it is not necessary to hinder and retard the efforts of an earnest people to rise, simply because they lack faith in the ability of that people.
5. With these duties in mind and with a spirit of self-help, mutual aid and

> co-operation, the two races should strive side by side to realize the ideals of the republic and make this truly a land of equal opportunity for all men.[92]

Take for example, the second axiom. Instead of such an idealistic formulation, he could have couched this sentiment in the quasi-technical language of natural rights. He could have argued that blacks, whether or not they 'make the best of themselves,' and whatever that might mean, simply cannot be deprived of equal opportunity and treatment. The language he did use represented a conscious choice to do otherwise. The third proposition betrays equally blatant moralizing, along with the implication that some blacks will not manage to attain the 'standards of modern civilization.' In the fourth proposition, the use of the words 'debauchment' and 'rise' suggest that while black Americans may be an 'earnest people,' their 'civilization' is nonetheless inferior to that of white Americans. In the last proposition, the language of rights and equal opportunity finally makes an appearance, but only after the moralizer has conveyed his message that the oft-alleged inferiority of his people may not be an illusion.

The remainder of 'A Final Word' offers many more examples of the juxtaposition of documented analysis and passionate moralizing. For example, 'There is no doubt that in Philadelphia the centre and kernel of the Negro problem so far as the white people are concerned is the narrow opportunities afforded Negroes for earning a decent living. Such discrimination is morally wrong, politically dangerous, industrially wasteful, and socially silly. It is the duty of the whites to stop it, and to do so primarily for their own sakes.'[93] Here Du Bois obviously violates his duty of self-restraint as a social scientist by openly expressing his outrage at the facts. Elsewhere, he is better able to mask his outrage while painting a credible portrait of the effects of racial conflict in Philadelphia:

> No matter how well trained a Negro may be, or how fitted for work of any kind, he cannot in the ordinary course of competition hope to be much more than a menial servant.
>
> He cannot get clerical or supervisory work to do save in exceptional cases.
>
> He cannot teach save in a few of the remaining Negro schools.
>
> He cannot become a mechanic except for small transient jobs, and cannot join a trades union.

> A Negro woman has but three careers open to her in this city: domestic service, sewing, or married life.[94]

While Du Bois's admonitory remarks were most often directed at lower-class blacks – the urban lumpenproletariat – his regard toward the top of the social hierarchy, the small upper class that he viewed as steadily breaking away from the more populous middle classes, tended toward the elitist. Weighing the economic and cultural factors responsible for the rise of this class, Du Bois celebrated and projected a somewhat idealized future upon it. Such exaltation of the upper class may seem surprising in a radical like Du Bois, but it was in fact central to his ideology at this stage. His essay 'The Talented Tenth' (1903), published in a volume of essays edited by Booker Washington, explicitly laid out a model of hope, a redemptive utopia for blacks embroiled in racial conflict, in the form of a group of elite black intellectuals who would guide the future of their race: 'The Negro race, like all races, is going to be saved by its exceptional men. The problem of education, then, among Negroes must first of all deal with the Talented Tenth; it is the problem of developing the Best of this race that they may guide the Mass away from the contamination and death of the Worst, in their own and other races.'[95]

What with the prevailing ideological climate (white and black) and the embryonic state of sociology, Du Bois was unable to contain himself within the role of the pure scientist. The experience of researching and writing *The Philadelphia Negro,* which brought him into contact with the small Philadelphia black elite, very probably catalyzed his singular utopian vision of a great cultural emancipation orchestrated by the most talented members of his cultural group. As the appearance of *The Souls of Black Folk* and 'The Talented Tenth' in 1903 indicates, Du Bois was then in the prime of his intellectual career. Besides becoming a noted figure among the black intelligentsia right at the start of the century, he had already assured his posterity. In a fine recent work, *The Future of the Race*, the literary critic Henry Louis Gates, Jr, and the philosopher Cornel West demonstrate this by reevaluating 'The Talented Tenth' one hundred years or so after its publication. In many respects, they argue, the work still provides topical enlightenment for 'the future of the race.'

The Sociologist in His Time

How was Du Bois's social science work received in contemporary sociological circles? For the Anglo-American establishment, the answer is simple: *The Philadelphia Negro*, that magnum opus published the same year as Thorstein Veblen's *Theory of the Leisure Class* and sharing its iconoclastic spirit, was totally ignored by the only sociological journal of the time, the *American Journal of Sociology*. Nary a commentator today hesitates to attribute this fact to racial prejudice.[96] But another factor potentially explaining Du Bois's exclusion was his no-holds-barred rhetorical style. He never minced words in describing what he saw as the purely speculative science of certain of his European and Anglo-American peers, who ignored his inductive and empirical approach. From this angle, the *American Journal of Sociology*'s silence smacks of a reprisal against an author paddling too vigorously and, perhaps, too arrogantly against the current of conventional wisdom. This judgment is reinforced when one notes the *Journal*'s lukewarm reviews of only two of the works he published during his time at Atlanta University: the edited conference proceedings titled *The Negro Artisan* and the essay collection *The Souls of Black Folk*. During the same period the *Journal* regularly noted the publication of works by known racists, reviewing them with a mixture of flattering and arbitrary observations.[97]

As for the possibility that Du Bois might actually publish a paper in the *Journal*, it was completely out of the question; in fact, under Small's reign, the *Journal* published only a very few articles on blacks in the United States or elsewhere, all of these written by whites and, in most cases, exhibiting obvious racial bias. To take just one example, H.E. Belin (see p. 31) described slavery as 'the most humane and the most practical method ever devised for "bearing the white man's burden."'[98] Du Bois was clearly the victim of a racist double standard at the sociology journal of record in his time.[99]

Beyond all these reactions from varied institutional sources, a basic problem burdened the sociology that Du Bois had cultivated since 1897 in Atlanta, a problem he did not appear to notice or, if he did, had no idea how to resolve. While the bank of raw facts was being enlarged with each new monograph in the Atlanta University Studies, his founding interpretive framework of empiricist positivism remained static, undergoing no substantial revision. Lacking a more modern framework, he was unable to offer a systematic interpretation of all these facts. He was at the epistemological dead end to which empiricist positivism inevitably leads, for the great flaw of this ideology is its tendency to eschew systematic theorization in attempting to produce scientifically valid knowledge.[100]

One might posit that Du Bois took the tack of complete and impartial fact-finding about race relations in an effort to gain scientific legitimacy for his work and thus to counter the harmful effects of the gross racism pervading Anglo-American sociology. However, it may also have been a consequence of his intellectual isolation. Working alone at Atlanta University, cut off from his peers in the North and the East, he was unable to carry on the critical dialogue that would have helped him mature conceptually by making him aware, among other things, of the need for theoretical generalization in science.[101] To be sure, it was factors extrinsic to science that precipitated his withdrawal from sociology in 1910, but it is clear that Du Bois would have run into major cognitive difficulties if he had pursued his scientific career. Seen in this light, one might even say that those other factors saved him by averting a major cognitive crisis from which he might not have been able to extricate himself. This failing, moreover, clearly pointed the way for his successors after 1918 toward the further construction of an authentic black American sociology.

All of this leads to the general conclusion that Du Bois's scientific legacy was limited. It was fortified by the strengths of one of the era's keenest minds even as it was marred by his weaknesses. His great scientific merit is to have founded a bona fide black American sociology based on an essentially historicist model of race relations. It was indeed a revolution, one that challenged the Anglo-American conventional wisdom and its deeply racist bias.[102] But it was not an epistemologically pure model, for it, too, showed traces of race reification and essentialism, albeit of the sociocultural rather than the biological variety. This shortcoming proves that Du Bois was not free, in his innovations, of the teleological reveries of the Enlightenment. In fact, throughout his many engagements, he lovingly drew on these sources to nourish both his mythology and his practice.

Finally, one should not neglect, in summarizing his accomplishments, his exemplary institution-building work at Atlanta University. Integral to his heritage is the tour de force of having implemented a complete center for scholarly initiation to an original form of American sociology before the First World War. Before Du Bois, there was nothing; with his arrival came the brisk wind of hope along with the conviction of entitlement to a place within world academia, not just the American university. And this was only as it should be, for Du Bois, in his tireless quest for authenticity, was in the habit of invoking the universal.

5 Four 'New Negroes'

Du Bois's premature withdrawal from academia left the work of building an original black American sociology tragically unfinished. The void was not filled until after the war by a new generation of southern blacks who were motivated, among other things, by the antiracist ideological movement in which the founding of the NAACP and its journal *Crisis* (1915) were milestones. Deeply opposed to segregation and intellectually ambitious, these self-styled 'New Negroes' were keen to advance their education at northern universities. However, they did not all conceive of sociology and its application to the black condition in the same way; in fact, one of the more interesting things about this cohort is that they did not all reside on the left of the ideological spectrum. Charles Spurgeon Johnson, Horace Roscoe Cayton, and J.G. St Clair Drake, all discussed in this chapter, were moderate reformers, fitting comfortably into the mold of the University of Chicago where they did their graduate work. Oliver Cromwell Cox, the least orthodox of the group, passed through Chicago but parted company with the school to found his own iconoclastic, Marxist-inspired brand of sociology. E. Franklin Frazier, the pivotal figure in this new cohort (to whom chapter 6 is devoted), sat somewhere along the spectrum between reformer and radical. It was he who would leave the richest scientific legacy, one that has remained influential to this day.

Johnson: The Activist as Organization Man

Charles Johnson was born in Virginia in 1893 to an emancipated slave who had become a Baptist minister. After obtaining his undergraduate degree, he went to the University of Chicago for graduate work with

Robert Park, becoming his first black student.[1] The climate in the city at the time was one of great social tension. The First World War had created a demand for labor in the North, and black migration from the South had grown accordingly. New black competition for jobs led many whites to clamor for restricted housing, education, health care, recreational sites, and so forth. In the summer of 1919, Chicago witnessed one of the worst race riots in the country's history.[2] Johnson, on Park's recommendation, was commissioned by the Illinois government to write a report of inquiry going beyond the facts to examine the broader issues of race relations (published as *The Negro in Chicago*).

It was in Chicago that Johnson made the acquaintance of Small, Burgess, and the philosopher George Mead, and began to develop a personal approach to the construction of social science. In 1921 he left for New York, where he spent the next five years as research director of the National Urban League. Simultaneously, as editor of *Opportunity,* he transformed the journal into a forum for Harlem Renaissance writers, poets, and artists. In 1927 he decided to go back to academic research. On Park's recommendation he was hired to head the social science department at Fisk University in Tennessee, a position he would hold for the rest of his career. It was here that he produced most of his important scientific papers.

Without interrupting his research activities, he now had access to the small circle of American donors interested in funding race relations research, and he proved an efficient administrator of this money. He set up a social science graduate program, founded university presses, and organized conferences.[3] Moreover, he pulled off a coup by hiring Robert Park to the Fisk faculty in 1936. In addition to his dynamic work at the university, Johnson sat on various national public policy commissions, including a special commission formed by President Hoover on housing conditions for blacks. He served under Roosevelt as a consultant and researcher to the Tennessee Valley Authority, the Southern Commission on the Study of Lynching, and the Southern Regional Council. In the early 1940s, Johnson became involved in educational issues, serving on the White House Conference for Children. He developed special expertise on southern black youth education and served as an adviser to the NAACP on the *Brown* v. *Board of Education* decision that made school segregation illegal. After the Second World War he joined the first American delegation to the United Nations Educational, Scientific and Cultural Organization (UNESCO) in Paris. As Richard

Robbins observes, this and other extra-academic commitments were in keeping with his University of Chicago training:

> His committed activism in a moderate key – the work with the foundations, the advisory role as a race statesman, his contribution to formulating public policy, which he called his 'sidelines activism,' his quiet but effective role in the organization of protest movements – was grounded in his belief, rooted in his University of Chicago training, in the essentiality of research. And research, in providing a foundation for an informed activism, advances activism's cause.[4]

In 1947 Johnson was appointed president of Fisk University while retaining his position in the social science department. His new responsibilities limited his productivity as a researcher but enabled him to create a remarkable institutional legacy. By the time of his death in 1956, he had made Fisk University the center for the sociological study of racism in the South, as well as a clearinghouse for all American groups and movements engaged in antiracist struggle. Johnson's published work consists of seventeen authored or coauthored monographs, fourteen books to which he contributed one or more chapters, and more than sixty major papers.

Published Work

The Negro in Chicago (1923) was, on its face, a topical report on a specific event; however, because it went much further, it remains a document of undeniable value even today. It examines the complex relationship between black-white relations in Chicago and the constantly changing context in which they evolved. Johnson adhered to the human ecology model used by Park in his 'The City' (1915), then the conceptual standard for urban studies. He assigned great importance to migration, the continuous flow of population from the South and its impact on the sociocultural context of life in Chicago. Though written under the direct influence of Parkian ecologism, the core of *The Negro in Chicago* is largely descriptive and empirical. It notes the many ways in which the sudden arrival of blacks in white neighborhoods altered race relations within a wide variety of institutional and informal settings. The city is envisaged as a sort of psychophysical mechanism (a Parkian construct) either separating or bringing into interaction its inhabitants under a multitude of different circumstances as a result of continuous, uninterrupted change. The book offers no deep theoretical interpretation; nevertheless, it represents an important stride toward the rigorous understanding of race relations in an urban context marked by growing instability.[5]

In New York in 1925, influenced by the ferment of the Harlem Renaissance, Johnson and his Harvard-educated colleague Alain Locke edited a special issue of the *Survey Graphic* (the journal of the social survey movement; see p. 209) symbolically titled *The New Negro*. This publication did more than introduce a new group of black writers, poets, and musicians: it sought to disseminate a cultural model of a new African American that was poles apart from Booker Washington's complacent, subjugated citizen; an African American proud of his or her race and unwilling to settle for less than full equality in American society. This movement represented a continuation of the cultural emancipation undertaken fifteen years earlier by Du Bois and his acolytes with the foundation of the NAACP and *Crisis*. Johnson identified with this liberatory thrust and sought to mobilize gifted blacks to express their creativity in all recognized intellectual genres.

The publication in 1930 of *The Negro in American Civilization*, edited by Johnson, enhanced his renown as a researcher and research coordinator. The work was commissioned by sixteen national associations involved in the improvement of race relations and seeking to hold a major conference on the theme. In preparation for the conference, they invited Johnson to submit a synthesis of the relevant existing knowledge. The work was an up-to-date compilation of statistics on demographics, health, education, industry, agriculture, leisure, housing, crime and delinquency, and justice, along with critical commentary. The work was especially valuable in 1930, when few reliable sources of data on African Americans existed. It was a timely scientific contribution as the country sank into depression and black nationalism became increasingly assertive.

Johnson's third work, *Shadow of the Plantation* (1934), was the product of several years of applied research thanks to a grant from the Julius Rosenwald Fund. Working under a mandate from the United States Public Health Service, Johnson studied the plantation economy in Macon County, Alabama, one of the poorest areas in the state. While the original goal had been to ascertain the social factors causing a high incidence of syphilis in the South, Johnson broadened the research to encompass all aspects of life for rural blacks in Macon. In his introduction to the work, Park stressed that its main challenge was to interpret the rural culture: 'There are no special difficulties in describing the external forms and the obvious expressions of a local culture. The difficulty consists in making that culture intelligible; in discovering the meaning and the function of usages, customs, and institutions.'[6]

As regards methodology, Johnson drew upon the best known empirical research techniques of the time, including interviews with a sample of six hundred black families (from which he published a large number of excerpts). He compiled statistics on work, education, income, and socioeconomic status for these families. His main objective was to probe the workings of the cotton plantation economy and, in the process, to do away with the racist myth of happy blacks living lazy lives in the cotton fields. The main problem facing blacks on the plantations, he contended, stemmed from the decline of the slave economy and its replacement by a feudal economy of cotton tenantry:

> The present Negro population of these old plantation areas can best be understood by viewing it in the light of this plantation tradition, with its almost complete dependence upon the immediate landowner for guidance and control in virtually all those phases of life which are related to the moving world outside ... Such families as escape from the prevailing economy of dependence into the new responsibilities which go with independence find economic complications and shades of social conflict which manifest themselves in various ways, sometimes prompting them to migration, but as often leading to resignation and relapse from the ownership status to tenantry. The gradual decline in Negro ownership and the increase in the tenant class are evidences of this struggle.[7]

Chapter by chapter, the book builds its case that the plantation economy was a vast system of social exploitation. Illiterate black sharecroppers were both economically dependent (indebted to) and culturally dependent (for bookkeeping) on the white landlords. Meanwhile, the landlords were themselves in debt to the banks. The exploitation of southern blacks thus took the form of a vicious circle of indebtedness in which the person at the bottom, the sharecropper, bore the heaviest burden:

> To the Negro tenant the white landlord is the system; to the white landlord the capital of the banks is the system. The landlord needs credit by which to advance credit to the tenants ... but the advantage is always with the

white landlord. He dictates the terms and keeps the books. The demands of the system determine the social and economic relations, the weight of which falls heaviest upon those lowest down.[8]

The scientific interest of Johnson's book lies, in part, in his refusal to pathologize the behavior of poor rural blacks. He persuasively argued that it was the plantation system that was largely responsible for their cultural marginalization – indeed, for the maintenance of the whole region in a state of chronic underdevelopment:

The community studied reflects a static economics not unlike the Mexican *hacienda*, or the condition of the Polish peasant – a situation in which the members of a group are 'muffled with a vast apathy.' It is unquestionably the economic system in which they live, quite as much or even more than the landlords, that is responsible for their plight ... From the nature of the external conditions determining the early social organization of this group it has taken form, naturally, outside the dominant current of the American culture ... The situation is one clearly of isolation and cultural lag.[9]

Johnson could not help but point the finger at the exploitation he observed in Macon County, but his accusation was never explicit; rather, it transpired from the data that he coolly presented: 'It is, of course, impossible to determine the extent of exploitation of these Negro farmers, so long as the books are kept by the landlord, the sale price of cotton known only by him, and the cost and interest on rations advanced in his hands.'[10]

The book provides a wealth of ethnographic material, including many hitherto uncompiled details of family behavior among Macon's black residents, their religious practices, and scattered efforts to reduce illiteracy and help the population emerge from cultural isolation. The conclusion gives a clear indication of the political and ideological position to which Johnson adhered: 'The greatest pressure is being felt at present by the tenants, dulled and blocked in by a backwardness which is a fatal heritage of the system itself. But the fate of the tenant is but an aspect of the fate of the southern farmer generally and the plight of all of these awaits a comprehensive planning, which affects not merely the South but the nation.'[11] In calling for national planning to tackle underdevelopment, he was looking to the liberal Roosevelt administration to carry it out within an overall strategy of progressive reform. Like the southern liberals, Johnson supported reasoned (i.e., science-based) policy on race relations. An example was a 1935 report that he and two directors of the Rosenwald Foundation presented to Roosevelt's cabinet in which they called for measures to turn black sharecroppers into landowners, the solution then favored by southern liberals.[12]

Johnson enlarged his sociological expertise about the South with *Growing Up in the Black Belt* (1941), a study of black youth funded by the Youth Commission, an important public agency. The quantitative and qualitative study focused on eight counties in five states of the Black Belt (North Carolina, Tennessee, Mississippi, Georgia, and Alabama). His premise was the existence of a close correlation between cultural environment and personality development, where personality was defined as 'the organization of the individual's habits and behavior patterns in adjustment to his environment and in his effort not merely to survive but to achieve a career.'[13] Even more than in the previous book, Johnson strove here to assemble a scientifically reliable data set. He administered a questionnaire to a sample of more than two thousand teenagers and subjected the raw data to various statistical tests. He used the results to sketch personality profiles and describe youth in action in a variety of social settings. His conclusion was that black southern teenagers were the product of both an omnipresent racial system and socialization within a complex microsociety involving youth of different ages, genders, classes, and rural or urban origins.

While *Shadow of the Plantation* barely grazed the phenomenon of black social stratification, *Growing Up in the Back Belt* gave it pride of place. Johnson defined three social classes as a composite of ownership, income, education, occupation, stability of residence, and other criteria. The upper class accounted for 6 percent of the rural population, the middle class for 12 percent, and the large class of 'folk Negroes' studied in *Shadow of the Plantation,* itself divisible into subgroups according to various economic and cultural criteria, for 82 percent.

It was evident to Johnson that the worldview of the white majority distorted the personality of black teenagers of all classes. But, he contended, qualitative modification could be effected through a series of minute, gradual changes to the effective system of social relations as a result of blacks' struggle to improve their status and abolish the caste system. He had no illusions about the extent and depth of institutional racism in the South but believed that tangible changes were taking place: 'The southern race system does not ... appear to meet fully the description of a caste system.'[14]

In the same vein was *Patterns of Negro Segregation* (1943), an in-depth reworking of the research note on segregation that Myrdal had commissioned Johnson to produce (see pp. 92, 283), using survey data he had previously gathered in the South (Mississippi, Arkansas, North Carolina, Tennessee, Virginia, Alabama, Georgia, and Texas), in the border states of Maryland and Indiana, and in Chicago and New York. The book begins with a review of patterns of racial segregation and discrimination in these regions of the country. Johnson built on Park's idea of segregation as a mechanism of accommodation between races in conflict, defining segregation as a means of attenuating interracial conflict through the selective ordering of individuals and the creation of social distance. Any number of tangible social settings – schools, businesses, public and professional services, residential areas – served to demonstrate this mechanism. In the second part of the book, Johnson examined the behavioral response of blacks forced to undergo segregation under different circumstances. Here he boldly went his mentor one better, emphasizing the influence on blacks' behavioral reaction of sociological factors largely ignored by Park. Drawing on the class analysis of *Growing Up in the Black Belt*, he elucidated the range of behavioral responses to segregation and discrimination by different classes of southern blacks – a theme that would be taken even further by Frazier (see ch. 6).

Another important idea in *Patterns of Negro Segregation* is that the color barrier is as much a function of ideological representations as of customs or laws. This idea appears in the conclusion along with an undisguised interventionist message:

> The effects of the unrestrained operation of the principle of racialism are conceivably as dangerous to American society as the unrestricted play of free competition in the economic sphere.
>
> Logically, it would be appropriate for government to impose controls and regulations, as mandatory as those imposed on its economic life, to ensure to all its racial minorities not only free but equal participation in the economic and political life of the country.[15]

Three other works published by Johnson from 1943 to 1951 show the multifaceted nature of his concerns. The first, *To Stem This Tide* (1943), sought to demonstrate the existence of discrimination against blacks during the Second World War, both in the armed forces and in the war industries. The second, *Into the Mainstream* (1947), performed the same analysis for the postwar period, when the soldiers returned to mainstream life. The third, an essay titled *Education and the Cultural Crisis* (1951), appeared when Johnson was at the summit of his career and at leisure to philosophize at length on the subject of education, drawing on his experience as a field researcher and an administrator committed to the fight against segregation. He advocated 'fundamental education,' whose chief characteristic he defined as its democratic inclusiveness: 'The essential element of fundamental education, however, is that it involves all ages, without distinction as to sex, class, race, or creed. It is the education of the mass of people. It is opposed to any system of teaching founded on the existence of privileged classes or social or religious castes. It is thus one of the vital components of democracy.'[16] Such an inclusive educational system, if implemented, would represent a stride forward for humankind:

> One of the end results of this diffusion of a kind of mass education which is democratic in inspiration and faithful to the idea of minority rights, and which seeks to develop the best within a culture and includes all cultures, can be a blending of the goals of East and West and the discovery of common ground in those values which are a responsibility of the higher civilizations.
>
> The interdependence of the world, an irreversible fact and an aspect of the cultural crisis of the present, involves our own orientation to this conception of education.[17]

A posthumous work, *Bitter Canaan: The Story of the Negro Republic* (1987), stemmed from a 1929 international commission of inquiry into slavery and forced labor in the West African nation of Liberia. The issue was politically sensitive for the United States in view of its long-standing economic interests in the region. Because of his reputation as a race relations scholar, Johnson was asked by President Hoover to represent the United States on this commission, and he spent seven months in Liberia, his first African trip. He returned outraged and disgusted by a political and economic system in which the aboriginal people were exploited by the Americo-Liberian elite descended from African American immigrants. The elite were in open collusion with the neighboring European imperialist colonies and the local representatives (firms, industries, bureaucrats) of American capitalism. After delivering his report to the Secretary of State, Johnson continued to work on a longer version for many years.[18]

It was not until 1945 that he submitted the manuscript to the University of Chicago Press. The three academic reviewers made several unfavorable comments but did not reject the book as such; the publisher also asked him to update the facts in view of the long period elapsed and the major sociopolitical transformations that had taken place. He withdrew the manuscript, stating that as president of Fisk University he did not have the time to produce an in-depth revision. The work was finally published in 1987 by Transaction Books, a publishing house specializing in historical works by black Americans on topical issues for social science and politics.

Bitter Canaan is important because it illustrates several of its author's most salient intellectual traits. Rather like Frazier's *Black Bourgeoisie* (see pp. 225–30), *Bitter Canaan* offers a combination of documented description of social facts and explicit denunciation of injustice. Johnson rallied to the cause of the natives, drawing parallels with southern U.S. blacks and bringing to light an institutionalized system of oppression modeled on the one prevailing in the United States. Here, for the only time in his career, he resolutely broke with Park's rule of neutrality and emotional distance. His tone of unrelenting irony seems intended to demystify the absurdity of what he discovered. It is unfortunate that Johnson was unable to publish the work during the 1930s when it would have had the greatest impact on the situation of gross racism prevailing in Liberia.

A Critical Appraisal

Without a doubt, Johnson's work adheres to the Chicago paradigm, whose theoretical corpus and methods he appropriated nearly in their entirety. It was at Chicago that Johnson learned the value of synthesis in sociological theory, beginning with the race relations cycle. It was there that he was initiated into a research methodology combining statistical surveys with personal portraits. The best of his subsequent work adopted this approach, using statistics to provide a solid foundation for generalization and personal descriptions to bring the data alive.

But it would be unfair to Johnson to ignore the originality of his work vis-à-vis its Chicago sources. Much more than his mentors Park and Burgess, he dwelled on the concept of caste to explain southern segregation, going so far as to take up certain elements of Warner's competing paradigm. More importantly, he focused more on class and the conflicts ensuing from the profound distortion of social relations caused by racial prejudice. Perhaps his greatest scientific merit is to have repeatedly demonstrated that southern black culture, far from being a vehicle for pathological ways of thinking and living, represented a peculiar adaptation to restrictive, indeed debilitating environmental conditions. He was the first of the New Negroes to attempt to sociologically deconstruct this tenacious piece of Anglo-American conventional wisdom, thus adding new elements to the still-rudimentary edifice of black American sociology begun by Du Bois.

In parallel with his writing, Johnson engaged in numerous projects for the advancement of African Americans. Some regarded him as a forward-looking thinker, while others considered him an opportunist prone to obsequiousness before the white establishment in order to rise through the ranks. He and Frazier were intellectually of a piece until the mid-1930s; they parted ways then, siding with Warner and Park, respectively, in the caste/class debate. A homage to Johnson in the year after his death by Ernest Burgess, one of the last living founders of the Chicago School, provides a fair summation of his contribution as a black American intellectual and second-generation sociologist:

> The accumulated impact of his research has been tremendous because of his scientific objectivity, his caution in interpreting data, his understanding of the human element in social situations, and his discernment in coming to sound and practical application of his findings. He achieved first rank as a social scientist. He also developed as a great educator and as a social statesman to whom our government, our welfare, educational, and religious organizations and UNESCO frequently turned for counsel and guidance.[19]

From 1920 to 1945, Johnson stood apart as the leading black sociological expert on the social condition of African Americans in the southern United States. After the war, his role as an institution builder tended to crowd out his activities as a social scientist. Thus, his scientific originality was largely in the past just as Frazier was coming into his own as a sociologist.

Cayton and Drake: Theorists of the Ghetto

Toward the end of the 1930s, W. Lloyd Warner commissioned the sociologist Horace Cayton and the anthropologist J.G. St Clair Drake to produce the last book in a series on black American communities, this one focusing on the black community of Chicago's South Side. The result, *Black Metropolis* (1945) – to which I devote an in-depth analysis below – became a classic of black American sociology and a 'masterpiece of social research,'[20] fusing the best methods of its authors' respective disciplines.

Cayton was born in 1903 to a poor family in Seattle, Washington. Working his way through school as a stevedore, a sheriff's deputy, and at other odd jobs, he gained early experience of the rough realities faced by black Americans on the job market. In his undergraduate program at the University of Washington he studied under the human ecologist Roderick McKenzie, a close colleague of Robert Park's. In the late 1920s Park visited the university, met Cayton, and arranged a substantial graduate scholarship for him at the University of Chicago. The stimulating Chicago environment helped Cayton circumscribe his research interests in short order. An initial job as a research assistant gave him an opportunity to study the characteristics of neighborhood politicians and police officers and to familiarize himself with the numbers rackets that would come in for close analysis in *Black Metropolis* ten years later. A second research position, arranged for him by Charles Johnson, resulted in the publication of his first book, *Black Workers and the New Unions* (1939), written with George S. Mitchell.[21]

The book focuses on the factors affecting black workers' participation in labor unions in the face of stiff competition and 'racial antipathy.' Though it does not present itself as a contribution to sociological theory per se, it does put forward as its guiding hypothesis that racial antipathy exists and 'has been utilized in a rational and conscious manner by both labor and capital.'[22] The authors studied this hypothesis in relation to three industries: steel (which takes up more than half of the book), meatpacking, and railway car manufacturing, using a mixture of direct observation and some one thousand interviews with representative individuals over fifteen months of field research.

Blacks in the steel industry faced specific problems that whites were spared: 'The racial prejudice in the United States against Negroes manifests itself in the industrial sphere in the form of limited industrial opportunity. This is true in the North as well as in the South. It has been true in the steel industry, as in all industries.'[23] Consequently, they began to seek 'a dependable alliance with some group of white workers.'[24] They encountered considerable barriers, chief among them the company union,[25] a paternalistic structure with a long tradition in American labor relations as a means for employers to control their workforce. The founding of the Contress of Industrial Organizations (CIO) raised hopes, for '[o]ne of [its] first tasks ... was to plan a campaign for the organization of the steel industry.'[26] Thanks to the CIO's efforts, progress by black workers was already notable by 1939.

Overall, the authors observed the same situation in the two other industries, noting that black advancement there was much slower than in the steel industry. In their conclusion, they noted that 'at present there is no organization among Negroes which is devoted to the single task of integrating colored workers into the general labor movement.'[27] The book ends with an outlook section titled 'A Program for Negro Labor' in which they argued that fuller participation in the labor movement could only benefit blacks.

Apart from his autobiography (1965), Cayton wrote no other major works after *Black Metropolis*, nor was he involved in any long-term sociological research. He wrote regularly for the *Nation*, the *New Republic*, the *Chicago Sun*, and the *Chicago Tribune* and produced a weekly column for the *Pittsburgh Courier*. He was active until his death as a speaker and a member of numerous civil rights organizations, playing the role of 'race leader' or 'race man,' as he termed it. A doctoral thesis in sociology begun in the 1940s was never completed. Cayton died in 1970.

J.G. St Clair Drake (1911–90) grew up in Virginia, where he attended high school and college. As a boy, he traveled with his Barbadian American father to the Caribbean to promote Marcus Garvey's Universal Negro Improvement Association (see p. 55), thus gaining an early awareness of the worldwide struggle for equality by all oppressed cultures of African descent. When he entered the social anthropology program at the University of Chicago several years after Cayton arrived, he already had a strong background in empirical research, having worked as a research assistant on the project that led to Warner's *Deep South*.

After *Black Metropolis*, Drake would gravitate toward interests reflecting the worldliness he had acquired in his youth. In 1954 he obtained his doctorate in social anthropology with a concentration in African studies, producing a thesis titled *Value Systems, Social Structure and Race Relations in the British Isles*. In later life he was a frequent world traveler. In 1954 he taught for six months in Ghana followed by nine months in Nigeria. He returned to Ghana for a three-year stint in 1958 to head the sociology department at the University of Ghana. In between overseas trips, he worked with associations whose goals included encouraging African Americans to identify with the idea of a heightened African presence in world affairs. In terms of theory, he would produce nothing to equal *Black Metropolis*; later works included *The Redemption of Africa and Black Religion* (1970) and the two-volume *Black Folk Here and There: An Essay in History and Anthropology* (1987–90). He taught at Dillard University, the University of Chicago, Roosevelt University, Boston University, and Columbia University before holding his final position as director of the graduate program in African and Afro-American studies at Stanford University (1969–76).

Black Metropolis

While researching his first book, Cayton met Warner, who had recently been hired by the University of Chicago as associate professor of sociology and anthropology. Discussions between the two men led to the idea of applying for funding from the Works Progress Administration (WPA), the Roosevelt administration's federal employment agency, to produce a wide-ranging study of the Chicago black community. With Warner as his thesis adviser, Drake, too, quickly found himself a member of the research team, as Cayton wrote in his autobiography:

> Drake had been working with Dr. Allison Davis on a study of Natchez, Mississippi, and had come to the university to secure his doctor's degree in anthropology. He soon became a guiding force in our research and, though by and large a poor executive, he was by far the most creative supervisor on the project. While I was busy with administrative details and raising funds to provide the sponsor's contribution to the project, Drake was devoting all his energies to outlining research procedures and to the gathering and compiling of data.[28]

The 'mammoth community study'[29] that is *Black Metropolis* shows the influence of Warner's ideas about social stratification, but, more important, it represents the culmination of the tradition of holistic studies of black American communities dating back to *The Philadelphia Negro*. It owes its exceptional richness to an approach that goes beyond elementary statistical surveying techniques to present itself as an in-depth sociological investigation whose goal is to transform the social conditions of Chicago's black ghetto. According to William Julius Wilson, who wrote the foreword to the 1993 edition, the work represents 'a fundamental revision in the Chicago framework,'[30] while drawing on many aspects of it. The key innovation in their work was to elaborate on one of Frazier's important Depression-era insights:

> Frazier's awareness of the black urban condition in the 1930s led him to recognize and emphasize a problem ignored in the earlier work of Park and Burgess – namely the important link between the black family structure and the industrial economy. Frazier believed that upward mobility for African Americans and their eventual assimilation into American life would depend in large measure on the availability of employment opportunities in the industrial sector.[31]

In this way, the work departs from the Anglo-American conventional wisdom regarding urban communities. Without denying the existence of a complex process of morphological and ecological growth, the authors play up the importance of institutional practices and political decisions and, more generally, the multiple expressions of human behavior in a ghettoized living environment.

Black Metropolis opens with a solemn dedication to Robert Park,

> AMERICAN SCHOLAR AND FRIEND OF THE NEGRO PEOPLE; who once said: 'Anthropology, the science of man, has been mainly concerned up to the present with the study of primitive peoples. But civilized man is quite as interesting an object of investigation, and at the same time his life is more open to observation and study. Urban life and culture are more varied, subtle and complicated, but the fundamental motives are in both instances the same.'

Another unusual feature is a seventeen-page introduction by the black novelist Richard Wright. Wright became famous in 1940 with his *Native Son*, a tragedy about a Chicago black man whose plight symbolized the alienation experienced by all members of his race. Wright placed *Black Metropolis* in context, using rich, sober prose that evokes the universal as it attempts to raise the reader's awareness of the tragedy embodied by the denial of human freedom: 'In *Black Metropolis*, the authors have presented much more than the anatomy of Negro frustration; they have shown how *any* human beings can become mangled, how *any* personalities can become distorted when men are caught in the psychological trap of being emotionally committed to the living of a life of freedom which is denied them.'[32]

HISTORICAL CONTEXT

The work concerns the Chicago neighborhood of Bronzeville, where the authors lived for many years and practiced the technique of participant observation. They set their work in context by recounting the sociodemographic history of the Chicago black community in general, which had taken shape as a result of far-reaching processes such as the Great Migration: 'The earliest Negro migrants to Chicago, like those of later years, were refugees from the bondage of America's cotton kingdom in the South. They poured into the city by the hundreds between 1840 and 1850, fleeing slavery. Some remained; others passed through to Canada and points east.'[33] A Black Belt or 'Black Metropolis' had grown up around the city, swelling with new immigrants after the First World War:

> The five years from 1924 to 1929 were no doubt the most prosperous ones the Negro community in Chicago had ever experienced. A professional and business class arose upon the broad base of over seventy-five thousand colored wage-earners, and was able for a brief period to enjoy the fruits of its training and investment. Throughout the Twenties, additional migrants from the rural South swelled the size of the Black Belt market. The Fat Years were at hand.[34]

But then came the debacle of 1929. The New Deal programs provided some help during the Depression, and blacks, like everyone else, took advantage of them. However, they were discriminated against in this as in other areas of life. Meanwhile, the flow of migrants from the South continued unabated. The Second World War produced an enormous number of jobs in Chicago and accelerated the flow of migrants, with 60,000 arriving from 1940 to 1944.[35] The authors took the resulting problematic social situation as their focus: 'There were plenty of jobs, but the already troublesome problems of inadequate housing, congestion, inferior recreational facilities, and overcrowded schools in the Black Belt were aggravated by the influx ... The Negro was once more becoming a "problem" and racial conflict seemed to loom in the offing.'[36]

DISCRIMINATION AS A BYPRODUCT OF THE ECONOMIC CRISIS

The first problem they examined was discrimination, popularly known as the 'color line.' In public life, where contacts tended to be anonymous or impersonal, discrimination was (with some exceptions) generally not too flagrant: 'Negroes in Midwest Metropolis experience a degree of "freedom to come and go" and a measure of political equality denied them in the South. Discrimination in public places is not widespread and, being illegal, can be fought. Yet there are two areas in which the color-line is tightly drawn – employment and housing.'[37] Blacks did not have the opportunity to compete for jobs on an equal basis. Before the great migration, they had largely been confined to domestic occupations. In the 1920s, the bulk of the black population worked at dangerous, low-paying jobs. The Second World War enabled many of them to hold a wide variety of technical and clerical positions, but there was no guarantee that they would be able to keep their jobs once the economy shifted off a war footing. Meanwhile, housing discrimination became particularly stigmatizing: 'The Job Ceiling *subordinates* Negroes but does not *segregate* them. Restrictive covenants do both. They confine Negroes to the Black Belt, and they limit the Black Belt to the most run-down areas of the city.'[38]

The dual phenomenon of subordination and segregation was inevitably a source of tension and violence:

> The conflict over living space is an ever-present source of potential violence. It involves not only a struggle for houses, but also competition for school and recreational facilities, and is further complicated by the fact that Negroes of the lowest socio-economic levels are often in competition with middle-class whites for an area. Race prejudice becomes aggravated by class antagonisms, and class-feeling is often expressed in racial terms.[39]

Crossing the color line – that is, entering into an interracial marriage – was not legally prohibited but neither, to say the least, was it approved of.[40] This stricture was one of many ways of keeping blacks 'in their place.' By comparison, interracial extramarital relations and sexual encounters were quite frequent. The clearest indication of the existence of a color line in Chicago was the presence of the Black Belt or black ghetto:

> The native-born, middle-class, white population is the group that sets the standards by which various people are designated as desirable or undesirable. The attitudes of this middle-class group are probably decisive in restricting Negroes and other groups to special areas of the city ... The areas in which these groups are concentrated become stigmatized as 'slum neighborhoods,' and there is a tendency to blame the group for the condition of the area.[41]

Blacks did not accept forced segregation, but they did not have much choice in the matter: 'Black Metropolis has become a seemingly permanent enclave within the city's blighted area.'[42] And just as there was a black ghetto, there were 'Negro jobs': Pullman porters; domestics in white homes; washerwomen; and employees of hotels, rooming houses, athletic clubs, and brothels. Because of the large pool of unemployed people, blacks often met with fierce competition from whites for these largely unskilled jobs. If the color line and all its concomitant prejudices persisted, it is because they were deeply rooted in the Anglo-American mind:

> Since the early days of the slave trade, dark skin-color has been considered a mark of inferiority – social, economic, and political – in the Anglo-American world. Africa has become the master-symbol of benightedness and savagery, its people being thought of as lowest in the scale of culture and civilization – perhaps even not fully human. A vague belief permeates the society that Negroes are 'closer to the apes.'[43]

But there was hope that this line could be erased, not through divine intervention but by the efforts of blacks themselves. Nearly all blacks felt that they were advancing, but they also realized that their efforts had to be focused on the specific goal of lifting the 'job ceiling.' Only a small number of them had managed to do so by their own efforts, while for the majority, education had an important role to play: 'The process of lifting the Job Ceiling ... involves also the problem of educating the Negro – educating him to want the job, to get it, and to keep it. Negroes have for so long had a subordinate "place" in American life that many find it hard to conceive of themselves or other Negroes except in that place.'[44] The two main labor unions, the AFL and the CIO, were working on behalf of black labor mobility without making any spectacular gains:

> The demands of a war economy broke the Job Ceiling at various points ... In this process of breaking the Job Ceiling, the new labor unions have played a perhaps subsidiary, but nevertheless very important, role. Within the new labor movement, a new Negro leadership has emerged which speaks not only for Negroes but often for white workers as well.[45]

BRONZEVILLE: CITY WITHIN A CITY

Part three of *Black Metropolis*, making up nearly half the book, is a detailed study of Bronzeville, the South Side community at the core of the Black Belt. Drawing on human ecology concepts developed by Park, as well as Frazier's *The Negro Family in Chicago* (see pp. 212–16), Drake and Cayton began by describing the physical and social morphology of the community in terms of its 'centers of orientation,' 'which claim the time and money of Bronzeville – the "axes of life" around which individual and community life revolves[.] The most important of these are: (1) Staying Alive; (2) Having a Good Time; (3) Praising God; (4) Getting Ahead; (5) Advancing the Race.'[46]

The 'city within a city' described by the authors was structured around four major institutions that determined Bronzeville's system of social relations: the church, the black press, black businesses, and the lottery. Between the Civil War and the Great Migration, the church had become the most influential institution in Chicago's black community. This influence was exerted through face-to-face contact between the minister and his congregation. The pulpit was a source of both information and spiritual inspiration, with the minister acting as a newsmonger as much as a moral and religious guide. By the Second World War, however, the former role had largely been taken over by Bronzeville's five weekly newspapers: 'The church remained a center for the formation of public opinion, but the Negro press emerged as a victorious competitor.'[47] The black population of 300,000 had high expectations for their churches and newspapers: 'The Negro newspaper is a business institution which Bronzeville expects to "serve The Race." The Negro church is ostensibly a "religious" organization, but Bronzeville expects it, too, to "advance The Race." There are nearly 500 churches in Black Metropolis, claiming at least 200,000 members and distributed among over thirty denominations.'[48]

The church was no longer as central to community life as it had been in the North and still was in the South, but it still had an important function: 'It is probable ... that the church's main attraction is the opportunity it gives for large masses of people to function in an organized group, to compete for prestige, to be elected to office, to exercise power and control, to win applause and acclaim.'[49] One way for the church to work for the advancement of the 'race' was to encourage black businesses. In the black community, a business was more than a profit-making enterprise; it was a symbol of racial advancement, and everyone expected clergymen to exhort their congregations to shop there. In Bronzeville, the largest retail stores and half of the smaller businesses belonged to whites and did not hire many blacks. Black businesspeople were few and far between, but several were able 'to compete with whites for the Negro market, and some have even been able to develop businesses competing in the general city market.'[50] In its most extreme form, the dream of controlling their own market visualized a completely separate black economy, but this was far from the reality in which 'nine-tenths of Bronzeville's money is spent with whites.'[51] And not all blacks in the community were attracted by the idea of being merchants: 'the average college-trained Negro, if he is not a professional man, is more likely to go into insurance or real estate, publishing or printing, than into the hurly-burly of retail merchandising.'[52]

The industry in which blacks had been most successful in competition with whites was insurance. They had been able to amass capital and secure trained personnel, such that '[i]n 1940 there were four such companies with home offices in Chicago. They were valued at over $10,000,000 and employed over 2,000 persons.'[53] Though blacks were outcompeted by whites in most lines of retail business, there were three professions – undertaker, barber, and beautician – in which blacks competed only among themselves.

The fourth characteristic institution of Bronzeville, the lottery, was more than just a highly lucrative game; according to the authors, it was a '"protected business," operating in defiance of Illinois State Statute No. 413, but under the benevolent patronage of the city political machine.'[54] The lottery in Bronzeville was also something of a cult. Drake and Cayton depicted it as being shrouded in mystery, using an esoteric language and having a structuring effect on the lives of the individuals participating in it. Profits from the lottery were derived from sales at some five hundred 'policy stations,' which provided employment for about two thousand persons. Above this front-line structure was the syndicate, whose job was to do everything necessary – paying bribes or kickbacks, for example – to keep the police, the Illinois bureaucrats, and a host of reform groups from interfering with the smooth running of the business. It was a racket, of course, and a very popular one indeed: 'The strength of the "policy racket" in the Negro community may be due to Bronzeville's penchant for gambling, but it is perpetuated by the intricate tie-up with the "downtown" political powers, who render protection not only from the police, but also from attempts of civic leaders to interfere with the game.'[55] Few in the black community were opposed to the lottery, and anyone who got his own station or, better still, joined the syndicate was thought of as a 'policy king,' hence a race hero. Clergymen tended not to oppose the lottery too stridently since many of them played the numbers themselves. In sum, the lottery institution was a prime example of the second 'center of orientation' mentioned above – having a good time.

THE CLASS SYSTEM

'Everybody in Bronzeville,' wrote Drake and Cayton, 'recognizes the existence of social classes, whether called that or not.'[56] The authors identified the existence of upper, middle, and lower classes, the first of these being constructed as follows: 'At the top of the social pyramid is a scant 5 per cent of the population – an articulate social world of doctors, lawyers, schoolteachers, executives, successful business people, and the frugal and fortunate of other occupational groups who have climbed with difficulty ...'[57] Holding positions of responsibility in major black institutions, cooperating with liberal whites who gave them financial and moral support, this black upper class came to symbolize the potentialities of the race, which did not prevent it from 'displaying all of the intraclass conflicts which a highly competitive social and economic system has made characteristic of any group in an insecure position – as this upper class certainly is.'[58]

The members of the upper class were not necessarily the richest people in Bronzeville, but they possessed better-than-average levels of education and were generally recognized as 'leading citizens':

> These physicians and their wives, along with the majority of the dentists, lawyers, and the more prominent businessmen, social workers, schoolteachers, and public administrators, make up the core of Bronzeville's upper class. With family incomes ranging from $3,000 to $50,000 a year, their prestige is based not primarily on income ... but rather on education and professional status, and upon a definite way of life.[59]

Some one thousand families, or about five thousand persons, acknowledged one another as making up the upper class of Black Metropolis. They recognized one another as equals, meaning good business partners, marriage partners, or sincere and durable friends. Social ritual dominated life in the Black Belt and was generally the wives' affair. So-called civic virtues were highly valued: 'Most upper-class men have a life-pattern of activity and interests which combines devotion to a career, a restrained good time, and participation in organized community "uplift" and "racial advancement." At least half of the upper-class wives are either career-women or persons who accept occasional white-collar employment. The others are "the pillars of Society."'[60] The attitude of the upper class toward people below them on the social ladder was marked by ambivalence:

> As people whose standards of behavior approximate those of the white middle class ... [t]hey emphasize their *differentness.* But, as Race Leaders, the upper class must identify itself psychologically with 'The Race,' and The Race includes a lot of people who would never be accepted socially ... The whole orientation of the Negro upper class thus becomes one of trying to speed up the processes by which the lower class can be transformed from a poverty-stricken group, isolated from the general stream of American life, into a counterpart of middle-class America.[61]

The lower class made up a substantial majority of the adult population:

> The Chicago adult world is predominantly a working-class world. Over 65 per cent of the Negro adults earn their bread by manual labor in stockyard and steel mill, in factory and kitchen, where they do the essential digging, sweeping, and serving which make metropolitan life tolerable ...
>
> A part of this working class constitutes the backbone of Bronzeville's 'middle' *social* class, identified by its emphasis on the symbols of 'respectability' and 'success.' The largest part of this working class is in a 'lower' *social* position, however, characterized by less restraint and without a consuming drive for the symbols of higher social prestige.[62]

The physical environment of lower-class Bronzeville was composed of second-hand clothing stores, taverns, cheap movie theaters, storefront churches, commercial dance halls, dilapidated houses, and overcrowded kitchenettes. It was a complex world:

> Basic to it is a large group of disorganized and broken families, whose style of life differs from that of the other social classes, but who are by no means 'criminal' except so far as the children swell the ranks of the delinquents, or the elders occasionally run afoul of the law for minor misdemeanors. Existing side by side with these people is a smaller, more stable group made up of 'church folks' and those families ... who are trying to 'advance themselves.' In close contact with both these groups are the denizens of the underworld – the pimps and prostitutes, the thieves and pickpockets, the dope addicts and reefer smokers, the professional gamblers, cutthroats, and murderers.[63]

Lower-class people participated in very few organized activities apart from the church. The Baptist denomination had the largest number of faithful, most of whom were women: 'Bronzeville lower-class churches are sustained by what the ministers like to call "the faithful few." Probably less than 10,000 people (two-thirds of them women) form the core of Bronzeville's lower-class church life.'[64] Preachers were influential figures ('With over 700 preachers competing for 500 churches, the struggle is always keen')[65] but also, in many cases, came in for criticism of the jarring discrepancies between their virtuous sermons and the private avarice to which many of them were prone. At any rate, religion was far from the center of gravity of lower-class life in Bronzeville. The great majority structured their daily lives around the baser commercial pleasures, most notably the lottery.

As for the middle class, the authors wrote, 'About a third of Bronzeville is in a social position between the "uppers" and the "lowers" – an amorphous sandwich-like middle class. Trying with difficulty to maintain respectability, they are caught between the class above into which they (or at least their children) wish to rise and the group below into which they do not wish to fall.'[66] A small number of middle-class people were white-collar workers, while many performed manual labor. Only a few had the relative security of civil service jobs. What marked this class off from the lower class was neither occupation nor income but 'a pattern of behavior expressed in stable family and associational relationships, in great concern with "front" and "respectability," and in a drive for "getting ahead." All this finds an objective measure in standard of living – the way people spend their money, and in *public behavior*.'[67] Nevertheless, the middle class could itself be subdivided by income, occupation, and education:

> Near the top are the upper middles, oriented toward the upper class and very conscious of the 'big shots' above them. Within the upper middle class are many persons who are anxious to strengthen their ties with the people above them or to so train their children as to push them into that set. At the other end are the people socially and financially much closer to the lower class. Life for these becomes a constant struggle to keep from falling back, and to maintain a middle-class standard of living and conduct against the pressure of the lower-class world.[68]

The dominant tone of middle-class life was characterized by 'getting ahead,' which meant having the right contacts as well as a stable family and sex life. The institutions of greatest importance to this class were the church, recreational clubs of all sorts (athletic, artistic, musical, social), and the more respectable civic organizations. Most middle-class congregations exhibited a combination of lower- and middle-class features in their rites and organizational customs, marrying noisy, enthusiastic singing with more sober ceremonial aspects. But secular organizations were even more central to social organization. Among these, the social clubs – men's, women's, and mixed – were highly valued: 'social clubs express and reinforce the middle-class ideals of restrained public deportment and "respectability."'[69] More than just places to meet, they were places where members of the middle class could consolidate ties of racial solidarity in their efforts to get ahead.

Each class contained what Drake and Cayton called 'shadies' – people working in illicit or otherwise disreputable industries such as the lottery, prostitution, liquor sales, cabarets, and nightclubs. The most socially mobile of the 'shadies,' or 'upper shadies,' consisted of the best-off 'policy kings' and their wives, a few lawyers, and some retired entrepreneurs. Their lives largely revolved around conspicuous consumption (luxury goods, expensive pastimes, travel). They managed to compete with the 'respectable' members of the upper class, but instead of showing them contempt, sought 'to secure prestige in the eyes of this group by assuming many aspects of its behavior pattern, and by attempting to become Race Leaders even to the extent of supporting the organizations of the upper and middle classes, becoming the patrons of the arts, and entering legitimate business.'[70] While the 'real uppers' regarded them askance, the 'shadies' aspired to supplant them:

> What the 'shadies' hope ultimately to do, perhaps, is to displace the older upper class, to outshine it, to incorporate sections of it within their own circles, and to emerge as the *bona fide* upper class. They have the money, but they are keenly aware that there are some things money won't buy. But they know that once they become known as good Race Men, Bronzeville will forget the source of their income and accord them honor and prestige. And in the eyes of many Bronzeville people they are already *the* upper class.[71]

The physical boundaries between these three classes were fluid; all three could and did live side by side in the same neighborhoods. The area inhabited by the Bronzeville lower class was near the Chicago business district (the Loop): 'It is a world of old and decaying homes, and it contains three-fourths of all lower-class churches, and innumerable taverns and poolrooms and policy stations, where people of slender means and education may freely enjoy themselves.'[72] The middle class, however, exhibited a singular distribution: 'Instead of middle-class *areas* Bronzeville tends to have middle-class *buildings* in all areas, or a few middle-class blocks here and there.'[73]

The class system in Bronzeville was structured to allow for both upward and downward social mobility within a general context of social control. The upper class protected its lifestyle while allowing the most tenacious, determined individuals to join it. Individuals and organizations typical of the upper class became models for everyone else to follow as well as incentives to social mobility. A 'New Negro' middle class was gradually being forged from this process of stratification:

> The older Negro middle class was church-centered; not so the 'New Negro.' During his leisure time he sees nothing wrong in enjoying life, in playing cards, dancing, smoking, and drinking. At the same time he often maintains membership in a church, attends its services regularly, and helps to raise money for it; but he takes its theology with a grain of salt or ignores it completely, and puts pressure on his minister to work for 'racial advancement.' He believes in 'Negro business' and admires a Race Man.[74]

But Bronzeville, in this respect, was a very different community from other Chicago ethnic communities: 'The number of such "New Negroes" is set, however, by the iron bands of the Black Ghetto and the pressure of the Job Ceiling. Their future and the future of their children is largely beyond their control.'[75]

GENERALIZING THE EXPERIENCE

In part four, the epilogue to their work, Drake and Cayton developed comparisons between Chicago's black community and those of other U.S. cities: 'The story of the growth of Black Metropolis between the Civil War and the Depression is, with minor variations, the story of the Negro in New York, Detroit, Philadelphia, Pittsburgh, and a number of other cities in America's northeastern and east-central industrial areas.'[76] After the Second World War, a similar statement could be made for Los Angeles, San Francisco, and the other cities of the West Coast. The conclusion was inescapable: 'Negroes in America are becoming a city people, and it is in the cities that the problem of the Negro in American life appears in its sharpest and most dramatic forms. It may be, too, that the cities will be the arena in which the "Negro problem" will be finally settled.'[77] Since this problem was observable in all major cities, why a sociological study of Chicago in particular? What made this city unique?

> A study of Negro life in Chicago is important not only because it is typical of northern urban communities, but also because it involves one of the cities in which change is taking place most rapidly and where in the next decade friction, and even conflict, between capital and labor, Negroes and whites, will probably reach its most intense form, and where a new pattern of race relations is most likely to evolve.[78]

The authors explained black-white relations in Chicago with reference to the concepts of free competition and fixed status:

> Negro-white relations in Midwest Metropolis always involve two contradictory principles of social organization: *free competition* and *fixed status*. In industry, politics, and the use of public services the principle of *free competition* is dominant but is checked and limited by the principle of *fixed status*. In the realm of housing, on the other hand, the principle of *fixed status* predominates but is challenged by the principle of *free competition*. In 'social' affairs the principle of *fixed status* operates almost unchecked.[79]

The black community embraced free competition and rejected fixed status in all areas of economic and political life, including the heavily disputed area of housing. The two principles functioned as basic social processes whose interaction at any given time determined blacks' position within the social structure. Moreover, the inevitable conflicts caused by the operation of the fixed status principle in some areas and the free competition principle in others affected the individual personalities of black people. In a northern city like Chicago, imbued with the characteristically urban ideology of democracy and liberty, blacks inhabited both the white world and their own:

> [A black person] becomes aware of the contradiction between the ideology of democracy which emphasizes free competition and the efforts of the white world to fix his status. While in the South there is little doubt how he is expected to act, in a city like Chicago he is often not at all sure. He may work for a white man and receive recognition for his skill and capabilities, but he must not 'marry the boss's daughter.' He may be awarded a degree from a university, but he cannot expect to practice medicine in a white hos-

> pital, or to be pledged to a white fraternity ... there is no strict rule to guide him.[80]

Whence the existence of a 'marginal personality' among Chicago's blacks: 'What has been termed the marginal personality (and all Negroes in Chicago are to some degree marginal) results from this dual position in society. The fact that in a supposedly democratic society they are allowed to compete for some values but not for others sets up a conflict in most Negroes' minds.'[81] This, the authors contended, was the essence of the 'Negro problem' in Chicago as it had evolved up to the time of the Second World War. This major conflict was not unrelated to the fact that the difficulties of black Americans had developed within the broader perspective of a profound clash of values within American culture, as Myrdal explained in *An American Dilemma*. But the 'Negro problem' in Midwest Metropolis had not found a solution. Perhaps, suggested the authors, none existed:

> It is conceivable that the Negro question – given the moral flabbiness of America – is incapable of solution. Perhaps not all social problems are soluble. Indeed it is only in America that one finds the imperative to assume that all social problems *can* be solved without conflict. To feel that a social problem cannot be solved peacefully is considered almost immoral. Americans are required to appear cheerful and optimistic about a solution, regardless of evidence to the contrary.[82]

For the time being, 'most Chicagoans view[ed] Negro-white relations negatively – solely in terms of preventing a riot.'[83] A repeat of the Chicago riot of 1919 in the postwar period was not impossible. Faced with this prospect, the authors showed their colors as sociopolitical reformers:

> Any attempts to effect a moving equilibrium which will prevent racial outbursts must involve the following processes: (1) the continuous interpretation of the Negro's aspirations and demands to all sections of the white community; (2) the actual progressive relaxation of discrimination and segregation, beginning immediately; (3) the inclusion of Negroes in all postwar plans on an equitable basis; (4) the strengthening of social controls – familial, associational, and governmental – within the Black Belt; (5) the constructive channelizing of the Negro's mass resentment into successful action-patterns of nonviolent protest.[84]

As imperative as it seemed to implement such a plan of action, it was equally necessary to keep the situation in Chicago in larger perspective: 'the problem of Bronzeville and of the American Negro is not an isolated problem. The fate of Black Metropolis is dependent on the fate of Midwest Metropolis, of the country, and of the world. Forces which are in no sense local will in the final analysis determine the movement of this drama of human relations toward hope or tragedy.'[85]

Myrdal, too, as we have seen, viewed the 'Negro problem' as one that could not be studied in isolation, being an integral part of the larger problems characteristic of American civilization. Indeed, the authors argue, a correct analysis of the problem demanded a worldwide perspective:

> The fate of the people of Black Metropolis ... depends not so much on what happens locally as on what happens in America and the world ... The problems that arise on Bronzeville's Forty-seventh Street encircle the globe ... The people of Black Metropolis and of Midwest Metropolis and of all their counterparts are intertwined and interdependent. What happens to one affects all. A blow struck for freedom in Bronzeville finds its echo in Chungking and Moscow, in Paris and Senegal. A victory for Fascism in Midwest Metropolis will sound the knell of doom for the Common Man everywhere.[86]

The bulk of the research leading to the publication of *Black Metropolis* was, of course, done by the authors, but Lloyd Warner played an important role as well, one for which he was explicitly thanked, named codirector of the enterprise, and asked to write a methodological afterword. In it he noted that if Chicago was chosen as the book's subject, it was because of its ability to illustrate the differences between North and South generally. *Black Metropolis,* he contended, broke ground by showing that even though the status of black Americans had improved and would continue to do so, 'the *type* of status relations controlling Negroes and whites remains the same and continues to keep the Negro in an inferior and restricted position. He cannot climb into the higher group although he can climb higher in his own group ... In short, there is still a status system of the caste type.'[87] Warner's note aimed to remind the reader that the central social system of Bronzeville was a combination of class and caste (although the authors almost never used the latter word in the book). Entrenched inequality played a decisive role in determining social status in Chicago.

Cayton and Drake: A Critical Appraisal

A comparison of Cayton's and Drake's sociology with that of Johnson shows the kinship of their respective approaches despite widely distinct areas of research. Insofar as Cayton and Drake borrowed Park and Burgess's ecological model to explain the gradual settlement of Bronzeville as part of a 'natural history' beginning just after emancipation, they applied the same reasoning as did Johnson to southern blacks. Bronzeville was a geographical area in which there coexisted a wide variety of forms of thought and action *adapted* to the restrictive environmental conditions that Chicago placed on black migrants, and these conditions obviously arose from the dominant and discriminatory white culture. Where Johnson used ecological theory to prove that southern blacks were kept sociologically underdeveloped and isolated from the rest of the country, Cayton and Drake used it to shed light on the structural crisis (especially in the area of employment) afflicting the inhabitants of Bronzeville during the Great Depression. They showed the harmful effects of this crisis on the South Side ghetto, particularly the heightened racial discrimination and the institutional disorganization of the community.

To this analysis they added an interpretive tool that set them apart from Johnson: conflict theory, which served to explain the fundamentally unequal class dynamics between white and black Chicagoans. As they saw it, an emancipatory process was at work in the Bronzeville of the 1940s. Its main manifestation was the arduous but undeniable rise of a small middle class in the face of economic discrimination and other environmental constraints. This black middle class was noteworthy, they argued, for symbolically illustrating the progress of the race in the broader society. For the time being, though, its effective impact on history through vertical mobility was severely limited by the intensity of racial conflict. The core of Cayton and Drake's theory of racial conflict between unequal classes consisted of a juxtaposition of the contradictory principles of free competition and fixed status, with the latter predominating and controlling white-black relations in the development of Bronzeville within Midwest Metropolis.

They made no direct reference to Du Bois in this connection, but their interpretive framework greatly resembles a sociological transposition of the concept of 'double consciousness' that he envisaged in his *The Souls of Black Folk* at the turn of the century,[88] or the 'compound identity' thoughtfully described by Todd Gitlin in a recent work.[89] Blacks had to be both what whites expected them to be based on their representations (fixed status) and what they believed themselves to be when away from white influence (free competition).

Apart from Du Bois, the most important influence on Cayton and Drake was surely E. Franklin Frazier.[90] In addition, they borrowed from Myrdal's *American Dilemma* a diagnosis of the 'Negro problem' as a primarily moral problem, as well as his innovative approach to rational social intervention. As such, *Black Metropolis* contained not only normative judgments but also, in the conclusion, explicit prescriptions for action, thus breaking Park's abiding rule of neutrality. Johnson had done the same, in his way, and Frazier would have no great scruples on this point either. In the spirit of Du Bois, this cohort of 'New Negroes,' each within his own area of study, was working to gain scientific legitimacy for an activist sociology.

Finally, the scientific model developed by Cayton and Drake contains a universalist dimension; for, they contended, 'Bronzevilles' could be found in other large U.S. cities, and broad generalizations could be drawn from a systematic comparison of these separate empirical cases. Indeed, enlarging the comparison still further, they saw many parallels with systems of oppression the world over. When, in their lyrical closing paragraphs, they spoke of the need for worldwide solidarity against fascism, they were perhaps ending as they had begun, with homage to Robert Park, for in his last writings the older man had expressed a desire to see black Americans weld their emancipatory struggle to that of all the world's oppressed peoples.

Cox: Innovator and Iconoclast

Oliver Cox (1901–74) was a contemporary of Frazier and Johnson, a member of their scientific generation, but he also lived to see the rise, in the 1960s, of a new phase in the evolution of American black sociology. Working with fierce independence, never collaborating on research, Cox wrote some five books and thirty-five papers. Though initially cast in the mold of the University of Chicago, where he obtained his doctorate, he was subsequently ostracized by both the sociological establishment and the other black sociologists, and spent the bulk of his career at several obscure peripheral institutions. He never worked at Atlanta, Fisk, or Howard, the 'hottest' universities of color. His extensive use of Marxian theory and bibliographical sources made him unique among the black sociologists of his generation.

Cox was born into a middle-class family in Port-of-Spain, Trinidad, and came to the United States at the age of eighteen for a higher education. After obtaining a bachelor of laws from Northwestern University in 1929, he was afflicted with polio, and his severely reduced mobility as a result of the disease forced him to change his career plans. He opted for economics, in which he obtained a master's degree from the University of Chicago in 1932. He then switched to sociology, for reasons that are not entirely clear:

> It may have been that sociology offered a wider framework for analysis and theorizing than did economics; further, if Cox wanted to study race relations, as he ultimately did, there was no better place then [sic] this department of sociology, which had an ongoing teaching and research program and attracted more black graduate students than that of any other academic institution in the United States.[91]

Park had left Chicago by this time, but on Ellsworth Faris's recommendation Cox took preparatory courses for the doctorate, including classes with Ogburn and Blumer. He also became acquainted with Wirth's historical approach to social problems and institutions. The methodology for his thesis, 'Factors Affecting the Marital Status of Negroes in the United States,' supervised by Ogburn, unambiguously betrayed his preference at Chicago: 'Cox was attracted to the quantitative methods emphasized by Ogburn and Samuel Stouffer, rather than the more qualitative case-study method and ecological approach developed by Park, Burgess, Blumer, and their students.'[92]

After completing the doctorate in 1938, Cox looked for an academic job. Despite his qualifications in both economics and sociology, there was no question of his finding one at the country's best white institutions. He had to content himself with the black schools, and was hired by a small Texas college in 1939. Five years later he moved to the Tuskegee Institute in Alabama. In the meantime, he had begun to publish papers in journals such as *Social Forces, American Sociological Review,* and the *Journal of Negro Education*. These early papers find him taking exception to Warner's theory of caste and class as dual determinants of social organization. Since this theory was rapidly gaining credence among social scientists, the result was to establish Cox's reputation as a maverick.

At Tuskegee he taught undergraduate economics and sociology as well as a graduate course on race and culture. Since the institution was primarily a vocational school, few students were interested in graduate work, a source of some frustration to him. In 1948 he published his first book, *Caste, Class and Race: A Study in Social Dynamics*, which cemented his heterodox reputation as a Marxist. It was a dangerous position that could have resulted in costly reprisals. But he did not lose his job, undoubtedly because he 'had many friends, and there was great respect for his ideas – which in any case often seemed more radical than he was. He was personally austere and conservative in his ways, and did not espouse a particular political philosophy publicly.'[93] Unlike Frazier, he was not an activist who carried on sustained relations with the left. He did not attend unruly demonstrations, never riled the crowds from a stage, never sat on the editorial committees of left journals. He was a solitary theoretician who enjoyed working with and arguing over abstract ideas. Presumably, he was too retiring in habits to be perceived as a threat by the authorities, and was left alone for this reason.

Cox left Tuskegee in 1949 for Lincoln University in Missouri, apparently because the institute was no longer supporting his research to his satisfaction. By that time, thanks to good contacts, he had already published more than twenty papers in prestigious journals. He taught at Lincoln until his retirement in 1970, continuing to publish papers (including one in an Indian journal) and books: *The Foundations of Capitalism* (1959), *Capitalism and American Leadership* (1962), and *Capitalism as a System* (1964). In this trilogy, he examined the historical origins and development of the world capitalist system while attempting to lay the foundations for an explanation of the economic and political aspects of race relations. After retirement he accepted a position as visiting professor at Wayne State University, a black institution in Detroit, where he continued to write controversial papers and teach part-time. The posthumous work *Race Relations: Elements and Social Dynamics* (1976), unfinished at the time of his death, was intended as a general theory of race relations. This ambitious work – inspired by the black nationalist currents of the 1960s and 1970s, the civil rights struggle spearheaded by Martin Luther King, Jr, the Black Power movement, and the debate around the putative black underclass – was an ultimately unsatisfactory attempt at a comprehensive theory of race relations.[94]

Why was Cox sidelined by his peers? Obviously, the hysterical anti-communism of the immediate postwar era did not lend itself to a favorable reception for a Marxist sociological analysis of race. But Cox's personality, his fierce intellectual independence verging on intransigence, undoubtedly had much to do with his ostracism as well. For example – and in striking contrast to Johnson and Frazier – he never showed any deference to Robert Park, the standard of reference on race for all American sociologists of his generation; on the contrary, criticism of Park's theories was a public and prominent feature of his writings from his first book onward. Cox paddled against the scientific current and paid the institutional price.

The Published Work

With *Caste, Class and Race*, published as the anticommunist witch hunts reached their paroxysm, Cox boldly took on the conventional ideological wisdom of his day. He clearly indicated his intent to dispense with neutrality from the outset: 'the social scientist ... should be passionately partisan in favor of the welfare of the people and against the interests of the few when they seem to submerge that welfare ... the reason for the existence of the social scientist is that his scientific findings contribute to the betterment of the people's well-being.'[95] Thus it was out of the question for him to cultivate Park's ideal of pure objectivity. To be complete, argued Cox, the social science practitioner must be *engaged*. He or she must work openly for the socioeconomic promotion of the masses and must demystify anything hindering that promotion.

Most importantly, he or she must unmask the arbitrary, debilitating marriage of racism and capitalism, the essentially artificial or factitious link between the two. This phenomenon was not specific to American blacks but had become quasi-universal over the course of time: 'Our hypothesis is that racial exploitation and race prejudice developed among Europeans with the rise of capitalism and nationalism, and that because of the world-wide ramifications of capitalism, all racial antagonisms can be traced to the policies and attitudes of the leading capitalist people, the white people of Europe and North America.'[96] In keeping with this hypothesis, Cox produced a closely argued treatise that may be broken down into three distinct and complementary components, discussed in the following sections.

RACE RELATIONS: A BYPRODUCT OF CLASS CONFLICT UNDER CAPITALISM

Racial prejudice was not observable in older civilizations, where cultural and religious differences determined the social hierarchy. It was only with the birth of a capitalist economy as the outcome of interactions between labor, capital, and profit that race relations had emerged as an integral part of class conflict:

> the fact of crucial significance is that racial exploitation is merely one aspect of the problem of the proletarianization of labor, regardless of the color of the laborer. Hence racial antagonism is essentially political-class conflict. The capitalist exploiter, being opportunistic and practical, will utilize any convenience to keep his labor and other resources freely exploitable. He will devise and employ race prejudice when that becomes convenient.[97]

This Gordian knot was, wrote Cox, perhaps the most important socio-historical construction of modern times. Following his logic, one of today's black Marxists describes the specific case of the United States as follows: 'More than any other modern nation in the world, with the possible exception of South Africa, the United States developed from the beginning, a unique socio-economic structure and a political apparatus which was simultaneously racist, stubbornly capitalist, and committed to a limited form of bourgeois democracy: a racist/capitalist state.'[98]

CLASS: A MULTIFARIOUS CONCEPT

The concept of class was obviously central, but it was also ambiguous, being assigned all sorts of putatively scientific meanings that even Marxists could not agree upon. Three different concepts had to be distinguished: the estate, the social class, and the political class. As to the first:

> The term 'estate' in the English language, like *Stand* in the German and *état* in the French, has a variety of meanings. It may be correctly employed to mean status, degree of rank, position in the world, state, public, property, profession, social class, and so on. But the meaning with which we shall be concerned is that of a social order or stratum of society, and we shall mean by an estate system a society divided into estates.[99]

Estates, Cox contended, formed the strata of static, hierarchical, pre-capitalist social systems in which rank was determined by custom or law. Social classes, however, are unique to modern urbanized societies. Not necessarily organized as hierarchies, they present themselves as heuristic constructs including a status system and allow for loose, shifting boundaries; no class consciousness is exhibited. The contemporary social order is such a system: 'While there may still be vestiges of the social estates in some Western countries, today the individual in cities especially has no estate; he belongs to a social-class system ... Probably the crucial characteristic of a social-class system is individualism.'[100]

Political classes, by contrast with social classes, have clearly demarcated boundaries and are structurally much more specific: 'political and social classes are distinct phenomena. Social classes form a system of co-operating conceptual status entities; political classes, on the other hand, do not constitute a system at all, for they are antagonistic. The political class is a power group which tends to be organized for conflict; the social class is never organized, for it is a concept only.'[101] Class cohesion or solidarity plays an essential role in the organization of political classes: 'These classes ... are not thought of as social-class strata but as organizations arrayed face to face against each other. Furthermore, unlike the social class, the political class seeks to attract members to itself, and group solidarity is highly valued. Social solidarity is not a characteristic of social classes ...'[102]

In short, political classes are organized according to a specific objective, that of class struggle; the dominant class seeks to preserve it while the subordinate class seeks to obtain it. From this standpoint, control of the state is a major object: 'Since the power of the ruling class is always concentrated in the organization of the state, the oppressed class must aim directly against the mechanism of the state. Every class struggle is thus a *political struggle,* which in its objectives aims at the abolition of the existing social order and at the establishment of a new social system.'[103]

Class conflict is not haphazard but follows a rational plan in which class consciousness is prominent.[104] Violence is a practically inevitable outcome of class struggle between antagonistic groups:

> The aim of the attacking class is not co-operation; it does not want law and order, since law and order means perpetuation of the old order ... The end of the attacking class is the vanquishing not only of the old leaders but also of the old system itself – a problem which the ruling class cannot be expected to discuss. Therefore, the struggle for power tends to be involved with a succession of conspiracies, imprisonments, and summatory conflicts, while compromise and appeasement may postpone but not settle the basic antagonism.[105]

THE PREDOMINANCE OF POLITICAL CLASS CONFLICT

What are the essential characteristics of political class conflict in modern Western capitalist societies? Cox began by defining the ruling class: 'In a capitalist society, the economic system, as is well known, is run by businessmen principally for their benefit; free workers are exploited for profit. Roughly, then, businessmen constitute our ruling class ...' The position of power held by the members of this class was a historically recent phenomenon; they first had had to triumph over the landowners who constituted the ruling class in the Middle Ages 'through bitter and bloody struggle ...'[106] Businessmen took power by controlling the means of production and fashioning laws to serve their own interests. The result was inevitably a social system of exploitation based on free enterprise and a state that serves the specific interests of the capitalist class while giving the appearance of benefiting all members of society. Cox defined the relationship between capitalism and the state as follows: 'Capitalism is a social system based upon free enterprise and upon production, by means of large quantities of capital goods, for private profit. The state is set up to administer and to defend this system. The capitalist State is not a spiritual product; its function, from its inception in the medieval town, has always been primarily to secure the interest of a certain class.'[107]

But capitalism is also supported in modern Western society by another class, that of 'free' workers who have become proletarianized.[108] Besides being a particular political class, the proletariat was an inevitable outgrowth of capitalism.[109] Revolutionary change orchestrated by the proletariat was a possible scenario for Western society, but '[i]n modern political-class antagonism nothing needs to be more clearly realized than that the proletariat will never supplant the capitalists peacefully.'[110] Just as the bourgeoisie had differentiated itself from feudalism, a proletarian revolutionary movement would emerge in the struggle against the ruling class. Such a movement would ultimately be provoked by the economic disorder caused by the capitalist system of profit along with any direct repression exercised by the powerful. The revolution would logically be inclined toward socialism, which would have to be won through political class struggle: 'capitalism cannot be transformed into socialism by means of the institutions and values of capitalism ... socialism cannot be instituted on the system of ethics developed by capitalism; consequently, a labor party seeking to gain the power must be prepared to ignore bourgeois concepts of right and wrong and to *force* the bourgeoisie to accept a new system of ethics as a mandate of the people.'[111]

It is unlikely, asserted Cox, that true democracy can take form within contemporary capitalist society. For this to happen, the great mass of people would have to control society's economic resources and also possess the political clout to determine their own destiny. Democracy and capitalism are antagonistic entities, and so the political class struggle between capital and labor is intrinsically a struggle for democracy: 'The problem of racial exploitation, then, will most probably be settled as part of the world proletarian struggle for democracy; every advance of the masses will be an actual or potential advance for the colored people.'[112]

While the emancipation of American blacks demanded class solidarity with other peoples of color around the world, and while this was the best historical trajectory for progressive elimination of segregation, it did not follow that blacks had to sociologically withdraw from the larger society in which they had been embedded for three centuries. On the contrary, the essential goal of class struggle in their particular case was *assimilation*:

> The race problem, then, is primarily the short-run manifestations of opposition between an abiding urge among Negroes to assimilate and a more or less unmodifiable decision among racially articulate, nationalistic whites that they should not ... The solidarity of American Negroes is neither nationalistic nor nativistic. The group strives for neither a forty-ninth state leading to an independent nation nor a back-to-Africa movement; its social drive is toward assimilation.[113]

This, thought Cox, was tantamount to a natural law of white-black equilibrium in the United States, a law that had been well understood by a sagacious French observer: 'Many years ago, when Alexis de Tocqueville said, "The Negroes and the whites must either wholly part or wholly mingle," he saw clearly the only possibilities of a stable racial adjustment; and it is doubtful whether today anyone will seriously question the inevitability of the latter alternative.'[114]

These premises serve to situate Cox's thought along the spectrum of antiestablishment ideologies in the early postwar era, a spectrum ranging from moderate New Deal-style positions (viz. *An American Dilemma*) to various radical visions and more assertive modes of action.

Perhaps predictably, black intellectuals were significantly outnumbered by whites on the right but represented a substantially larger proportion on the left. Left-wingers – whether socialists or outright Communist Party members – were the persons most threatening to the Anglo-American powers that be, for they did not rule out a revolution of the masses to achieve their nationalist goal of black separatism. Though indeed a radical, Cox had no use for separatism; and while he believed in Marxist class struggle, he rather paradoxically refused to follow this belief to where it logically led – to revolution, by violence if necessary, in order to bring a fairer, more just society into being:

> Revolution ... cannot be initiated by Negroes. If it comes at all, it will be under the aegis of the democratic forces of the nation. Basically, therefore, Negroes as a whole are not radical. They tend to be conservative and forgiving, though not resigned. Their policy is that of whittling away at every point the social advantages of the whites. By continual advances, no matter how small, the Negro hopes to achieve his status of complete equality as an American citizen.[115]

Two disparate elements came together in Cox's emancipatory schema. On the one hand, the social fate of blacks was tied to the outcome of the class conflict waged by oppressed workers in all of the world's capitalist societies (the proletariat as a general Marxian concept), from the most rudimentary to the most advanced. However, the culmination of this conflictive process – revolution – was absent. On the other hand, the social fate of blacks depended on another type of emancipation within the American social structure, a gradual, nonviolent acquisition of unblemished citizenship and its concomitant power. It seems that Cox conceived of emancipation as the product of two interacting forces, one exogenous (universal proletarian solidarity), the other endogenous (systematic nonalignment with white racial standards), with no clearly delineated logical relation between them.

LATER WORKS

As noted, Cox also produced a critical review of world capitalism in the form of a trilogy written between 1959 and 1964. *The Foundations of Capitalism*, as the title of the first volume indicates, deals with the historical origins of capitalism as a socioeconomic system. Capitalism's primordial sources, he wrote, are to be found in the cities of medieval and early modern Europe: 'The national cities were the center of capitalist organization and action; they constituted the true home of capitalists. They succeeded in a very high degree to isolate themselves from feudalism and to develop a system of law and economic order.'[116] Of these 'national cities,' Venice deserved special attention. 'Venice the Progenitor,' Cox called it, meaning the progenitor of capitalism, which first flowered there not as a mature system but as a prototype of future capitalist societies. Venice was distinctive for its highly developed governmental structure, its political sovereignty, the preeminence of its merchant class, and the constitutional rights granted to its citizens. A city-state that controlled Mediterranean trade, it pointed the way for other European capitalist entities such as Florence, Genoa, Amsterdam, and Hamburg. None of these, however, succeeded in reproducing the unique Venetian model, wherein 'the capitalist citizen ... emerged as an active, self-seeking, responsible individual with a direct material interest in the state and a passionate allegiance to the country.'[117]

Capitalism and American Leadership, the second volume of the trilogy, situated the United States within Cox's historical account of the rise of capitalism. He posited the country as being in every respect (power, resources, productivity, leadership, etc.) in the vanguard of the world hierarchy of capitalist nations competing to produce and sell goods and services. This hegemony was essentially the result of a historical development, not a *coup de force*: 'The United States may be properly regarded as the lusty child of an already highly developed capitalism.'[118] He refers, of course, to the British experience of the seventeenth and eighteenth centuries, later eclipsed by that of the United States. 'The end of World War II found the country in a position of capitalist leadership more far-reaching and thorough-going than that of any preceding capitalist nation.'[119] Despite this international status, the country was wracked by profound internal tensions whose ethnic and racial aspects were particularly worrisome. A morally suspect class conflict was raging:

> The situation in the South has been such that the master class has been able to limit severely the education and folk participation of Negroes and thus to prolong its paternalism. In that area also the ruling group has succeeded in propagating race prejudice and utilizing it effectively as a retarding cultural force ... The dominant economic class has always been at the motivating center of the spread of racial antagonism.[120]

In their continuing historical resistance to oppression, blacks had been assisted by some whites: 'A fact, apparently not always fully realized, is that some of the most dedicated champions of the extension of full citizenship rights among Negroes have been white individuals and groups.'[121] But this remained insufficient:

> The South, unaided, apparently cannot pull itself out of the system contrived for it by powerful historical forces ... Negroes alone, though they have manifested a willingness to throw off the repressions, could never reform the power structure ... It would probably not be too far amiss to say again that upon the solution of the racial problem in the South and thus in the United States rests the fate of the world as it seeks to adjust to rapidly changing circumstances under American leadership.[122]

What were these circumstances? Cox referred here to a worldwide macrophenomenon – already underway, he believed, in all capitalist countries – consisting of a nonviolent shift from capitalism to socialism: 'Does the change from the capitalist system to one of planned economies necessitate utter deterioration or violent revolution in every global unit of the pre-existing order? There is reason to believe that it does not ... Modern socialism ... is a direct consequence of capitalism. The movement from capitalism to socialism, therefore, may be properly described as a transition.'[123] Again: 'The decline of capitalism thus involves an ineluctable transition rather than a civilizational decay. Modern socialism introduces new institutions but also consciously adopts and redefines capitalist cultural forms to meet the ends of social planning.'[124]

According to Cox, the United Nations had a pivotal role to play in this seismic shift. From its inception in 1946 onward, it had not been guilty of any socioeconomically 'immoral' act. It was therefore institutionally indispensable in the ongoing shift from capitalism to socialism, so as to ensure a peaceful equilibrium of forces in the emerging world configuration: 'In any consideration of the prospects of world-wide societal change, the United Nations must surely be recognized as a pivotal institution. Out of this organization will probably come the governmental system of a universe of cooperating communities which are in instant communication with each other and which have learned to settle minor or major differences without resort to war.'[125] But the United Nations was more than that. It was a supranational power, a social and moral authority that could help bring about the long-sought 'redemption' of the American black minority while preserving the legitimate, uncontested leadership of the United States in the putative new world constellation:

> it seems transparent that the U.N. will become increasingly important as a central agency in the new universal social and economic system. There are major problems ahead that only such a representative organization can properly cope with. Some of these are: the bringing of the backward peoples of Asia and Africa into cultural alignment with the more progressive areas; equitable distribution of the natural resources of the world; migratory rights and obligations of people; *provisions for human rights*, and restraints upon civil and religious authority ...[126]

Capitalism as a System revisits some of the themes of the previous work within a more general, theoretical framework. It lays out a model of the structure and territorial organization of the world capitalist system during the first two decades of the twentieth century, when Great Britain, Germany, and the United States were vying for leadership. Cox began by providing his definition of the structure of such a system: 'We may regard the elementary structure of the capitalist system as constituted of the whole network of its territorial units and their interrelationships. The nations, colonies, and dependent communities thus related tend to form a commercial and power-status gradient with its most energetic and prestigious component at the top.'[127]

This system gradually came into being in thirteenth-century Europe, when it revolved around centers of power in the Mediterranean and the Baltic. With the discovery of the New World, Holland emerged as the leader of a more unified capitalist structure. Later, under the leadership of Great Britain, 'the process of expansion and unification continued until practically the whole world became integrated into an interdependent, rhythmic unity with a single major nucleus. The system apparently reached its highest state of perfection between 1870 and the First World War.'[128]

Of the many criteria potentially useful in classifying the units of the system, 'the extent to which a community has been able to control its foreign commercial relations seems crucial.'[129] Germany, the United States, and Great Britain were the leaders of the capitalist world, the pace-setting nations, and 'no other country could then reasonably aspire to world leadership.'[130] Among these three countries of the capitalist elite, the United States would take the lead:

> Three factors seem to have decided the competitive position of the United States ... its superb capitalist organization, its freedom to employ the most advanced capitalistic techniques, and its vast natural resources. Given comparable forms of capitalist societal organization, the basis of victory in the international struggle for markets had now clearly become supremacy in mass industrial production. The relative size of the domestic market, making it possible to apply capitalist techniques in production to an ever larger number of commodities and continually to perfect existing methods, gave the United States a singular advantage over her competitors.[131]

Furthering his analysis of the factors that had helped the United States achieve this commanding status, Cox was inevitably led to discuss imperialism. Since foreign trade is indispensable to city-states and nation-states seeking to strengthen their position, imperialism is a fundamental structural component of capitalism. Imperialism enabled capitalist countries to acquire trading rights and privileges by gaining sway over local leaders. The latter, in an effort to improve their nation's economic well-being, opened it up to foreign exploitation without awareness of the consequences – for the age-old institution of imperialism is fundamentally one of exploitation: 'The role of imperialism as a fundamental component of the economies of leading capitalist nations has not changed in essence. It serves to maximize and stabilize domestic income at the expense of more or less backward peoples.'[132]

By its very existence, imperialism prevents underdeveloped countries from attaining the economic, political, and cultural standards of the advanced capitalist nations. This backwardness results in perpetual subordination to imperialist trade policies and objectives. Cox's logic ineluctably led him to revisit the theme of political class conflict in the context of world capitalism. Can class conflict generate social change on a global scale? In theory, yes, but in practice it depends on a country's position in the broader capitalist system:

> Class organization is a complex phenomenon, varying with the position of the country in the hierarchy of the capitalist system, as well as with the system's own historical stage of development. Moreover, the chances of success of the opposition class are not the same in different countries and at different times. The struggle necessarily involves not only a particular country, but also the entire system. One may generalize that the higher the nation stands in the system, the greater the consequences of its class struggle upon universal capitalism.[133]

Without disparaging the political and economic progress achieved by workers in the dominant Western nations, Cox contended that their historically privileged status by comparison with the underdeveloped countries would continue to bias them in favor of reform instead of revolution. They would be likely to display antagonism toward the demands of labor organizations in underdeveloped countries. Radical change, if it occurred at all, would come from these latter oppressed people, the real proletarians:

> Proletarian thinkers in the advanced countries have seen perhaps correctly that the workers constitute the real revolutionary force, but the social situation in these countries has not been heretofore conducive to revolution. The revolutionary areas have been the backward countries; hence it seems more accurate to say that the critical proletariat of capitalism resides in the backward countries of the system ... the social situation in the major backward countries is such that revolution is not only indicated, but also feasible and largely profitable. Hence revolutionary solidarity seems far more easily attainable among them.[134]

Cox: A Critical Appraisal

There is really only one approach to taking the measure of Cox's contribution to early black social science: he must be viewed as a thoroughly marginalized opponent of the mainstream approach to race relations. His early switch from economics to sociology adumbrates the iconoclastic path he was to follow: 'I felt that if economics did not explain what I wanted to know; if economics did not explain the coming of the depression; if economics did not help me to understand that great economic change, then I felt I did not need it.'[135] Once immersed in sociology, Cox persistently swam against the current. He discarded the qualitative case study methodology and the ecological approach developed by Park and Burgess in the 1920s and by Blumer and his students afterward, preferring the quantitative statistical methods of Ogburn and Stouffer. With the beginning of his teaching career in the Black Belt of the early 1940s, he made race relations his primary subject, taking as a scientific foil the competing theories of Warner and Park. *Caste, Class and Race* cuttingly rejects the former's idea that American race relations could be likened to caste relations: 'The race-caste assumption is sterile because it has no way of confronting the real dynamics of race relations. It goes happily past the meaning of the racial dichotomy in the

South ...'[136] Elsewhere Cox wrote, 'An astonishing characteristic of this caste school of race relations is its tendency to conceive of itself as being original. It believes not only that it has made a discovery, but also that it has "created" something. It is difficult, however, to determine wherein rests its originality ... the burden of the productions of this school is merely old wine in new bottles, and not infrequently the old ideas have suffered from rehandling.'[137] Similarly, Cox did not mince words in assessing Park's theory of race relations:

> Shorn of its censual and descriptive support, Park's theory of race relations is weak, vacillating, and misleading; and, to the extent that it lends 'scientific' confirmation to the Southern rationalizations of racial exploitation, it is insidious. His teleological approach has diverted him from an examination of specific causal events in the development of modern race antagonism; it has led him inevitably into a hopeless position about 'man's inhumanity to man,' a state of mind that must eventually drive the student into the open arms of the mystic.[138]

Having thus dispensed with the two most fashionable theories, Cox was ready to reconceptualize race relations around the sociological axis of social *stratification*, an approach he believed had been neglected by the humanities. His four works on the subject developed a complete explanatory system along a highly general discursive axis. The first begins with a recapitulation of the general historical principles giving rise to stratification, which Cox believed to be a nearly universal feature of human societies. A major premise first set out here became the key to his entire system of sociology: he contended that a worldwide capitalist dynamic of unequal development had engendered stratification in all human societies. Racial antagonisms were a by-product of this historical megaprocess woven from contradictions and injustices toward the proletariat, that supremely disadvantaged class. Cox's system is pervaded with Marxian concepts and culminates in a historical and structural macrosociology centered on world capitalism, a world-system perspective exhibiting affinities to that of Immanuel Wallerstein today.[139]

Cox relied throughout on an argumentative approach involving deduction from hypotheses, drawing on both history and pure logic. He attempted to conceptualize the black American identity as the expression of a strong form of racial exploitation as well as a particular case of alienation engendered by large industrial capitalism.[140] His model enabled him to make a clean break with the other models of black American sociology that we have examined. It was also a normative model, not only anticipating but prescribing, as the only acceptable historical outcome, the advent of a socialist society through the emancipatory efforts of the proletariat. Such an ideal society would rid itself of exploitation, discrimination, and segregation. Cox's model comprised no inductive or empirical methods. His basic data did not come from his own fieldwork but were taken from the existing black American, Anglo-American, and European literature. The 'field,' in this explanatory model, comprised competing theories of race as well as the classic works of Marxism and European socialism. His willingly abstract stance is reminiscent of that of Talcott Parsons.

As we have seen, the academic world was swift to marginalize him: 'With the publication of *Caste, Class, and Race* in 1948 ... Cox's label of Marxist sociologist was well established, as the many reviewers ideologically opposed to his ideas dismissed his work as "Marxist dogma" and "Communist propaganda," pernicious labels that were to shadow him throughout the rest of his career ...'[141] The whole of postwar American society was in the grip of anticommunist frenzy, and sociologists were no different from others in dismissing Marxist ideas out of hand:

> Marxism in those days was a dirty word. Sociologists generally believed that Marx was naive. The assumption that there are really only two important social classes was seen as a gross oversimplification. They did not blame Marx. Marx wrote in another time. But they thought that it was naive for people in this day to be spouting that out as contemporary sociology. The class system was seen as being much more complex.[142]

In fact, difficulties arose even before *Caste, Class and Race* came off the presses at Doubleday: 'At least one prominent sociologist, Howard Becker, refused to write an introduction to the book because of its putative "Marxist" orientation, and one publisher turned it down because the ideas were reminiscent of "Communism."'[143] To be fair, these perceptions of Cox's work were not entirely without foundation. To take just one example, a statement like the following seems almost designed to provoke such reactions: 'From the standpoint of degrees of development of democracy in the three great nations of the world – the United States, England, and Russia – the United States is probably most backward and Russia farthest advanced.'[144]

But in addition to his Marxism, Cox was criticized for flouting the mainstream Chicago paradigm and, more specifically, the teaching and example of Robert Park, still influential after his death. Whereas Park 'impressed upon his students a view of the scientific role of the sociologist' and 'believed that one's personal status depended on one's ability to gain access to unusual research sites and establish rapport with key respondents,'[145] Cox personified the antithesis of this way of doing science. Consequently, '[his] entire theoretical orientation was considered unscientific, deterministic, polemical, and incapable of addressing the complex problems of a modern industrial society.'[146] Cox was not much given to ad hoc rejoinders to such critiques, except in his occasional lapidary reviews of new works by the disciples of the Chicago orthodoxy. His real riposte is to be found in his books, whose writing he tirelessly pursued as a solitary observer. It was here that he settled scientific scores with his numerous adversaries. Since his ostracism from the sociological community was observed by both whites and blacks, it is not surprising to find texts in which he judges the latter harshly, indeed unfairly, perhaps out of pure envy. Here is another important factor in understanding Cox's relegation to the periphery of the field, not to say his outright exclusion from it. Vindictive by nature, he accused the two most prominent black sociologists, Johnson and Frazier, of having sold out to the Anglo-American academic establishment. Both (especially Frazier) riposted immediately.[147]

Such open rivalry between black American sociologists may seem surprising, but it was surely inevitable in an academic context where the few good positions for black graduates were always awarded with the support of the white academic barons. To be sure, there is more here than can be explained by stiff competition; in Cox's case, a particular conception of radicalism was at issue. Early in his career, he had cut ties with those he perceived, rightly or wrongly, to be puppets manipulated by white intellectual paternalism, and that meant nearly every black sociologist of his generation. At base, his radicalism meant a blanket refusal to compromise with or be duped by such paternalism, to practice a sociology in which value judgments were stifled behind a facade of scientific neutrality. He opted instead for one that situated racial problems within the major structural issues of the world.

Cox's utopia – the social redemption of blacks through international proletarian solidarity under the aegis of the United Nations – was very much out of step with world events at the start of the 1960s, when American radicals reacted vigorously to each new successful decolonization in Africa or elsewhere in the Third World. Castro's Cuban revolution electrified activists of all stripes, breathing new life into their struggle against segregation. Social classes were in open conflict; older American movements (e.g., the NAACP) were being rekindled and newer ones coming to the fore: the Congress of Racial Equality (CORE), the Student Nonviolent Coordinating Committee (SNCC), and the Southern Christian Leadership Conference (SCLS), among others. New life was being injected into political nationalism, and the way was being paved for those who would soon be chanting much more violent and intransigent slogans under the banner of the Black Panthers and Black Power. Alongside all of this, Cox's redemptive solution – even though expressed in Marxian terms – seemed eccentric, even surrealistic in its apparent neglect of the actual confrontation between classes. But Cox the social utopian, I would argue, was not much concerned with current events. He was a disenchanted observer of repeated failures to bring about genuine desegregation of social relations in the United States. He sought to circumvent this impasse by *imagining* a new locus of identity that would come into being over the long term. To this end, he called on black Americans to regard themselves as full-fledged partners in a global human enterprise under the auspices of cooperative socialism. And this, after all, is the purpose of a utopia: to offer the dream of an ideal 'elsewhere' in the absence of a fulfilling 'here.'

The black sheep of his generation of New Negroes, a distant and rather casual intellectual, Cox and his scientific merits were finally recognized several years before his death when, in 1971, he became the first laureate of the Du Bois-Johnson-Frazier Award, created by the handful of African American sociologists working at that time. In view of Cox's open conflict with two of these three men throughout his career, the honor was not lacking in historical irony. Marable sums up his major intellectual contribution as follows: 'Oliver Cromwell Cox was probably the first American sociologist to develop a Marxian analysis of comparative race relations ... limitations to Cox's analysis [included] his underestimation of the role of culture and nationalism within the working class ... But he prepared the field for later works by black social scientists who employed a Marxist method.'[148]

6 Edward Franklin Frazier

The years following Du Bois's withdrawal from sociology in 1910 saw the publication of a number of sociological works cast in the mold of his *Philadelphia Negro*: Mary White Ovington's *Half a Man: The Status of the Negro in New York* (1911), George Edmund Haynes's *The Negro at Work in New York City* (1912), and John Daniels's *In Freedom's Birthplace: A Study of the Boston Negroes* (1914).[1] These three works kept the emerging black sociology vital by extending Du Bois's empirical approach to the blacks of other cities. However, none of these works attempted to expand or renew Du Bois's conceptual framework. Particularly lacking was any attempt to theorize the issues and problems raised by what he had foreseen in 1899 as the great social challenge for black Americans in the next century: daily survival in the country's increasingly crowded cities and in the face of acute conflict with the white majority.

Among the members of the intellectual cohort emerging just after the First World War – the New Negroes – the most keenly aware of this problem of survival was undoubtedly Edward Franklin Frazier. Displaying great admiration for Du Bois and his groundbreaking work,[2] Frazier went on to produce a sociological oeuvre that displayed continuity with his predecessor's enterprise while surpassing some of its limitations, particularly on the plane of theory.

He was born in 1894 to a Baltimore bank employee who followed current events as they related to discrimination against black people and who regularly discussed the subject with his five children. He attended Howard University on a scholarship, graduating in 1916 from its classical education program. Howard was then a vibrant, politicized place where students were drawn into debate around current events. It was there that Frazier developed his socialist leanings and his taste for social and political activism. From 1916 to 1919, while he held teaching positions in Tennessee, Virginia, and Maryland, his interest in the race question and in sociology as a scientific discipline was kindled, and he decided to pursue graduate studies in sociology.[3] Thanks to a second scholarship, in 1919 he attended Clark University in Worcester, Massachusetts, where he wrote a master's thesis, 'New Currents of Thought among the Colored People of America,' under the supervision of Frank Hankins. In intellectual terms, it was a pivotal year for him, one in which he discovered the utility of sociology as a theoretical approach to the analysis of social problems.[4] He moved in 1920 to the New York School of Social Work, taking a year to conduct his first empirical study on black dockworkers. Next he went to Denmark to study rural cooperatives, which gave him the opportunity to make brief visits to France, Great Britain, and Germany. On his return to the United States he accepted a position as instructor of sociology at Atlanta University (Morehouse College) and director of the Atlanta School of Social Work, where he remained for five years. At the instigation of Robert Park, whom he had met during summer courses, he began to study the history and development of the black American family. This interest developed into a doctoral thesis that he pursued starting in 1923 in the form of summer courses at the University of Chicago. Frazier's tenure at Morehouse was cut short when he received death threats from the Ku Klux Klan and other racist groups after publishing a paper, 'The Pathology of Race Prejudice' (1927), in which he drew parallels between race prejudice and mental illness. He left for the University of Chicago to immerse himself in its stimulating social science community.[5]

His thesis on the African American family was completed in 1931 and published the following year as *The Negro Family in Chicago*. In the interim, he was hired as a sociology professor at Fisk University in the department headed by Charles Johnson. He remained there for five years before moving to Howard University to head its sociology department. For an intellectual of color in the 1930s, this was the zenith of one's academic trajectory, for Howard symbolized the color line abruptly dividing the American academic world into two hermetic parts. He stayed there for the rest of his career.[6] Toward the end of his doctorate, with the support of his thesis advisers, he applied for funding from the Social Science Research Council to conduct an in-depth study of the American black family, which culminated in the publication of his second important work, *The Negro Family in the United States* (1939). Publication of the work was delayed largely because of a hiatus that he took at the request of the mayor of New York, Fiorello La Guardia, to head up a commission of inquiry into the Harlem riot of 1935. Frazier spent the whole next year writing the corresponding report.[7]

In the 1940s, Frazier published two other works that helped to secure his scientific reputation. The first, undertaken under the auspices of the American Youth Commission, was *Negro Youth at the Crossways* (1940). The study concerned social factors affecting youth personality development in Washington, D.C., and Louisville, Kentucky. Factors that Frazier considered included family, neighborhood interactions, school, and the church, all within a general framework of class analysis. He examined the socialization of youth and their understanding of the urban living environment. The second work, *The Negro in the United States* (1949), an investigation of the complex and delicate phenomenon of American race relations, offers a substantial overview of his thinking on a subject central to his research. It is 'a comprehensive history organized around the race relations cycle and purporting to show how successive phases of Afro-American history exemplified the stages of the cycle.'[8]

In the 1940s Frazier was busy with many other academic projects, including close collaboration on *An American Dilemma*. He was among the small group of scholars whom Myrdal asked to comment on the research plan, and later (along with Wirth, who had been his professor at Chicago) read and wrote a generally positive critique of the manuscript. For this contribution he was publicly thanked by Myrdal, and the attendant prestige was a factor in his being named president of the American Sociological Association in 1948, the first black scholar to hold that position.[9]

He took a hiatus from Howard from 1951 to 1953 to head up the Applied Social Sciences Division of the United Nations Educational, Scientific, and Cultural Organization (UNESCO) in Paris. The sojourn gave him the opportunity to travel throughout Europe and to Africa and the Middle East. It is evident from Frazier's subsequent writings that this European period catalyzed a broadening of his focus on American race relations to encompass an international perspective. A paper that he gave at a 1954 conference in Honolulu begins, 'Although the problem of Negro-white relations in the United States has many unique features, it is, nevertheless, a phase of a world process.'[10]

The year 1957 saw Frazier publish his last two full-length works, *Black Bourgeoisie* and *Race and Culture Contacts in the Modern World* (for discussion of this latter, see pp. 232–4). *Black Bourgeoisie* focused on the phenomenon of stratification in northern black communities living with the effects of industrialization. The book was the crystallization of thirty years of writing on the subject. It contains an acerbic critique of the black middle class, which Frazier accused of dodging its responsibilities toward the minority group from which it had originated. Not surprisingly, the book provoked its share of controversy among cultivated blacks and in the broader academic world; nevertheless, it won the MacIver Award from the American Sociological Association for the best American work of sociology published in that year. (For further discussion of this work, see pp. 225–30.)

Before he died of cancer in 1962, Frazier had become embittered, his hopefulness giving way to pessimism, even cynicism, as to the likely outcome of race relations in a postwar context that remained as repressive to blacks as ever. This bitterness is evident in the title of his last article, 'The Failure of the Negro Intellectual' (1962). American intellectuals of color, he argued, had seriously defaulted on their critical mission by servilely conforming to the values, ideals, and behavioral models of white Americans.

The African American ideological and political culture of the 1960s had been transformed since his first days as a sociologist; where once the integrationist identity agenda had been regarded as conservative, it was now, in either of its two versions – the nonviolent civil rights movement of Martin Luther King, Jr, or the 'black power' movement of Malcolm X and the Black Panthers – considered radical. Frazier advocated for neither of these assertively integrationist scenarios. It is hard to say whether he grasped how the political landscape had changed, but it is certain that in the new climate of radicalism, his emphasis on worldwide black solidarity and his rediscovery of African cultural heritage were interpreted by his peers as a false identity solution, a retrograde form of escapism at a time when all the major issues had to be decided on the American front. But Frazier, and Du Bois as well, for that matter, had moved on. Their shared pan-Africanism in later life, though an honorable stance, had become an anachronism given what the black communities of New York, Chicago, or Los Angeles were confronting as the civil rights movement unfolded. Frazier's last political gesture, marking both his dissent from American societal trends and his faith in the possibility of world solidarity, was to bequeath his personal library to the revolutionary nationalist leader of Ghana, Kwame Nkrumah. It was officially housed in the University of Ghana library as of 9 July 1963.

The Committed Intellectual

When Frazier first came on the academic scene, the United States was experiencing waves of racist violence. Black urban workers were ruthlessly exploited, yet excluded from the American Federation of Labor and the other unions. From the black urban proletariat there had emerged a new middle class of no great economic significance whose political leanings ranged across the spectrum from the conservative accommodationism of Washington to the interracial liberalism of the NAACP and the National Urban League and on to socialism and nationalism, not to omit the popular versions of pan-Africanism promoted in the early part of the century by Garvey and Du Bois. All of these 'New Negroes,' regardless of affiliation, were confronting a segregationist old guard of whites who buttressed their power with fashionable forms of scientific racism (the most notorious and egregious being eugenics).

By 1920, in his master's thesis, Frazier's radical approach to these trends was evident. The thesis began with a review of the literature produced by what he termed the new radicalism: Du Bois's essays in *Crisis*, Garvey's pan-Africanism, and various critiques of Washington's accommodationist tradition. He identified four factors responsible for the emergence of this current of left-wing thought: the expansion of education, the failure of religious leaders to keep pace with the 'rise of the race,' the failure of the Republican Party to improve the social condition of the masses, and the effects of the war. He proceeded to analyze the content of *Messenger*, a socialist journal published by black intellectuals Chandler Owen and A. Philip Randolph, describing it and the socialist tendency revolving around it as 'the most fundamental and thorough movement ever initiated among Negroes.'[11] Though prudent and impartial in his appraisal of the new radicalism, Frazier concluded with a statement leaving no doubt as to his activist leanings: 'The new spirit which has produced the New Negro bids fair to transform the whole race. America faces a new race that has awakened, and in the realization of its strength has girt its loins to run the race with other men.'[12]

Four years later, in his first article for *Crisis*, he summed up what horrified him the most at this phase of his intellectual development, 'the greatest crime of the age,' as 'the denial of personality to the Negro.'[13] The 1920s (particularly the period 1922–7) saw him display his talents as an ideologue and polemicist with increasing assurance.[14] Since Frazier lived and worked in the Deep South, far from the vibrant northern intellectual circles, he appears to have compensated by devoting a great deal of his activist energies to the question of culture: '[He did] all he could to stay involved in what was happening in New York and other centers of Afro-American activism. He subscribed to the *Crisis, Messenger,* and *New Masses*. He took every opportunity to travel north, where he would inform anybody who would listen about southern atrocities while he learned about the latest political debates and controversies.'[15] His intellectual itinerary thus led him straight into the heart of the celebrated Harlem Renaissance movement.

The Princeton historian Arnold Rampersad gets at the cultural and sociological meaning of this movement when he writes that its members shared a 'growing sense of certainty that black America was on the verge of something like a second Emancipation – this time not by government mandate but by the will and accomplishments of the people, especially the artists and intellectuals.'[16] Similarly, David L. Lewis, in his introduction to an anthology of Harlem Renaissance literature, notes, 'if the factory, campus, office, and corporation were dehumanizing, stultifying, or predatory, the African American, largely excluded because of race from all of the above, was a perfect symbol of cultural innocence and regeneration. He was perceived as an integral, indispensable part of the hoped-for design, somehow destined to aid in the reclamation of a diseased, desiccated civilization.'[17]

Frazier's involvement in this vibrant movement began with an invitation to contribute to *The New Negro*, an anthology that is regarded as the movement's bible.[18] His contribution was a brief analysis of black middle-class culture in Durham, North Carolina. It was his first treatment of what would soon become a theme of predilection. In a moderate, conventionally academic register he presented the rising Durham middle class, or petty bourgeoisie, as an illustration of the progress of the race since the First World War. This class represented, for him, the 'promise of a transformed Negro.' He continued, 'in the composite portrait of the New Negro must be put the sharp and forceful features of the Negro man of business. Through his effort and success, the Negro is becoming an integral part of the business life of America ...'[19]

But Frazier's subsequent writings became increasingly critical of the New Negro movement. In a 1927 paper published in an anthology edited by Charles Johnson (then editor of the left journal *Opportunity*), he positioned himself on the movement's left wing by critiquing certain aspects of the nationalism that it championed. He warned of the dangers of excessive cultural isolationism, which would marginalize the American black community even more than it was already: 'any nationalistic program that made the Negro seek compensations in a barren racial tradition and thereby escape competition with the white man which was an inevitable accompaniment of full participation in American culture, would lead to intellectual, spiritual and material impoverishment ...'[20]

This critique is underpinned conceptually by Frazier's singular representation of culture. For him it was more than an amalgam of symbols and attributes necessary to the self-preservation of the group; it had to be consciously based on values serving the advancement of blacks as individuals and citizens. It had to draw on the founding principles of American democracy – justice, freedom, equality, responsibility, and integrity. In the American context, asserting one's culture necessarily entailed political struggle for civic equality and dignity – either with the whites or against them. Culture was both content and an instrument for collective affirmation.

The following year Frazier wrote a critical assessment of the New Negro movement for the socialist journal *Modern Quarterly* with the deliberately polemical title 'La Bourgeoisie Noire.' He leapt straight into the ring with a question then of great import to black progressives: 'Why does the Negro, the man farthest down in the economic as well as social scale, steadily refuse to ally himself with the radical groups in America?'[21] His answer began by explaining that, contrary to popular belief, the American black community was not monolithic or homogeneous but highly differentiated. More importantly, the social class best positioned to develop a revolutionary consciousness, the industrial workers, accounted for only a small percentage of the black labor force: '*the radical doctrines appeal chiefly to the industrial workers, and the Negro has only begun to enter industry.*'[22] And crucially (but controversially), the emerging class represented by the 'New Negro' was actually conservative, not radical, due to its impregnation with white bourgeois ideals:

> While the New Negro who is expressing himself in art promises in the words of one of his chief exponents not to compete with the white man either politically or economically, the Negro business man seeks the salvation of the race in economic enterprise. In the former case there is either an acceptance of the present system or an ignoring of the economic realities of life. In the case of the latter there is an acceptance of the gospel of economic success.[23]

Frazier's critique was not directed fundamentally against the new black businesspeople ('the Negro business man is winning out, for he is dealing with economic realities')[24] but against the new intellectual bourgeoisie who looked down upon black capitalism while adulating the customs and ideals of white businesspeople. This class of intellectuals, rather incredibly, thought of itself as nationalist and radical:

> There has come upon the stage a group which represents a nationalistic movement. This movement is divorced from any program of economic reconstruction ... It looks askance at the new rising class of black capitalism while it basks in the sun of white capitalism. It enjoys the congenial company of white radicals while shunning association with black radicals. The New Negro Movement functions in the third dimension of culture; but so far it knows nothing of the other two dimensions – Work and Wealth.[25]

Meanwhile, the black capitalist, although more firmly anchored in economic praxis, was busy being a consumer and had no interest in 'tear[ing] down social distinctions and creat[ing] a society of equals.'[26] He was just as alienated in his way as the New Negro:

> in seeking escape from economic subordination, the Negro has generally envisaged himself as a captain of industry. In regard to group efficiency he has shown no concern. For example, a group isolated to the extent of the Negro in America could have developed cooperative enterprises. There has been no attempt in schools or otherwise to teach or encourage this type of economic organization. The ideal of the rich man has been held up to him.[27]

Frazier's radicalism now comprised an analysis of economic and labor issues, but this did not mean that he had renounced his initial concern with culture:

> Many of those who criticize the Negro for selecting certain values out of American life overlook the fact that the primary struggle on his part has been to acquire a culture. In spite of the efforts of those who would have him dig up his African past, the Negro is a stranger to African culture. The manner in which he has taken over the American culture has never been studied in intimate enough detail to make it comprehensible. The educated class among Negroes has been the forerunners [sic] in this process.[28]

The key task for black Americans was to strive for cultural self-determination. No longer Africans, their roots were now in North America and had been since the end of slavery: 'The manner in which Negro slaves were collected in Africa and disposed of after their arrival in this country would make it improbable that their African traditions were preserved.'[29] There was nothing left but for blacks to draw on all their resources and compete with whites; to steadfastly blaze the trail toward full equality and successful integration into American society. Critically important to this process was that they avoid internalizing and thus becoming trapped within white racist representations of themselves, for they would then be incapable of freeing themselves from economic and social domination. The only solution was to develop race consciousness, and this most certainly entailed political struggle: 'The development of racial consciousness among Negroes may help the Negro to place a true valuation upon his personality ... Much of the fanfare about racial consciousness has been forced upon the Negro by white people who are only interested in making the Negro a lower caste ... The present problem of the Negro is to make white Americans recognize him as a citizen.'[30]

The Emergence of a Social Scientist

Frazier selected his first objects of sociological study during the decade in which he came into his own as a polemicist. It was during his early years in Atlanta that his ideas about the black family took shape and he took an interest in the twin processes of differentiation and stratification operating on it.[31] He described this personal trajectory as follows:

> Through the reading of the works of Burgess and Mowrer, I developed the idea that a more fundamental knowledge of the processes of disorganization and reorganization of Negro family life than was in existence at that time should be made available for social workers. Subsequently, when I entered the University of Chicago, I was very much impressed by the ecological approach to the study of social phenomena.[32]

It appears that Frazier the activist was quick to understand that if he rigorously studied the dynamics of the family – the social structure most vital to the black community – he would acquire a powerful asset in his fight for racial equality. He put this realization into practice most impressively with *The Negro Family in Chicago* (1932) and *The Negro*

Family in the United States (1939). The first of these works stays close to the Chicago School's methodological template, skillfully combining considerations of human ecology with the use of personal documents. The work's originality also stems from the way it links black family life to class differentiation in the urban black population. More generally, it sheds light on blacks' ways of adapting to their harsh living conditions in the fast-growing cities.

Human ecology, in 1932, was essentially the study of human populations with reference to Burgess's model of concentric geographical zones defined according to socioeconomic criteria, which he and others had applied to the city of Chicago. In *The Negro Family in Chicago,* Frazier used a modified version of this method that he had developed in an earlier paper.[33] The technique essentially consisted in a regrouping of the occupational designations used in the 1920 census into eight new categories. Frazier argued that this approach was more objective and precise and that it could highlight 'the variations in differentiation of the black population between cities ... and relate these to "the extent that the Negro participated in the whole community," which was linked to the status of racial segregation in these cities.'[34] Thus, he conceived of urban blacks not as a homogeneous community but as a stratified one. By compiling and comparing statistics on Chicago's different residential neighborhoods, Frazier determined that the geographical distribution of black population strata behaved as predicted by the human ecology model, being no different in this from any other ethnic group. The zones closest to downtown displayed the highest rates of disorganization and demoralization. They were inhabited by many single-parent families headed by women; low rates of schooling put many children on the road to delinquency. The number of stable families, as measured by variables such as long-lasting marriages, land ownership, participation in religious activities, and quality schools, increased along a gradient from downtown to the suburbs. The farthest outlying suburbs had the largest concentrations of upper-class blacks and the highest levels of schooling among them. All in all, it was a major finding that

> [t]he expansion of the Negro community was not a unique phenomenon, but was similar to the movements of other racial and immigrant groups in the city of Chicago. Like other racial and cultural groups of a low economic status, Negroes at first acquired a foothold in and near the center of the city where less resistance is offered to the invasion of alien elements ...

> As the city expanded, the segregation of the Negro population was the result of the general process of segregation of cultural and racial groups, which is an aspect of urban growth.[35]

Burgess had previously associated the concepts of disorganization and organization with that of growth; these concepts '[cooperated] in a moving equilibrium of social order toward an end vaguely or definitely regarded as progressive.'[36] Frazier echoed this observation when he asserted that disorganization – extremely common among blacks – should not be seen as pathological but rather as part of a larger process of 'civilization' and progress:

> The widespread disorganization of Negro family life must be regarded as an aspect of the civilizational process in the Negro group. It is not merely a pathological phenomenon ... As the Negro is brought into contact with a larger world through increasing communication and mobility, disorganization is a natural result ... In the large cities of the North, where competition is severe and family life in some sections of the population tends to disappear, a part of the population will die out. There will be a quantitative loss even among those who succeed in acquiring a relatively high status. This seems to be the inevitable price which the Negro must pay for civilization.[37]

In Frazier's eyes, the best elements of the black community corresponded to the people who were the most organized, cultivated, and civilized as well as the most prosperous. Social differentiation was a necessary condition for the progress of black Americans. Previously a uniform mass of slaves, blacks had gradually distinguished themselves through contact with white civilization and taken advantage of various possibilities for cultural enrichment and collective evolution. Free blacks and immigrants living in northern cities had served as role models for the newly arrived migrants. Frazier was struck by the severe social and moral disorganization of these migrants to downtown Chicago as compared with the high level of social stability and culture among mulattoes living in the outlying residential areas, most of them professionals and businesspeople. These reorganized families, he observed, were increasingly well integrated into white society, adopting the behavioral norms of the Anglo-American middle class. These same norms helped them keep their distance from the newcomers, with whom they refused to identify because of their socioeconomic success.

Frazier devoted an early chapter of the book to the history of the black family. In it, he explained the peculiarities of family behavior with reference to the radically different experiences of slavery and emancipation. During slavery, the only familial behavior possible was that of submission, since everything depended on the authority and control exercised by the white masters. It was impossible, in such a context, to innovate in any area. He termed this type of family the 'natural' family. After emancipation, the traditional normative controls faded and family behaviors changed accordingly. Frazier considered changes among ancestrally free blacks, many of them mulattoes, who had managed, from one generation to the next, a 'complete assimilation of the highest ideals of family life,'[38] and among freed slaves who stayed on the plantations, their family life coming to be based on 'sympathetic relationships'[39] induced by the poverty of their living environment. In this particular setting, and more visibly among the land-owning minority, the natural family gave way to a new type, the 'institutional' family, based on a legally sanctioned marital union reinforced by land ownership and tradition and characterized by greater paternal authority and conformity to the moral norms of the larger society. The institutional family undoubtedly favored blacks' integration into the majority culture. But the Great Migration subjected the institutional family to extraordinary stresses because of the complexity of the forces operating in the new environment. The family had to reinvent its stability.

In the years following *The Negro Family in Chicago*, Frazier published two short works devoted to the family as an object of sociological study. 'The Impact of Urban Civilization upon Negro Family Life' summarized his knowledge on black family life three years in advance of the publication of his masterwork, *The Negro Family in the United States*, the first book to win him widespread acclaim in American sociological circles. *The Free Negro Family* was part of a comprehensive study of the Negro family that Frazier conducted at Fisk University concurrently with an extension of his doctoral research for the University of Chicago. It was essentially a statistical compilation augmented by observations on the origins, expansion, and population distribution of free blacks before the Civil War. The aim of the work was to explore an observation made in *The Negro Family in Chicago* as well as to further the larger study on which Frazier had embarked:

> As a result of this approach to the study of the problem it was shown among other things that those families with a heritage of traditions and

> economic competency extending back before the Civil War have constantly played a stabilizing role in the population as the Negro has been compelled to make adjustments to our changing civilization. It is the purpose of the present study to show in a more thoroughgoing fashion how these families originated and became the vanguard in the cultural and economic progress of the race.[40]

Toward a More Radical Approach

In between *The Negro Family in Chicago* and *The Negro Family in the United States*, Frazier's thinking underwent a major ideological shift. In the early 1930s, his rhetoric was becoming sharper and more critical. Much more of his attention was devoted to economic considerations, which took their place alongside the political and cultural considerations of the previous decade. Two phenomena go far in explaining this transformation: the onset of the Depression and the rise of the Communist Party. Given the immensity of the crisis, it is no surprise to find Frazier more sensitive to the economic conjuncture and its impact on black Americans. A 1935 text shows that he had absorbed the influence of class analysis by then, and tended to reinterpret the history of race relations through the prism of economic exploitation:

> The introduction of the Negro into America was due to the economic expansion of Europe ... The fate of Negro slavery was determined by economic forces ... The economic dependence of the Negro in the South furnishes the key to the understanding of his status ... In the urban environment [the Negro] is showing signs of understanding the struggle for power between the proletariat and the owning classes, and is beginning to cooperate with white workers in this struggle which offers the only hope of his complete emancipation.[41]

Frazier's interaction with the Communist Party calls for comment. Founded in 1919, the U.S. Communist Party initially had very little contact with progressive black intellectuals and little interest in their political concerns. That changed in the 1930s, when the party's fortunes rose and it formally committed itself to the struggle for civil rights and racial equality. The figures are eloquent: the number of black party members rose from fewer than 200 (of a total of 14,000) in 1928 to more than 1,000 in 1930, 2,700 in 1935, and more than 5,000 in 1939.[42] It was to be expected that Frazier would discover affinities with the party on various issues, for most progressive intellectuals, white or black, were associated with it in one way or another.[43] From time to time he participated in party-sponsored panels or events; however, he never joined the party, and much less was he interested in becoming a party official or loyal disciple.[44]

Frazier's association with the communists led him to question (without ever abandoning) his socialist leanings and to become more active as a left-wing militant. In 1934 he allowed Nancy Cunard, a well-known British supporter of the U.S. Communist Party, to reprint 'The Pathology of Race Prejudice' in her anthology *Negro*. In 1935 Frazier joined the editorial committee of a new journal, *Race*, and coauthored the following remarks:

> The special system of discrimination against the Negro in America is so deeply rooted in the very foundations of the present social order and the vested interests of dominant capitalism that there is no complete 'solution' of this basic problem of American life short of a fundamental reconstruction of society, a social upheaval that will plow up our institutions to their very roots and substitute a socialist order for the present capitalist imperialist order.[45]

In 1936, he joined the editorial staff of the Marxist-aligned quarterly *Science and Society*, which brought together a broad collection of independent radicals, socialists, and communists. The next year he gave the keynote address at the May Day rally in Washington organized by the Communist Party. He spoke of the necessity of creating a workers' movement capable of uniting black and white workers in a single struggle.

The decade was the most politically active in Frazier's life, alongside his full-time work as a field researcher and director of the Howard University sociology department. To all appearances, American society was moving toward his political ideal; a solution to racism would soon be found by black workers in solidarity with white workers, in the form of a qualitative revolution in social relations. The solution would be domestic – that is, accomplished within the bounds of the American democracy with reference to its core founding values.

The Negro Family in the United States (1939) was cast in the mold of this unabashedly optimistic social vision. In its preface, Frazier clearly stated the void that the study was intended to fill: 'Thirty-one years ago a study of the American Negro family appeared in a pioneer series of monographs devoted to the application of objective methods to the study of the Negro's adjustment to modern civilization. Since then the Negro family as a subject of serious sociological interest has been neglected.'[46] Burgess, who wrote a second preface as the book's editor, praised it in the following terms: 'It is, in fact, the most valuable contribution to the literature on the family since the publication, twenty years ago, of *The Polish Peasant in Europe and America* by W.I. Thomas and Florian Znaniecki. For it is a basic study of the family in its two chief aspects – as a natural human association and as a social institution subjected to the severest stresses and strains of social change.'[47]

In this voluminous work, Frazier offers a comprehensive synthesis, in five chapters, of the state of knowledge on the black American family. The first part of the book reprises and extends *The Negro Family in Chicago* by examining the history of the black family up to the time of its arrival in the cities. The second part considers the effects of the Great Migration on family organization. Frazier used family biographies, local surveys, and various kinds of accounts to build a composite portrait of the black family, his interest being primarily to describe the general facts about these families rather than to systematically investigate their diversity. His key observation was that, after black people were uprooted from Africa and stripped of their cultural heritage, they essentially had to rebuild their family organization from the ground up. The form that the black family took at each stage of its evolution corresponded to the radical changes in environmental conditions that black Americans had to traverse – from slavery to sharecropping and on to the urban tumult of the Great Migration. During slavery, black people had stanched their loneliness and isolation with 'feelings of tenderness and sympathy toward those who shared [their] bondage.'[48] But blacks had also copied their masters' ideas and morals, and their marital and family relations reflected the stages of this gradual process. When material interests and economic forces began to destabilize these family ties after emancipation, resulting in increased marital instability, unwed parenthood, and higher rates of divorce, child abandonment, poverty, crime, and delinquency, family behavior in the southern plantations began to depart from Anglo-Saxon normative models. Matriarchy emerged as the dominant family structure, providing a minimum of emotional and material stability for childrearing under such difficult circumstances.

Frazier adhered to the Chicago School in elucidating the subjective dimensions of family behavior, but he also systematically highlighted environmental factors – the American context itself – as explanatory components of this new 'atypical' behavior. In so doing, he sought to refute prior interpretations whereby this behavior was considered a product of degeneracy and ascribed to inherent racial traits or cultural backwardness. The main environmental factors that he adduced were slavery and its damaging effects, continuously enforced social isolation, and the disorganizing influence of urban life for which black migrants were not suitably prepared, along with the prejudice and discrimination that made this last phase tremendously more difficult.

In the part of the book focusing on the consequences of the Great Migration for family organization, Frazier moved briskly to one of his favorite themes: the social differentiation that had emerged as a result of greater economic opportunities:

> One of the most important consequences of the urbanization of the Negro has been the rapid occupational differentiation of the population. A Negro middle class has come into existence as the result of new opportunities and greater freedom as well as the new demands of the awakened Negro communities for all kinds of services. This change in the structure of Negro life has been rapid and has not had time to solidify.[49]

The black middle class exhibited significant differences from the white middle class in terms of its lifestyle and consumption habits. A great many middle-class blacks actually favored segregation, believing that its disappearance would jeopardize their status. But for Frazier, the advancement of the middle class depended on the effacement of segregation, and more specifically on an increase in the number of salaried workers who assimilated with their white counterparts as racial barriers broke down:

> The process of assimilation and acculturation in a highly mobile and urbanized society will proceed on a different basis from that in the past. There are evidences at present that in the urban environment, where caste prescriptions lose their force, Negroes and whites in the same occupational classes are being drawn into closer association than in the past. Such associations, to be sure, are facilitating the assimilation of only the more formal aspects of white civilization; but there are signs that intermarriage in the future will bring about a fundamental type of assimilation. But, in the final analysis, the process of assimilation and acculturation will be limited by the extent to which the Negro becomes integrated into the eco-

> nomic organization and participates in the life of the community. The gains in civilization which result from participation in the white world will in the future as in the past be transmitted to future generations through the family.[50]

In addition to the middle class, a black lower class had emerged in the cities of the late nineteenth century: 'The most significant element in the new social structure of Negro life is the black industrial proletariat that has been emerging since the Negro was introduced into Western civilization. Its position in industry in the North was insecure and of small consequence until, with the cessation of foreign immigration during the World War, it became a permanent part of the industrial proletariat.'[51]

To summarize, the interwar period saw the rise among American blacks of a two-class system, which, in its morphology and internal dynamics, was intimately bound up with the fate of the family institution. Frazier drew eclectically upon history, social psychology, sociology, and elements of African American genealogy in his explanation of how the lower class, as it diverged from the ideals and values of the middle class and began to identify with the industrial workers, adopted the latter's typical family behaviors and thought patterns. As well, the concepts of class and class conflict were now informing his approach to race relations in a context of ongoing structural transformation in American society. Overall, he was still adhering to Park's perspective, but his two works of the 1930s showed him beginning to assert his originality.

The outbreak of the Second World War temporarily halted all movement toward any sort of social utopia, but Myrdal's appearance on the scene brought new hope. With the revolution of which he dreamed a distant prospect, Frazier saw Myrdal's approach as a palatable substitute that set aside laissez-faire for deliberate state and legal intervention as a means of palliating the injustices caused by racial segregation. Frazier's radicalism was further tempered by the collapse of the Communist Party and other left organizations after the war. Disillusioned, he set his sights overseas. 'A Negro Looks at the Soviet Union,' a paper given in 1943 on a panel in New York to commemorate the tenth anniversary of diplomatic relations between the United States and the Soviet Union ('The Soviet Union: A Family of Nations in the War'), outlines this shift in his thinking. Calling the Soviet Union a 'country free of racial prejudice,' he went on to state, 'Today once more Negroes are called upon to participate in a struggle in which the issue between democracy and the equality of races, on the one hand, and autocracy and the doctrine of racial inequality, on the other, is more clearly drawn. As a result of this struggle, their own battle for freedom and equality can no longer be an isolated domestic problem.'[52]

While cultivating what must be seen as a passionate commitment to internationalism, Frazier continued his domestic political activism in various left movements, eliciting harassment even before the onset of the McCarthy era: 'Frazier ... was identified by the House Un-American Activities Committee as working with various "Communist front" organizations as early as 1944, and he continued to be redbaited until his death in 1962.'[53] Intellectually, he ranged widely and rather confusingly, taking up all manner of ideas as long as they served the cause of racial equality.[54] It is clear that several different Fraziers – the political activist, the left essayist, the academic, the university administrator – coexisted and wrangled within the same man, making him a complex, ambivalent, and often contradictory individual. Unlike Johnson and others, he did not speak with a single, consistent, conceptual voice.

Topping the list of issues that catalyzed Frazier's radical shift was that of institutional racism. Early in his career, he had showed himself to be an astute observer of the racist machine and its effects on black communities, and his interest in this issue was not merely academic.[55] While the interwar period found him constantly reacting to a political and institutional climate in which the dominant ideas on black Americans ranged from arrogant defense of Anglo-Saxon superiority to charitable paternalism, the publication of *An American Dilemma* raised his hopes that segregation would not withstand a legal onslaught, and he went so far as to predict the advent of a 'common humanity' bringing blacks and whites together.[56]

His magnum opus, *The Negro in the United States* (1949), is a wide-ranging and comprehensive work that seeks to demonstrate how the successive phases of black American history obeyed Park's race relations cycle theory.[57] Despite the radicalization undergone by the author in the postwar years, his book makes no particular ideological plea, still striving for the reigning academic standards of neutrality and detachment. What made it stand out was his emphasis on the historicization of black history: 'The blend of historical events with sociological theory enabled Frazier to substitute specific events and tendencies as causal agents in place of the ahistorical generalizations used by other Chicago scholars. Thus instead of attributing race prejudice to biological or psychological factors he located it in the peculiar circumstances of American race relations as they had developed historically.'[58]

Frazier's essential concern was that of acculturation, which he defined as acquisition by blacks of white cultural characteristics. He viewed African Americans as being collectively favorable to assimilation: 'the Negro minority belongs among the assimilationist rather than the pluralistic, secessionist or militant minorities ... In his individual behavior as well as in his organized forms of social life he attempts to approximate as closely as possible the dominant American pattern. Whenever an opportunity for participation in American culture is afforded he readily seizes it ...'[59]

Historically, the cyclical process had begun with the first contacts between blacks and whites within the institution of slavery. With time, the plantations had become a channel through which white culture was transmitted to blacks. Masters and slaves came to be part of a single social organization: 'The planter's authority often assumed a quasi-patriarchal character and the lives of slaves and masters became intertwined in a web of social relationships. Under such conditions the social organization of the plantation provided the channel by which the culture of the whites was mediated to the blacks.'[60] Sparingly applying Park's theory to slavery, Frazier interpreted Reconstruction with reference to the concepts of conflict and accommodation. The conflicts of Reconstruction had largely consisted of class conflicts; accommodation had taken place within a caste system that limited, though it did not totally eliminate, conflicts between two groups with discrepant interests. The most important sociological phenomenon in the cycle, however, had been the Great Migration: 'From 1900 to 1940 the proportion of whites living in urban areas increased from 43 per cent to 57.8 per cent. During this same period the proportion of the Negro population resident in urban areas increased from 22.7 per cent to 48.2 per cent. Between 1900 and 1930, about two and a quarter million Negroes left the farms and small villages of the South for the cities.'[61]

Within his overall adherence to the ideas of Burgess and Park, Frazier highlighted the role played by economic forces in the ecological distribution of the urban black population. Though racial prejudice had certainly influenced this distribution, the locations of black neighborhoods in northern cities had largely been determined by the same overarching social and economic forces acting on other ethnic groups. As in all his works, he gave pride of place to social class stratification within the black community. He provided no formal definition of social class but presented as follows the development of a system of stratification among black Americans:

> The roots of the social and economic stratification of the Negro population go back to the period of slavery. Under the influence of slavery as a social institution, significant social distinctions appeared among the slaves. These social distinctions were related to the r[o]le of the slaves in the social and economic organization of the plantation. There was the distinction, first, between those who served in the house and those who labored in the fields ... Then, there was a division of labor on the plantation which provided an outlet for individual talent and skill ... Other distinctions came into existence ... These various types of social distinctions created a class structure in the Negro community that existed until the mass migrations during and following World War I. Then as the result of urbanization, which accelerated the operational differentiation of the Negro population, the class structure of the Negro community became more complex and some of the older social distinctions lost their significance.[62]

The new social class system appearing after the First World War was founded on the economic criteria of occupation and income rather than on cultural or social criteria. The system was composed of only two classes: a small middle class comprising professionals and businesspeople and a large lower class composed of the poor and illiterate. In the absence of an authentic black upper class, the newly arrived middle class imitated the customs and lifestyles of the white upper class without in any way constituting a sociological equivalent. The closest Frazier got to a formal definition of the middle class was as follows:

> The term 'middle class' as used here refers to the class having an intermediate status between the upper and lower classes in the Negro community. Only a relatively small upper layer of this class is 'middle class' in the general American meaning of the term. Moreover, 'middle class' as used here is essentially a social class though occupation and income play some part in determining its place in the class structure of the Negro community.[63]

It must be admitted that, in sociological terms, Frazier's conception of social classes in general, and the middle class in particular, was hazy, involving a rather unorthodox version of the classical Marxian approach to economic and political relations of production.[64] This haziness let the author combine into one middle class a wide array of trades and professions: preachers, entrepreneurs, intellectuals, lawyers, doctors, office employees, specialized workers, foremen, and so forth. The conjunction of these different job categories illustrated the fact that blacks were increasingly taking their place in all walks of life, an enormous step forward in historical terms. The negative aspect of this trend was that too many of these individuals became complacent with their success, forgetting that they accounted for a very small percentage of a large group of people who continued to suffer from intense racial discrimination. Ideally, the black middle class should have been working to create a society of equals within the larger American whole, but in fact it was being drawn off into consumerism and luxury spending, thus shirking its most important social responsibility. Frazier would have much more to say on this delicate and complex subject as his career went on.

The book concludes with some thoughts on the prospects for black integration into American society:

> The integration of the Negro into American society will be determined largely by the reorganization of American life in relation to a new world organization. The so-called 'Negro Problem' is no longer a southern problem or even an exclusively domestic problem ... The integration of the Negro into American society must be viewed in relation to the reorganization of American life which has been necessitated by the new world into which the United States must fit if it is to survive ... the integration of the Negro into American society becomes from the standpoint of the Americans themselves a question of a new organization of American life in relation to certain principles and values which are becoming dominant in the world today. These principles and values were implicit in the American system, from the beginning. There was the assumed basis of a 'common humanity' and the 'absence of fundamental racial characteristics.'[65]

In his conclusion, Frazier considered the important question of absorption into the white majority culture – assimilation. He still believed in eventual black assimilation (this belief waned in subsequent years) but hesitated to use the term, for, like Park before him, he was uncertain as to its scientific meaning, and he opted instead for 'integration' and 'acculturation.' A section titled 'Integration: From Secondary to Primary Group Contacts' describes the prospects for blacks' integration into American public life – the opportunities for them to hold socioeconomically advantageous positions. Frazier was evidently only too aware of the political sensitivity of the question and, accordingly, opted for more readily accepted and neutral terminology. (The major theme of assimilation in the works of the African American sociologists is the subject of further discussion in part three.)

The perhaps overly ingenuous optimism of the book's final pages, its expression of hope in a 'common humanity,' was dashed by the savage McCarthyist repression of the 1950s and, in its wake, the recrudescence of racist violence. Frazier's two-year stint in Paris with UNESCO resulted in a solidification of his cultural internationalism; he returned to the United States with his radicalism definitively transformed by the experience. He now considered racism and its concomitant issues and problems from a strictly internationalist perspective. Simultaneously, and inevitably, he had become increasingly detached from the long-held goal of comprehensive race relations reform within the United States in isolation from the rest of the world. He had, more generally, increasingly lost interest in academia and sociology. In his polemical work *Black Bourgeoisie* (1957), he turned his attention to his long-standing interest in the theme of power in its political and intellectual dimensions. *Race and Culture Contacts in the Modern World,* published the same year, was more scientific and derived much of its inspiration from a comparative approach. Together, the two books find Frazier eloquently articulating his disenchantment and reenchantment.

The Poverty and Greatness of the Black Middle Class

In order to grasp the critical impact of *Black Bourgeoisie* in its time, it is useful to trace the evolution of Frazier's thinking on the subject up to the time of its publication. The theme of power had been central to his works from the very first. It was closely tied to his interest in the stratification observable in the black community, a concern inherited from Du Bois. The middle class, in particular, was the focus of his ideological struggle throughout his career, and his analysis evolved in step with the general political situation of the United States. He sought to understand the complex relationships between this class and the other black and white social classes. Frazier first noted the rise of a dynamic and enterprising middle class in a few articles published in *Opportunity, The New Negro,* and *Modern Quarterly.* His first critical, though not overtly polemical paper devoted specifically to the subject appeared in 1928; here he termed this new class, with barely dissimulated irony, the 'black bourgeoisie.' The Atlanta experience had taught him that survival in academia meant expressing dissidence in subtle ways.[66]

Frazier berated this class for turning its back on the masses, defaulting on its duty to promote the status of all blacks, and having no greater ambition than to mimic the attitudes and behaviors of the white middle class. Who would fight for justice and equality if not the rising middle class, more educated and hence, presumably, aware of the deep roots of institutional racism so inimical to everyone's interests? With the greater ideological leeway afforded to radical thinkers and activists between the onset of the Depression and the McCarthyist clampdown of the 1950s,[67] Frazier's critique of the middle class intensified and its scope broadened. He had always kept a certain distance from the New Negroes' brand of cultural nationalism, of which the Harlem Renaissance was the aesthetic expression. Rightly or wrongly, he regarded it as a mythology whose effect was to distract blacks from the real challenge facing their community: that of organizing industrial workers into an international movement to counter white supremacy. Cultural nationalism remained fashionable in the 1930s, and Frazier focused his attacks on its spokespeople, most notably Du Bois, whom he accused of seeking to become a sort of king of the ghetto; other 'opportunists' and 'arrivistes' also came in for his criticism.[68] Late in the decade, the upward mobility of black businesspeople and the black middle class in general had tailed off sharply. Frazier rebuked them for embracing 'racial chauvinism' and entertaining the pipe dream of a 'black Utopia where the black middle class could exploit the black workers without white competition.'[69]

After 1945, upward mobility resumed, and black lawyers, politicians, realtors, and others took their place alongside the ministers and teachers who had always formed the core of the black middle class. Frazier accused these individuals of profiting obscenely from the existing system of segregation; of securing acquired rights from which they derived various social and material benefits: 'only certain elements in the Negro community have a vested interest in segregation ... It is the Negro professional, the business man, and to a less extent, the white collar worker who profit from segregation. These groups in the Negro population enjoy certain advantages because they do not have to compete with whites.'[70]

But their efforts were vain, a depressing historical sidelight, as he would take great pains to point out in his most controversial work. *Black Bourgeoisie* was first published in French and remains a product of the European phase of his career. On its American publication two years later, it left few indifferent.[71] Frazier the polemicist used the opportunity to settle scores with the black businesspeople who thought of themselves as race heroes but actually held a marginal position in the national economy.[72] Previously, in 1955, he had curtly denounced what he saw as a trap into which the postwar black middle class had fallen:

> The attempt of the middle class Negro to escape from the realities of his position in American life is really an attempt to escape from himself ... the middle class Negro pretends that he is proud of being a Negro while rejecting everything that identifies him with Negroes. He pretends that he is a leader of Negroes when he has no sense of responsibility to the Negro masses and exploits them whenever an opportunity offers itself.[73]

Black Bourgeoisie presented no new analytical or interpretive elements in Frazier's treatment of his favorite themes – the gentrification of the black middle class, its divorce from the masses, its utter rejection of political activism – but his style had become much more acerbic and polemical. Here is his description of the political ineptitude of a class that saw itself as an example of historic success:

> Since the black bourgeoisie is composed chiefly of white-collar workers and since its small business enterprises are insignificant in the American economy, the black bourgeoisie wields no political power as a class in American society ... In the political life of the American society the Negro political leaders, who have always had a middle-class outlook, follow an opportunistic policy. They attempt to accommodate the demands of Negroes for better economic and social conditions to their personal interests which are tied up with the political machines, which in turn are geared to the interests of the white propertied classes.[74]

The second part of the book, titled 'The World of Make-Believe,' denounced the tenacious but, according to Frazier, completely spurious myth of a black business world: 'The myth of Negro business thrives despite the fact that Negro businessmen can best be described as a "lumpen-bourgeoisie." The myth of Negro business is fed by the false notions and values that are current in the isolated social world of the Negro, a world dominated by the views and mental outlook of the black bourgeoisie.'[75] Striving to demystify these phenomena, Frazier kept up his mordant attack until the very last pages:

> the black bourgeoisie have shown no interest in the 'liberation' of Negroes except as it affected their own status or acceptance by the white community ... Because of its struggle to gain acceptance by whites, the black bourgeoisie has failed to play the role of a responsible elite in the Negro community ... When the opportunity has been present, the black bourgeoisie has exploited the Negro masses as ruthlessly as have whites ... The single factor that has dominated the mental outlook of the black bourgeoisie has been its obsession with the struggle for status. The struggle for status has expressed itself mainly in the emphasis upon 'social' life or 'society' ... Middle-class Negroes who have made real contributions in science and art have had to escape from the influence of the 'social' life of the black bourgeoisie ... The emphasis upon 'social' life or 'society' is one of the main props of the world of make-believe into which the black bourgeoisie has sought an escape from its inferiority and frustrations in American society.[76]

This world of make-believe did reflect the values of American society, Frazier conceded, but was not grounded in the facts of economics. By isolating themselves within this world, the members of the black middle class had ceased to identify with blacks as a group and with their traditional culture, resulting in a deep sense of anomie among them:

> Through delusions of wealth and power they have sought identification with the white America which continues to reject them. But these delusions leave them frustrated because they are unable to escape from the emptiness and futility of their existence ... The black bourgeoisie suffers from 'nothingness' because when Negroes attain middle-class status, their lives generally lose both content and significance.[77]

Black Bourgeoisie is imbued with the spirit of globalism that Frazier had acquired during his Paris sojourn. One finds him now comparing the black American middle class with its equivalents around the world. In a similar vein, 'The Failure of the Negro Intellectual,' a lecture given at Atlanta University in 1962, took aim at what Frazier regarded as the self-delusion of black American intellectuals. Within the opening sentences he produced this lapidary observation: 'anyone knows that after 250 years American Negro intellectuals cannot measure up to African intellectuals.'[78] This, he maintained, was because African thinkers, unlike their American counterparts, analyzed the root causes of the conflicts affecting their people:

> All African intellectuals begin with the fact of the colonial experience of the African. They possess a profound understanding not only of the colonial experience and its obvious effects upon their traditional social organization, but of the less obvious and more profound effects upon the culture and the African personality.
>
> The American Negro intellectual goes his merry way discussing such matters as the superficial aspects of the material standard of living among Negroes and the extent to which they enjoy civil rights. He never begins with the fundamental fact of what slavery has done to the Negro or the group which is called Negroes in the United States. Yet it is as necessary for the American Negro intellectual to deal with these questions as it is for the African intellectual to begin with the colonial experience.[79]

Unlike their African counterparts, black American intellectuals had lost sight of their mission to help the members of their racial group. In particular, they had become lost in reveries of assimilation with the dominant culture: 'The African intellectual recognizes what colonialism has done to the African and he sets as his first task the mental, moral, and spiritual rehabilitation of the African. But the American Negro intellectual, seduced by dreams of final assimilation, has never regarded this as his primary task.'[80] Frazier argued that black intellectuals had to reconceive the black American historical experience and to rehabilitate it in mental, moral, and spiritual terms. They had failed utterly to do so:

> I am referring to his failure to dig down into the experience of the Negro and bring about a transvaluation of that experience so that the Negro could have a new self-image or new conception of himself.
>
> It was the responsibility of the Negro intellectual to provide a positive identification through history, literature, art, music and the drama.[81]

It was, moreover, a serious error for black intellectuals to suppose that integration and eventual assimilation meant physical, cultural, and spiritual annihilation. Frazier berated them for failing to develop emancipated patterns of thought:

> educated Negroes ... have failed to achieve any intellectual freedom. In fact, with the few exceptions of literary men, it appears that the Negro intellectual is unconscious of the extent to which his thinking is restricted to sterile repetition of the safe and conventional ideas current in Ameri-

can society ... Most Negro intellectuals simply repeat the propaganda [in regard to national and international issues] which is put out by people who have large economic and political interests to protect ... One of the most important results of the lack of freedom on the part of Negro intellectuals has been their failure to produce men of high intellectual stature who are respected by the world at large.

We have no philosophers or thinkers who command the respect of the intellectual community at large.[82]

If they had failed to achieve intellectual freedom, it is because black intellectuals had, through unconscious conformism, become mired in a paradigm of assimilation, absorption, and disappearance of their own identity, as theorized by whites. They could escape from this trap and overcome their alienation if they gave up the idea of assimilation:

> The Civil War is supposed to have been the result of a misunderstanding of two brothers, white brothers, of course, and the Emancipation of the Negro is forgotten. Confronted with this fact, the Negro intellectual should not be consumed by his frustrations. He must rid himself of his obsession with assimilation. He must come to realize that integration should not mean annihilation – self-effacement, the escaping from his identification ... But this can be achieved only if the Negro intellectual and artist frees himself from his desire to conform and only if he overcomes his inferiority complex.[83]

However, they could not do it alone – they needed Africans to help them:

> In a chapter entitled, 'What can the American Negro Contribute to the Social and Economic Life of Africa' in the book, *Africa Seen by American Negroes*, I pointed out that the American Negro had little to contribute to Africa but that Africa, in achieving freedom, would probably save the soul of the American Negro in providing him with a new identification, a new self-image, and a new sense of personal dignity.[84]

The essay ends with the following paragraph, in which pride triumphs over an element of fatalism: 'It may turn out that in the distant future Negroes will disappear physically from American society. If this is our fate, let us disappear with dignity and let us leave a worthwhile memorial – in science, in art, in literature, in sculpture, in music – of our having been here.'[85]

For a Comparative World Sociology

One straightforward explanation for Frazier's doggedly ideological stance is his natural indignation at the injustices caused by racial oppression, his passion for the cause of racial equality. But if he fought so tirelessly, it is also because, as a scientist, he realized that he was pursuing an extremely rewarding and promising line of sociological research; namely, the analysis of the fundamental sources of racism within a global framework of class relations.

The precursor to Frazier's key work on this subject, *Race and Culture Contacts in the Modern World*, was his 1954 paper 'The Negro in the United States.' In it, he assessed the status of black Americans 'as an aspect of the world-wide contact of European and non-European races.'[86] He stated his intention to work within a broad analytical framework built around the idea that different race relations systems are determined by fundamental economic and political factors, and that mores influence racial relations and attitudes. Frazier considered, in turn, the demographic, economic, political, social, and psychological dynamics of the North American race relations system from the Civil War to the mid-twentieth century, closing on a somber note: after 350 years, this system was still blocking blacks' effective integration into American society. In order to break this peculiarly American impasse, an enlarged, internationalist perspective was necessary:

> Although the problem of the Negro in the United States appears to be unique in many of its manifestations, it involves economic, political, and cultural elements similar to those in other areas where there are widespread contacts between large settlements of Europeans and non-Europeans. Therefore, the Negro situation provides a case study in which the interaction of economic, political, and cultural factors in race relations may be studied.[87]

Certain facts made such a comparative analysis particularly promising, Frazier thought. For one, the experience of black Americans was unique in that they had been cut off from their ancestral culture, the vestiges of which were rapidly lost in the new environment. There was no way for the resulting community to be founded on that heritage. For another, nationalist or racialist movements had not thus far played an important role in black American struggles to improve their status in society. It would be useful, Frazier felt, to seek comparisons with other regions where Europeans and non-Europeans were interacting within evolving societies, resulting in the emergence of new peoples.[88]

Race and Culture Contacts in the Modern World elaborates on these ideas. It takes Park's analytical schema as a starting point only to diverge from it in important respects, revealing the scientific originality of which the mature Frazier was capable. In particular, it is structured around the grand thesis of a 'world process' that allegedly shaped race relations over the centuries:

> The world-process ... had its origin in the economic expansion of Europe during the fifteenth and sixteenth centuries. This economic expansion coincided with the technical and intellectual revolution which enabled Europe to gradually establish its dominance over the rest of the world. During the period when European nations were establishing their dominance over non-European peoples, there arose the idea of the superiority of the white race. Although this idea could not be maintained on scientific or moral grounds, it nevertheless served as a means of separating the white and colored races and of justifying political and economic domination by the Europeans. The separation of the races was facilitated by differences in culture and standards of living which were employed in conjunction with the race concept to stamp non-European peoples as inferior races. Consequently, racial ideologies and race sentiment must be analyzed in relation to cultural differences in studying the problems which have resulted from the contacts between the white and colored peoples in the modern world.[89]

This process manifested itself first and foremost as a complex, sweeping, world-historical phenomenon. Its outcome, modern interracial and intercultural relations, constituted a sociological problem in that these relations involved human beings who displayed a dual identity: they were at once individuals involved in interpersonal relations and members of groups differentiated by physical features and cultural characteristics. Sociology and the other social sciences could not fully characterize race relations without careful study of the effects of geography and technological development as well as economic and political institutions on the people involved.

Having established this multidisciplinary framework, Frazier embarked on a comparative analysis of racial and cultural contacts around the world.[90] The primary theoretical instrument that he used for this analysis was the Chicago model. He examined the ecological and demographic transformations that had taken place in each of six areas and, adhering to his theoretical template, analyzed economics, political organization, social organization, culture, and personality. More than any of his predecessors, Frazier dwelled on the variable of political power, defined as white control over peoples of color. His conclusion, 'Federated Cultures and Cosmopolitanism,' revisited the economic and political components of the world process of interracial contacts:

> Except in the United States and Canada, the establishment of white domination was associated with the creation of a large mixed population. In the West Indies, in Central America, and in a large part of South America, economic and political developments indicate that the native Indian and Negro populations as well as the mixed bloods will increasingly acquire economic and political power and thereby destroy the pattern of white domination.[91]

> It is in the multiracial communities that the economic relations of white and colored peoples are complicated by political and social factors, including personal relations. Racial problems in the area of economic relations do not arise as long as there is a racial division of labor based upon an impersonal competitive process ... The United States and the Union of South Africa, which is entering a period of industrialization, are the two areas in which competition between white and colored peoples has been restricted.[92]

Though the world exhibited a marked trend toward cosmopolitanism, an imminent fusion of the races was not to be expected:

> The increasing mobility of both white and colored peoples ... will encourage a certain cosmopolitanism. That means that there will be a growing number of marginal people who will break away from their cultural roots ... This does not mean that the three major racial groups will become fused in a new racial stock, or that, in the words of Tagore, the 'colourless vagueness of cosmopolitanism' will cover the earth.[93]

Nor was it likely to find the different human cultures merging into a great uniform culture or world federation – an interesting but not an imminent prospect. Yet this would not necessarily imply the continuation of the present oppressive situation:

> In the foreseeable future the great masses of the various cultural groups in the world will continue to be identified with some national or racial group.

> Indeed, for the great masses of people a national or racial tradition will provide the basis of their solidarity as well as the basis of their personal identification. As imperialism and colonialism based upon color disappear, racial and cultural differentiation without implications of superiority and inferiority will become the basic pattern of a world order.[94]

Another task for Frazier in this work was to compare the black American middle class with what he called the 'colored middlemen' and 'compradors' of the world.[95] His extensive travels outside the United States, his stay in Paris, and his numerous contacts with European and other left intellectuals had convinced him of the strong similarities between the black middle class, who felt increasingly alienated and frustrated in the white man's world, and the new bourgeoisie of the decolonized nations who resembled 'derelicts, frantically seeking some foothold of security for body and mind.'[96]

Yet the middle class was not ineluctably condemned to conservatism and co-optation. In the emancipatory utopia envisioned by Frazier at this period of his intellectual maturity, Africa and the rest of the world figured as a liberatory solution to their oppression. He particularly admired Kwame Nkrumah, leader of the Ghanaian Convention People's Party and later president of Ghana,[97] whom he viewed as a role model for black American elites wishing to rethink their approach to nationalism in a country marked by accelerated cultural change and increasing globalization of trade. Internationalism dominated his discursive approach, while the scientific basis of his work remained the multidisciplinary corpus (history, anthropology, comparative sociology) assembled in *Race and Culture Contacts*. By adopting internationalism, however, Frazier did not abandon the values he saw as central to American democracy; on the contrary, he venerated them his whole life, as no less an observer than W.E.B. Du Bois would later recall: 'In the best sense of the words, E. Franklin Frazier was more fundamentally American than most Americans. He believed the ideals of democracy were genuine and that men equally sharing responsibility could and would improve themselves. He pursued Truth and revealed the reasons for society's confusions and fears.'[98]

The Importance of Theory

In the spirit of Du Bois but alone among his black American peers, Frazier thoroughly understood the importance of developing a solid theoretical framework for his observations. This was a sine qua non if the field of race relations studies was to acquire real credibility. He never cultivated general theory as did Parsons or Merton, to take the classic examples of his generation. Still, it is easy to detect in the earliest of his important 1930s essays an original treatment of the ecological theory with which he had been inculcated at Chicago. More significantly, Frazier saw it as essential to carry on a critical discourse – in essence, an epistemological discourse – on the act of theorization as an essential pillar of black race relations theory, as well as continuing to infuse theoretical considerations into his empirical work. Four examples of relevant articles serve to illustrate the point.

In 'Sociological Theory and Race Relations,' a paper presented to the 1946 annual conference of the American Sociological Association, Frazier took stock of American sociological theory on race relations starting from its origins. As we have seen, the first two sociological works published in the United States, those of Hughes and Fitzhugh, were deeply racist. The works of the founding fathers (Ward, Sumner, Giddings, Small, Cooley, and Ross) that followed, despite differences among them, did not represent a significant departure.[99] However, the same period saw the emergence of an independent theory of race, first set out by Thomas in his 'The Psychology of Race Prejudice,' and later, in similar terms, by Park.

Park rapidly became the premier American sociologist of race: 'Park's theories ... represent the most comprehensive and systematic sociological theories of race relations developed by American sociologists and have had the greatest influence on American sociology ...'[100] However, until the 1930s, Park's model of competition, conflict, accommodation, and assimilation was somewhat static: 'His theory ... contained the fatalism inherent in Sumner's concept of the mores. His theory was originally based upon the assumption that the races could not mix or mingle freely.'[101] Still, Park had perfectly grasped the changes taking place in the United States and elsewhere, and he refined his theory to take account of them.[102] After his death, it had fallen to his students and other researchers to advance his theoretical agenda so as to achieve an even more precise conceptual formulation: 'What is needed is the further development of a dynamic sociological theory of race relations, which will discard all the rationalizations of race prejudice and provide orientation for the study of the constantly changing patterns of race relations in American life.'[103]

Frazier's 1948 presidential address to the American Sociological

Association, titled 'Race Contacts and the Social Structure,' is in a very similar vein. His aim here was to review the 'general orientation of studies of the Negro by American sociologists,'[104] and he discerned three chronologically appearing groups of scholars. The first, comprising the generation of the founding fathers, did not study race relations specifically but to a large extent derived their theories from European researchers interested in the universal phenomenon of interracial contact. In the second phase, represented by Thomas and Park, a great leap forward was made: 'Park ... did not study the Negro as a "social problem" but as a subject of sociological research.'[105] The third group, comprising the caste and class theorists, based its work on an organic conception of sociology and society. It contended that sociologists should focus their attention on the social processes and the organized aspects of life arising from communication and interaction instead of conceiving of society as an aggregate of individuals and attempting to explain it by studying individual behavior. But this theory was at an embryonic stage, whence the importance of a new approach: 'Since my aim is to show how the study of race contacts in the context of social relationships will increase our understanding of this aspect of human relations, it is necessary to give some attention to the social world of the Negro.'[106]

By 'social world,' Frazier meant the social structure of the world in which blacks lived. His idea, in short, was to highlight the relationship between nonpersonal factors in the structure of the black social world and race relations, a cause-and-effect relationship derived from his organic representation of society and sociology: 'I shall begin by considering the effects of the spatial segregation of the Negro community on race contacts.'[107] He continued by considering other nonpersonal and social factors such as the family and the church as influential cultural institutions, as well as the range of norms and values of the black communities, which influenced racial contacts but also served to isolate black Americans. He put forward the following hypothesis about social organization:

> The social organization of Negro life and its dominant values act as a social prism through which ideas, patterns of behavior, and values current in the larger American community are refracted or distorted. I would even suggest the hypothesis, which might be tested by empirical studies of racial contacts, that the degree of refraction or distortion is in inverse ratio to the extent that Negroes participate in the larger American society.[108]

At the end of the paper, Frazier stressed that the variable of urbanization should have pride of place in the structural sociological approach to race relations:

> Since the social structure of both the Negro community and white community has been undergoing rapid changes, the analysis of race contacts should be related to a changing structure of social relationships. The most important factor which has been responsible for the change in race contacts has been the urbanization of the Negro population ... Urbanization has changed the structure and function of every institution and association in the Negro community and their role in race relations.[109]

In short, Frazier found, the future of the sociological theory of interracial contact would inevitably require meticulous analysis of the behavior of individuals as members of social groups.

'Theoretical Structure of Sociology and Sociological Research,' a condensation of three lectures given at the University of London in 1953, is probably the most elaborate of Frazier's theoretical papers. Sociology, he wrote, is the science of human nature viewed as the product of association among human beings. This presupposes interaction made possible by various forms of communication. Subjectivity inevitably plays a role in the process, since human beings rely on symbols to understand and organize their collective existence. The result – institutions and other structured forms of behavior – determines individual conduct. This view of things is 'essentially an organic conception of social life, since, according to this view, individual acts become meaningful or socially significant as the result of the organization of the behaviour of individuals. This view is opposed to the atomistic conception which regards society as an aggregate of individuals whose behaviour is to be explained in terms of the similarity of individual responses and attitudes.'[110] He added, 'The various systems of social relationships which come into existence as the result of association are, according to our view, the proper subject matter of sociology.'[111]

Systems of social relationships include institutions, such as the family; associations, such as labor unions, or larger ensembles, such as the nation. The peculiar features of each system are determined by factors such as spatial distribution of population, division of labor, social stratification, existing institutions, and the nature of contacts and communication between members of society. Only empirical data can reveal the exact nature and boundaries of any particular social system. It is not sufficient, he argued, to focus on the investigation and measurement of attitudes to the exclusion of economic and political factors, or to develop vague concepts such as mores and customs as sui generis sociological phenomena – the approach taken, he claimed, by the majority of his sociological contemporaries: 'According to our point of view, sociological analysis must include economic and political factors relevant to the analysis of a particular system of social relations which is being studied. This is quite different from claiming that sociology is a general social science discipline confronted with the impossible task of synthesizing the data of all the social sciences.'[112]

Taking account of such factors forces one to radically revise the standard explanation of race relations in the southern United States, in which racial antagonisms and prejudices stemmed from attitudes rooted in slavery or from mores spontaneously arising from the association between the races. On the contrary, 'the sociological explanation of the system of racial separation and the disfranchisement of the Negro is to be found in the unresolved class conflict and the resulting political struggles among the whites in the South.'[113]

The next part of Frazier's argument consists of an examination of the genesis of racial and cultural contacts in the modern world. The first phase of such contacts brought together human groups that did not make up a single moral order, and so there was no common code of behavior to regulate the conflicts that inevitably ensued. Notwithstanding these conflicts, interactions like trade and barter were possible. During this initial phase, 'the ecological organization of race relations is taking form and ... is influenced by such factors as climate, geographic and demographic factors, but more especially by the type of economic exploitation.'[114] The transition from the first to the second phases of race and culture contacts had been aptly described by others, according to Frazier, as a transition from barter to slavery. The essential feature of the second stage was that economic relations assumed an organized or institutional character. From this perspective even slavery, as dehumanizing as it was, could be viewed as a type of industrial institution. But it could hardly be characterized as only that and nothing more. Slavery could not be viewed independently of politics, since the plantation system generated traditions and means of social control that transformed it into a particular species of sociopolitical institution. This tended to happen where slavery became an established way of life and brought masters and slaves into close association: 'Social control is not maintained simply by physical force and fear of punishment. Traditions, custom, and habits become more important elements in social control.'[115]

The final phase in the development of race and culture contacts gave rise to the problem of social organization. Where these contacts developed beyond the stage of slavery, the classical form of social organization was typically a caste system – a hierarchical division of society along racial lines: 'This type of social organization represents a form of accommodation in which conflicting interests are resolved, if not permanently, at least to the extent that a collective life is possible.'[116] Another possible outcome was biracial organization, in which racial groups live separately, side by side, possessing their own institutions and associations, and – at least in theory – being equal in social status. The essential sociological problem at the last phase of contact, according to Frazier, is 'the manner in which the racial division of labour is broken down and racial competition in the economic sphere gives way to competition on an individual basis and political power is identified with class rather than race.'[117] At this phase the 'marginal man' comes to play an important role in social organization, and particularly in nationalist movements, whose ideology must unavoidably come to grips with the issue of social organization: 'The marginal man is a cultural hybrid since he is the product of two cultural worlds and is not at home in either ... The marginal man may become an intellectual and he may develop an objective attitude toward both the minority and the dominant racial group. Very often it is these marginal men who become leaders of nationalistic movements.'[118]

Frazier found that debate over race and culture contacts had been obfuscated by the failure to distinguish among the three concepts of amalgamation, acculturation, and assimilation:

> Amalgamation will be used to designate the results of the mating of members of different racial stocks. Amalgamation ... may occur within or without marriage ... acculturation, which is a social process, refers to the process by which a person takes over the culture of the group or one group takes over the culture of another group ... Although the process of assimilation is closely related to acculturation, it should be differentiated from the latter because it includes something more fundamental than the latter. It involves complete identification with a group. Thus, American Negroes have been amalgamated to a large degree with whites and they are acculturated in respect to European culture. But they are not assimilated in

> American society, since they are regarded as American *Negroes*, seldom even as Negro *Americans*, and they think of themselves as Negroes first and only secondarily as Americans.[119]

He proceeded to consider the family and its role in acculturation and assimilation, leading him to propound a distinction between the 'natural family' and the 'institutional family.' The first is based on matriarchy and does not necessarily presuppose marriage, while the second is based on marriage. The institutional family is characterized by stability and continuity and tends to influence the individual's status in the community. During slavery, there existed large numbers of natural families, which played a considerable role in the acculturation and assimilation taking place at that stage. However,

> When we consider the role of the institutional family in assimilation we must confront the stubborn fact that the institutional family constitutes a barrier to the assimilation of divergent racial elements. In order to continue its function of conserving the traditions and values of a society, it must maintain a certain exclusiveness. This does not mean that the institutional family cannot play an important role in assimilation.[120]

The African American institutional family played this role in a rather specific way. It had appeared before the Civil War among free southern mulattoes who had acquired property and built patriarchal families similar to those of white slave owners. Some had even owned slaves. They had, in short, assimilated several traits of the majority culture:

> They took over the ideals and values of the aristocratic slaveholding whites and took pride in their relationship to this class ... After emancipation it was the descendents of these same families who constituted an upper class in the Negro communities and became the leaders of the Negroes. A study of the institutional life which developed among Negroes after emancipation reveals that they established schools and churches and businesses and became the leaders in the professions. This accounts for the fact, for which American sociologists have often sought an explanation in biology, that during the first decade of this century the vast majority of the educated leaders and successful men and women among Negroes were mulattoes or mixed-bloods.[121]

With the sweeping changes brought by urbanization in the early twentieth century, another variety of black institutional family came to the fore. Its members, descended from slaves, increasingly inhabited northern cities, where their day-to-day contact with the white culture led them to assimilate many of its traits. With time, 'from these same families came the most ambitious members in the Negro communities ... It was from these families that came the most efficient and stable workers who entered industry.'[122] These families were now changing rapidly, and the changes were having repercussions on their core values, traditions, and behavioral models:

> As the result of their new contacts in the urban environment and their new relation to the great body of American industrial workers, these families are changing. But the point of interest here is that the new outlook on life and the new values and patterns of behaviour which members of these families have acquired through wider contacts with American life are becoming a part of their family traditions.[123]

Frazier closed his article with a discussion of methodology, observing: 'The question of methods and techniques in sociological research just as in other fields of scientific enquiry is inseparable from the conceptual organization of the discipline.'[124] Many problems concerning human beings might be interesting without being sociological problems, either because of the way in which they have been defined or because the data involved cannot be studied within a sociological frame of reference:

> In many so-called sociological studies this simple fact is forgotten and virtuosity in the use of methods and techniques becomes an end in itself. Therefore, the first task in sociological study is to define or formulate a problem *in terms of the concepts of the discipline*. Then the problem of methods and techniques resolves itself into one of utilizing the appropriate methods and tools.[125]

This task must not be confused with the search for new concepts, which Frazier felt was not urgent:

> According to our point of view, there is no pressing need for new concepts ... Often when the attempt has been made to introduce new concepts into sociology, it has resulted in a substitution of new verbal symbols for old terms. The conceptual tools of sociological research – whether labeled by

old or new verbal symbols – will become more precise as they are utilized to reveal significant relationships between social phenomena.[126]

By 'significant relationship between social phenomena,' Frazier meant 'the organic relation between the data on human behaviour.'[127] Many statistical studies lack sociological significance because this organic relationship is not clearly discernible in their analytical method. To the objection that his own approach involved subjective evaluations and judgments, Frazier responded that this is inevitable given the state of sociological methodology and that, at any rate, it is not certain that all aspects of social reality lend themselves to statistical treatment. But sociologists must not to give up the study of fundamental problems merely because they lack the appropriate tools of research. Only during sustained study of sociological problems will the scientific tools necessary to enhance the validity of analysis and generalization be created. Contemporary sociologists had to be particularly aware of this issue because

> [they were] being called upon to study the pressing problems of the modern world. Chief among these problems are those posed by the new societies which are coming into existence in Africa and Asia as the result of the impact of Western civilization. The study of these problems provides a great opportunity for sociology to become a serious and respected social science discipline. But the achievement of this end will depend upon the extent to which sociologists have a clear conception of their distinctive field of enquiry and are willing to deal with significant problems in the area of social relations.[128]

'Desegregation as an Object of Sociological Study,' the fourth example of Frazier's original contributions to sociological theory, posited a continuum ranging from segregation to desegregation and proceeded to verify its existence in the case of black Americans. This intention is set out in the first paragraph: 'scarcely any studies have been concerned primarily with the manner in which the organization and social life of the Negro community and its interaction with the wider American community influence the nature and extent of desegregation. It is the purpose of this essay to explore and analyze this phase of the process of desegregation.'[129] Frazier immediately provides the relevant conceptual definitions:

> Desegregation and integration are often used interchangeably. There is some justification for this usage since desegregation and integration are correlated aspects of the same social process. Generally speaking 'desegregation' refers to the process by which Negroes are being integrated into the institutional and other phases of the social life of the wider American community or American society. Unfortunately, however, the term 'integration' is often used to refer to assimilation, which has a more restricted or specified denotation.[130]

Blumer's 'Social Science and the Desegregation Process,' wrote Frazier, had elaborated a clear distinction between two types of racial segregation, one a natural ecological process, the other resulting from conscious social policy: 'It is with the effect upon desegregation of racial segregation as an ecological process that the sociological study of desegregation should begin. Racial segregation resulting from social policies should be considered as a phase of the conflicts arising over the status of the Negro in the social organization.'[131] Segregation as an ecological process had been operative since the introduction of Africans into the American colonies. As a result of this process, free blacks before the Civil War had concentrated in cities and other areas outside the plantation system, and it was here that some degree of desegregation had first been seen. This type of settlement, Frazier argued, had to be distinguished from the segregation operative in the newer cities of the South, or in cities whose spatial pattern was determined by industry and commerce. Furthermore, 'The location of the Negro communities in the Border cities tends to conform to the pattern of Southern cities, though there are large concentrations of Negroes similar to those in Northern cities ... The concentration of Negroes in certain areas of Northern cities was the result of the same economic and social processes as were responsible for the segregation of other minority groups.'[132]

Ecological segregation, Frazier argued, is important to the sociologist because 'the spatial pattern of the community is the basis of a moral order.[133] It is an indication of the place of the racial group within the organization of the community and the interactions of people within the community.' In the sociological study of blacks in particular, racial segregation as an ecological process 'provides an index to the absence of communication between Negroes and other peoples and their moral isolation.'[134] In counterpoint to segregation, the forces of desegregation worked to create economic dependence on the wider American society:

> Although the Negro community is more or less isolated spatially from the wider American community and the social life of Negroes revolves around the institutions and associations of the Negro community, Negroes are, nevertheless, dependent economically upon the economic institutions of the American community ... as Negroes have moved into cities their dependence upon the economic institutions of the American communities has increased.[135]

The integration of African Americans was accelerated in the northern cities as they entered white economic and professional spheres. When analyzing the black community from the standpoint of desegregation, Frazier wrote, 'the first fact which should be considered is the stratification of the Negro community.'[136] Spurred on by urbanization, stratification represented a move from the older, simpler system based on social distinctions to a more complex system based on socioeconomic classes. The change was more rapid in the North than in the South, where restrictions on black labor mobility persisted. In the North, blacks were largely stratified according to occupation and income. The class system comprised a slim upper class and a larger middle class. Strictly from the standpoint of desegregation as a process, Frazier argued, sociologists must be attentive to differences between the new black middle class and the white middle classes:

> The new Negro middle class, which has become increasingly important in the Negro community, has a social heritage which differentiates it from the white middle classes. In fact, the social heritage of this class is a mixture of the so-called 'aristocratic' heritage of mulattoes or Negroes who were free before the Civil War and the heritage of the Negro folk who have risen to middle-class status. Therefore, they have a style of life and set of values which do not permit them to participate easily in the social world of white middle classes.[137]

In studying this process, the sociologist must include the variable of change in his or her conceptual paradigm: 'A study of the changing class structure of the Negro community is important in order to understand the social heritage and attitudes of the new strata which are rising to middle-class status and are assuming leadership in the process of desegregation.'[138]

The powerful Negro church, according to Frazier, encapsulated all that was most traditional about the black community and, as such, presented 'one of the most important barriers to desegregation.'[139] Other black institutions, such as fraternal associations, social clubs, or long-standing professional associations, were additional barriers.

One particular area of interest for sociologists was black integration in the areas of sports and entertainment. Frazier thought that such integration revealed important facts about blacks' changing social status and about the relationship of desegregation to the changes in the organization of American life:

> first ... the Negro has always been able to secure an acceptance more easily in those areas of American life which were outside of conventional society; and, secondly, the change in the organization of American life – urbanization, the growth of gigantic corporations, and the growth in power of labor unions. As a result of the change in the organization of American life, the assimilation of Negroes has become a process of assimilation in secondary groups.[140]

It seemed clear that urban blacks were subjected to the opposing forces of desegregation and segregation: 'The Negro is being incorporated into the institutions and associations of the metropolitan communities and he is acquiring the superficial uniformity and homogeneity of manners and fashions characteristic of cosmopolitan groups. But his loyalties and deepest attachments are still rooted in the Negro community or the social world of the Negro.'[141]

In his conclusion, Frazier's theoretical argument came full circle: to understand desegregation as a sociological process, one must study the effect upon it of racial segregation as an ecological phenomenon. This is the starting point because the ecological structure of a community is the basis of its social organization. It is important for sociologists to study the social organization of black people and of the wider community because 'desegregation is the result of the interaction between both the Negro and white communities, both of which are undergoing changes.'[142] Consequently, sociologists should pay particular attention to 'those areas of interracial contacts which are on the fringe or outside of the traditional or conventional social organization of both the white and Negro communities. It is in these "vulnerable" areas of social life that desegregation progresses most rapidly.'[143]

Frazier, like Park, was not especially gifted at the systematic exposition of his ideas. As may be seen from the above discussion, his arguments repeat from one paper to another and at points become vague or obscure. Nevertheless, he provides ample illustration of his keen awareness of the importance of the theoretical imagination in sociology, if only to keep the field from lapsing to a pre-scientific level of impressionism or intuitionism. He was the only black sociologist of his cohort to set out formal theoretical guideposts for his work, and in so doing was very much in tune with the mainstream sociology of his day. This mature theoretical penchant is most notable in the last two essays discussed above.

Frazier's Originality

Frazier's originality is not readily apparent early on, but emerges as the product of a slow taking of distance from the established scientific corpus in his field. His trajectory at Chicago was different in many respects from that of Johnson. When he began his doctorate there at the age of thirty-three, he had already published several papers and gained a respectable amount of teaching experience; moreover, his was a multifaceted intellect:

> Frazier came to Chicago willing to learn from Park and others, but he did not arrive as a tabula rasa. He came with well-formed, strong views about racism; a wealth of personal and practical experience in the South; a compelling political interest in race relations and socialism; and a commitment to activism. He had also already absorbed ideas about theory from a variety of sources and had definite views about the functions and obligations of intellectuals.[144]

In the seventeen years between *The Negro Family in Chicago* and *The Negro in the United States*, Frazier incorporated the Chicago corpus syncretically, along with a large number of conceptual borrowings from elsewhere. His family studies of the 1930s illustrate this strategy. To a general framework taken from Du Bois (a 1908 work in the Atlanta University Studies series) he adds Park's race relations cycle; Burgess and Mowrer's ecological approach, including a theory of the impact of urban processes on family structure; the twin concepts of disorganization and reorganization from *The Polish Peasant in Europe and America* by Thomas and Znaniecki; and the natural history methodology of these last two authors and Park.

The Negro in the United States summarizes his research to the end of the decade but also constitutes an epistemological turning point. While much of his argumentation still takes the race relations cycle and Burgess's ecological theory as givens, Frazier adjusts the cycle theory to better fit the realities of postwar African American life. Competition, conflict, and accommodation are still present, but he replaces the stage of assimilation with that of integration.[145] A further refinement is the adoption of Cooley's distinction between primary and secondary institutions. Most importantly, though, Frazier is now departing significantly from the Chicago School by introducing class considerations into his analysis of race relations.[146] The concept of class itself demands a structural approach, something that was sorely lacking in the mid-century Chicago paradigm. Moreover, this conception of conflict is markedly different from Park's, which was essentially an *ahistorical* generalization. Frazier's class theory enables him to explain conflict as the result of contingent social events that are measurable and analyzable within a historical time frame that is also that of the sociologist. Conflict evolved from the great divide between the proletarian masses and the small black middle class that was increasingly uninterested in the fate of African Americans, an alienated class that devoted itself to imitating whites' conspicuous consumption in the hope of thereby becoming 'true Americans.' Conflict was historically conditioned and embodied the antagonism between opposing class consciousnesses. Frazier maintained this theoretical referent until the end of his career, seeking to generalize its applicability to the whole world, as we have seen. The end result was a hybrid model combining the ecological heritage of Park and Burgess with an original, non-Marxist theory of class conflict.

This brings us to the need to set the historical record straight as to the introduction, in the 1930s, of class and class conflict as explanatory principles in race relations theory. A number of authors have too readily taken Park's sole authorship of these ideas for granted, relegating his African American colleagues to the status of imitators – an injustice to Frazier and Johnson. As Chapoulie notes, 'The addition of a class-based analysis to the analysis in terms of ethnic (or race) relations appeared at this period as a normal extension of Park's perspective, as confirmed by the [1954] thesis of Helena Znaniecka Lopita on the Polish-American community, supervised by Wirth, Blumer, and Hughes.'[147] He is right about the widespread *perception* among 1950s white sociologists that these concepts were fundamental analytical components of Park's sociological perspective; but while Park did employ the concepts in certain instances,[148] the reality is that he was not fundamentally a class theorist, and it is incorrect to present class analysis as the 'normal extension' of his perspective.[149] That being the case, how did the corresponding perception arise? As the product of a feint used by Park in his later work, in which the meticulous class analysis of Johnson and Frazier was drawn upon *without citation*. Park also presented as his own certain conceptual developments concerning the relevance of expanding class analysis in the field of race relations, yet these were derived directly from Frazier's original thinking on the subject. In this way, Park sustained the false impression of a self-driven renewal of his ideas on race, when the authorship of those ideas was in fact attributable to Johnson and Frazier. Historical accuracy demands that this perception be corrected, especially given the academic discrimination that they and other African American scholars faced. Contemporary European researchers who insist on seeing Frazier in particular as no more than a carbon copy of Park would do well to consider this thought: 'Frazier was no one's intellectual lackey, least of all Park's, according to Park himself ...'[150]

But as innovative as it was, the theoretical amalgam that Frazier produced was also fragile in that it necessitated a reconciliation of two divergent explanatory approaches, one drawing on the events of real history, the other evoking a vast unilinear evolution of human progress in the form of successive stages leading, *in principle*, to greater interracial harmony. This internal inconsistency in his work – which Frazier never resolved, since it is unresolvable – is part and parcel of his scientific singularity, as was his fierce intellectual independence.

PART THREE

From Explanation to Comprehension

> One must consider not only the genealogy of ideas but also their institutional setting, their meaning and relevance for contemporaries, and their depth of penetration, both inward into individual consciousness and outward through society's many levels.[1]

Here – in a sentence that might have served as an epigraph for this work – we have an exhaustive definition of a research program (*sensu* Lakatos) in the sociology of scientific knowledge. This formulation suggests the need to break down such a program into at least six different analytical dimensions, each suitable material for one or more sociological research projects. For my purposes here, I shall first concentrate on the genealogy of American sociological ideas about race, casting a critical look at the cognitive cores of the two major scientific constructions reconstituted in the preceding chapters. The question to answer is this: Can it be said that there was an *original* African American sociology during the founding period from 1896 to 1964?

Having answered this question, I shall go on (following Haskell) to consider an aspect that I have discussed only tangentially up to this point: the institutional setting in which this scientific knowledge was produced – the American university. This setting was common to both white and black sociologists and may be thought of as a social microenvironment or, paraphrasing Merton's analytical vocabulary in the sociology of science, a particular social structure. I have illustrated the various ways in which the early black sociologists were victimized by segregation. Not only were they second-class citizens in the wider society, but as intellectuals they were shut out of mainstream academia and the power and prestige that it conferred. The sporadic honors that Du

Bois, Frazier, or Drake enjoyed were a pittance by comparison. I shall elucidate the strategies adopted by African American sociologists as they attempted to overcome this obstacle and stake out a legitimate place within the university.

Two Sociologies, One Society

Three authoritative observers, using different arguments, have challenged the very basis and scientificity of the American sociology of race relations as it stood in the 1960s. As Everett Hughes, in his 1963 presidential address to the American Sociological Association, wondered, 'Why did social scientists – and sociologists in particular – not foresee the explosion of collective action of Negro Americans toward immediate full integration into American society?'[2] He blamed this failure on the ineptitude of the sociological imagination and on the conceptual isolation – the disconnect – between the discipline of race relations and the broader processes that were modifying the larger social structure and raising many complex questions. Four years later Lewis Coser addressed the same issue in an essay devoted to the status of Marxist thought in Western sociology:

> The fact that American sociology was so ruefully unprepared for the civil rights revolution of the last few years is connected with its systematic neglect of social conflict and of the mobilization of power and interests in racial contentions. Being wedded to the belief that only increased understanding between the races and successful mobilization of guilt about the American dilemma among the dominant racial majority would lead to the gradual erosion of prejudice and discrimination, American sociology was by and large unprepared for the emergence of a situation in which a major part of the initiative for change did not come from the white man but rather from the black. American sociology has systematically neglected analysis of the conditions that gradually led to the emergence of a new self-consciousness among younger Negroes and to the development not only of alienative tendencies in the Negro community but of a militant type of alienation as well. Much professional embarrassment might well have been avoided had attention been paid to certain Marxian leads ...[3]

Marxism is, of course, only one of several legitimate scientific approaches to the study of social conflict. William Julius Wilson, in the work that launched his career as a distinguished black American sociologist, wrote, 'Race relations analysts were shackled for several decades by the narrow perspectives of assimilation models and by the heavy preoccupation with theories of prejudice, and therefore found themselves unprepared to predict or explain the violent confrontation of ghetto revolts, the emergence and growth of the Black Power Movement, and the rapid rise of cultural nationalism within the black community.'[4]

All three of these analysts get at a fundamental cognitive difficulty in the 1960s sociology of race: it was trapped within overly narrow interpretive limits, making it incapable of predicting the course of even near-term historical events. This was a fatal flaw, for it called into question the structure of the theory itself. For Hughes, sociologists lacked the conceptual imagination to theorize racial phenomena on a general scale; for Coser, they failed to conceptualize social conflict, power, and interest when considering race; and for Wilson, the ball and chain of assimilationism and the excessive fixation on prejudice inhibited their theories' predictive capacity and prevented the theorists from conceiving of alternative evolutionary scenarios for American race relations.

The Mainstream Sociology of Race

It is not surprising that Wilson directed the brunt of his attack at the concept of assimilation, for this was truly the foundation of Anglo-American thinking on race relations, as we have seen in this book and as many other scholars have stressed.[5] The obsessive focus on assimilation and the failure to question the corresponding assumptions had made it the equivalent of intellectual wallpaper, the unseen and unquestioned figure in the carpet. The concepts of race and racial prejudice occupied a similar status in the work of many Anglo-American authors. I shall proceed to subject this conceptual triptych to an epistemological analysis designed to elucidate the causes of the major cognitive difficulties discussed above.

THE CONCEPT OF ASSIMILATION

We saw in chapter 1 that the concept of assimilation made its appearance in the earliest works of American sociology. Its adoption as an explanatory principle was the logical result of increasing recognition that dynamic processes were taking place within society viewed as a totality. Lester Ward, typifying this approach, came at the notion of assimilation in the following terms:

> [Paul] Lilienfeld has likened the process which takes place through conquest to fertilization in biology, comparing the conquering race to the spermatozoa and the conquered race to the ovum, the former active and aggressive, the latter passive and submitting, resulting in a crossing of strains. Similarly [Gustav] Ratzenhofer compares this race amalgamation to conjugation in biology, and says that hordes and clans multiply by division. There certainly is a remarkable 'analogy' between the process called karyokinesis in biology and that which goes on in societies formed by the conquest of a weaker by a stronger race.[6]

Once the 'conquest' was complete, synergy – another principle dear to Ward – took over, leading in successive stages to the formation of a 'synthetic people' characterized by shared national affiliation.[7] The biosocial analogy impelled Ward to conceive of *social* assimilation in terms of a biological process (karyokinesis) as he understood it. Thus, from its earliest introduction into sociology, the concept of assimilation was an interloper, or, looked at another way, an exile from its natural context of meaning. It was inevitably ambiguous, imprecise, diffuse, approximate, and suggestive rather than rigorously explanatory. Ward was notable among the early sociologists for placing assimilation at the center of a complete, theoretically ambitious sociological system, but as we saw in chapter 1, nearly all the founding fathers followed him in taking up the biological analogy. Here, then, we find the origins of a major conceptual stumbling block.

Pursuing the genealogy of assimilation and related notions, its next important theorists among race relations scholars were Park and Burgess.[8] Park endorsed the borrowed concept in his very first paper, though he wisely acknowledged the inevitable transfer of connotations along with it: 'Assimilation, as the word is here used, brings with it a certain borrowed significance which it carried over from physiology where it is employed to describe the process of nutrition. By a process of nutrition, somewhat similar to the physiological one, we may conceive alien peoples to be incorporated with, and make part of, the community or state.'[9]

But eight years later, in their sociology textbook, Park and Burgess came up with a new definition owing nothing to physiology or biology: 'Assimilation is a process of interpenetration and fusion in which persons and groups acquire the memories, sentiments, and attitudes of other persons or groups, and, by sharing their experience and history, are incorporated with them in a common cultural life.'[10] This became the standard mainstream definition of assimilation – conceptual progress, to be sure.

It will also be recalled that this same work conceptualized assimilation as the final phase in a typology beginning with competition, conflict, and accommodation, a typology formalized as the race relations cycle in 1926 and remaining central to Park's thinking until near the end of his career.[11] While an undeniable advance over biological analogies, this schema is problematic from the standpoint of scientific knowledge. In particular, the definition of assimilation is semantically vague, elastic, and polysemic, encompassing psychological adjustment, cultural adaptation, and sociostructural integration.[12] Park revisited the definition in his 1930 article for the *Encyclopedia of the Social Sciences*, elaborating on its cultural aspects and discussing its uses in sociology, though not discarding its psychological aspects. But it remained a vague notion, a nimbus of multiple meanings in which the cultural connotation predominated, and this state of affairs would continue for several decades. As late as 1967, a critic of assimilation as a concept in race relations theory could write, 'The field of race relations has come to resemble a theoretical no-man's-land between psychology, sociology, and anthropology.'[13]

Perhaps an even more serious problem with Park's and Burgess's treatment of the concept is that, while regarding assimilation as a purely societal process, they were also capable of writing, 'As social contact initiates interaction, assimilation is its final perfect product.'[14] This is illogical: if assimilation strictly designates a process, it cannot also be a product of that process. More problematically, there is clearly nothing scientific about the use of a phrase like 'perfect final product.' It is an *ideological* construct that contaminates not only the work of these two scholars but also the work of their followers. This becomes even clearer in the discussion by Park and Burgess of the popular usage of the term 'assimilation' in the United States, which is derived from the country's experience as a haven for immigrants. They refer to the process of Americanization, as prophetically expressed in the parable of the 'melting pot' by the dramatist Israel Zangwill in his play of the same name. But, as Bash notes, this highly ideological usage pervades and distorts the thinking of Park and Burgess themselves: 'Their "sociological" notion of assimilation does not appear to depart significantly from its popular, social specification as a "magic crucible ..."'[15] Combine this with the race relations cycle and it becomes evident that, in Park and Burgess, assimilation as the perfect final product is being conflated with the successful Americanization of immigrants – a process, incidentally, that could be accelerated by the politically fashionable expedient of social intervention.

The now classic work of Peter Berger and Thomas Luckman and of Burkart Holzner,[16] establishing and codifying a clear distinction between social and scientific constructions of reality, clarifies why this concept of assimilation has no epistemological legitimacy or validity. Social and scientific constructions are two incommensurate, though in some respects complementary or mutually influencing, levels of interpretation. Modern standards of epistemology rule out the possibility of any social construct's interfering with theorization or dictating scientific conceptualizations on its own terms. The fundamental epistemological rule is that scientific theories, whether in sociology or any other field, must present themselves as abstract *reconstructions* of any social, popular, or commonsense conception derived from a completely independent source (generally, though not necessarily, another theoretical construct). Putting it plainly, one must take care never to confound knowledge with the objects of that knowledge.

This exposition enables us to see that what Park developed as sociological *science* was fundamentally ideological in nature. His race relations cycle was a social construct – assimilation into the melting pot as the inevitable final stage of a cycle – passing itself off as theory. Such was his epistemological mistake. Granted, even though ideology is not science or theory, it is a highly important construction within its own discursive space. Still, theory relates to an entirely different, asocial construction: it is the core of an abstract system founded on logical coherence: 'The elements of scientific systems are concepts and their referents. Concepts are symbols, not observables. Conceptual meaning cannot be reduced to a set of empirical observations. Instead concepts gain meaning by their relation to other concepts at the theoretic level. They are not identified with their empirical referents but are connected to them through abstraction.'[17]

This is, of course, an ideal definition of science, and it is far from certain that all scientific constructs, even today, fully meet its conditions. That said, Park and his contemporaries should have been more sensitive to the need to formulate the concept of assimilation in abstract language as a neutral concept inscribable within a neutral theoretical structure. As it was, their concept of assimilation was largely dictated by the *empirical* early-twentieth-century American experience, characterized by competition between recent immigrants and older-stock citizens for integration into the new society. Clearly, such social science is normative and hence illegitimate, whereas it should ideally be free of external influence.[18] In fairness to Park, he was a white American in an era profoundly marked by the 'scientific' ideology of evolutionism (a highly normative construct), which situated the United States on the cutting edge of societal progress. Under such circumstances, the temptation for a sociologist to be normative was acute: his discipline, after all, embraced societal change. If one accepts this argument, the question then becomes, What general orientation was supported by Park's normativity and that of his followers, whether they knew it or not? The following answer is, in my view, quite satisfactory, provided, again, that assimilation is understood as an ideological not a scientific or sociological concept, much less a theoretical one; that it is seen as a peculiar type of interpretive perspective: 'The Assimilationist Perspective, the inclination to approach race and ethnic relations phenomena with a predisposition to perceive, document, analyze and explain ... assimilative processes to the relative neglect of others, fits squarely into this order-celebrating orientation of the conservative sociological tradition.'[19]

Park could indeed be considered one of the more open-minded of the *conservative* Anglo-American sociologists of his time, fitting comfortably within the following description by Bramson: 'the 20th century American sociologists of conservation were concerned with maintaining the American norm and assimilating vast numbers of "deviants" (both from within and without) to that norm ...'[20]

Turning to Myrdal, his conception of assimilation as an imminent social eventuality is as polysemic as Park's, gravitating among psychological, cultural, and social meanings, and is no more scientific. We need not dwell on it here at any length, except to say that it is an ideological construct wrapped in putatively rigorous, systematic language. Where he departs from Park, it is to insist on the race problem as a *moral* dilemma. This difference may perhaps be explained by the fact that Myrdal was dealing specifically with the status of African Americans, who had always been considered unassimilable (by whites) and treated as such, while Park's interest in assimilation was as a general concept applicable to a variety of different situations. There is no error, though, in stating that Myrdal's approach helped maintain the dominance of the assimilationist perspective among race relations scholars after Park's death, and did nothing to dissipate the semantic haze surrounding the concept of assimilation.

THE CONCEPTS OF RACE AND PREJUDICE

As to the epistemological status of race and prejudice, it can be said that their early theorization in Anglo-American sociology went through two phases. In the first, embodied by the slavocrats Hughes and Fitzhugh and their ideological kin, race was a fundamental biological fact subordinating culture and giving rise to social and cultural differences. In the second, beginning at the turn of the century, a subtler amalgam of nature and culture took over as more northern scholars entered the fray. Ward, for example, drew inspiration from the biological wisdom of his time, embracing Darwinism (though he rejected Galton's eugenics as an improper extrapolation from it). As for Sumner, he gave explanatory weight to culture when he wrote in *Folkways* that race must not be used to explain what are in fact mores and customs. However, it is difficult not to read racism into Sumner's refusal to countenance the assimilation of black people for fear of impairing the mores and customs of the majority culture. All of the founding fathers, in sum, were laboring under powerful ideologies of hierarchy, and their treatment of race is fatally colored by it.[21] The prevailing racialist vision of social phenomena had pervaded the construction of common sense and, by the same token, the more sophisticated language of sociology.

After the First World War, American social science took a decisive turn on the delicate and complex question of race. Under the influence of Boas, sociologists, while certainly not expunging the term from their vocabulary, sought to move the frame of reference definitively from nature to culture. Moreover, they were now concentrating less on innate or acquired human traits and more on intergroup and especially intercultural relations. This general shift in Anglo-American social theory was clearly catalyzed by the case of the African American minority: 'What developed in the USA in the twentieth century, first in rudimentary form, then with greater precision in the 1920s – after blacks had served in the American ranks in the First World War and, particularly, when they began to move in large numbers into the great northern industrial cities – was a sociology of "race relations."'[22]

Park had much to do with this conceptual transmutation, and there is a profound tension in his work that makes for both its innovativeness and its epistemic ambiguity. Recapitulating the discussion of chapter 2, what he did was to embark on a highly promising *cultural* construction of race and racial prejudice by setting these concepts within a historical evolutionary perspective. In general terms, he argued that race relations belonged to the modern period of history; they were the product of European colonization with its train of demographic, political, economic, religious, and ideological changes. Race relations in such a context would normally be expected to attenuate with the advance of modernity, with the source of intergroup differences shifting from race to culture and class. Late in his career, Park in fact predicted that future racial conflict would be confounded with or even superseded by class conflict. Restricting the analysis to the United States, where race relations were epitomized (though not, of course, exhausted) by the relations between whites and blacks, there had been no race relations *sensu stricto* in the antebellum South because blacks were excluded from the sphere of social competition. Nor did race relations emerge afterward with the instatement of the caste system and its emphasis on 'etiquette,' in which blacks' status was determined by a social regime designed to enforce racial cooperation. The era of race relations proper had been ushered in at the turn of the century by sweeping societal changes, especially the exodus of rural blacks to the cities and the gradual rise of a black middle class and intelligentsia. As blacks came into increasing competition with whites, relations between them took the form of physical, geographical, economic, and/or cultural contacts and conflicts of all kinds. These phenomena were perfectly tangible and capable of being studied. As we have seen, Park carried out a wide-ranging applied sociological research program devoted to the study of American race and ethnic relations, focusing on the relationships between minority groups (most notably but not exclusively blacks) and the white majority.[23] It was in this empirical context that he interpreted prejudice as a tool used by whites to prevent or hinder blacks from competing with them.

Park's innovations in this area were many. However – and here is the central tension in his work – races were for him not just subjective contributors to society: they were also a matter of objective fact. One recalls his definition of race relations as relations between peoples distinguished by *marks* of racial origin; one thinks of his definition of race consciousness, as real in his eyes as caste or class consciousness, or the passage in *Introduction to the Science of Sociology* describing the 'temperament' of black people, their distinctive, biologically transmitted characteristics, their alleged propensity to be emotionally expressive but not enterprising (see p. 61). Apart from the ambiguity here, the potentially racist undertones, it is Park's *reification* of race – for that is what it is – that makes the concept highly suspect as a scientific construct. It is an ideological construct, and its presence demonstrates Park's lineage with the grand racialist theories of the early twentieth century. He oscillates between nature and culture, as he did with the concept of assimilation. Therefore, his 'race' cannot be assigned any rigorously scientific status; on the contrary, the concept mirrored the social and intellectual context in which it evolved.[24]

It might be thought that Park's immediate successors Dollard and Myrdal would improve on the epistemological soundness of race and prejudice theories, but it was not so. Race was still being conceived of unscientifically as an objective fact underlying individual and collective inequality, this despite the mid-century remonstrances of eminent contemporaries in fields such as physical anthropology.[25] The durability of this misapprehension in the face of clear evidence to the contrary confirms the intrusion of ideology into the epistemic space of Anglo-American race relations theory and highlights its distorting effects on the corpus that was being assembled.

Beginning with Dollard's *Caste and Class in a Southern Town* and continuing with Myrdal's *An American Dilemma,* the focus in analyzing prejudice shifts from races to racists – from the distinctive traits of minority peoples to the psychology of the individual members of the (white) majority interacting with them. After allowing that prejudice is rooted in a race relations system, Dollard defines racism as 'a defensive attitude intended to preserve white prerogatives in the caste situation and aggressively to resist any pressure from the Negro side to change his inferior position.'[26] Wieviorka explains what is taking place:

> with Dollard ... [p]rejudice is no longer the instrumental rationalization of a domination, or, at least, it is no longer merely that. It becomes a mode of resolving problems and tensions which have their origin elsewhere than in contact between races: namely, in the lived experience of the members of the racializing group, who find in the racialized group an outlet for their social and psychological difficulties.[27]

An American Dilemma takes the same tack. When Myrdal writes in his introduction, 'it became increasingly evident that little, if anything, could be scientifically explained in terms of the peculiarities of the Negroes themselves,'[28] it is clear that he has no interest in biological essentialism, that he conceives of African Americans as social subjects. For him, racism is an attitude founded on ignorance, giving rise to behavior aimed at 'classifying the Negro low and the white high,'[29] an utterly irrational means of keeping blacks in their lower status and even rendering them invisible. Revisiting an idea previously expressed by Weber and Tocqueville, Myrdal argues that prejudice against blacks was rooted in the behavior of poor southern whites. As blacks gained on them socially, the poor whites practiced prejudice as a way of maintaining their superior status and projecting the frustrations engendered by their relations with other whites onto a scapegoat. One would expect, therefore, to find higher-class whites exhibiting less racism, relieved as they were by the poor whites of having to bear this 'painful task necessary to the monopolization of the power and the advantages.'[30] In an attempt to get at the psychosocial underpinnings of prejudice, Myrdal limits consideration of the social context, race relations, in which prejudice manifests itself, though he does not ignore it completely: 'the chief virtue of his reasoning ... is an acceptance that, in order to understand racism, one should turn aside from the concrete experience of the relations between blacks and whites – though this is, in fact, also covered to a considerable extent – and give priority to examining the ideological work carried out by whites on themselves, to looking at their internal contradictions, their dilemmas.'[31]

I have drawn upon the analysis in the first part of this book in concluding that mid-twentieth-century Anglo-American sociological theories of race and prejudice were derived from two different models, one focusing on race relations and the other on the individual actor. Claims of blacks' inferiority had shifted to invoke cultural rather than biological arguments. Meanwhile, the work of theorization was not impermeable to the new tendency, rooted in Myrdal's contribution, to favor direct professional intervention in society as a way of attenuating conflicts caused by prejudice.

The Peripheral Sociology

How epistemologically sound were the comparable theories of race and prejudice put forward by the African American sociologists?

THE FIRST GENERATION: DU BOIS

W.E.B. Du Bois devoted considerable efforts to theorization, for he understood its fundamental importance in establishing a new discipline. His early conceptualization of race (even before *The Philadelphia Negro*, it will be recalled) is completely out of step with the Anglo-American approach to human inequality at that time, not to mention the widespread faith in white supremacy. Du Bois configured race as an essentially sociohistorical construct, a fact of culture and not of biology; indeed, this was one of the principal tenets of his great work of 1899. In a context of great hostility, he had to fight alone for his sociological cause, even though his empiricist model was, in scientific terms, decades ahead of the mainstream:

> Du Bois's sociological studies on Negro life stood virtually alone against a flood of nonscientific and virulently racist dogma – which included Charles Carroll's *'The Negro a Beast'; or 'In the Image of God'* (1900); Thomas Dixon's *Leopard's Spots* (1902); Robert W. Shufeldt's *The Negro, A Menace to American Civilization* (1907); and William Graham Sumner's *Folkways* (1907). The latter explained that racial 'folkways' were 'uniform, universal in the group, imperative, and invariable.' At a period when white social scientists and novelists denied the humanity of Afro-Americans, Du Bois established their sociological diversity and integrity.[32]

For the good of his own sociology but to the detriment of his career, Du Bois directly challenged scientific racism. At times, though, he gave way to pressure and reproduced his adversaries' logic in spite of himself. It was unfortunately not possible for him to completely transcend the historical and ideological dictates of his era: 'DuBois, in bitterness and frustration over prejudice against members of his race, responded at one point by appealing to a counter-racism based upon the supposed superiority of Negroes to whites.'[33] He countered assimilation, the governing idea at the heart of Anglo-Saxon sociology, with its opposite, isolationist nationalism. For example, 'The Conservation of Races' contains passages clearly indicating that he entertained the rejection of any form of absorption or assimilation into white society: 'if in America it is to be proven for the first time in the modern world that not only Negroes are capable of evolving individual men like Toussaint, the Saviour, but are a nation stored with wonderful possibilities of culture, then their destiny is not a servile imitation of Anglo-Saxon culture, but a stalwart originality which shall unswervingly follow Negro ideals.'[34]

Like several black contemporaries, Du Bois was convinced that African Americans had been misled by history as to their identity within American society. Forced to grapple with their identity confusion ('What, after all, am I? Am I an American or am I a Negro? Can I be both? Or is it my duty to cease to be a Negro as soon as possible and be an American?'),[35] they could look to the following solution:

> We are Americans, not only by birth and by citizenship, but by our political ideals, our language, our religion. Farther than that, our Americanism does not go. At that point, we are Negroes, members of a vast historic race that from the very dawn of creation has slept, but half awakening in the dark forests of its African fatherland. We are the first fruits of this new nation, the harbinger of that black to-morrow which is yet destined to soften the whiteness of the Teutonic to-day. We are that people whose subtle sense of song has given America its only American music, its only American fairy tales, its only touch of pathos and humor amid its mad money-getting plutocracy. As such, it is our duty to conserve our physical powers, our intellectual endowments, our spiritual ideals; as a race we must strive by race organization, by race solidarity, by race unity to the realization of that broader humanity which freely recognizes differences in men, but sternly deprecates inequality in their opportunities of development.[36]

To all those, white or black (e.g., Washington) who espoused assimilationism, Du Bois responded by defending cultural pluralism (or cultural differentialism, which amounts to the same thing). But this concept, at this stage of his intellectual progression, was not a pure theoretical construct free of the ideological interference suffered by his adversaries, for he was a fervent adherent of pan-Africanism. His conviction that black people in America had to make common cause with blacks elsewhere while differentiating themselves from the other races colored his theories with ideology. It was a misstep analogous to the one taken by his adversaries.

Du Bois is on more sound scientific footing in his treatment of race, rooted in the worldview of empiricist positivism. Here one finds the epistemological wellspring of his sociology, the anchor of its credibility in the face of his rivals' abstract, dogmatic imaginings. His advance with respect to the mainstream resides precisely in his American 'quest for objectivity' – the subtitle of a modern work on early American sociology in which, most ironically, the name 'Du Bois' is nowhere to be found.[37] His sociology was such a quest because it countered the arbitrary Anglo-Saxon interpretation of race with a construction of it as a sociohistorical phenomenon. In *The Philadelphia Negro* and the Atlanta University Studies, he offered a meticulous empirical analysis of the descriptive variables making up race, an approach that would be adopted by the whole of mainstream sociology long after Du Bois had moved on.

THE SECOND GENERATION: FRAZIER AND COX

In this section, I shall focus on the epistemological merits of the work of the two second-generation African American sociologists who most radically departed from the Chicago School: Frazier and Cox – the former's departure being, as we have seen, a long-term, gradual process while the latter's was an abrupt leap. (As for Johnson, his work tended to mimic the Parkian assimilationist model that he had internalized, while Cayton and Drake brought in elements from Frazier and Myrdal.)

The evolution of Frazier's conception of assimilation and race can be divided into three cognitive phases.[38] If one considers as a prelude the initial years in which he believed that assimilation made sense largely because of white resistance to the idea of African Americans as full-fledged citizens, the first phase involves a theorization of the two concepts according to a historical macroevolutionary perspective borrowed from the part-sociological, part-philosophical work of Giddings in his *Principles of Sociology*. In several review articles, Frazier conceptualizes race relations as a long-term societal process that was aborted at the time of emancipation, leaving blacks' assimilation into American society an unfinished process. The process could be restarted given three prerequisites: stimulation of black racial pride and continuance of black heritage, acceleration of blacks' acculturation to white middle-class values and customs, and reduction of their economic dependence.[39]

The second phase in Frazier's trajectory as a race theorist corresponds to his captivation with Park's ideas, starting in 1927: 'not only did [Park's ideas] legitimize his earlier thinking by revealing that assimilation was the inevitable outcome of an irreversible social process but they also provided him with a scientific model that he could follow in order to realize his racial goals.'[40] The scientific sophistication of his sociological theory took a great leap forward. Race became, for him, a purely sociohistorical category, the race relations cycle his primary interpretive instrument. The result was that assimilation became as ideologically rooted in Frazier's theory as it was in Park's, or even more so.[41] He would remain a rather strict Parkian on race relations until after the Second World War. The culmination, and also the terminal point, of this phase was *The Negro in the United States*, in which he asserted that blacks had successfully come through the first three stages of the race relations cycle (competition, conflict, and accommodation) and were about to make their definitive entrance into American cultural life. Frazier's optimism, in sharp contrast to Park's pessimism, was shared by others of his time who, 'through works like Gunnar Myrdal's *An American Dilemma* ... proclaimed their belief in the ultimate elimination of racial injustice.'[42]

The third phase began after 1950 when Frazier added considerable sophistication to his conception of race relations by positing that the phenomenon of 'assimilation by fusion,' for which he claimed to have found considerable historical evidence around the world, was totally inapplicable to the United States. He therefore theorized a second sociohistorical model, that of cultural differentialism, for the apparently exceptional American situation. This epistemological bimodality, limpidly expressed in Frazier's 1950s' work, is a central feature of its originality with respect to its Chicago antecedents.[43]

Contrary to Dale Vlasek's interpretation in 'E. Franklin Frazier and the Problem of Assimilation,' Frazier's late works – *Black Bourgeoisie*, 'The Failure of the Negro Intellectual,' and others – were not last-ditch attempts to rescue the possibility of assimilation in the United States. As an ideologue, Frazier might deplore that it had never occurred, but as a sociologist he had been deeply convinced of its empirical impossibility. Therefore, he urged black Americans who hoped to integrate into a viscerally hostile cultural environment to rebuild their own cultural identity. The impossible dream of fusion with white society had to be discarded, he wrote in 1962: 'the American Negro intellectual [has been] seduced by dreams of final assimilation ... the Negro intellectual should not be consumed by his frustrations. He must rid himself of his obsession with assimilation.'[44] On race in America, Frazier was neither an optimist nor a pessimist: he displayed a realism grounded in science, wedding it to an activist's combativeness. To black people, his message was a hard-hitting one of commitment to true emancipation, of willingness to fight the good fight until victory. The conceptual structure of Frazier's mature thought was like an egg with a double yolk, comprising two separate approaches, something that was not visible in any of his sociological contemporaries. But the very thing that made him original in epistemological terms – his radical attempt to combine the opposing concepts of cultural pluralism and assimilationism within a single paradigm – also created a problem of internal consistency. How did he tie these two together? In a word, with the thread of ideology. *Race and Culture Contacts in the Modern World* and many of his comparative sociology papers from the same period are filled with admiring remarks about foreign intellectuals and political figures, particularly Africans, whom Frazier felt had taken decisive steps toward racial democracy in their respective countries thanks to the support of their oppressed countrymen. Their example, he argued, should guide black American intellectuals, the black middle class, and the masses of black people in standing up as a people to white racism. Slow, inevitable assimilation would no longer do: it was time for collective emancipation, through open conflict if necessary.

For many decades, the imposing figure of Park had interposed itself between Frazier and his progenitor Du Bois. As Park's influence faded after mid-century, the two thinkers rediscovered their commonalities, their shared commitment to emancipatory radicalism. Du Bois was, of course, no longer institutionally involved in the advancement of African American sociology; he was, however, close to Frazier ideologically and supported him while the latter, following the trail once blazed by the former, placed stone after stone on the foundations laid in *The Philadelphia Negro*.

A similar statement applies to Frazier and Cox, and a close examination of their writings at this period points up rather surprising similarities between them. Like the others of his cohort, Oliver Cox was up against a wall of racist rejection in American mainstream academia.[45] Given this situation, his straightforward self-definition as a Marxist on the issue of race was one of great temerity, for Marxism was never the dominant current even among black social scientists.[46] Yet Cox's definitions of race and race relations in his *Caste, Class and Race* seem at first sight to be directly derived from the Chicago interactionist paradigm:

> It is evident that the term 'race relations' may include all situations of contact between peoples of different races, and for all time. One objection to the use of this term is that there is no universally accepted definition of race. The biologist and the physical anthropologist may indeed have considerable difficulty with this, but for the sociologist a race may be thought of as simply any group of people that is generally believed to be, and generally accepted as, a race in any given area of ethnic competition. Here is detail enough, since the sociologist is interested in social interaction ... The sociologist is interested in what meanings and definitions a society gives to certain social phenomena and situations.[47]

> We may think of race relations, therefore, as that behavior which develops among peoples who are aware of each other's actual or imputed physical differences. Moreover, by race relations we do not mean all social contacts

between persons of different 'races,' but only those contacts the social characteristics of which are determined by a consciousness of 'racial' difference.[48]

It becomes clear, however, that for Cox, race is no natural category to which people have instinctive reactions but a byproduct of historical exploitation: 'What then is the phenomenon, the beginnings of which we seek to determine? It is the phenomenon of the capitalist exploitation of peoples and its complementary social attitude. Again, one should miss the point entirely if one were to think of racial antagonism as having its genesis in some "social instinct" of antipathy between peoples. Such an approach ordinarily leads to no end of confusion.'[49]

For Cox, then, 'race relations' are a form of conflict deriving from a pre-existing situation of capitalist exploitation, a fundamentally unequal system of societal relations. Given his Marxist leanings, the kind of conflict he considered important was conflict between classes – the bourgeoisie versus the proletariat. This emphasis on capitalist exploitation logically led to the following definition of prejudice: 'Race prejudice ... developed gradually in Western society as capitalism and nationalism developed. It is a divisive attitude seeking to alienate dominant group sympathy from an "inferior" race, a whole people, for the purpose of facilitating its exploitation ... race prejudice is peculiar to the system of capitalist exploitation.'[50]

This conceptual apparatus is much more than an extension or a carbon copy of Park's race relations theory: it was the only starkly different epistemological alternative to Park's model, or even Myrdal's, in the mid-century American academic and ideological arena. As a Marxist alternative, it was also an irritant of the first order.

Cox devoted considerable space to the concept of assimilation in the last chapter of *Caste, Class and Race,* whose opening sentences posit it as a central feature of African American life: '[Blacks'] social drive is toward assimilation. In this respect Negroes are like most other American immigrants; it is well known that the social tendency toward assimilation is an American cultural trait.'[51] Thus, blacks' inclination to assimilate was an empirical social fact analogous to the same inclination among other subgroups of Americans. Such an inclination degenerated into a social problem when obstructed by discriminatory practices: 'In the United States white foreigners are ordinarily encouraged to assimilate, but peoples of color are not.'[52] How could this debilitating barrier be overcome? For one thing, argued Cox, it had been erected not by black Americans but by whites, and for their own benefit, yet the problem of its resolution had fallen to blacks: 'To be assimilated is to live easily and unobtrusively in the society. One must be at home, so to speak, with the dominant social organization. So long as a group is identified or remembered as alien, it will be forced to have a divided allegiance. Naturally, the assimilation ideal of American Negroes is to be recognized as unqualified Americans.'[53]

Those striving for assimilation could envisage two possible strategies for attaining it. The first was to continue to do so without help – an unpromising path if the past was any indication of the future: 'It is possible that Negroes are farther away from ultimate oneness and belonging in the general American social order than any white European group that might currently enter the country. If this is so, then Negroes in America are less well assimilated than any conceivable white immigrant group.'[54] The second strategy to be considered, then, was alliance-building. Pursuing this line of thinking, Cox suggested that a broadened perspective might be necessary: 'acculturation alone may not be sufficient for assimilation; in other words, the mere assumption of the dominant cultural patterns has not been sufficient to assure complete integration of the group.'[55] He devotes the rest of the chapter to topics tenuously related to assimilation, but returns to it tangentially in his conclusion when he suggests a new interpretive approach to the race problem – a broad worldwide proletarian front: 'The problem of racial exploitation, then, will most probably be settled as part of the world proletarian struggle for democracy; every advance of the masses will be an actual or potential advance for the colored people. Whether the open threat of violence by the exploiting class will be shortly joined will depend upon the unpredictable play and balance of force in a world-wide struggle for power.'[56]

In sum, Cox's theory of race and assimilation, which forms the core of *Caste, Class and Race,* is far removed in both its premises and conclusions from the theories of Park, still influential in 1948. Starting from his annunciatory final paragraph, he proceeded to expand the focus in three subsequent works, seeking to develop the guiding idea that while American racial conflict has its peculiarities, it is far from unique: comparison with the rest of the world shows that it is just one example of a broader pattern. He contended that the resolution of any racial conflict, regardless of where it occurs, is closely linked to, in fact contingent upon, the outcome of the power struggle between the bourgeoisie and the proletariat. Interestingly, Cox's three later works ignore the theme of assimilation completely. Why? The wrong answer is that it no longer interested him, that he considered himself to be of Caribbean, not American heritage, or that the years after 1950 saw him pursuing a macrosociological, transhistorical, comparative agenda that led him to see the American racial situation in a different light. The right answer, in my view, is that the enlargement of his Marxist-aligned perspective to encompass the entire world, while not excluding or invalidating assimilation as a topic of interest, puts it in perspective within the broader framework of the class struggle found wherever capitalism has reigned supreme. Thus Cox joined Du Bois and Frazier in theorizing that the historical forces that might one day dissolve the American racial conflict were in fact world-historical; that the international proletariat would inevitably be an important agent of this transformation, and that emancipation was an imaginable empirical outcome for all the black people of the world, while American blacks represented a particular and not necessarily typical target of white racial oppression.[57]

The Originality of Black Sociology

Let us return to our starting question, which may now be paraphrased: Can the early black American sociology of race relations legitimately aspire to the major epistemological status of a distinctive tradition equal in validity to its mainstream counterpart? The discussion to this point suggests that the answer is yes. Du Bois, Frazier, Cox, and to a lesser extent Johnson, Cayton, Drake, and others were responsible for the genesis and gradual differentiation of an indigenous *space of the imagination* that was not reducible to any other of its time. Its richness derives from the broad reservoir of ideological and other representations that the African American community produced in order to survive as a cultural entity in the face of rampant racism. It was a social imagination that almost literally (in the terms of Fernand Dumont's theoretical model) served as the lifeblood of the community:

> Societies interpret themselves; when science leaves behind it the interpretation that gave birth to it, it is via an ever-incomplete argumentation that it asserts its autonomy ... it is true that representations derive their conditions of production from the social system, but couldn't they be given central importance in attempting to understand how a social imagination serving as a point of reference for both scientists and social subjects is constituted?[58]

The collective representations at the core of the social imagination encompass ideologies, historiography, and literature; together, they sketch out a 'spectrum of changing dialectics'[59] within the culture. These in turn engender, in various ways, more circumscribed constructs such as a scientific imagination, from which theories emerge as if by some singular process of crystallization. My essay has been concerned all along with a polyphonic sequence of such interpretive voices.

But another crucial question must be addressed in regard to the early African American sociologists: To what extent can one detect the systematic interference or intrusion of ideology into their production of scientific knowledge about race? I have maintained that the whole of mainstream sociology during this era was shot through with the ideology of inexorable and unilinear social progress, and that in Park this ideology dictated the construction of his central concept of assimilation. But ideological contamination is also evident in the work of Du Bois, Cox, and Frazier. Their shared assumptions about patterns in American race relations converged toward pluralism or cultural differentialism – the opposite of assimilation. In Du Bois it took the form of a quasi-utopian pan-Africanism, while in Cox and Frazier it was another species of political utopia: world solidarity among oppressed black people, a prospect described in Marxist language by the former and in more moderate, perhaps quasi-Marxist terms by the latter.

Does this mean that both Anglo-American and black sociology were afflicted with one of science's incurable infirmities? Not so, says Dumont in his classic work on ideologies: 'science constitutes and reconstitutes itself by delimiting, through ideological discourses, its sphere of operation ... It should be emphasized that science is discourse or ideological practice not only in its beginnings but in the whole of its trajectory and the totality of its statements.'[60] Thus, the close cohabitation of science with ideology in this case need not threaten its claim to objectivity, provided that the factors conditioning the genesis of knowledge are meticulously kept separate from the theoretical discourse that seeks to push the bounds of knowledge and satisfy, according to the rules set by the scientific community, one's critical intelligence of reality:

> The fact that science finds its beginnings in a broader environment, social context, or interweaving of pre-existing sciences does not predetermine its truth or falsity. Nor does the fact that throughout its evolution it relies on these initial suggestions as a sort of norm to guide its progress predetermine its validity. That merely shows that one does well to distinguish

more clearly, for the sciences, the problem of the construction of the object from the problem of truth.[61]

Thus the originality of American black sociology vis-à-vis the mainstream was in large part due to its different ideological affiliations. However, returning to the criticisms of Hughes, Coser, and Wilson discussed earlier, another problem afflicts both traditions in the American sociology of race. I am not, of course, referring here to a methodological issue, for by now it should be clear that the Chicago School background of the sociologists in question gave them a panoply of valid qualitative and quantitative procedures with which to work. The problem deplored by the three critics – a problem they saw as calling into question the very scientificity of race relations sociology – was rather the lack of systematicity at the heart of their cognitive constructions. The early sociologists did not succeed in building an abstract system of concepts that could interrogate social facts at a high level of generality and predict their likely empirical outcomes. If such cognitive maturity had been attained by the 1960s, then these theories should have predicted, at least in broad outline, the kinds of radical transformations in white-black relations that took place.

That such structural imperfections should have marred the postwar sociology of race is surprising given the existence of at least three major contemporaneous currents in the social sciences in which systematization was identified as a key stage in the valid and complete construction of the study object. Talcott Parsons, in parallel with his wide-ranging structural-functionalist program, wrote at length about the importance of systematic theory in general sociology after 1945.[62] Gaston Bachelard's epistemology, with its insistence on the need for 'rupture' with commonsense or social 'theories' of reality (such as ideologies), was much debated during that time. And the critical Marxian epistemology of the Frankfurt School, spearheaded in the United States by Theodore Adorno and Max Horkheimer, made systematicity a cardinal norm of the production of explanatory theories in sociology.

The sociology of race relations would have taken quite a different form if its practitioners had engaged in dialogue with any of these currents of thought. If, for example, Park, Myrdal, Frazier, or Cox had grasped the importance of Bachelard's epistemological break (*rupture*), they would undoubtedly have taken distance from their respective ideological convictions. They might then have theorized unilinear assimilationism or cultural differentialism, as the case might be, as legitimate objects of knowledge within an abstract conceptual framework, a true explanatory system. If Frazier and Cox had absorbed the insights of the Frankfurt School, they would have had at their disposal a rich conceptual heritage derived from Hegel, Marx, and Weber with which to theorize racial conflict as a particular expression of the alienation, reification, and mystification operative within universal historical and social praxis.[63]

Isolated from these critical trends that were profoundly remaking postwar Western norms of scientificity,[64] the early American sociologists of race may be fairly said to have missed an opportunity. Not only did they fail to make use of available materials that would have enabled them to move toward systematicity, they failed to comprehend the epistemological necessity thereof. Without such a conceptual apparatus, they were unable to foresee the African American 'revolution' of the 1960s.

Why did the race relations theorists operate in so isolated a fashion? If they passed over Parsons, it was because he had long been considered beyond the pale for being the main architect of the sole paradigm competing with that of the Chicago School. Moreover, Parsons himself never exhibited much interest in the phenomenon of race before the 1960s, his only work on the subject being his contributions (including the introduction) to *The Negro American* (1966). One wonders why Cox and Frazier were not drawn to the Frankfurt School, considering the convergence of their scientific and political concerns with those of its members. I would posit that Frazier kept his distance from it for nationalistic reasons, preferring the influence of black American radical sources (e.g., Du Bois) to German sources. Cox, on the other hand, ignored them entirely, making a point of referring only to Marx and Engels directly, not their heirs. He worked on his own to reconstruct the issues of class struggle and apply them to the specific case of race relations. As for Bachelard, there seems to have been total ignorance of his rewarding critical insights into science.

All this being the case, can it be said that these sociologists produced bad science? Yes and no. Judged with reference to the epistemological breakthroughs of their era, what they produced was a backward sociology of debatable cognitive value. But if African American sociology in particular is judged by its trajectory from Du Bois onward, a different verdict is reached. Though the works produced by his successors are undistinguished in epistemological terms, they exhibit undeniable progress in terms of explanatory theory and research methods, admittedly influenced in this by the interwar conceptual developments of the Chicago School. Field research and data interpretation methods had gained in reliability, and what Johnson, Cayton, Drake, and Frazier called theory was the outcome of that process. Their theory essentially consisted of first-level generalizations – descriptive typologies, hierarchical rankings – that amounted to genuine advances in sociological knowledge, given the context in which they were produced. For example, the Marxian comparative historical generalizations of Cox, the pure theoretician of the group and a man of considerable erudition, represented a non-negligible achievement even if they infringed the modern rules of abstract systematization in science. In short, the African Americans produced a respectable but imperfect body of knowledge that distinguished itself from mainstream sociology.[65] Moreover, they all truly displayed great courage in persisting in the face of a formidable ideological obstacle – institutional racism.

Breaking Down the Barriers: Racism in Academia

If the content of Anglo-American sociology was colored by racism, as should by now be obvious, the institutional environment in which African American sociologists worked was equally so. And if the amalgam of ideas and practices known as racism pervaded American academia, it is because certain features of the university as a social system predisposed it to do so. In this section I shall examine the broad social factors due to which the American university developed as a site of both open inquiry and rampant racism, repression, and intolerance. I shall go on to consider why Du Bois's efforts to break through the wall of academic racism met with total failure while those of his intellectual heirs, Frazier, Johnson and the rest, were more fruitful.

The American university was a creation of the seventeenth and eighteenth centuries, when the first private universities (Harvard [1636], Yale [1701], Princeton [1746], etc.) were founded; they were followed by the state universities. However, a much more typical structure of higher education from the colonial regime until after the Civil War was the college. Most of these were small religious or sectarian institutions that saw their role as attending to the classical moral and intellectual education of young Americans: 'The American college in the first half of the nineteenth century was centered in tradition. It looked to antiquity for the tools of thought, to Christianity for the by-laws of living; it supplied furniture and discipline for the mind, but constrained intellectual adventure. Like most institutions anchored to tradition, the ante-bellum college was also paternalistic and authoritarian.'[66]

The status of the college in the American educational system eroded steadily and appreciably after 1865. The rapid expansion of scientific and technical knowledge, the growing secularization of American culture, and the appearance of new needs linked to the resumption of economic and industrial activity caused the college to give way to a more complex structure that was better adapted to the new circumstances: the 'modern' university.[67] With the rise of the university came the creation of advanced programs of study and research at specialized institutions such as Johns Hopkins (1876), Clark (1887), Stanford (1891), and Chicago (1892). The result was heightened competition among both private and public universities, leading in turn to the injection of considerable sums of money into the university system so as to recruit qualified students and professors. Another consequence was the emergence of a hierarchy among institutions of higher learning in which authority was concentrated in specific geographical areas:

> Certain places came to stand out in the cognitive map. These were either the new universities like Johns Hopkins, Clark, Chicago, and Stanford, the slowly self-transforming older universities of the Eastern seaboard or the state universities of the Middle West and California. These were the centers, the influence of which helped to create the intellectual consensus about problems and procedures in each field. The consensus in a given field about what was true and important emanated from the center.[68]

This emerging hierarchy inevitably instilled in academics a self-awareness as members of an intellectual elite, a group different from the rest of society and amply deserving of their independence.[69] Another key aspect of the modernization of the American university in the late nineteenth century was the phenomenon of professionalization: 'By and large the American university came into existence to serve and promote professional authority in society. More than in any other Western country in the last century, the development of higher education in America made possible a social faith in [the] merit, competence, discipline, and control that were basic to accepted conceptions of achievement and success.'[70]

This cognitive and professional authority, manifested through various channels (associations, journals, conferences, symposia), gave academics enviable prestige and symbolic power. Moreover, the momentum created by the expansion of higher education reaffirmed the new American middle class, giving rise, among other things, to the culture of professionalism that is one of the hallmarks of American society:

> The American university has served as a primary service organization, a professional service institution which has made possible the functions of many derivative institutions serving the middle class ... a special relationship has developed between the kinds of training given in universities, the kinds of problems Americans can define in their lives and attempt to solve, and the kinds of people who succeed in acquiring status, power, and wealth.[71]

In the age of positivism, when science was largely rid of religious or metaphysical considerations, the foregoing structural characteristics combined to make the American university a powerful, exemplary, influential social institution whose stated normative purpose was the disinterested pursuit of knowledge at the highest levels and its transmission through teaching, specialized publishing, and popularization. But simultaneously the institution was coming under pressure from the industrialists who were busily transforming the face of the modern United States. Apart from inflecting the course of the work being done at the universities, they wanted to sideline those academics who were speaking out too loudly against industrial interests. Such external pressures threatened the independence of the university, which defended itself by staking out the boundaries of academic freedom within the institution:

> Ever since the modern university took its present form at the end of the nineteenth century, the concept of academic freedom has been periodically debated and redefined. Rarely were these reappraisals stimulated by what was happening on campus; the academy usually revised its notion of academic freedom in response to external demands for the removal of individual dissenters ... in order to keep outsiders from intervening in such sensitive matters as the hiring and firing of teachers, faculty members and administrators scrambled to show their critics that they could handle their political problems on their own. They did this by claiming that all personnel decisions within the academy were technical ones, determined by the intellectual demands of each discipline, and thus beyond the competence of anyone who lacked a Ph.D.[72]

This defense of the university's independence had consequences for both administrators and professors. For the administrators, it represented a useful and ostensibly objective way to circumscribe the bounds of allowable dissent: 'It created an intellectually defensible zone of political autonomy for the professoriat, which ... was sufficiently circumscribed so as to exclude as unscholarly whatever political behavior the leading members of the academic community feared might trigger outside intervention.'[73] Correspondingly, the professors now had to cope with a rigid mechanism of control that could easily give way to intolerance or repression as circumstances demanded. The late-nineteenth-century social situation of intense populist agitation in the face of triumphant capitalism militated in favor of rigid control and strict censorship of what was taught and written at the university: 'By 1895 it was clear that the academic profession was not going to accept the advocacy of controversial social or political reforms as legitimate scholarship. Academic victims of political repression could, it seems, retain their jobs if they kept quiet and gave up their political activities.'[74]

Thus, the modern American university must, at that stage of its development, be decoded as a politically and ideologically repressive institution that had no room for radicals. After an exceptional period of progressiveness from 1907 to 1914, this repressive character became accentuated and reached a peak with the war and in the 1920s. War hysteria exacerbated the university administrators' insecurity, and they reacted by clamping down on academic freedom.[75] These developments therefore coincided with the time when Johnson, Frazier, and the other African Americans of their generation were embarking on their academic careers. While both whites and blacks were targeted, the risks were much greater for the latter:

> Although many young Afro-American intellectuals like Frazier were eager to go to graduate schools ... they quickly found themselves in an academic milieu that, though socially liberal compared with black colleges, was extremely paternalistic and demanded a high level of ideological conformity. Dissent was tolerated only within limited parameters ... During World War I an informal loyalty oath was administered, and dissidents were fired for any expression of an unpatriotic attitude.[76]

Institutional loyalty was the order of the day. Despite the liberalism they publicly espoused, the universities valued their outward reputation more highly than the intellectual debate taking place within their walls, even where that debate aimed to advance the cause of objectivity: 'In almost every situation, faculty members and administrators responded to outside pressures for the dismissal of dissenting faculty members in accord with what they believed would best protect or enhance their school's reputation.'[77] It was not until the onset of the Great Depression that political repression in the American university system eased somewhat, influenced by the nationwide popularity of left-wing social movements and the Communist Party.

The irony of history had it that during the same period when enforcement of ideological conformity through repression and intolerance was becoming a key structural feature of the university, those university intellectuals with the greatest capital of credibility and prestige (*sensu* Bourdieu) were proponents of the pernicious theory of biological racialism:

> We misinterpret the strength of the racism of the period ... if we imagine that its most formidable proponents were emotional bigots like the Ku Kluxers. It is essential to understand that quite a large number of people eminent in the sciences and the social sciences were then genuinely convinced that races vary greatly in innate intelligence and temperament ... It is natural that in the histories of the period the views of the extremists have been accorded more attention, but *it was mainly the academic writers on racial differences who made racism respectable.*[78]

Structurally, then, the intellectual authority of the proponents of biological racism found its parallel in the entrenched practices of institutional racism. The respectability of scientific racism introduced racist practices into the university, whose repressive character caused them to proliferate. It was a self-sufficient social system whose outward manifestation was an informal but generally accepted code of suitable behavior, a culture of conformity, within an academic environment divided along lines of color. This code, undergirded by the scientific norms of the day, prescribed that truth lay with the white racist intellectuals, that nonracists were in error, and that antiracists should be denounced as subversives. It seems to me that, broadly speaking, Bertram Doyle's idea of an etiquette of race relations in the South can be readily transposed to the university setting, where it sheds light on the social function of the practice and culture of academic racism: 'While etiquette and ceremonial are at once a convenience and a necessity in facilitating human intercourse, they serve even more effectively to preserve the rank and order of individuals and classes ...'[79] In short, it was a system whereby white academics had the latitude to assert their authority and ascendancy over blacks.

To summarize the foregoing discussion, the American university was, during the half-century from 1880 to 1930, a dynamic social institution enjoying abundant resources largely derived from private or corporate endowments. It had become a more complex institution as the result of increasing specialization and professionalization, leading to the emergence of prestigious and influential occupations. It was an institution that made it a point of honor to encourage high-caliber research and education in the name of the disinterested pursuit of truth. Simultaneously, it was the locus of a struggle for power among different social actors, notably on the basis of skin color. Intramural academic relations were ruled by an etiquette of race relations that directly contradicted the American democratic ideal of 'one nation indivisible.' Ultimately, the limits placed on the exercise of academic freedom from within made the university a model of ideological conformism, despite its public espousal of the liberal credo.

Impacts on Black Academics

The effects of this singular social system on the institutional trajectory and fate of black intellectuals, particularly the sociologists discussed in this book, were pernicious to say the least. Any of them who aspired to study and eventually work at the country's best universities faced a daunting obstacle:

> Until relatively recent years, a virtually impermeable racial barrier excluded Negroes from white universities and their superior facilities for teaching and research. In addition, the Negro scholar has found himself isolated in Negro colleges and universities which were themselves marginal financially and intellectually, existing precariously on what Edward Shils has called ... an 'intellectual periphery.'[80]

Because of systemic racism, the American university system bifurcated into two largely unconnected networks: the northern, eastern, and Midwestern universities – Shils's 'center' – where only whites could hope to pursue their careers, and the southern 'periphery,' below the color line, where blacks worked and studied. A parallel bifurcation in academic standards developed in which the southern network labored with much more limited resources and acquired a largely deserved reputation of inferiority. It should be noted that the oldest southern colleges and embryonic universities were already segregated by the time scientific racism became accepted in polite society. During and after Reconstruction, white supremacists had taken control of these institutions and expunged all mention of black and African history from the curriculum. As long as white control persisted – until late into the twentieth century – so did the discriminatory practices that went along with it. Thus, for example, Fisk had to wait until 1946 for its first black president, Charles Johnson, and other universities even longer. The only notable exception was Howard University, whose first non-white president was appointed in 1926. (It is not in the Deep South but in Washington, where liberal trends may have taken hold earlier.) The historian Ellen Schrecker, in her discussion of white academics who lost their jobs during the McCarthy era, presents a detail that speaks volumes about the persistence, even at that late date, of the divide between the two university networks: blacklisted white academics, it seems, had no place to go but south:

> Though it was all but impossible for the blacklisted professors to get regular academic appointments at a mainstream college or university, they could sometimes find positions in the periphery ... To get such a job, a full-time, tenure-track position in an American college, a blacklisted professor would have to go to the South, to the small, poor, denominational Negro colleges that were so desperate for qualified faculty members that they would hire anybody with a Ph.D., including teachers other educational institutions dared not touch.[81]

Given this context, one is led to wonder what were the social strategies used by the pioneering African American sociologists to achieve their goals, beginning with the goal of making a personal contribution to a new American science of race. How did they respond to systemic racism in academia?

DU BOIS

Let us first consider the case of W.E.B. Du Bois. If he had begun his academic career in, say, 1965, not 1895, his future would surely have held tenure-track positions, emeritus appointments, honorary doctorates, and all the distinctions befitting an academic star. The Ivy League schools would have competed to attract him to their faculties. Consider: within his first decade in academia, he had received a Harvard undergraduate fellowship, studied in Europe with the leading lights of German sociology, rapidly completed a doctorate, published numerous papers, and written a book that anticipated methodological standards still twenty years in the future. But in his time, Du Bois was kept out of the northern university circuit. As we saw in chapter 4, he had no choice but to work at a southern school, where he was increasingly starved of funding and resources. All the strenuous efforts that he dedicated to building durable collaboration between sociologists in the two university systems were for naught. And with all of that, there was nothing (at this period) even slightly subversive about his goals; he proceeded most conservatively, seeking only to enhance the status of the southern system in the hope that it might eventually join the mainstream.

There was surely no 'right' strategy that would have enabled Du Bois to accomplish what he sought to accomplish, nothing that he perhaps missed out of ignorance, myopia, or underestimation of his adversaries. The proof of his structural exclusion, his failure to break through the wall of systemic racism in academia, is provided by what took place later, when the New Negroes came on the scene. While their objectives were similar to Du Bois's, the university landscape of the 1920s and afterward had changed substantially since his day. Most important, a number of highly respected white social scientists in the dominant university system now presented themselves as the ideological *allies* of black people. Park, Burgess, and their Chicago colleagues were perfectly positioned to help their graduate students of color achieve many of their professional goals in spite of the institutional racism that stood in their way.[82] No such support was available to Du Bois. Structurally speaking, he was trapped within one of two hermetic epistemic spaces, something he would regretfully discover with the lapse of time.

If history had had it so, there were two contemporaneous white sociologists who might conceivably have taken up his cause: Robert Park and William Thomas. But while Park was active on the intellectual scene by the first decade of the twentieth century, he had no stable university affiliation at that point. More fatally for Du Bois, Park was a close friend and collaborator of Booker T. Washington, Du Bois's most formidable political and intellectual opponent. And while Thomas was teaching at the University of Chicago by the time of Du Bois's appointment to Atlanta, his deconstruction of the false premises of biological racism dates from around 1910, when Du Bois was about to abandon sociology for good. The very scarcity of such potential instances of synchronicity shows how total and intellectually damaging was his isolation, how impossible it was for him to amass the capital of scientific credibility that would have allowed him to make headway in the dominant university system. With reference to Bourdieu's model discussed in the last chapter, Du Bois did not exist as a respectable scientific agent to anyone who mattered in northern academia; he had no way to bend the scientific field to his will. In institutional terms, he was consigned to oblivion by the pernicious power of academic racism.[83]

THE SECOND GENERATION

Racism persisted in academia after the First World War, but its effects on the New Negroes were different because of their improved opportunities for social interaction with eminent and powerful members of the dominant university network; as well, the sociohistorical context for this interaction was rapidly changing. As racism intensified with the 'Red Scare' of 1919–20 and its witch hunts, a sort of sinister echo to the Russian revolution, the New Negroes rose in opposition to these phenomena, speaking in a single ideological voice of open protest against the racism that had poisoned academia at all levels: 'The challenge to racism on the campus broke forth with unprecedented force during the 1920s ... The wave of rebellion that engulfed most of the leading black colleges of the 1920s was one of the most significant aspects of the New Negro protest movement.'[84]

Another structural factor improving the outlook for African American sociologists at this juncture was the exceptional progressiveness of the University of Chicago sociology department by comparison with other academic settings of its time. Under Park's direction, the department boldly turned toward the study of race relations as an essentially societal phenomenon, with pride of place being given to field research. Interracial conflict was no longer perceived as an inevitable evil produced by the interplay of biosocial forces. Of this major development, Park was the ideological, scientific, and institutional linchpin. He had been profoundly marked by his direct and extensive experience with southern blacks. He knew better than other whites the poverty that they were fleeing when they came north, and he had developed great sympathy for them and their struggles.[85] Moreover, it was Park's wisdom to shrink from any self-identification as an activist or propagandist among his peers. He neither fought nor advocated politically for the cause of racial equality but presented himself as an open-minded moderate. As such, he was able to make his way through the academic hierarchy without arousing suspicion that his ambitions might be more radical in nature. Finally, his scientific competence was nearly unanimously recognized in sociological circles on both sides of the color line. Although his reputation had not yet reached its peak, it was sufficiently established by the 1920s for him to make race relations a sociological object of study in its own right. Park held the privileged position of gatekeeper in the country's most important scientific networks. His personal capital of credibility allowed him to wield tremendous influence.

A burning question remains about Park, however: given his enormous influence in academia, why didn't he arrange for either Johnson or, more likely, Frazier (who had a doctorate by 1931) to obtain a professorship in sociology at the University of Chicago? Wouldn't this gesture have made good on the progressive principles that he claimed to espouse? Why did he not take this honorable step before his retirement in 1934, rather than encouraging Johnson and Frazier to accept positions with peripheral institutions? After all, there can be no doubt that their qualifications for such a position were the equal of those of any competing white scholar.[86] On this subject, there is little that can enlighten us in Park's sparse autobiographical writings or in the critical works devoted to him. One hypothesis is that, given the implacable racism pervading white academia in the 1930s, he may have considered it prudent for his talented disciples to be shielded from the hostility that surely awaited them there and instead to be given the chance to establish their careers in 'safe' black institutions. It is also not impossible that Park was a more circumspect progressive than he has been depicted as being. Certainly he was willing to do a great deal for his black students, but could it be that he was not willing to cross the line that would place them on an equal footing with himself and his white colleagues? Perhaps there is truth to the critique of the 'liberal' Chicago culture presented by Oliver Cox in his introduction to Nathan Hare's *The Black Anglo-Saxons* (see p. 202). Yet another possibility was that Park declined to wield his influence on Johnson's and Frazier's behalf out of profound respect for them not only as individuals but also as members of a cultural group. Perhaps he felt that African Americans had to go it alone in breaking through the thick walls of academic racism, that the privilege of changing the course of history had to be theirs and theirs alone. The question of Park's rationale in this matter is crucial to the fates of the black scholars discussed in this book, and remains open.

To summarize, it was the progressive environment of the University of Chicago, combined with the activism of the New Negro movement, that effected a historic shift in American academia in the 1920s.[87] There was new connectivity between two previously mutually impregnable worlds, as educated blacks entered the dominant university system and formed new relationships with white scholars. What interpretive model best accounts for the complexity of the structure and social workings of these relationships? In my view, the model that best does so is one of reciprocity-based *exchange* between members of different racial groupings – in large part Warren Hagstrom's model in *The Scientific Community*, with elements of Bourdieu's model brought in to explain the fundamentally competitive framework in which academic action takes place. However, one must also account for the highly unequal roles and statuses of the participants. What I suggest is that the white sociologists, with their quasi-monopoly on power and influence, operated according to the logic of *patronage*, while the African Americans had little choice other than *accommodation* if they were to derive maximum cognitive, economic, and symbolic advantage in the alien environment they were being admitted to.[88]

An example will serve to illustrate the explanatory power of this sociological model. When Charles Johnson was admitted to the University of Chicago sociology department in 1917, the school's empiricist orientation placed it in the vanguard of the field. In assigning the younger man to report on the race riot of 1919, it was Park's intention to instill this orientation in him and to ensure that he derived the benefits of it, seeing to it, for example, that Johnson's name appeared on the cover of the voluminous report published in 1922 by the prestigious University of Chicago Press. In this exchange, Park was the patron. He provided knowledge, research proficiency, and influence, and the result was to put Johnson on the sociological map. In return, Johnson provided Park with his scientific and institutional loyalty. The asymmetry of the relationship meant that the latter was obliged to accommodate if he was to gain professional status in the highly competitive world of social science. Johnson was, among his cohort, the sociologist who was most comfortable in this role of protégé with respect to Park and Burgess, for whom he always showed the greatest respect. As discussed in chapter 5, he played the role well – throughout his career, in fact – and it enabled him to become 'the black scholar most highly regarded in foundation circles in the late 1930s.'[89] Moreover, it is fair to assert that his own tenure at Fisk University was faithfully modeled on the asymmetric exchange in which he had participated.

The initial trajectories of Frazier, Cayton, Drake, and Cox followed a similar pattern. Frazier, for example, reproduced the essential approach of Park's and Burgess's sociology of race in his doctoral thesis and subsequent 1930s writings. In exchange he was given institutional visibility, editorial support, research money, and conference invitations. His store of scientific credibility grew rapidly, earning him a career at Howard University and the opportunity to inflect the Chicago model itself. In the case of Cayton and Drake, Lloyd Warner was the main white patron, while Park played an auxiliary role. It was in large part thanks to Warner that *Black Metropolis* was accepted for publication by the University of Chicago Press, bringing visibility to its coauthors, while Warner could expect his reputation to be enhanced through his connection with the promising research carried out by his assistants of color. The case of Cox differed in that his patron, William Ogburn, through whom he was able to publish in the best social science journals of the 1940s, was not primarily a race relations theorist.

Again, it is important to remember that these relations of exchange took shape within a fundamentally asymmetric framework of center and periphery. To make them work, the participants had to exploit breaches in the still-oppressive color line. The race barrier still kept the African American sociologists who played the game of strategic accommodation locked out of the North; they could look forward to no better than a position in the peripheral southern university circuit.[90] Academic mores in the dominant circuit had evolved since the days of Du Bois, thanks notably to Park's racial progressivism and his great prestige and influence, but the color line still governed the American university system. And not only did it keep scholars physically separate, but the work they produced was codified as peripheral sociology or true sociology depending on which side of the line it came from.[91]

MYRDAL AND THE BLACK SOCIOLOGISTS

With a few important nuances, the same model of patronage and accommodation comfortably encompasses the relations between Myrdal and the African Americans. In the late 1930s Myrdal was naturally looking for competent contributors to help him fulfill his Carnegie-funded mandate. The influence of Park and Chicago had slipped but was still quite pervasive: 'By the late 1930s, the Chicago Department of Sociology had begun to lose its preeminent position within the discipline, as Park's successors lacked the intellectual and personal cohesion to extend the influence of the Chicago school. Nevertheless, Park and his students had produced the most significant body of research on race relations that Myrdal would confront.'[92] Myrdal therefore, in addition to soliciting the cooperation of the leading white race relations specialists (Dollard, Odum, Wirth, Warner, Boas, and Herskovits), turned to Park's students, Johnson and Frazier foremost.[93]

Johnson had three assets that made him a particularly valuable colleague: thorough practical knowledge of the difficult economic and social conditions of southern blacks; all-important contacts among granting bodies; and – like Myrdal but unlike Park – a worldview favorable to government planning and social reform.[94] Johnson's part in the project was to prepare the research note that later became *Patterns of Negro Segregation* (see pp. 163–4). As for Frazier, his chairmanship of the sociology department at Howard University placed him in a hotbed of radical thought whose non-Marxist character Myrdal was likely to find acceptable.[95] All Frazier's Howard colleagues were, like Myrdal, fervent assimilationists who viewed race as a white myth designed to justify exploitation as well as an instrument manipulated by the black bourgeoisie to enhance their status within their community. Frazier received two offers, one early in the project to produce several monographs, the second toward the end of the research in 1942 to critically review the manuscript of *An American Dilemma*.[96] He was flattered by the assignment, which enhanced his scientific credibility, and in return wrote an overall positive critique of the book.[97]

The services of Drake and Cayton were also solicited, the first for a paper on 'Negro Churches and Associations in Chicago,'[98] the second for a small research project.[99] Here again, the logic of patronage and accommodation was operative. In return for their contributions to the research project, the African American scholars received symbolic support in the form of citations, authorship of sections of the main text or appendices – in short, explicit recognition that enhanced their scientific credibility (in Cayton's case there was also monetary remuneration). It should be said in his favor that Myrdal's attitude toward his African American collaborators was highly unorthodox. He treated them as the scientific equals of their Anglo-American counterparts, paying no attention whatsoever to the prevailing institutional codification of white and black as center and periphery. In the same egalitarian vein, he made a point of visiting Du Bois twice during his mandate, even though he had not been included in the research team,[100] and in his final text writing that '[his] study of the Philadelphia Negro community ... stands even today as a most valuable contribution ...'[101] Du Bois appreciated

Myrdal's recognition and, in return, wrote a glowing review of *An American Dilemma*.[102]

This attitude of open-mindedness and authentic consideration from an outsider like Myrdal – someone with no corporatist interest to defend or any professional advancement agenda to pursue, someone unanimously respected for his great intellect and scholarly achievements – had great symbolic resonance. Once again, it is Bourdieu who provides the conceptual keys to an understanding of the events. To his central concept of a scientific field he adds the concept of autonomy: 'The concept of field serves to designate this relatively autonomous space, this microcosm possessing its own laws ... And one of the big questions that will be asked about scientific fields (or subfields) is indeed the degree of autonomy they enjoy.'[103] He proceeds to define autonomy in terms of the capacity of a scientific discipline or some other microcosm to withstand or even free itself from external constraints so that it can 'recognize only its own internal determinations.'[104] He refers here to an ideal social process: the acquisition by a discipline of increasing autonomy with respect to its competitors. This, in my view, was precisely what the early African American sociologists were attempting: to secure the autonomy of a scientific subfield while laboring under systemic racism. In that context, Myrdal's actions were a needed public affirmation of their scientific respectability, on the strength of which they could legitimately assert their autonomy with respect to the mainstream. In fact, many years later Myrdal contended that these individuals' radicalism had been a key asset in rendering their discipline autonomous within American sociology, thus corroborating Bourdieu's hypothesis that the end result of autonomy must be won through an emancipatory process vis-à-vis an obstacle or constraint in the environment.[105]

Then there is the mold-breaking Oliver Cox. During his time at Chicago he practiced accommodation like the others, though his approach was more selective. He took advantage of the resources available to him in an academic structure governed by the etiquette of race relations; but after Chicago, he chose to reinvent American race relations theory in a bold break from the traditions with which he had been inculcated. Instead of accommodating to the theories of the white establishment, he opted for a strategy of open confrontation. We have seen how he summarily disposed of the race theories of Park and Warner; similarly, his Marxist alignment led him to condemn Myrdal's enterprise as a 'mystical approach,'[106] arguing that it ignored the economic sources of the American race problem – the exacerbation of racial tensions by the white governing classes so as to better exploit the masses. His exemplary punishment for his systematic attempts to discredit the leading theories of race relations and replace them with a competing sociology derived from Marxism – in essence, for the crime of lèse-majesté – was to be relegated to the most obscure institutions of the southern periphery. Indeed, his institutional misfortune points to the existence of a qualitative hierarchy within the southern university system itself, a hierarchy analogous to the one existing in the North. If Frazier and Johnson were able to rise to the top of that hierarchy, it is clearly because they had the prudence never to attack Park, Warner, Odum, or the others directly. In the terms of the model presented above, Cox's refusal to accommodate earned him rejection and institutional marginalization in place of patronage.

In conclusion, the mid-century cohort of black sociologists paid the humiliating price of accommodation to a fundamentally racist academic hierarchy; they had no other choice if they hoped to pursue their professional advancement and maximize their chances of developing and promoting an authentic African American sociology. Not only did they succeed within these structurally absurd constraints, they transcended them by producing original, provocative scientific work with respect to the canons of the American sociology of race.

The Solace of Culture

According to the eminent contemporary historian John Hope Franklin, each of the African American sociologists of the generation I have been discussing faced a cruel dilemma in his situation of profound isolation: 'whether he should turn his back on the world, concede that he is the Invisible Man, and lick the wounds that come from cruel isolation, or whether he should use his training, talents, and resources to beat down the barriers that keep him out of the main stream of American life and scholarship.'[107] It is clear that they chose the opposite of invisibility and resignation: they chose to fight for intellectual emancipation. But since their isolation was not random but the result of a racist social construction, severe structural harm was done to their attempts to achieve their fundamental objective: the institutionalization of a new sociological paradigm as legitimate and credible as the mainstream paradigm, if judged by the epistemological standards of the day. In other words, their physical isolation gave rise to a *structural* isolation whereby they were hindered from progressing as a distinct *epistemic community* within the American scientific field – the end point, for Bourdieu, of the institutional establishment of any system of knowledge. By 'epistemic community,' I mean the configuration that African American sociologists would have had to form in order to occupy a stronger and more influential position as competent producers of knowledge in the general scientific field (viz. Holzner, a community of knowledge 'unified by a common epistemology and frame of reference').[108] This community would have had to be associated with an essentially radical vision of African American history, as Myrdal understood; all manner of forums and opportunities should have been available for black sociologists to consider how to effect an in-depth transformation of American society so that blacks could live free of racist constraints. There should have been mechanisms for the sharing and coordination of the resources necessary to achieve autonomy and self-determination for the new discipline. Absent the structural advantages enjoyed by their colleagues in the sociology department of the University of Chicago (or, to take another example, Columbia University), with its strong internal cohesion as a *social* system of scientific production, the black sociologists had to compete intellectually as outlying individuals. By dispersing and isolating them in the peripheral southern circuit and by provoking futile, artificial rivalries among them, academic racism functioned as a formidable structural hindrance to the creation of such an epistemic community.[109] Yet even so, they managed to create and disseminate an original sociological paradigm, breaking down many barriers in order to do so.

But to focus narrowly on the isolation of these sociologists within institutional settings is to miss a promising alternative sociological explanation for their perseverance. One is tempted to posit that that they drew solace and inspiration from the broader cultural forces operative in African American society during the same period of time; in particular, from the vibrant cultural movement known as the Harlem Renaissance. It comprised talented black intellectuals from a wide range of disciplines, such as the poets Claude McKay, Jean Toomer, Langston Hughes, and Arna Bontemps; the novelists Countee Cullen, Zora Neale Hurston, Nella Larsen, and Wallace Thurman; the philosopher Alain Locke; the artist and essayist Romare Bearden; the performing artist Paul Robeson; and the playwright Joseph Cotter, among many others (including W.E.B Du Bois). Simultaneous with this outburst of artistic achievement, America entered the age of urban jazz and blues, which came into their own with the commercialization of new sound recording techniques.[110] New York during this time was alive with the rhythms of this authentically American music as well as with readings of fiction and poetry produced by a close-knit group of some forty-five authors, who mingled with painters, stage actors, and lyric artists. It was a brilliant manifestation of creative imagination and pure energy taking place just as the pioneering generation of African American sociologists was coming up. One can only suppose that the black artistic community of the early twentieth century did much to counterbalance the isolation and oppression imposed by systemic racism. It must have served as an osmotic, energizing social milieu for postwar black intellectuals sold short by the wider society; in short, as a locus of exchange and interaction, encouragement and stimulation.

The Literary Connection

In fact, a more direct link between sociology and other forms of African American culture may be descried in the work of renowned novelists such as Richard Wright and Ralph Ellison, who, although best known for their fiction, also produced nonfiction of notable sociological import.

Wright was born in Natchez, Mississippi, in 1902 to a poor family. He attended school sporadically, spending time in an orphanage after the family was abandoned by his father. In 1927 he moved to Chicago. where he went from job to job, continued his education, and devoted himself to writing. It was a period of intense literary creation for him, as well as a time during which he moved to the left of the political spectrum, joining the Chicago John Reed Club and the Communist Party in 1933. In 1937 he left Chicago for New York and helped found the left magazine *New Challenge* while working as an editor at the Harlem office of the *Daily Worker.* The publication of his *Native Son* in March 1940 'made Richard Wright one of the great names among American novelists of the forties ... Wright was acclaimed as one of the most perceptive social critics of his time and hailed for his exceptional command of dramatic narrative.'[111]

The 1940s saw him produce work in a variety of literary genres including novels, autobiography, screenplays, and poetry. He had become increasingly disaffected with the Communist Party and broke with it in 1942, although continuing to identify himself as a radical writer comfortable with the Marxist perspective. His August 1944

Atlantic Monthly article 'I Tried to Be a Communist' aroused the party's enduring hostility. His reputation now international, Wright traveled to France in 1946 at the invitation of the French government, a life-changing move that led to his taking up French citizenship the next year. He returned to the United States only briefly thereafter (e.g., to Chicago to shoot a film derived from *Native Son*).[112] He reaffirmed his stature as a novelist with *The Outsider* (1953), which was deeply influenced by his association with the French existentialists. He traveled widely (in Africa, Spain, and Scandinavia, for instance) and focused on writing journalistic essays replete with powerful social criticism. The year 1958 saw him return to the novel form with *The Long Dream*, which was adapted for Broadway. His health was failing by then, and he died of a heart attack while working on a book of short stories in November 1960 at the age of fifty-two.

I have mentioned Wright's preface to *Black Metropolis* (see p. 171), and its existence is indicative of his closeness to professional sociology and its practitioners. He was a close friend of Horace Cayton, whom he met in Chicago in 1933, but in fact all Wright's works of fiction double as fascinating sociological documents,[113] demonstrating that he was a faithful comrade in arms of more radical sociologists such as Frazier and Cox. Wright's 'Blueprint for Negro Writing,' for example, defined the theoretical line of *New Challenge*. Writing as a convinced communist, he discussed what he saw as the close relationship between literature and politics and the equally close relationship between class perspective and ethnic culture. The text takes the form of a series of exhortations of literary and ideological if not sociological breadth. For example, 'Negro writers must accept the nationalist implications of their lives, not in order to encourage them, but in order to change and transcend them. They must accept the concept of nationalism because, in order to transcend it, they must *possess* and *understand* it. And a nationalist spirit in Negro writing means a nationalism carrying the highest possible pitch of social consciousness.'[114] He proceeded to associate the concept of social consciousness with that of responsibility or historical engagement:

> The Negro writer who seeks to function within his race as a purposeful agent has a serious responsibility. In order to do justice to his subject matter, in order to depict Negro life in all of its manifold and intricate relationships, a deep, informed, and complex consciousness is necessary; a consciousness which draws for its strength upon the fluid lore of a great people, and moulds this lore with the concepts that move and direct the

> forces of history today ... a new role is devolving upon the Negro writer. He is being called upon to do no less than create values by which his race is to struggle, live and die.[115]

To fully perform their role in society, writers have no choice but to draw on Marxism:

> it is through a Marxist conception of reality and society that the maximum degree of freedom in thought and feeling can be gained for the Negro writer. Further, this dramatic Marxist vision, when consciously grasped, endows the writer with a sense of dignity which no other vision can give. Ultimately, it restores to the writer his lost heritage, that is, his role as a creator of the world in which he lives, and as a creator of himself.[116]

But the authentic writer cannot stop at that:

> for the Negro writer, Marxism is but the starting point. No theory of life can take the place of life. After Marxism has laid bare the skeleton of society, there remains the task of the writer to plant flesh upon those bones out of his will to live. He may, with disgust and revulsion, say *no* and depict the horrors of capitalism encroaching upon the human being. Or he may, with hope and passion, say *yes* and depict the faint stirrings of a new and emerging life.[117]

Native Son is written in this spirit. It is, without doubt, a powerfully dramatic work of fiction, but it can also be read as sociology, shocking the reader by the extreme gravity of the 1930s racial situation it depicts. Fortified by his Marxist convictions, Wright described with fierce realism the effects of economic and racial oppression on his protagonist, Bigger Thomas, who breaks the supreme taboo of Anglo-Saxon America when he kills a white woman. The author uses the incident to reflect upon the huge question of revolutionary consciousness and violence.

Another of his works that makes the link between literature and sociology explicit is the essay *Twelve Million Black Voices*, which recounts the history of African Americans from slavery through Reconstruction to the massive upheaval caused by migration to the North. Wright's poetical prose style here was described by a contemporary, Arna Bontemps, as being in the authentic tradition of blues and spirituals. But there is nothing lyrical about the conclusion of *Twelve Million Black Voices*: it is a gauntlet thrown down to racist America, a prelude of sorts to the civil rights movement and to more militant African American currents of thought. If *Native Son* is a literary work rich in sociological insights, *Twelve Million Black Voices* is the opposite: a work of sociology written with great literary flair. Indeed, its combination of Marxist sociological discourse on American racism and sumptuous poetics rivals the best academic studies of the Chicago School and has few parallels in radical literature. His biographer describes how Wright accomplished this feat:

> His friend Horace Cayton was now director of the recently opened Parkway Community House ... Wright collected a great deal of material for the book, interviewing the young people who used the library or the clubs and consulting the notes of his friend Cayton, who generously shared the information he had gathered for *Black Metropolis*, a monumental study of the South Side, which came out four years later. Cayton also provided him with some broad general concepts, such as the sociological differences between urban capitalists and large landowners, on which Wright based his chapters 'Lords of the Land' and 'Bosses of the Buildings.'[118]

At a party given by the Caytons, Wright was given guidance on his independent study of sociology[119] and acknowledged his debt to sources such as *The Negro Family in the United States*, Wirth's 'Urbanism as a Way of Life,' and *Black Workers and the New Unions* in the foreword to the essay.[120]

He continued along these lines with two other works, *The Outsider* and *White Man Listen!* (a collection of lectures). *The Outsider* represented a major advance in his thinking. It repudiated both fascism and communism as models of society, substituting for them an attempt to problematize the human drama as a quest for balance between individual freedom and social order. Under the influence of the existentialists, he sought to redefine the idea of racial oppression as a universal and not solely American phenomenon, pursuing a globalism parallel to or convergent with the ideas of Frazier and Cox. As for *White Man Listen!*, it described the various ways that African Americans were torn between the pull of ancestral African traditions and beliefs and the demands of modernity. Here again, Wright explored a radical internationalist approach similar to those of Frazier, Cox, and Du Bois.[121]

Ellison's Invisible Man

Ralph Waldo Ellison was born in Oklahoma in 1914. From 1933 to 1936 he attended the Tuskegee Institute, where he was introduced to music and sculpture; literature remained, for him, a secondary interest, though he devoted considerable time to reading the great modernist works. It was his meeting with Wright toward the end of the decade that placed him firmly on the path of writing.[122] Wright gave Ellison his first publication opportunity, printing his review of *These Low Grounds* by Waters E. Turpin in a 1937 issue of *New Challenge*. Until after the Second World War Ellison's fiction output would remain slim. A Marxist like Wright, he aspired to be known for his critical essays, which he published in left-wing magazines such as *New Masses* and *Negro Quarterly*. Nevertheless, it was the experience of Marxism itself that brought him to novel writing: 'Like so many intellectuals who came of age in the thirties, Ellison became involved not only in social and political activity, but with the Marxist movement. His conscious decision to devote himself to the novel was simultaneous with his introduction into the orbit of the Communist Party.'[123]

In the 1940s Ellison periodically published short fictions amid his more abundant critical essays and reviews. Then, in 1952, came the masterwork, *Invisible Man*, winner of the National Book Award and the Russwurm Award. No one really saw it coming: its author went from obscurity to fame overnight. The book reveals a writer in full possession of his powers, someone who has found his distinctive voice. With this one inspired book, Ellison's stature as a major twentieth-century novelist was secure, though he never produced anything to equal it. His published work also includes two essay and interview collections, *Shadow and Act* (1984) and *Going to the Territory* (1986) as well as a dozen short fictions. Ellison died in 1994.

Many years after *Invisible Man*, Ellison admitted that the theme for the book had come about as the crystallization of a long intellectual progression starting from his work as an essayist and propagandist of communism during the 1930s and 1940s.[124] The theme, in a nutshell, is that of the African American's quest for identity in the confrontation with white society. The novel's nameless narrator, a young southern black man, embarks in ignorance (or naiveté, or lack of self-awareness) on a long and arduous process of coming to awareness and finally to self-affirmation through revolt against white values. He burns with ambition to climb the social ladder through his own determination and tenacity, but comes to grips with brutal reality in the form of repeated and devastating failures. His innocence prevents him from grasping the meaning of his successive experiences in the white people's world. The narrator's trajectory ultimately leads him to fall into an actual black hole: a manhole left open on the sidewalk. His fall into the darkness metaphorically touches off a salutary awakening. Now physically invisible, he realizes that he has always been socially invisible while in the grips of a formidable illusion of visibility. His identity has consisted of a sequence of social roles through which he has been set up for failure in the white man's world. The novel concludes with a moment of illumination and a promise of progress through suddenly acquired knowledge.

> Using his own mind for the first time, [the narrator] reviews his experiences and imposes a significant order on a chaotic world. His account is an ironic tale, for he is both narrator and protagonist. As narrator, he tells his tale from the dark underground where he has become newly sighted; as protagonist, he is willfully, if unconsciously blind, a part of the enveloping chaos. The account of his journey is *Invisible Man*, an affirmation and a first step in his ascent from the underground.[125]

More than a purely literary experience, *Invisible Man* may be read as a careful exercise in critical sociology. Ellison presents his hero as a black man acculturated from birth to the Washingtonian tradition of accommodation (also a key phase in Park's race relations cycle, as we know). The interpretation and representation given this concept, as a model of behavior, is one of rationalized submission and humility, as per one of Washington's most famous dictums: 'united with others of our country in everything pertaining to the common good, and, in everything social, separate like the fingers of the hand.'[126] Writing with acerbic irony, Ellison presents accommodationism as illustrative of the repression and alienation programmed into the white social order, the dehumanizing codes of conduct governing black people. His narrator, inculcated with the accommodationist delusion, represses the emotional conflicts caused by the indignities and humiliations to which he is daily subjected. He endeavors to conform to the dehumanizing standards of the majority society and accepts without complaint, even with enthusiasm, all the social roles assigned to him. In so doing, he places himself on the road to failure, but when it occurs, as it regularly does, he is taken unawares, understanding nothing of what is happening. It takes a fall into a manhole to bring him to consciousness.

Quite obviously, Ellison is mocking Washington's accommodationism and the Chicago School's placement of the concept of assimilation at the center of its theoretical corpus. Against this he pits his own brand of sociology, delivered with a novelist's gift for irony. Unlike Wright, Ellison never admired, much less borrowed from, the principal sociological paradigm of his day.[127] Rather like his contemporary John Dos Passos, he kept a prudent distance from American sociologists, mocking them (mostly the whites) on more than one occasion. He deviated from this course only once, in 1944, producing one of the subtler and more incisive reviews of *An American Dilemma*.[128] His aptitude for plying an intellectually independent course at the risk of controversy and incomprehension only heightens his stature as one of the greatest and most uncompromising figures of twentieth-century American literature.[129]

Summing Up

I now return to the question with which this final section began: how was it that the most imaginative of the African American sociologists managed to create a rich and original scientific oeuvre despite their systematic marginalization by white academic racism? The answer can now be formulated as follows: they clearly understood that while they felt a *duty* to help black Americans break free of this stultifying condition, they did not have to 'go it alone'; they could work in synergy with the writers and artists (notably the novelists) of their cultural community. Each of them, whether an artist or a sociologist, was working on the great task of ideological demystification within a social context that he had not chosen. Fernand Dumont is clear on this essential point: 'In any community of interests, literature is subjected to social conditions, a fact betrayed by its effort to break free of them. It would be pointless to try to free it from that which nourishes its transcendent fervor.'[130]

Frazier, Johnson, Cox, Cayton, and the other African American sociologists of their generation witnessed such 'transcendent fervor' whenever the great works of Wright, Ellison and others were published, or when they heard the great blues and jazz numbers that immeasurably enriched the twentieth-century musical heritage of the United States. The first African American sociologists had the chance to live in a time of intense creative energy bursting out of all the disciplines of their distinctive culture. They came to maturity in a time of great scientific, musical, literary, poetic, and philosophical vibrancy. Academic ideas and artistic creations were both parts of a provocative whole, a revolt against the unacceptable. Above and beyond differences of interpretation and explanation, the black community was surely united by an awareness that they and they alone were the source of this creativity. This, in my view, must have been significant compensation for the academic sociologists who never, unlike their white counterparts, came to form a real epistemic community, and therefore never collectively enjoyed the institutional power and authority that such a status confers. They all had profound personal knowledge of the terribly persistent barriers in their way, but they also knew that they were not alone in the struggle to beat them down (returning to John Hope Franklin's image). Therein lies all the difference. To borrow a concept dear to Park and also espoused by his African American peers, they could take symbolic consolation in the knowledge that they were working together to articulate and disseminate – to Americans and to the whole world – an authentic, noble race consciousness.

Postface: Imagining a Different History

With his phenomenal longevity, W.E.B. Du Bois was the figure who had the longest and most continuous involvement in the societal upheavals of the period covered by this book. By the first decade of the twentieth century, he had become an inspiration to many African Americans on the strength of prophetic pronouncements such as this one, from 1900: '[t]he problem of the twentieth century is the problem of the color-line, – the relation of the darker to the lighter races of men in Asia and Africa, in America and the islands of the sea.'[1] Lawrence Young and Lynn England speculate as to how sociology might have developed if Du Bois at Atlanta University had had access to the financial largesse of Rockefeller, or if an African American had been given a position at the University of Chicago or a comparable institution. They ask, 'How would a sociology with a more liberal political focus and an immediate experience of poverty and discrimination have looked?'[2]

One may surmise that this hypothetical sociology would have been unified rather than split into white and black variants by the insidious action of scientific and academic racism. It would have arisen and developed within a completely different zeitgeist. Supposing further that the African American hired by a first-rank northern university before the turn of the century had been Du Bois (one of the very few black intellectuals of the era to possess the requisite academic credentials), it is highly likely that his *Philadelphia Negro* would have been praised as the first objective sociological study of poverty, discrimination, unemployment, crime, and all the other phenomena adversely affecting the lives of the black people recently arrived in the cities of the North. Simply put, the course of scientific events would have been changed by this groundbreaking study; a new research tradition would have arisen and spread throughout the entire American university system.

There is also no doubt that his contemporaries would have noticed and appreciated, in Du Bois's published work, a conceptual richness going beyond the bounds of positivism and empiricism. In his early years at Harvard and Berlin, he had come into contact with a philosophical tradition very different from the Comtian and Spencerian tradition that then dominated Anglo-American sociology; to wit, the Hegelian phenomenology and neo-Kantian idealism taught to him by William James, George Santayana, Adolph Wagner, and Gustav Schmoller.[3] His early masterpiece, *The Souls of Black Folk* (1903), is cast in the mold of this philosophical tradition, which inspired an equally original sociological one. As things transpired, the preeminence of evolutionist positivism in mainstream sociology meant that this tradition would be ignored in its time.[4] Today, due recognition has been given to the sociological and philosophical originality of Du Bois's work, particularly in terms of the pertinence of the concepts treated in *Souls* to certain issues in contemporary sociology. For instance, 'We suggest that Du Bois's conceptions of Self and community are relevant for issues now being raised in conjunction with global migration. The Self is now theorized in terms of cosmopolitanism and hybridity ... which is quite consistent with Du Bois's conceptions in *Souls*. We also indicate that Du Bois's works are relevant for how sociologists pose questions about social justice.'[5]

If the Darwinian version of evolutionary positivism eclipsed the rich conceptual matter presented in *Souls*, it is because, racism being what it was in 1903, white sociologists had no more formidable weapon than 'scientific' theory with which to relegate blacks to the lowest level of the racial hierarchy. If, in an alternative historical scenario, scientific racism had not been the zeitgeist of the era, *Souls* would have met with a very different intellectual fate. It would have been celebrated as a major sociological work in the vein of phenomenological idealism, one of the early American classics in that tradition.[6]

But all this, of course, is in the realm of the historical counterfactual. All of the African American pioneers of sociology bore the scars of their ceaseless struggle against the sinister commandment – 'Stay in your place!' – that ruled both the university and the wider society. Because of this shameful state of affairs, the pioneering sociologists may be regarded as players on the stage of an authentic modern tragedy, as genuine tragic figures, given what they created under such limiting social, ideological, and institutional circumstances.

Du Bois, Frazier, Cox, and the other scholars examined in this book carried the burden of institutional racism throughout their lives. At the same time, with each of their works, they brought forward an entirely different representation of their true place in social science and society alike. Of course, there was no way for them to break down all the barriers of racial discrimination, but their constructive resistance to it was crucial to what scientific success they had. By refusing to internalize the degrading image of the black minority embodied in the dominant white model, by refusing to apply the stereotyping language of the Other to themselves, they succeeded in the task of inventing an original African American sociology, an academic tradition that is carried on today by William Julius Wilson, Elijah Anderson, Manning Marable, Tukufu Zuberi (Antonio McDaniel), Joyce Ladner, Orlando Patterson, and many others.

The black pioneers of sociology met and overcame innumerable hurdles along their way. They were subjected to ridicule and humiliation, but together with their peers in other academic disciplines and in the arts – in music, philosophy, poetry, and literature – they remained steadfast in their shared construction of a remarkable tradition of *protest* that has enriched twentieth-century American intellectual life. Had they lived long enough, they would certainly have savored the consecration of a great black voice in emancipatory literature that occurred when, in 1993, Toni Morrison was awarded the Nobel Prize – history's revenge, surely, and perhaps an object lesson for any people who, finding themselves an oppressed minority within an ostensibly democratic society, remain profoundly lucid in the face of such a strange circumstance.

Notes

Introduction

1 Parsons borrows the question from Crane Brinton, *English Political Thought*, 226.
2 Howard Winant, 'Dark Side,' 538.
3 Ibid.
4 Steven Seidman, *Contested Knowledge*, 97–8.
5 Charles Taylor, *Multiculturalism*, 26.
6 Benjamin Matalon, *La construction*, 90.
7 Ibid., 15.
8 Raymond Boudon, 'Les deux sociologies.'
9 Internalism is espoused in the work of its originator, Robert Merton, as well as in that of Warren Hagstrom and Stephen and Jonathan Cole, all of them working in the shadow cast by the philosopher of science Karl Popper.
10 The standard-bearers of externalism include a constructivist like Bruno Latour as well as relativists such as Karin Knorr-Cetina, Michael Mulkay, Barry Barnes, Steve Woolgar, David Bloor, and Harry M. Collins. If anyone's shadow is being cast here, it is that of the American historian of science Thomas Kuhn or the Austrian philosopher Paul Feyerabend.
11 Joseph Ben-David and Pierre Bourdieu typify this sociological approach to science.
12 Or to use Bourdieu's concept, 'constitutive norms of the [scientific] field'; Pierre Bourdieu, *Pascalian Meditations*, 111.
13 Paul Ricoeur, *Lectures on Ideology*, 8.
14 Fernand Dumont, *Récit*, 189–90.
15 As the dominant figure in his sociological generation, Park set the tone for much thinking on American race relations; I cover his ideas in detail in ch. 2. Sumner's ideas are discussed in ch. 1.

16 Lipset's argument is that the United States has always considered itself an exception among the world's nations because of the ideals of the revolution that gave birth to it. This vision has engendered various conflicts and paradoxes within contemporary American society, particularly along the broad and complex spectrum of racial and ethnic relations. Since the thesis of exceptionalism was never taken up by the authors covered in this book, to bring it into the discussion here would have unduly encumbered the task of elucidating their work in its social and intellectual context.
17 Loïc J.D. Wacquant, 'De la "Terre promise,"' 44.
18 Jean-Michel Chapoulie, *La tradition*, 430.

Part One: Anglo-American Sociology and the Race Question

1 Herbert Blumer, 'Reflections,' 4.
2 Tukufu Zuberi, *Thicker Than Blood*, xviii.
3 William Julius Wilson, *Bridge over the Racial Divide*, 14–15. See also, for a more historical perspective, G.M. Fredrickson, *Racism.*

1. From the Civil War to the First World War

1 'In the late nineteenth century, sociology was less an emerging specialization than a central intellectual perspective for the social sciences in general (and the social sciences included applied social reform and philanthropy).' Craig Calhoun, 'Sociology in America,' 19.
2 Stephen Turner and Jonathan Turner, *Impossible Science*, 12–13.
3 This process is described in great detail in Harry Scheiber, Harold Vatter, and Harold Faulkner, *American Economic History*, ch. 13, 'Expansion, New Frontiers, and Economic Development after 1865,' 193–206.
4 Harold U. Faulkner, *American Economic History*, 347.
5 Ibid., 306–7.
6 'The burst of city growth peaked in the two decades immediately preceding the Civil War ... In 1820, only twelve cities exceeded 10,000 inhabitants, and only two had greater than 100,000. Just 40 years later, in 1860, 101 cities numbered more than 10,000 people, eight cities held over 100,000, and New York had already hit the 1,000,000 mark.' Zane L. Miller and Patricia M. Melvin, *Urbanization*, 31–2.
7 Ibid., 40.
8 Howard Zinn, *People's History*, 259.
9 Ibid., 258–9.
10 Steven Seidman, *Contested Knowledge*, 95–6; see also J. Graham Morgan, 'Contextual Factors.'

11 Seidman, *Contested Knowledge*, 96, 98.
12 Roscoe C. Hinkle, *Founding Theory*, 267.
13 Turner and Turner, *Impossible Science*, 17.
14 Ibid., 68. The Spencerian source of this representation is described in more specific terms as follows: 'Spencer's society is an integrated whole that is naturally occurring, continuous with the natural world, and subject to transhistorical laws of evolution. Sociology is therefore by this definition, a holistic, naturalistic, and evolutionary science of society.' Daniel Breslau, 'American Spencerians,' 40.
15 Turner and Turner, *Impossible Science*, 22.
16 Hinkle, *Founding Theory*, 71–2.
17 United States, Bureau of the Census, *Historical Statistics*, vol. 1, 14.
18 August Meier and Elliott M. Rudwick, *From Plantation to Ghetto*, 123.
19 Ibid., 156.
20 United States, Bureau of the Census, *Historical Statistics*, vol. 1, 14.
21 Stanford M. Lyman, preface to Henry Hughes, *Selected Writings of Henry Hughes*, ix.
22 John Shelton Reed, *One South*, 46.
23 '[E]ven as late as the end of the seventeenth century it was held that "the Negro was not a man but a wild beast, hardly superior to the monkey in intelligence, and with habits far more debased"'; Bertram W. Doyle, *Etiquette*, 34, quoting Philip Bruce, *Economic History*, 2:64.
24 Franklin H. Giddings, *Elements of Sociology*, 236, 238.
25 Ibid., 350.
26 Franklin H. Giddings, *Principles of Sociology*, 328–9.
27 Lester F. Ward, *Pure Sociology*, 230.
28 Ibid., 273–4.
29 A strict Darwinist adheres to the revolutionary idea whereby, through natural selection alone, 'one species evolves into another'; Zuberi, *Thicker Than Blood*, 23. The idea was revolutionary because it challenged the centuries-old Western religious representation of the world known as 'the Great Chain of Being,' in which each species was created by God in its existing form and structure.
30 Lester F. Ward, *Applied Sociology*, 110.
31 Lester F. Ward, 'Evolution of Social Structures,' 604.
32 As were all of the early sociologists, or nearly so: 'Pioneered by the English sociologist Herbert Spencer in the late nineteenth century, Social Darwinism became the dominant theory of sociological thought and played an important role in the prevailing ideology of racism.' Zuberi, *Thicker Than Blood*, 23.
33 William G. Sumner, *Folkways*, 16.

34 Ibid., 77.
35 Ibid., 78.
36 Ibid., 110–11.
37 Edward Ross, *Social Control*, 8.
38 Ibid., 14.
39 Ibid., 432–5.
40 Ibid., 433.
41 Edward Ross, *Foundations of Sociology*, 185.
42 Ross, *Social Control*, 52.
43 Ibid., 336.
44 Charles Cooley, *Social Process*, 245.
45 Charles Cooley, *Social Organization*, 71.
46 Cooley, *Social Process*, 19.
47 Cooley, *Social Organization*, 209ff.
48 Ibid., 347.
49 Cooley, *Social Process*, 407.
50 Ibid., 406.
51 Cooley, *Social Organization*, 118.
52 Cooley, *Social Process*, 354ff.
53 Charles Cooley, 'Genius.'
54 Cooley, *Social Organization*, 218.
55 Ibid., 219.
56 Ibid., 220.
57 I am indebted to Vernon J. Williams, *From a Caste*, whose analysis greatly enriched the following treatment.
58 Joseph Tillinghast, *Negro in Africa*, 2–5.
59 Ibid., 96.
60 Jerome Dowd, *Negro Races*, 432, 447–8, quoted in Williams, *From a Caste*, 38.
61 On this point, see Meier and Rudwick, *From Plantation to Ghetto*, ch. 2, 'Negroes in Agrarian America: Slavery and the Plantation,' 23–4. See also John Hope Franklin, *From Slavery to Freedom.*
62 Dowd, *Negro Races*, quoted in Williams, *From a Caste*, 38–9. My emphasis.
63 H.E. Belin, 'Southern View.'
64 Ibid., 520.
65 Walter L. Fleming, 'Reorganization.'
66 Ibid., 499.
67 See, for example, Carl Kelsey, 'Evolution of Negro Labor.'
68 Howard Odum, *Social and Mental Traits*, 274–5.
69 Ibid. My emphasis.

70 Ibid., 276–85.
71 Ibid., 286–91.
72 Alfred H. Stone, 'Is Race Friction between Blacks and Whites in the United States Growing?'
73 Ibid., 682.
74 Ibid., 687–94.
75 Walter F. Willcox, 'Discussion.'
76 Ulysses G. Weatherly, 'Discussion.'
77 James W. Garner, 'Discussion'; John S. Bassett, 'Discussion.'
78 'Many early sociologists were systematic racists, and both evolutionary theory and the rise of social statistics were shaped by racialist projects.' Craig Calhoun, 'Sociology in America,' 27–8.
79 Thomas P. Bailey, *Race Orthodoxy,* 93.
80 John S. Haller, *Outcasts*, 94.
81 James B. McKee, *Sociology and the Race Problem*, 25.
82 Spencer's position would be deplored by William Thomas, a somewhat more critical sociologist than the others, to whom we return: 'There is, however, a prevalent view, for the popularization of which Herbert Spencer is largely responsible, that primitive man has feeble powers of inhibition.' William I. Thomas, 'Mind of Woman,' 442.
83 Franz Boas, 'Human Faculty.'
84 Franz Boas, *Mind of Primitive Man*, 249.
85 Ibid.
86 McKee, *Sociology and the Race Problem*, 31.
87 Thomas, 'Mind of Woman,' 441.
88 Ibid., 447, 449.
89 William I. Thomas, 'Psychology of Race-Prejudice,' 607, 610.
90 Ibid., 609–10.
91 Miller and Melvin, *Urbanization*, 81.
92 Gary M. Walton and Ross M. Robertson, *History of the American Economy,* 401. For more details, see my *Park, Dos Passos, metropolis*, ch. 1, 'Une société en mutation,' 23–48.
93 Excellent illustrations of this phenomenon are given in Melvyn Dubofsky, *Hard Work.*
94 See Raymond Mohl, ed., *Making of Urban America.*
95 Ibid., 100.
96 Vernon J. Williams, *From a Caste*, 92.
97 Ibid., 81.
98 William I. Thomas, 'Race Psychology,' 745.
99 Ibid., 726.

100 Ibid., 727.
101 Ellsworth Faris, 'Mental Capacity,' 618.
102 Cooley, *Social Process*, 275.
103 Ibid., 276, 278

2. The Rise of the Chicago School

1 Stephen Turner and Jonathan Turner, *Impossible Science*, 39.
2 'Robert Park and Ernest Burgess, in elaborating Chicago-School human ecology, explicitly used the Spencerian analogy to the organism, though transposing it into geographical terms, to describe the city as an organism.' Daniel Breslau, 'American Spencerians,' 61.
3 Turner and Turner, *Impossible Science*, 40.
4 'The most distinctive feature of the American sociological tradition may be its resolutely empirical character.' Donald Levine, *Visions*, 251; see also the section titled 'Pragmatism and American Sociology,' 260–8.
5 Andrew Abbott, *Department and Discipline*, and Jean-Michel Chapoulie, *La tradition*, provide a useful overview.
6 'Harper offered $7000 to department heads, an unprecedented sum at the time ... He recruited to the faculty eight former college presidents, including [Albion] Small ... reduced the teaching load to 8 to 10 hours per week, and publicly proclaimed that promotion would depend more on research than teaching.' Anthony Oberschall, 'Institutionalization,' 194.
7 Albion Small, 'Seminar Notes,' 113.
8 Albion Small, *General Sociology*, ix.
9 Albion Small, 'Fifty Years,' 763.
10 'Sociology emerged as a discipline more at the University of Chicago than anywhere else ... It became less politically engaged and activist as it became more disciplinary and professional – and as a new generation led by Robert Park and Ernest Burgess distinguished themselves from their founding predecessors.' Craig Calhoun, 'Sociology in America,' 20.
11 'In fall 1913 Robert Park delivered an address at the University of Chicago on "Racial Assimilation in Reference to the Negro." In 1914 he gave his first course in the university's Department of Sociology and Anthropology: *The Negro in America* ... He thus pursued, in a new setting and with new colleagues, the subject of his work in the South.' Winifred Raushenbush, *Robert E. Park*, 77.
12 'Thomas's connection with the University of Chicago ended in April 1918. In that month he was arrested at a Chicago hotel in company with a Mrs. Granger ... President Judson, supported by the trustees, moved directly to dismiss Thomas ... The matter might be dealt with in different ways, but

universities of the period were wholly intolerant of what they judged moral laxity.' Martin Bulmer, *Chicago School*, 59–60.

13 Turner and Turner, *Impossible Science*, 46.

14 Raushenbush, *Robert E. Park*, 30.

15 Robert E. Park and Ernest W. Burgess, *Introduction*, 42.

16 'Lakatos's central idea was that not all elements of a research program have the same status; rather, a research program is composed of two parts, a hard core made up of inalterable hypotheses – the orthodoxy, the dogmas – and a protective outer layer that can be modified in response to new data without affecting the hard core. It is to this latter part that one attempts to make the necessary changes where empirical refutation casts doubt on the theory.' Benjamin Matalon, *La construction*, 98. The classic work of use here is Imre Lakatos, 'Falsification.'

17 Bulmer, *Chicago School*, 7.

18 'Park taught sociology by example and eschewed both formal statements of methodology and theory. Thus, the model was not readily transmitted as either a theoretical or methodological doctrine; at Chicago, it was taught through immersion and osmosis.' Turner and Turner, *Impossible Science*, 49. For a contrary view, see Jean Burnet, 'Robert E. Park.'

19 Luigi Tomasi, 'Tradition,' 3. See also Abbott, *Department and Discipline*, ch. 1, 'The Historiography of the Chicago School,' 4–33.

20 Matalon, *La construction*, 98.

21 Bulmer, *Chicago School*, 78.

22 '"[C]ase study method" [was] seen then as the key qualitative approach; it subsumed "life history" and "personal documents" as types of data.' Jennifer Platt, 'Chicago Methods,' 92.

23 The settlement movement, emerging in the late nineteenth century, was an early example of social welfare. Established in many cities of the United States, most famously at Hull House in Chicago, it provided a wide range of social, cultural, and educational services for working-class people, many of them recent immigrants.

24 Platt, 'Chicago Methods,' 90.

25 Park and Burgess, *Introduction*, 54.

26 Turner and Turner, *Impossible Science*, 50.

27 Roscoe C. Hinkle, *Developments*, 159. The three later works by Park are *Race and Culture* (1950), *Human Communities* (1952), and *Society* (1955), all published posthumously by the Free Press of Glencoe.

28 'Park's importance in developing the sociology of race can scarcely be exaggerated; he is eclipsed by few figures besides DuBois.' Howard Winant, 'Dark Side,' 552.

29 The total population grew from 106.4 million in 1920 to 123 million in 1930,

while the black population grew from 10.9 million to 12.5 million during the same period. United States, Bureau of the Census, *Historical Statistics*, vol. 1, 9.

30 'The flood of black humanity increased steadily: 170,000 migrants in 1900–10; 454,000 in 1910–20; 749,000 in 1920–30. Black migration dropped during the Great Depression decade, 1930–40, with only 349,000. From 1940–50, the movement accelerated again, totalling 1,599,000 for the decade.' Manning Marable, *Race, Reform and Rebellion*, 8–9. Taking account of urban emigration to the West, a discernible though much less prominent phenomenon, McKee presents the following figures: 'In 1910 there were 637,000 blacks in cities of the North and West; by 1930 there were 2,228,000.' James B. McKee, *Sociology and the Race Problem*, 128,

31 Vernon J. Williams, *From a Caste*, 114. A pseudo-scientific ideology concocted in the age of triumphant Darwinism, nativism essentially maintained that Anglo-Americans formed a race superior to all others in the United States since they had founded the nation in the early seventeenth century. With the arrival of masses of illiterate immigrants at the turn of the century, nativism provided ideological succor for old-stock whites from the 'inferior races,' 'the unassimilable immigrants,' which included blacks. The movement was very much alive and well in the 1920s.

32 Chapoulie points out that the NAACP at first 'offered legal representation for blacks charged with crimes after race riots, challenged certain segregational practices, and attempted to gain recognition for blacks' constitutional and especially political rights. It later changed course,' emphasizing defense of black labor rights. Chapoulie, *La tradition*, 298.

33 Garvey's organization was the largest mass movement in African American history, with claimed membership of more than a million at its zenith, and the prime example of the 'back to Africa' tendency in American black culture; see William L. Van Deburg, ed., *Modern Black Nationalism*. It was an instance of a broader category of black nationalist movements called pan-Africanism, which holds that people everywhere of African descent should unite to achieve their common goals. The historical prototype of this tendency is to be found in the work of the abolitionist Martin Delany (1812–85): 'As co-editor with Frederick Douglass of the leading Abolitionist organ *The North Star* founded in 1847, Delany's presence reflected the nationalist element of the embryonic Nationality versus Integrationist conflict within the Abolitionist movement (which also had its white faction).' Harold Cruse, *Crisis*, 6.

34 Robert E. Park, 'An Autobiographical Note,' vii–viii. This note, written in the 1930s, was discovered posthumously.

35 Robert E. Park, 'Negro Home Life.'
36 Because of his recent experience in the South, it was his natural microcosm for observation: 'Park's years working and traveling in the South had allowed him to observe the creation of a sense of community and race consciousness among Southern Negroes. Although blacks were drawn together by common interests, the mobilization of the black community had been intensified by the segregationist policies of whites. Their growing sense of solidarity was related to their segregation and accordingly was stronger in the South than in the North.' R. Fred Wacker, *Ethnicity*, 45.
37 Robert E. Park, 'Racial Assimilation,' 207.
38 Ibid., 209.
39 Ibid., 208–9.
40 Ibid., 209.
41 Ibid., 213–14.
42 Ibid., 214–15.
43 Ibid., 217.
44 Ibid., 216–17.
45 Ibid., 217.
46 Ibid., 218.
47 Ibid., 220.
48 Robert E. Park, 'Race Prejudice,' 227.
49 Ibid.
50 Ibid., 228.
51 Ibid., 228–9.
52 Robert E. Park, 'Education,' 267.
53 Ibid., 264.
54 Ibid., 280.
55 Ibid., 282–3.
56 Chapoulie, *La tradition*, 317.
57 Park and Burgess, *Introduction*, 735–7.
58 Robert E. Park, 'Assimilation, Social,' 281.
59 Robert E. Park, 'Our Racial Frontier,' 150. Park had just returned from a trip to the Hawaiian islands, an experience that undoubtedly influenced his ideas on the subject. These ideas met with generalized approval: 'Much of the race relations literature accepted Park's race relations cycle ... This cycle specified the ways social change occurred and the process by which variegated groups became full-fledged Americans.' Aldon D. Morris, 'Sociology of Race,' 507.
60 Robert E. Park, 'Negro Race Consciousness,' 294–5.
61 Robert E. Park, 'Concept of Social Distance,' 259.

62 Ibid., 260.
63 Ibid., 258.
64 Robert E. Park, 'Behind Our Masks,' 254. Note that in Park, the term 'moral' refers to mores rather than morality as such, as he explains in 'Human Ecology.'
65 Park, 'Our Racial Frontier,' 150.
66 Robert E. Park, 'Bases of Race Prejudice,' 233.
67 Robert E. Park, 'Mentality of Racial Hybrids,' 392.
68 Park, 'Bases of Race Prejudice,' 243. Park would revisit the theme of biracial organization once again after 1930, never abandoning it entirely.
69 Chapoulie, *La tradition*, 324.
70 See Roscoe C. Hinkle, *Developments.*
71 Earle E. Eubank, *Treatise*, 49.
72 Turner and Turner, *Impossible Science*, 73.
73 Eubank, *Treatise*, 386.
74 Parsons, *Structure*, 768. My emphasis.
75 Edward Shils, *Calling of Sociology*, 5.
76 Robert Lynd, *Knowledge*, 19.
77 Ibid., 250.
78 Robert E. Park, 'Human Migration.'
79 Robert E. Park, introduction to Charles S. Johnson, *Shadow*, 67.
80 Ibid., 76.
81 Robert E. Park, introduction to Bertram W. Doyle, *Etiquette*, 183.
82 Ibid., 186.
83 Ibid.
84 Robert E. Park, 'Race Relations Cycle,' 195.
85 Barbara B. Lal, 'Black and Blue,' 236.
86 Robert E. Park, 'Nature of Race Relations,' 116.
87 Robert E. Park, 'Modern Society,' 337–8.
88 Robert E. Park, 'Race Ideologies,' 311.
89 Ibid., 315.
90 Chapoulie, *La tradition*, 322.
91 Quoted in Horace R. Cayton, 'Robert Park,' 8.
92 W. Lloyd Warner, 'American Caste,' 234.
93 John Dollard, *Caste and Class*, 32.
94 Ibid., 391.
95 Ibid., 280.
96 Ibid., 405.
97 Allison Davis, Burleigh Gardner, and Mary Gardner, *Deep South*, 9, 59.
98 Ibid., 59.

99 Ibid., 15.
100 Ibid., 65.
101 Ibid., 228.
102 Ibid., 230.
103 Ibid., 250.
104 Ibid., 4.
105 Ibid., 12.
106 Ibid., 533.
107 Ibid., 538.
108 Ibid., 539.
109 Williams, *From a Caste*, 166–7.
110 Elaine O. McNeil and Horace R. Cayton, 'Research,' 183.
111 See Harry H. Bash, *Sociology, Race, and Ethnicity,* for a discussion of the ideological contamination of the concept of assimilation, a matter to which we return in the critical discussion at the end of part two.
112 W. Lloyd Warner, 'Methodological Note,' 782.

3. From the Second World War to the 1960s

1 From 123 million in 1930 to 132 million in 1940, 151 million in 1950, and nearly 181 million in 1960, this last peak being caused by the postwar baby boom; United States, Bureau of the Census, *Historical Statistics*, vol. 1, 9.
2 'In the five years from 1941 to 1945, the federal government spent more money than in the previous century and a half. Combined with the mobilization of millions of Americans (16 million in four years), this ineluctable government spending policy was such that unemployment disappeared within a few years.' Pierre Mélandri, *Histoire*, 148.
3 'Beset by Cold War anxieties, Americans developed an obsession with domestic communism that outran the actual threat and gnawed at the tissue of civil liberties ... In the barrage of accusations that rumbled through the late 1940s and early 1950s, reputations were made or ruined, careers blasted or created, lives and families shattered.' Richard M. Fried, *Nightmare in Red*, 3.
4 'In the 1950s ... nearly twice as much [was invested] overseas than in the entire period from the founding of the Republic to 1950. Direct US investments rose from $11.8 million in 1950 to $31.8 million in 1960.' Mélandri, *Histoire*, 176.
5 A great deal of literature is available for those interested in pursuing this theme further; see, for example, Harold R. Kerbo, *Social Stratification*, ch. 3 in particular, and Dennis Gilbert and Joseph Kahl, *American Class Structure.*

6 Thomas C. Wright, *Latin America*, 69.

7 The key event in the process was a 1963 meeting of Central American presidents at which Kennedy declared, 'Communism is the chief obstacle to economic development in the Central American region.' Allan Nairn, 'Exclusive Report,' 20–9.

8 Gunnar Myrdal, *American Dilemma*, ix.

9 Frederick Keppel, foreword to Myrdal, *American Dilemma*, vi.

10 Myrdal, *American Dilemma*, x.

11 Ibid., x–xi.

12 Ibid., xiv.

13 Ibid., xvii.

14 Ibid., xlv.

15 Ibid., xlvii.

16 Ibid., li.

17 Ibid., 8.

18 Ibid., 9.

19 Ibid., 24. The problem was exacerbated by '[a]nother cultural trait of Americans[: their] relatively low degree of respect for law and order'; ibid., 14.

20 Ibid., 32.

21 Ibid., 44–5.

22 Ibid., 101.

23 Ibid., 216.

24 Ibid., 489.

25 Ibid., 573.

26 Ibid., 575.

27 Ibid., 676.

28 Ibid., 677.

29 Ibid., 678.

30 Ibid., 761.

31 Ibid., 763.

32 Ibid., 879.

33 Ibid., 879–80.

34 Ibid., 902.

35 Ibid., 998.

36 Ibid., 1001, 1005.

37 Ibid., 1010.

38 Ibid.

39 Ibid., 1014.

40 Ibid., 1021–2; these remarks echo Myrdal's belief that '[t]he Negro problem is primarily a white man's problem.'

41 '[W]e assume that it is to the advantage of American Negroes as individuals and as a group to become assimilated into American culture, to acquire the traits held in esteem by the dominant white Americans.' Ibid., 929. Or again: 'The only thing Negroes ask for is to be accepted as Americans.' Ibid., 1007.
42 Ibid., 1035.
43 Ibid., 1043–4.
44 Ibid., 1045.
45 Ibid., 1052.
46 For more on this point, see Chapoulie, *La tradition*, 359.
47 Myrdal, *American Dilemma*, 928.
48 Ibid., 929.
49 Ibid., 930.
50 Ibid., 1030–1.
51 Ibid., 529.
52 Ibid., 518.
53 Ibid., 853.
54 James B. McKee, *Sociology and the Race Problem*, 251.
55 Robert MacIver, *More Perfect Union*, 2,10.
56 Ibid., 15.
57 'The threat to democracy posed by domestic and international forms of intolerance and bigotry brought to the sociology of race relations a new angle from which race could be defined as a social problem ... racial and ethnic intolerance now constituted threatening evidence of the potential for antidemocratic forces to effect an authoritarian reality.' McKee, *Sociology and the Race Problem*, 277.
58 Theodore W. Adorno et al., *Authoritarian Personality*, 975.
59 'During the late 1930s and 1940s Chicago sociology as a whole lost its institutional dominance ... the style of research embodied in the Chicago perspective on race and ethnicity declined in popularity.' R. Fred Wacker, 'Sociology of Race,' 136.
60 '[T]he Chicago perspective flowing from Park was linked to a subjectivist and processual set of assumptions and techniques of research which were out of fashion in a more activist era and one in which forms of "structural-functionalism" dominated.' Ibid., 150.
61 See, for example, Edward Shils, 'Tradition,' a particularly enlightening treatment; see also Fred H. Mathews, *Quest*, and Edward Tiryakian, 'Significance.'
62 Louis Wirth, 'Problem of Minority Groups,' 347.
63 Ibid., 347–8.

64 Ibid., 348.
65 Ibid., 349.
66 Ibid., 354.
67 Ibid., 357–8.
68 Ibid., 361.
69 Ibid., 362–3. Wirth took care to emphasize that 'this typology of minorities is a theoretical construct, rather than a description of actually existing groups. We should not expect to find any one of these types to occur in pure form either in history or in the present. All minorities contain within themselves tendencies and movements in which we can discern the characteristic features of one or more of these types.' Ibid., 364.
70 Ibid.
71 An activist throughout his intellectual career, Wirth had taken his distance from the classical Parkian mold by the end of the 1930s: 'Wirth was very important as an organizer of social scientists and citizens interested in alleviating racial tensions and responding to racial conflicts. Wirth was a leader of the American Council of Race Relations, an umbrella organization which coordinated civic action and some research during the postwar years.' Wacker, 'Sociology of Race,' 141.
72 Jean-Michel Chapoulie, 'E.C. Hughes,' 34.
73 Everett C. Hughes, 'Race Relations,' 883.
74 'Although he had maintained a close relationship with Park, he did not teach race and ethnic courses at Chicago. He did teach and study racial and ethnic relations (along with industrial relations) within the context of collective behavior. Blumer took over Park's course on "The Crowd and the Public" upon Park's retirement in 1933 and was an important figure in the later development of the fields of collective behavior and social movements.' Wacker, 'Sociology of Race,' 142–3.
75 Herbert Blumer, 'Social Science,' 140–3.
76 Herbert Blumer, 'Recent Research,' 408. Blumer also had words of praise for the work of Oliver Cox, Mozell Hill, Charles King, and others. Nevertheless, as Wacker points out in his commentary on Blumer's 1958 review, sociologists of color were living on a fundamentally different academic planet from mainstream white sociologists: 'Among the ironies of his praise, of course, is that no matter how valuable the early research of these scholars ... they were hampered severely as African Americans from getting jobs in research universities'; Wacker, 'Sociology of Race,' 144.
77 Wacker, 'Sociology of Race,' 145.
78 Blumer, 'Recent Research,' 433.
79 Ibid., 438.

80 Herbert Blumer, 'Industrialisation,' 221.
81 Ibid., 235.
82 Ibid., 239.
83 Ibid., 253.
84 Stow Persons, *Ethnic Studies*, 1–2.
85 Ibid., 6.

Part Two: The Genesis of African Sociology, 1896–1964

1 Henry C. Carey, *The Slave Trade*, 18.
2 John Bracey, August Meier, and Elliot M. Rudwick, *Black Sociologists.*
3 Ibid., 1. The Jim Crow laws officially entrenched segregation in public spaces such as buses, trains, restaurants, and cinemas. But there was much worse: 'The most dramatic and terrifying instrument in the repression of Blacks was lynching. According to the Department of Records and Research at Tuskegee Institute, between 1882 and 1968 there were 4,743 cases of death by lynching in America, with the period between 1892 and 1902 recording the most intensive activity.' Cedric J. Robinson, *Black Movements*, 105. The courageous black suffragist Ida B. Wells-Barnett gained national and even international recognition for leading a vigorous campaign against lynching during the terrible years 1890–1910, when the NAACP was also founded. On this history, see Adam Fairclough, *Better Day Coming*, 23–39.
4 Stow Persons, *Ethnic Studies*, 14.

4. W.E.B. Du Bois: Scientific Sociology and Exclusion

1 W.E.B. Du Bois, *Autobiography*, 149.
2 'Philadelphia in the mid-1890s had over 45,000 blacks, the largest Negro population of any city in the North. For over a year Du Bois was a participant-observer in the Seventh Ward, "the historic centre of Negro settlement in the City," where about one-fifth of the community's blacks lived.' Elliott M. Rudwick, 'W.E.B. Du Bois,' 28.
3 Morris Janowitz, introduction to James Blackwell and Morris Janowitz, eds, *Black Sociologists*, xiii.
4 'Du Bois firmly rejected the Black assimilation thesis that served as a key pillar of the white perspective.' Aldon D. Morris, 'Sociology of Race,' 513.
5 Throughout his long association with the NAACP, Du Bois oscillated between his principal belief in a political and cultural nationalism hostile to any alliance with whites and certain integrationist concessions designed to

secure recognition for black civil rights. Put differently, Du Bois's positioning on the black identity spectrum gave rise to an emancipatory rhetoric in which the moderate discourse of civil rights advocacy and the radical discourse of visionary black nationalism were uppermost at different times in response to changes in the political landscape.

6 For Du Bois's personal account of this event, see his *Autobiography,* 319.

7 Dan S. Green and Edwin D. Driver, introduction to W.E.B. Du Bois, *W.E.B. Du Bois on Sociology,* 28.

8 Randall Collins and Michael Makowski, *Discovery,* 194.

9 Green and Driver, introduction to W.E.B. Du Bois, *W.E.B. Du Bois on Sociology,* 5.

10 W.E.B. Du Bois, *Suppression,* v.

11 W.E.B. Du Bois, 'Program,' cited in Green and Driver, introduction to W.E.B. Du Bois, *W.E.B. Du Bois on Sociology,* 32.

12 W.E.B. Du Bois, 'Conservation of Races,' 239.

13 Ibid.

14 Ibid., 240.

15 Ibid.

16 Michael B. Katz and Thomas J. Sugrue, *W.E.B. Du Bois,* 24.

17 W.E.B. Du Bois, 'Conservation of Races,' 241–2.

18 Ibid., 242.

19 Ibid.

20 Ibid.

21 Thomas Holt shows this clearly, emphasizing that for Du Bois, historical contingency took explanatory precedence over any other postulate: 'There is no denying that he was certainly mesmerized by an almost teleological notion of what he called "the race idea, the race spirit, the race ideal," which was "the vastest and most ingenious invention for human progress." Through race consciousness each group develops its unique, divinely ordained mission, which is "to develop for civilization its particular message." But ... the ultimate roots of this consciousness are socioeconomic. Each group –whether city, nation, or race – develops perspectives and talents in the course of its particular struggles ... in life.' Thomas C. Holt, 'W.E.B. Du Bois's Archaeology,' 67. While it is true that Du Bois's conception partook of racial essentialism, it was entirely different from the biological essentialism cherished by his white contemporaries. It was a philosophical or ontological – indeed, almost mystical – essentialism.

22 W.E.B. Du Bois, 'Conservation of Races,' 243.

23 Ibid.

24 Ibid., 247.

25 On this fascinating issue, which is beyond the scope of this book, see Nancy L. Stepan and Sander L. Gilman, 'Appropriating the Idioms,' and Kevin K. Gaines, *Uplifting the Race.*

26 W.E.B. Du Bois, 'Study,' 72–3.

27 Ibid., 75–6.

28 W.E.B. Du Bois, *Autobiography,* 195.

29 W.E.B. Du Bois, *Philadelphia Negro,* 120.

30 Ibid., 134–5. Here Du Bois applies to specific cases the definition of 'social problem' that he had propounded the previous year: 'A social problem is the failure of an organized social group to realize its group ideals, through the inability to adapt a certain desired line of action to given conditions of life ... a social problem is ever a relation between conditions and action, and as conditions and actions vary and change from group to group from time to time and from place to place, so social problems change, develop and grow.' W.E.B. Du Bois, 'Study of the Negro Problems,' 71.

31 Du Bois, *Philadelphia Negro,* 193–4.

32 Ibid., 284.

33 Ibid., 74.

34 Ibid., 81.

35 Ibid., 305.

36 Ibid., 5.

37 Ibid., 309.

38 Ibid., 310–11.

39 'Its members usually felt compelled, as the elite of the race, to spend more than their white neighbors on clothes and entertainment.' Rudwick, 'W.E.B. Du Bois,' 35.

40 Du Bois, *Philadelphia Negro,* 315–16.

41 Ibid., 311.

42 Ibid.

43 Ibid.

44 Ibid., 311–15.

45 Ibid., 220.

46 Ibid., 201.

47 Ibid., 207.

48 Ibid., 394.

49 Ibid., 389–90.

50 Ibid., 392.

51 Mia Bay, '"World Was Thinking Wrong,"' 41.

52 David L. Lewis, *W.E.B. Du Bois: Biography,* 209. This work won the Pulitzer Prize in 1994.

53 'He focused his survey so as to define and capture the social dynamics of the African American community of Philadelphia. Unlike Booth's, Du Bois's study was focused on a community and what might be done to understand and change its social problems rather than the examination of a social problem like poverty. Du Bois did study poverty, but African American poverty was not the object of his study. The object of Du Bois's study was the African American community of Philadelphia.' Tukufu Zuberi, *Thicker Than Blood*, 83.

54 'It is the earliest large-scale empirical study in the history of American sociology. Gunnar Myrdal, in *An American Dilemma*, referred to *The Philadelphia Negro* as the best model of "what a study of a Negro community should be."' Green and Driver, introduction to W.E.B. Du Bois, *W.E.B. Du Bois on Sociology*, 113. On the general ignorance of Du Bois as a scientific pioneer, it is troubling to note the absence of any major difference in conceptual design between *The Philadelphia Negro* and, say, Everett Hughes's *French Canada in Transition*, published nearly fifty years later.

55 Robert C. Bannister, *Social Darwinism*, 188.

56 Du Bois, *Philadelphia Negro*, iv–v.

57 This, in my view, is a clear example of what Fernand Dumont calls a pre-scientific construct, the purpose of which is to bring a new type of science into being.

58 Jean M. Converse, *Survey Research*, 23. Booth and Hull House are specifically cited in the introduction to *The Philadelphia Negro* by S.M. Lindsay, the University of Pennsylvania professor who appointed Du Bois.

59 Bay, '"World Was Thinking Wrong,"' 49–50.

60 Bay, '"World Was Thinking Wrong,"' 49, quoting Lewis, *W.E.B. Du Bois: Biography*, 190.

61 W.E.B. Du Bois, 'Program for a Sociological Society,' 51.

62 W.E.B. Du Bois, 'Study of the Negro Problems,' 80.

63 Green and Driver, introduction to W.E.B. Du Bois, *W.E.B. Du Bois on Sociology*, 6.

64 Lewis, *W.E.B. Du Bois: Biography*, 201–2, quoting W.E.B. Du Bois, *Dusk of Dawn*, 51.

65 He wrote, 'I was approached by President Horace Bumstead of Atlanta University in 1896 and asked to come to Atlanta University and take charge of the work in sociology, and of the new conferences which they were inaugurating on the Negro problem. With this program in mind, I eagerly accepted the invitation.' Du Bois, *Autobiography*, 209.

66 Du Bois, *Dusk of Dawn*, 62.

67 Du Bois, *Autobiography*, 228.

68 Pierre Bourdieu, *Les usages*, 16.
69 Ibid., 17.
70 Ibid., 19.
71 W.E.B. Du Bois, 'Laboratory,' 62.
72 Du Bois, *Autobiography*, 213–14.
73 Ibid., 215.
74 'With two large, critically acclaimed monographs published by age thirty-one, a major essay in Weber's arbitral *Archiv* ... Du Bois's professional achievements placed him in the vanguard of social-science scholarship in America. Atlanta seemed admirably positioned to become the great research center he had come from Philadelphia to make it. Foundation grants had not materialized so far, and he could have no inkling in the first few years of his eventual failure to win their full support; yet Du Bois had already begun to feel dissatisfied. Having made an international reputation as a social scientist and historian, the Atlanta University professor found himself becoming impatient that the world went along as before, unreconstructed in its rabid racism in the South and in its sublime cynicism in the North, and leaving his own material and professional prospects about as much unchanged.' Lewis, *W.E.B. Du Bois: Biography*, 225.
75 Du Bois, *Autobiography*, 229.
76 'Washington was advocating a conciliatory and gradualist philosophy. He minimized the extent of race prejudice or discrimination and referred to Southern whites as the Negro's best friends. He held that discrimination and prejudice were basically the Negroes' own fault ... Washington accepted segregation and criticized political activity. He believed that economic accumulation and the cultivation of morality were the methods best calculated to raise the Negro's status in American society. Agricultural and industrial training was far more appropriate for the mass of Negroes, just then, than education for the professions.' August Meier and Elliott M. Rudwick, *From Plantation to Ghetto*, 180.
77 For a recent sympathetic yet critical appraisal of Washington's philosophy, see Adam Fairclough, *Better Day Coming*, ch. 3, 'Booker T. Washington and the Strategy of Accommodation,' 41–65. For example: 'If Washington gave black Southerners a strategy for survival, self-respect, and individual self-improvement, he devised no realistic strategy for breaking the chains of racism and poverty that shackled the great mass of black people. He insisted that industrial education, wedded to sobriety and thrift, and assisted by white good will, would eventually solve the race problem. It was a simplistic belief. Education was a necessary but hardly sufficient condition for black progress' (53–4).

78 'Industrial education was widely adopted because philanthropists encouraged it and because Southern whites saw it as keeping Negroes in the subordinate position of working with their hands rather than preparing them for professional careers ... many Negro leaders found industrial education appealing, partly because philanthropy subsidized it, and even more because it fitted the moral-economic ideology of advancement that was in the ascendancy. And though clothed in a philosophy of racial advancement, its advocates – from Samuel Chapman Armstrong to Booker T. Washington – saw it as a platform of compromise and accommodation between the North, the South, and the Negro.' Meier and Rudwick, *From Plantation to Ghetto*, 178.

79 'He served as political adviser on Negro affairs to Presidents Roosevelt and Taft. All colored men who were appointed to office by Roosevelt, and most appointed by Taft, were recommended by Booker T. Washington ... Washington wielded more power within the Negro community than anyone else had ever done. This authority derived from his political influence and from his popularity with the philanthropists. No Negro schools received contributions from Carnegie, Rockefeller, and lesser donors without Washington's approval. In short, ambitious men and institutions found it difficult to get ahead without the Tuskegeean's support.' Ibid., 181. See also Hermann Schwendinger and Julia R. Schwendinger, *Sociologists of the Chair*, ch. 65, 'The Business Domination of University Life,' 503–11, in which the skirmish between Du Bois and Washington is subjected to a subtle analysis convergent with mine.

80 W.E.B. Du Bois, *Souls*, 58–9.

81 'In Du Bois's view, the Negro race could be saved only by the "Talented Tenth" – i.e., the minority who had received a liberal arts education and thus were in a position to elevate Negroes both culturally and economically ... Du Bois was disturbed by Washington's exclusive preoccupation with industrial education and the financial support whites gave it at the expense of Negro colleges ... he reminded Washington that many of the teachers of the industrial and elementary schools had attended liberal arts institutions, and that until many more did so, Negro leadership and the Negro race would be seriously retarded.' Meier and Rudwick, *From Plantation to Ghetto*, 184.

82 Du Bois, *Autobiography*, 223–4. The cutoff of funding is confirmed by recent scholarship: 'White philanthropists, supported by the powerful Black leader Booker T. Washington, largely closed the research coffers to DuBois. Additionally, because of DuBois's academic marginalization, he was never in a position to mentor students who could have assisted him in develop-

ing a DuBoisian school of race on a par with the Chicago school.' Morris, 'Sociology of Race,' 533.

83 Meier and Rudwick, *From Plantation to Ghetto*, 184.

84 Green and Driver, introduction to W.E.B. Du Bois, *W.E.B. Du Bois on Sociology*, 20.

85 'During the decade ending in 1910, he became convinced that scientific investigation was not sufficient to solve the problems of black Americans. The problems were not, as he had initially and idealistically assumed, those of ignorance, but were instead based on the conscious determination of one group to suppress and persecute another.' Green and Driver, introduction to W.E.B. Du Bois, *W.E.B. Du Bois on Sociology*, 19. In short, Du Bois was becoming a 'public sociologist'; see Morris, 'Sociology of Race,' 526–8.

86 These characteristics were probably inevitable in *The Philadelphia Negro* given the mixture of scientific and political aims of the parties who commissioned it: 'W.E.B. Du Bois's pioneering study *The Philadelphia Negro* was at once an intellectual effort at understanding and a political project of persuasive documentation – conducted at the invitation of Philadelphia city officials as well as the University of Pennsylvania.' Craig Calhoun 'Sociology in America,' 12.

87 Du Bois, *Philadelphia Negro*, 63.

88 Ibid., 66, 351.

89 Ibid., 392.

90 Lewis, *W.E.B. Du Bois: Biography*, 210.

91 Ibid., 189.

92 Du Bois, *Philadelphia Negro*, 388.

93 Ibid., 394.

94 Ibid., 323.

95 W.E.B. Du Bois, 'Talented Tenth,' 33.

96 For example, see Michael B. Katz and Thomas J. Sugrue, introduction to Katz and Sugrue, eds, *W.E.B. Du Bois*, 26. Similarly, Rudwick recalls that Albion Small, the editor of the *American Journal of Sociology* in the year that Du Bois's monograph was published, had also been Schmoller's student and thus initiated into the same sort of empirical sociology as Du Bois. '[I]n spite of this similarity in professional background, and although the *American Journal of Sociology*, in addition to publishing theoretical articles, devoted many pages to social welfare problems, Du Bois's work was clearly considered of minor importance. Except for reasons of racial prejudice, it is difficult to account for his being shunted aside.' Elliott M. Rudwick, 'Note on a Forgotten Black Sociologist,' 305.

97 His exclusion from the journal was not, however, absolute. It did publish his 'Race Friction,' a reply to Alfred Holt Stone's paper discussed above (see pp. 33–4). Furthermore, it included his response to a questionnaire on teaching sociology (in L.L. Bernard, 'Teaching of Sociology'); his views on the study of sociology in educational institutions (in Frank L. Tolman, 'Study of Sociology,' 114); and his views on Americanism as part of a symposium conducted by the journal's editorial board (in *American Journal of Sociology,* 'What Is Americanism?,' 463). Finally, Du Bois's 'The Development of a People' (1904) was noted and abstracted in the *AJS* by 'E.B.W.' (1904).

98 H.E. Belin, 'Civil War,' 266.

99 Beyond professional sociology circles and among southern blacks, his work enjoyed a more sympathetic reception: 'The unsigned reviews in *The Nation, The Literary Digest*, and *The Outlook* were typical of the establishmentarian response to *The Philadelphia Negro*, allowance made for the decision of the *American Journal of Sociology* to ignore the monograph completely. "A very exhaustive study," *The Nation* decreed, commending it to readers for "the lesson taught by this investigation ... of patience and sympathy toward the South, whose difficulties have been far greater than those of the North." Concurring, *The Literary Digest* decided that the book proved the southern business wisdom of Booker Washington, while *The Outlook* approvingly noted that Du Bois made no attempt "to bend the facts so as to plead for his race." In its comprehensive treatment, *The American Historical Review* rejoiced that the author was "perfectly frank, laying all necessary stress on the weakness of his people." ... [In addition] Du Bois must have been gratified by *Yale Review*'s praise of *The Philadelphia Negro* as "a credit to American scholarship, and a distinct and valuable addition to the world's stock of knowledge concerning an important and obscure theme."' Lewis, *W.E.B. Dubois: Biography,* 206–7, 210.

100 Du Bois was not alone in exhibiting this flaw; I have shown that it also characterized the work of one of the paragons of early Anglo-American sociology, William Sumner. See my *William Graham Sumner.*

101 For example, the opportunity for critical dialogue greatly aided – or perhaps even saved – Park at the University of Chicago, given his mediocre aptitude for theorization.

102 'DuBois's sociology of race ... broke radically from the white perspective. His conceptual framework was driven in a novel direction because of its insistence from the beginning that sociological interpretations should rest on empirical data rather than grand theorizing; it rejected the thesis of Blacks' inferiority and its associated claims of Blacks' assimilation as foundational principles; and it conceptualized races as socia1 constructions rather than immutable categories.' Morris, 'Sociology of Race,' 514.

5. Four 'New Negroes'

1 He did not get a PhD but rather a PhB (1918); Adelaide M. Cromwell, 'Frazier's Background,' 38.

2 'On Sunday, July 27, 1919, there was a clash of white people and Negroes at a bathing-beach in Chicago, which resulted in the drowning of a Negro boy. This led to a race riot in which thirty-eight lives were lost – twenty-three Negroes and fifteen whites – and 537 persons were injured. After three days of mob violence, affecting several sections of the city, the state militia was called out to assist the police in restoring order. It was not until August 5 that danger of further clashes was regarded as past.' Chicago Commission on Race Relations, quoted in Naomi Farber, 'Charles S. Johnson's *The Negro in Chicago*,' 210.

3 Unlike Du Bois and Frazier (as we shall see), his ideology was steeped in moderate pragmatism, which served his personal cause and that of the powers that be. As Chapoulie suggests, Johnson was an astute organization man who seized every opportunity that came his way: 'from the 1930s on, he belonged to the little world of administrators of foundations that funded race relations research. Thanks to the advantages procured by this position, he developed a clearinghouse on the status of blacks and race relations in the South, organized the compilation and publication of statistical data, and published several works on the status of blacks.' Jean-Michel Chapoulie, *La tradition*, 300.

4 Richard Robbins, *Sidelines Activist*, x.

5 'If, in *The Negro in Chicago*, Johnson did not offer a comprehensive theory of race relations in the urban context, he did achieve an empirical study of the highest quality that is informative, theoretically suggestive and remarkably subtle in its "feel" for human relations.' Farber, 'Charles S. Johnson's *The Negro in Chicago*,' 213.

6 Robert E. Park, introduction to Charles S. Johnson, *Shadow*, xii.

7 Charles S. Johnson, *Shadow*, 3. Johnson draws inspiration here from Ulrich Phillips, 'Decadence,' 37–41.

8 Johnson, *Shadow*, 128.

9 Ibid., 208–9.

10 Ibid., 120.

11 Ibid., 212.

12 Charles S. Johnson, Edwin Embree, and Will Alexander, *Collapse*.

13 Charles S. Johnson, *Growing Up*, xvii.

14 Ibid., 325.

15 Charles S. Johnson, *Patterns of Negro Segregation*, 324.

16 Charles S. Johnson, *Education and the Cultural Crisis*, 93–4.

17 Ibid., 94.
18 'For almost two decades, *Bitter Canaan* was Johnson's labor of love, created in the "cracks" of a busy career'; John Stanfield, introductory essay to Charles S. Johnson, *Bitter Canaan*, vii.
19 Ernest W. Burgess, 'Charles S. Johnson,' 321.
20 Randall Collins and Michael Makowski, *Discovery*, 202.
21 'I received a call from Charles S. Johnson, the Negro sociologist from Fisk University. Over lunch he offered me a job as Special Assistant to Secretary of the Interior Ickes, to study the effects of New Deal legislation on Negro labor. I immediately accepted and soon afterward I left for New York. There I met George S. Mitchell, a professor of economics at Columbia, who was to be my colleague on the study, and for the next year I traveled all over the country interviewing, and observing the formation of the Congress of Industrial Organizations, the C.I.O., and the role of the Negro worker in the steel, meat-packing, and railroad car shop industries.' Horace R. Cayton, *Long Old Road*, 207.
22 Horace R. Cayton and George S. Mitchell, *Black Workers*, ix.
23 Ibid., 17.
24 Ibid., 41–2.
25 Ibid., 55.
26 Ibid., 192.
27 Ibid., 371.
28 Cayton, *Long Old Road*, 239.
29 Howard Winant, 'Dark Side,' 556.
30 William J. Wilson, foreword to Horace R. Cayton and J.G. St Clair Drake, *Black Metropolis*, xlviii.
31 Ibid., xlvii.
32 Richard Wright, introduction to Horace R. Cayton and J.G. St Clair Drake, *Black Metropolis*, xxvi. See pp. 288–90 for more about Wright's connections to professional sociology.
33 Horace R. Cayton and J.G. St Clair Drake, *Black Metropolis*, 32.
34 Ibid., 78.
35 Ibid., 90–1.
36 Ibid., 91.
37 Ibid., 111–12.
38 Ibid., 113.
39 Ibid., 114.
40 Ibid., 129.
41 Ibid., 174–5.
42 Ibid., 206.

43 Ibid., 266.
44 Ibid., 300.
45 Ibid., 340.
46 Ibid., 385.
47 Ibid., 398.
48 Ibid., 412.
49 Ibid., 423–4.
50 Ibid., 437.
51 Ibid., 439.
52 Ibid., 456.
53 Ibid., 462.
54 Ibid., 470.
55 Ibid., 484.
56 Ibid., 521.
57 Ibid., 522.
58 Ibid., 523.
59 Ibid., 528–9.
60 Ibid., 540.
61 Ibid., 563.
62 Ibid., 523.
63 Ibid., 600.
64 Ibid., 619.
65 Ibid., 629.
66 Ibid., 524.
67 Ibid., 661–2.
68 Ibid., 662–3.
69 Ibid., 689.
70 Ibid., 525.
71 Ibid., 550.
72 Ibid., 602–3.
73 Ibid., 660.
74 Ibid., 714.
75 Ibid., 715.
76 Ibid., 755.
77 Ibid.
78 Ibid., 755–6.
79 Ibid., 757.
80 Ibid., 759.
81 Ibid.
82 Ibid., 766.

83 Ibid.
84 Ibid.
85 Ibid., 766–7.
86 Ibid., 767.
87 W. Lloyd Warner, 'Methodological Note,' 781.
88 '[A] peculiar sensation, this double-consciousness, this sense of always looking at one's self through the eyes of others, of measuring one's soul by the tape of a world that looks on in amused contempt and pity. One ever feels his two-ness, – an American, a Negro; two souls, two thoughts, two unreconciled strivings; two warring ideals in one dark body, whose dogged strength alone keeps it from being torn asunder.' W.E.B. Du Bois, *Souls*, 3.
89 Todd Gitlin, *Twilight*, 59.
90 Frazier, Myrdal, and Warner were all cited six times in the book, Du Bois four times, and Park and Johnson, two each.
91 Herbert M. Hunter and Sameer Y. Abraham, *Race*, xx.
92 Ibid., xxi.
93 Ibid., xxv.
94 Ibid., 67.
95 Oliver C. Cox, *Caste*, xvi.
96 Ibid., 322.
97 Ibid., 333.
98 Manning Marable, *Race*, 2.
99 Cox, *Caste*, 123.
100 Ibid., 147–8.
101 Ibid., 154.
102 Ibid., 155.
103 Ibid.
104 Cox borrowed his concept of class consciousness from Werner Sombart, *Socialism*, 110.
105 Cox, *Caste*, 168.
106 Ibid., 177.
107 Ibid., 179.
108 Ibid., 180.
109 '[T]he capitalists and the proletariat are twin-born of the same economic matrix, capitalism'; ibid., 187.
110 Ibid., 198.
111 Ibid., 200.
112 Ibid., 583.
113 Ibid., 545. These remarks begin section 25, titled 'The Race Problem in the United States' (545–83).

114 Ibid., 501.
115 Ibid., 571.
116 Oliver C. Cox, *Foundations*, 27.
117 Ibid., 48.
118 Oliver C. Cox, *Capitalism and American Leadership*, 3.
119 Ibid., 58.
120 Ibid., 230.
121 Ibid., 255. Cox did not provide any examples of such support.
122 Ibid., 257–8.
123 Ibid., 262–3.
124 Ibid., 288.
125 Ibid., 303.
126 Ibid., 306–7. My emphasis.
127 Oliver C. Cox, *Capitalism as a System*, 3.
128 Ibid., 3–4.
129 Ibid., 4.
130 Ibid., 5.
131 Cox, *Capitalism and American Leadership*, 18–19.
132 Cox, *Capitalism as a System*, 141.
133 Ibid., 186.
134 Ibid., 198.
135 Quoted in Hunter and Abraham, *Race*, xx.
136 Cox, *Caste*, 495. Cox held the view (p. 3) that only India had a true caste system.
137 Ibid., 505, 507.
138 Ibid., 474.
139 Wallerstein himself agrees: 'Oliver Cox expounded in the 1950s and 1960s virtually all the basic ideas of world-systems analysis. He is a founding father, albeit one who is hardly recognized as such and is neglected, even today.' Immanuel Wallerstein, 'Oliver C. Cox,' 174.
140 Interestingly, though, Cox did not reject the capitalist system per se as a social system, for he saw it as an undeniable advance of civilization: 'In our present day of crisis and transition the achievements of capitalism should not be minimized. They involve preeminent cultural gains for mankind.' Cox, *Foundations*, 16.
141 Hunter and Abraham, *Race*, xxv.
142 Ibid., xxxiv.
143 Ibid., xxxii. The publisher in question was Public Affairs Press, and its editor, William B. Selgby, wrote the following letter to Cox (August 1946): 'Dear Professor Cox: It's no use, I can't stomach the communist line. Sincerely yours, Wm. B. Selgby'; Hunter and Abraham, *Race*, xxxiii.

144 Cox, *Caste*, 223.

145 Hunter and Abraham, *Race*, xxxiv, quoting James T. Carey, *Sociology and Public Affairs*, 155.

146 Ibid.

147 There was no way, however, for Frazier to respond to the following example of Cox's bitter criticism published eight years after his death: 'His professional career had to be contrived on the tight-rope set up by the associational establishment. He won many prizes and honors, but the exigencies of winning involved his soul and his manhood. Sometimes *Black Bourgeoisie* is compared to the *Theory of the Leisure Class* and to *White Collar*. It is, in my opinion, nothing of the sort. Had Frazier assumed the posture of Veblen or Mills, he would doubtless have been even more completely consigned to outer darkness to endure in silence the agony of his ways. He hardly confronted even tangentially a real power structure.' Cox attributed Frazier's alleged timidity to his having assimilated the ideas of Faris, Ogburn, and especially Park at Chicago: 'they were profound liberals ... possessed of praiseworthy attitudes toward Negroes, but still strongly opposed to any definition of them as fully equal to whites; they were willing to do many things *for* Negroes but sternly opposed to Negroes taking such initiative as would move them along faster than a *proper* pace; and they would rather turn conservative than tolerate independent thinking or acting Negroes.' Oliver C. Cox, introduction to Nathan Hare, *Black Anglo-Saxons*, 28, 30. The very title of this work was a deliberate slight of scholars such as Frazier.

148 Manning Marable, 'Black Studies,' 41–2.

6. Edward Franklin Frazier

1 Haynes was the first African American to obtain a doctorate in sociology (Columbia University, 1912). In addition to the above-mentioned book, he produced several other empirical studies on the Great Migration.

2 He wrote that Du Bois had produced 'the first attempt to study in a scientific spirit the problems of the Negro in American life'; E. Franklin Frazier, *Negro in the United States*, 503.

3 '[S]ociology ... appealed to him as the social science which most nearly provided an explanation and understanding of race and class conflicts.' G. Franklin Edwards, 'E. Franklin Frazier,' in James Blackwell and Morris Janowitz, eds, *Black Sociologists*, 90.

4 'It was Frazier's view that the year spent with Hankins at Clark marked the beginning of his work as a sociologist.' G.F. Edwards, 'E. Franklin Frazier: Race, Education and Community,' 112.

5 'Frazier absorbed the basic ideas of the [Chicago] school as they related to racial and ethnic topics.' Stow Persons, 'E. Franklin Frazier,' 252.

6 'Frazier came to Howard ... with great hopes. It was the leading black university in the country. Moreover, it was the only one in the North that provided tenure-track positions for black intellectuals prior to World War II ... He had many opportunities to leave Howard for research, short-term visiting appointments, and lecture tours, but he was apparently never offered a full-time position at a major university in the United States. He started and ended his career in a segregated educational system.' Anthony M. Platt, *E. Franklin Frazier*, 103.

7 Since he did not use the term 'race riot' (several whites had also participated), the mayor refused to make the report public.

8 Persons, 'E. Franklin Frazier,' 255.

9 And for the best of reasons: 'When E.F. Frazier was elected president of the American Sociological Association in 1948 ... he was already recognized as the leading scholar on the black family and one of the important theorists absorbed in the dynamics of social change and race relations.' James E. Teele, editor's introduction to *E. Franklin Frazier*, 2.

10 E. Franklin Frazier, *Negro in the United States*, 339.

11 E. Franklin Frazier, *New Currents*, 19.

12 Ibid., 71.

13 E. Franklin Frazier, 'Negro and Non-Resistance,' 213.

14 'During these five years ... he built his reputation as a leading Afro-American intellectual and activist. By the time he left the South, he was widely known for his scholarly writings, polemics, controversial politics, and battles against racism ... During these same five years, he was an extraordinarily prolific writer, publishing thirty-three articles, plus several book reviews, in leading academic, professional, and civil rights journals (including *Crisis, Opportunity, Journal of Social Forces, Southern Workman, Messenger, Howard Review, The Nation*, and *Forum*).' Platt, *E. Franklin Frazier*, 63.

15 Ibid., 64.

16 Arnold Rampersad, introduction to Alain Locke, ed., *New Negro*, xiv.

17 David L. Lewis, editor's introduction to *Portable Harlem Renaissance*, xviii.

18 Rampersad, introduction to Locke, ed., *New Negro*, ix.

19 E. Franklin Frazier, 'Durham,' 339–40.

20 E. Franklin Frazier, 'Racial Self-Expression,' 121.

21 E. Franklin Frazier, 'La Bourgeoisie Noire,' 173.

22 Ibid., 176.

23 Ibid., 178.

24 Ibid.

25 Ibid., 181.
26 Ibid., 179.
27 Ibid.
28 Ibid., 179–80.
29 E. Franklin Frazier, 'Negro Slave Family,' 203. On this point Frazier was in lifelong opposition to the anthropologist Melville Herskovits, who had been formidably arguing the contrary thesis since his 1927 work *The Myth of the Negro Past.*
30 E. Franklin Frazier, 'Group Tactics,' 31.
31 On this subject, see G.F. Edwards, introduction to E. Franklin Frazier, *On Race Relations*, xi–xx.
32 E. Franklin Frazier, 'Rejoinder,' 314.
33 In 'Occupational Classes among Negroes in Cities,' Frazier acknowledged Park for having 'called attention to the significance of the differentiation of the Negro population,' (719), then reminded the reader that the subject was first addressed, albeit imperfectly, by an earlier sociologist: 'Du Bois, in his study of the Philadelphia Negro, defined four grades in the Negro population on the basis of the families he studied ... The four grades of the Negro population as defined by Du Bois were based mainly upon subjective evaluations' (727).
34 Jean-Michel Chapoulie, *La tradition*, 343–4, quoting Frazier, 'Occupational Classes,' 737.
35 E. Franklin Frazier, *Negro Family in Chicago*, 91.
36 Ernest W. Burgess, 'Growth,' 54.
37 Frazier, *Negro Family in Chicago*, 252.
38 Ibid., 45.
39 Ibid., 47.
40 Ibid. There were 488,070 free blacks in 1860 versus 3,953,760 slaves; United States, Bureau of the Census, *Negro Population*, 53.
41 E. Franklin Frazier, 'Status,' cited in Platt, *E. Franklin Frazier*, 164. Note Frazier's use of the word 'proletariat,' largely absent from Park's lexicon.
42 Theodore Draper, *American Communism*, 551–2.
43 See my *Park, Dos Passos, metropolis* for various illustrations of this point.
44 'Frazier related to the CP in much the same way that he related to other organizations. On issues in which he was in agreement, he did not hesitate to work with Communists or CP-led organizations. On matters of difference, he did not hesitate to express his disagreements ... Ideology aside, Frazier moved in CP circles because they provided an interracial forum in which to mix and discuss important political issues and international events. Frazier liked to be around smart, stimulating people, and it was a

rare opportunity for him to be able to engage class-conscious, world[l]y intellectuals'; Platt, *E. Franklin Frazier*, 181. Nevertheless, his proximity to the Communist Party marked him as a 'subversive' to the authorities. Frazier became one of the FBI's many targets, a circumstance that would cause him untold nuisance until the end of his life. Unlike Du Bois, he was never prosecuted or deprived of his civil rights, but he would always feel the psychological effects of his being in the sights of a preeminent symbol of white American power.

45 E. Franklin Frazier et al., 'Editorial,' 3, cited in Platt, *E. Franklin Frazier*, 184. The journal ceased publication after its second issue in the summer of 1936 for lack of funds.

46 E. Franklin Frazier, *Negro Family in the United States*, xix. The volume he refers to is W.E.B. Du Bois, ed., *Negro American Family.*

47 Ernest W. Burgess, editor's preface to Frazier, *Negro Family in the United States*, ix.

48 Frazier, *Negro Family in the United States*, 41.

49 Ibid., 485.

50 Ibid., 488. See below, in the discussion on *The Negro in the United States* (1929), for Frazier's treatment of the concept of assimilation.

51 Ibid., 486.

52 E. Franklin Frazier, 'A Negro Looks,' 16.

53 Platt, *E. Franklin Frazier*, 176. The committee's origins are to be found in the early 1930s, when the House of Representatives formed a committee to investigate Nazi propaganda in the United States. This mandate was given short shrift, and the committee turned to investigating alleged Communist infiltration of New Deal agencies.

54 'Frazier, like Du Bois, held a multitude of competing ideas, and which ones came forth depended on the situation. His background of Chicago sociology, neo-Marxism, and latent black nationalism made him difficult to decipher.' David W. Southern, *Gunnar Myrdal*, 92.

55 For example, this sentence from 1924: 'We hold that if a Negro is treated in any situation different from other citizens because he is a Negro, there is a denial of democratic justice ...' E. Franklin Frazier, 'Negro and Non-Resistance,' 214.

56 E. Franklin Frazier, *Negro in the United States*, 704.

57 The book is introduced by Louis Wirth and bears the following dedication: 'To W.E. Burghardt Du Bois and to the memory of Robert E. Park, two pioneers of the scientific study.'

58 Persons, 'E. Franklin Frazier,' 255.

59 Frazier, *Negro in the United States*, 680–1.

60 Ibid., 44.
61 Ibid., 191.
62 Ibid., 273–4.
63 Ibid., 301.
64 Some commentators have, however, detected an unambiguous lineage with Marx's classic ideas on social class: '[B]y class Frazier did not mean prestige groups or the so-called "social classes" which Warner popularized; he used class in the European tradition that followed Marx'[s] definition of class as an economic group ... It is remarkable that in spite of this strong current [Warner's] in American stratification research, Frazier nevertheless consistently followed the Marxian tradition in his own writings and analysis.' Bart Landry, 'Reinterpretation,' 212.
65 Frazier, *Negro in the United States*, 703–4.
66 'After World War I and during the 1920s, Frazier confronted a conservative and racist academic system that expected its young Afro-American intellectuals to be compliant, apolitical, pious, and grateful for the opportunity to enter its doors. If Frazier's politics were not always self-evident, that is partly because it was risky for academics to express any viewpoint to the left of conventional liberalism. In the 1920s, when Frazier was working in the South, such a viewpoint was literally life-threatening, as Frazier found out in Atlanta.' Platt, *E. Franklin Frazier*, 176.
67 See Richard Pells, *Radical Visions*, for an instructive portrait of this development.
68 E. Franklin Frazier, 'Quo Vadis?,' 129–31.
69 E. Franklin Frazier, 'Some Effects,' 496–7, cited in Platt, *E. Franklin Frazier*, 152.
70 E. Franklin Frazier, 'Human, All Too Human,' 286–7.
71 '*Black Bourgeoisie* caused a stir because it was widely reviewed and made Frazier a controversial celebrity who was in demand as a speaker and who provided good copy in the Afro-American press.' Platt, *E. Franklin Frazier*, 153.
72 Frazier, *Negro in the United States*, 409–12.
73 E. Franklin Frazier, 'New Negro Middle Class,' 31–2.
74 E. Franklin Frazier, *Black Bourgeoisie*, 86.
75 Ibid., 173.
76 Ibid., 235–7.
77 Ibid., 237–8.
78 E. Franklin Frazier, 'Failure,' 57.
79 Ibid., 57–8.
80 Ibid., 65.

81 Ibid.
82 Ibid., 58–60.
83 Ibid., 66.
84 Ibid.
85 Ibid.
86 E. Franklin Frazier, 'Negro in the United States,' 340.
87 Ibid., 369.
88 Ibid., 369–70.
89 E. Franklin Frazier, *Race and Culture Contacts*, 6.
90 'According to our classification, there are six areas in which race and culture contacts have been created as a result of the development of European settlements. These were located in the United States; Latin America, including Mexico, Central America, and South America; the West Indies and the Guianas; South Africa; and Australia and New Zealand.' Ibid., 11–12.
91 Ibid., 327–8
92 Ibid., 331.
93 Ibid., 335.
94 Ibid., 338.
95 Ibid., 148–9.
96 Ibid., 295, quoting Jawaharlal Nehru, *Discovery*, 360.
97 'Nkrumah, who had a deep understanding and sympathy for the aspirations of the masses of Africans, wanted to make the nationalistic movement a mass movement.' Ibid., 293.
98 Cited in Platt, *E. Franklin Frazier*, 221. This text was part of an epitaph read by Du Bois's wife at the official presentation of Frazier's personal library to the University of Ghana.
99 'The sociological theory in regard to race relations which was current during the first two decades of the present century was doubtless not unrelated to public opinion and the dominant racial attitudes of the American people.' E. Franklin Frazier, 'Sociological Theory,' 35.
100 Ibid., 37.
101 Ibid., 40.
102 Ibid. Frazier refers here to Park's thinking during the last five years of his life.
103 Ibid., 42.
104 E. Franklin Frazier, 'Race Contacts,' 44.
105 Ibid., 45.
106 Ibid., 50.
107 Ibid.

108 Ibid., 56–7.
109 Ibid., 59–60.
110 E. Franklin Frazier, 'Theoretical Structure,' 4.
111 Ibid.
112 Ibid., 5. There is a tacit allusion here to Talcott Parsons.
113 Ibid., 5–6. Here Frazier departs significantly from classical Chicago ecological theory, which paid little attention to class conflict or to politics in general.
114 Ibid., 10.
115 Ibid., 12.
116 Ibid.
117 Ibid., 16. It must be admitted that Frazier's definition of this sociological problem is not particularly limpid.
118 Ibid., 16–17.
119 Ibid., 13.
120 Ibid., 22–3.
121 Ibid., 23–4.
122 Ibid., 26.
123 Ibid.
124 Ibid., 27. In short, they are inseparable from theory.
125 Ibid. My italics are designed to show that Frazier was conversant with the idea of abstract conceptualization.
126 Ibid., 27–8. We shall see in part three how such a restrictive view of conceptualization in science leads to epistemological difficulties.
127 Ibid., 28.
128 Ibid., 29.
129 E. Franklin Frazier, 'Desegregation,' 309.
130 Ibid., 309–10.
131 Ibid., 310.
132 Ibid., 313–14.
133 This is an explicit reference to Robert E. Park, 'Urban Community.'
134 Frazier, 'Desegregation,' 314.
135 Ibid., 315.
136 Ibid., 317.
137 Ibid., 318.
138 Ibid.
139 Ibid., 320.
140 Ibid., 321.
141 Ibid., 321–2.
142 Ibid., 322.

143 Ibid., 323.
144 Platt, *E. Franklin Frazier*, 90.
145 In this he follows Emery Bogardus, 'Race Relations Cycle.'
146 Persons, 'E. Franklin Frazier,' 258.
147 Jean-Michel Chapoulie, *La tradition*, 351.
148 See, for example, Robert E. Park, *Bases*, 243.
149 See my extensive analysis of this issue in Pierre Saint-Arnaud, 'Sur le concept de "classe sociale."'
150 Christopher A. McAuley, *Mind*, 40. Platt notes that 'there were some significant differences between Park and Frazier regarding sociological theory. Frazier, for example, did not accept the moral neutrality that was supposedly the bedrock of the Chicago School ... He always admired intellectuals whose work demonstrated that the "race problem was *made*" and therefore people "can *unmake* it"'; Platt, *E. Franklin Frazier*, 166–7. Another excerpt clearly establishes Frazier's independence from Park the icon: '"Whenever I want a damn good fight," Park used to tell Frazier, "I know right where to come"'; cited in Platt, *E. Franklin Frazier*, 90.

Part Three: From Explanation to Comprehension

1 Thomas L. Haskell, *Emergence*, 1.
2 Everett C. Hughes, 'Race Relations,' 879.
3 Lewis Coser, *Continuities*, 148–9.
4 William J. Wilson, *Power*, 4.
5 One further example: 'On the basis of the established literature through 1970, and to a considerable extent since then, the predominating American sociological approach to race relations reflects a celebration of "assimilation" as a reigning "theoretical" principle.' Harry H. Bash, *Sociology*, 29.
6 Lester F. Ward, *Pure Sociology*, 205.
7 Ibid., 208.
8 Harry Bash expresses the essential character of their conceptual model as follows: 'If Ward fixed upon a widely-held but loosely-formulated *bio-social notion* and structured it ... into an overarching *psycho-social principle* of institutional development, then it remained for Robert E. Park and Ernest W. Burgess to trim the explanatory implications from that principle, reduce it to the dimensions of an *analytic concept*, and establish it as a fundamental category of social process for American sociologists.' Bash, *Sociology*, 67–8.
9 Robert E. Park, 'Racial Assimilation,' 209.
10 Robert E. Park and Ernest W. Burgess, *Introduction*, 735.

11 See Robert E. Park, 'Our Racial Frontier.'

12 Park and Burgess were not the only ones in the interwar period to conceive of assimilation as a characteristic societal process; for other statements of this view, see Edward C. Hayes, 'Some Social Relations,' and Floyd N. House, 'Social Relations.'

13 Pierre Van Den Berghe, *Race and Racism*, 6.

14 Park and Burgess, *Introduction*, 736.

15 Bash, *Sociology*, 114.

16 See the former's *The Social Construction of Reality* and the latter's *Reality Construction in Society*.

17 Judith Willer, *Social Determination*, 32. This representation of science as a system of abstract, logically unified concepts has increasingly come to characterize contemporary sociology, as witness the works of Jeffrey Alexander, Niklas Luhmann, Anthony Giddens, and others.

18 Such normativity improperly does away with the falsification procedure necessary to any authentic and legitimate science; see Karl Popper, *Logic*.

19 Bash, *Sociology*, 145. See also, on this subject, Hermann Strasser, *Normative Structure*.

20 Leon Bramson, *Political Context*, 51. The norm in question here is, of course, the white social order. Another persuasive approach to Park's work homes in on the fatalist strain running through it: 'While less conservative than Social Darwinist William Graham Sumner, Park and many of his pupils were bound by a similar fatalism. Park's observations of social conditions led him to acknowledge the power of what he liked to call "natural forces." His sociological system embodied a *systematic tendency* to ignore practically all possibilities of modifying the social effects of "natural forces" by conscious social intervention.' Robert L. Hall, 'E. Franklin Frazier,' 54.

21 Wilson explains the infiltration of racism into the era's belief systems: 'During the first two stages of American race relations, racial belief systems were quite explicitly based on assumptions of the black man's biological and cultural inferiority, and, therefore, have been appropriately identified as ideologies of racism'; *Declining Significance*, 9.

22 Michel Wieviorka, *Arena*, 11. The exposition in the next few paragraphs is indebted to this work.

23 See Barbara B. Lal, *Romance*, for an interesting recent reading of Park's race relations theory.

24 'Perhaps no notion illustrates this tendency toward reification better in sociology, than that of "race." Much like the concept of assimilation ... "race" slipped into the discipline from its popular and *ideologically-conditioned* use in everyday life, as well as through adoption from another scien-

tific discipline, in this case from population genetics in particular, and human biology in general.' Bash, *Sociology*, 194. My emphasis.

25 See, for example, Ashley Montagu's *Man's Most Dangerous Myth: The Fallacy of Race* (1942), written at the height of the Nazi terror in Europe. The Nazis' claims of Aryan superiority were the topic of much debate among American academics that could not have been missed by Myrdal and his contemporaries.

26 Dollard, *Caste*, 439.

27 Wieviorka, *Arena*, 18.

28 Gunnar Myrdal, *American Dilemma*, li.

29 Ibid., 41.

30 Ibid., 68.

31 Wieviorka, *Arena*, 20.

32 Manning Marable, *W.E.B. Du Bois*, 29. Du Bois was the first black intellectual to rigorously and methodically challenge Anglo-Saxon Eurocentric racism (in which Europe is regarded as the cradle of civilization and high culture) using empirical data; see Tukufu Zuberi, *Thicker Than Blood*, 173.

33 Thomas F. Gosset, *Race*, 410. For the nuances of Du Bois's ideas on race, see W.E.B. Du Bois, *Dusk of Dawn*.

34 W.E.B. Du Bois, 'Conservation,' 243–4. Toussaint l'Ouverture was a Haitian leader greatly admired by African Americans for his courageous fight against Napoleon's troops in 1802, when they invaded Haiti.

35 Ibid., 244.

36 Ibid., 245.

37 Robert C. Bannister, *Sociology and Scientism*.

38 The best analysis of the issues dealt with here is Dale R. Vlasek, 'E. Franklin Frazier,' to which my discussion here is indebted.

39 Ibid., 144ff.

40 Ibid., 148.

41 'Frazier was a more thorough-going assimilationist than either Park or Charles Johnson. Where Park and Johnson saw assimilation as a distant prospect, Frazier emphasized that black migration to the cities was breaking down the older peasant culture and that blacks were adopting the values of white American culture'; Walter A. Jackson, *Gunnar Myrdal*, 104.

42 Vlasek, 'E. Franklin Frazier,' 151.

43 Here I depart from Vlasek's interpretation (152ff) in which Frazier was solely a believer in 'assimilation by fusion' after 1950. In my view, this is only one of the possibilities that he developed.

44 E. Franklin Frazier, 'Failure,' 65–6.

45 'The vast majority of white scholars did not recognize the existence of the

black community prior to the 1960s, and the works of black intellectuals were extremely rare within white institutions. At best, for liberal paternalists, the Negro was an object to be studied, a litmus test on the viability of American democracy. At worst, the Negro was genetically inferior. In either case, Afro-Americans were not viewed as active creators of culture or political and social thought.' Manning Marable, 'Black Studies,' 35.

46 Ibid., 42.

47 Oliver C. Cox, *Caste*, 319.

48 Ibid., 320.

49 Ibid., 321–2. In a footnote Cox cites Park's preface to Steiner's *The Japanese Invasion* in which he allegedly put forward a definition of racial prejudice as an instinctive phenomenon. Cox writes: 'We shall attempt to show that this instinct hypothesis is too simple.'

50 Ibid., 399–400. This is the 'social attitude' to which Cox clearly refers in the previous citation.

51 Ibid., 545.

52 Ibid., 546.

53 Ibid., 547.

54 Ibid.

55 Ibid.

56 Ibid., 583.

57 In this vein, see the interesting remarks on Cox and other twentieth-century black intellectuals in Cedric J. Robinson, *Black Marxism.* However, Du Bois's approach differed from that of Cox in that Cox 'denied the importance of Black agency by arguing that Blacks would be led to the promised land only by white proletarian revolutionaries.' Aldon D. Morris, 'Sociology of Race,' 523.

58 Fernand Dumont, *Genèse*, 339–40.

59 Ibid., 347.

60 Fernand Dumont, *Les idéologies*, 97, 100.

61 Ibid., 101.

62 See, for example, Talcott Parsons, 'Present Position.'

63 As early as 1937, Horkheimer's 'Traditional and Critical Theory' offered the keys to such an approach.

64 For an insightful commentary on this and related subjects, see Jean-Michel Berthelot's introduction to his *Sociologie.*

65 The history of African American sociology written by Marable, Wilson, Zuberi, and others since the 1970s has made appreciable cognitive progress thanks to the conceptual reformulation of race in more abstract and systematic terms. This process has been helped along by a fruitful and methodical

dialogue with other disciplines, such as demography, human genetics, history, statistics, and economics; in a word, thanks to *interdisciplinarity*, a key scientific practice of our time.

66 Walter P. Metzger, *Academic Freedom*, 4. See also Alain Touraine, *Université et société*.

67 See Laurence Veysey, *Emergence*, a classic work on the subject. Authorities such as Edward Shils argue that the idea of the modern university was in the air much earlier: 'The idea of the modern university was a creation of the end of the eighteenth and the beginning of the nineteenth centuries. By the beginning of the twentieth century, that idea had approached fulfillment.' Edward Shils, *Order*, 40.

68 Shils, *Order*, 19–20.

69 'These movements within the central constellation and between the centers and the concentric peripheral circles consolidated the collective self-image of the academic order and the position of the central constellation within it. It led many of its members to conceive of themselves as parts of a mighty regiment, somewhat distinct from the rest of American society, contributing to it, criticizing it, supported by it, and harassed by it. It also induced in academies an image of themselves as separated from the other intellectual institutions of the learned and the literary worlds.' Ibid., 21.

70 Burton J. Bledstein, *Culture*, x; see also Haskell, *Emergence.*

71 Bledstein, *Culture*, 289–90.

72 Ellen W. Schrecker, *No Ivory Tower*, 13–14.

73 Ibid., 14.

74 Ibid., 16. Schrecker adduces documented cases of professors (Richard Ely, Edward Bemis, Edward Ross, and others) who were censured for political dissidence by their respective institutions between 1890 and 1900.

75 Notably, a 1915 report by Arthur A. Lovejoy for the American Association of University Professors 'imposed restrictions on the professoriat's freedom of speech that [went] far beyond existing laws. Essentially, it refused to protect professors who indulged in any type of anti-war activity, whether that activity was legal or not. Thus, draft resisters and people who counselled draft resistance were beyond the pale of academic freedom, but so, too, were people who merely discouraged "others from rendering voluntary assistance to the efforts of the government."' Ibid., 21.

76 Anthony M. Platt, *E. Franklin Frazier*, 44.

77 Schrecker, *No Ivory Tower*, 23.

78 Gosset, *Race*, 373. My emphasis.

79 Bertram W. Doyle, *Etiquette*, 171. Robert Park, in his introduction to this work (p. xviii), wrote, 'Etiquette, so far as it can be conceived to be a form

of government or control, functions only insofar as it defines and maintains "social distances."'

80 Michael R. Winston, 'Through the Back Door,' 678. Winston's reference is to Shils, 'Color.' For Shils's theoretical work on the concept of periphery, see Edward Shils, *Center and Periphery*.

81 Schrecker, *No Ivory Tower*, 288–9. See also Schrecker, *Many Are the Crimes*, her classic general work on McCarthyism.

82 Johnson recalled, 'I met Dr. Robert E. Park in my first quarter of study. His course on "Crowd and Public" seemed challenging and I signed up for it with no prior intimation of his personality as a teacher. It was not long before he was on a basis of easy and stimulating exchange with individual members of the class ... A second [revelation] came when it dawned on me that I was being taken seriously and without the usual condescension or oily paternalism of which I had already seen too much. The relation of teacher and student grew into a friendship.' Cited by Winifred Raushenbush, *Robert E. Park*, 101.

83 No doubt, W.E.B. Du Bois was able to accomplish a great deal during his tenure at Atlanta University. I am sensitive to the position of Shaun L. Gabbidon and Earl Wright II that a genuine school of sociology was developed at Atlanta from the last three years of the nineteenth century through the second decade of the twentieth. Was it the first such school in the United States? I do not possess the historical and documentary competence necessary to properly assess this issue. However, it is important to note that the institutional trajectory of this school underwent a significant decline in the years following the departure of its intellectual architect, since no figure of comparable scientific stature came along to replace him. Wright tacitly acknowledges this fact when he notes that only two monographs were published after 1914, while the annual conferences were gone within a decade. Earl Wright II, 'Deferred Legacy!,' 199.

84 Raymond Wolters, *New Negro*, 16–17.

85 See Raushenbush, *Robert E. Park*, for more insightful commentary on this point.

86 'Today, one is tempted to imagine the actual relations between Frazier and Johnson and Frazier and Cox. They were all outstanding scholars but of different temperaments and caught in an academic environment barely accepting of black scholars ... One wonders how Park really felt about these three outstanding men. Did he evaluate them differently? In any case, none was offered a faculty position.' Adelaide M. Cromwell, 'Frazier's Background,' 38–9.

87 Actually, Columbia University was the first to grant a doctorate in sociol-

ogy to an African American (1912). But the war and the postwar recrudescence of racist prejudice interceded to make this a largely isolated event. What began at Chicago in the late 1920s was an enduring structural shift toward admission of blacks to the country's top schools.

88 Abbott offers a similar interpretation in which academic interactions at Chicago were the predictable social result of the unequal relations between Park the patron and his black protégés. Wishing to break into a world over which they had no direct control, they had much to gain by assimilating and reproducing the 'master's' theories: 'Park's theories of race relations profoundly shaped American conceptions of race, both directly and through their effects on major African American writers like Frazier, Johnson, Cayton, and Drake.' Andrew Abbott, *Department and Discipline*, 23.

89 Ibid., 102.

90 Frazier's trajectory illustrates this point with crystal clarity: 'For all his accomplishments – he was the first African American president of the American Sociological Association (1948); author of *The Negro in the United States* (1949), the first serious textbook on the topic; consultant to the United Nations – he was never offered a tenure-track job in a predominantly white university, and the praise he received from his professional peers for his contributions as a *Negro* social scientist was intentionally backhanded.' Anthony M. Platt, 'Between Scorn and Longing,' 72–3.

91 This is the structural source of a blunt paradox characterizing 'probably the most liberal among outstanding universities of the day' (Adelaide M. Cromwell, 'Frazier's Background,' 38), the University of Chicago. On the one hand, this distinguished institution did not hesitate to enroll nonwhite students, notably black ones, helping them further their academic training and intellectual autonomy; on the other, it denied them employment. Another illustration of the paradox is that Chicagoan 'stars' like Park or Burgess could and did entertain excellent personal relations with their black students while keeping the 'appropriate' institutional distance from them, occupationally speaking.

On this specific issue in mid-century academia, Mary Jo Deegan offers an interesting interpretation, though its scope is confined to the University of Chicago sociology department: 'While sociology was being established at Chicago, racism flourished in America. From the 1880s until at least the late 1950s, the United States was sundered by legal, separate worlds for Black and white people ... Du Bois referred to this external structural pattern of racism as the "color line." It generated an entire lifeworld surrounding Black people that Du Bois called the "Veil." Life within the Veil divided the self into a double-consciousness with a sense of "twoness" corresponding to the divisions emergent from the color line ... African-American sociologists in the Chicago school suffered specific, even greater divisions within their "selves" than other African Americans. As sociologists, they were empowered to speak about racism through their formal knowledge about race relations and the social construction of inequality. Simultaneously, they lived within multiple layers of discrimination as African Americans and sociologists in a white-defined, hegemonic school and lifeworld. The professional self of African-American sociologists generated a particular reality and experience that rarely informed the everyday practice and theoretical knowledge of "white sociology." I call this especially liberating and oppressing practice of American sociologists the "Veil of sociology," and the particular practice of this phenomenon in Chicago the "Veil of the Chicago school of race relations," referring to the different power, marginality, and legitimacy of white and Black sociologists within this structure of knowledge and higher education ... All African-American sociologists lived behind the Veil, and this common experience generated a different *epistemology* and network from their white colleagues at Chicago. For example, Frazier was a friend of Robert Park and Du Bois, and often added a "Marxist" dimension to his thought, while Park opposed Du Bois and Marxism.' Mary Jo Deegan, 'Oliver C. Cox,' 279–80. My emphasis. Deegan's 'veil of sociology' is the rough equivalent of what I am calling 'academic racism' for the American university system as a whole.

92 Jackson, *Gunnar Myrdal*, 95. Jackson's analysis informs the following discussion. See also David W. Southern, *Gunnar Myrdal*, as well as the special issue of *Daedalus* titled '*An American Dilemma* Revisited.'

93 Du Bois, too, though a much more marginal figure than he had once been, represented a resource for Myrdal: 'Although he had made pioneering studies in the sociology of blacks in *The Philadelphia Negro* (1899) and the *Atlanta University Studies*, Du Bois was a peripheral figure in the social sciences in the late 1930s. His marginality was not only the result of racism and institutional isolation. He had spent twenty-four years outside the academy as an editor and civil rights leader, and his strident advocacy was considered unscientific in an age that so highly esteemed objectivity and value neutrality. Du Bois's literary and historical writings were seen as further evidence of amateurism and dilettantism by a generation of social scientists so keenly conscious of professionalism and disciplinary boundaries.' Jackson, *Gunnar Myrdal*, 101.

94 'Although he was denounced by younger black radicals as a conservative, Johnson basically worked within the framework of reform offered by the

New Deal while publishing studies that revealed the damaging effects of segregation. Deeply committed to building the social sciences at Fisk University, he played the role of interracial diplomat and cultivated the good will of southern white moderates and foundation executives.' Ibid., 103.

95 'Although none of these thinkers advanced an explicitly Marxist theory of race relations, all gave great weight to economic factors in explaining the historical development of racial inequality in the United States ... Bunche, Harris, and Frazier condemned the New Deal as halfhearted reformism and envisaged some kind of social democratic solution to the United States' economic crisis.' Ibid., 103–4.

96 The second invitation came about in the following way: 'As the project neared completion, Myrdal grappled with the sticky problem of deciding who should read the manuscript ... Despite his spats with Wirth, Myrdal had come to respect his editorial prowess, so he chose him as the white social science critic. Myrdal wanted a black critic, not just as a token but because he respected the minority point of view. Since blacks made up the weakest group in America, a factual or an interpretive mistake, Myrdal reasoned, would hurt them more than whites. After a great deal of deliberation, he selected E. Franklin Frazier because of his fierce independence, his lack of sentimentality, and his keen insights.' Southern, *Gunnar Myrdal*, 39.

97 E. Franklin Frazier, 'Race: An American Dilemma.' 'Frazier clearly was the kindest critic. He argued initially with Myrdal's use of the concept "caste" as too static to capture the changing racial situation ... Frazier even lauded the dilemma thesis, but he thought that Myrdal had overplayed it. The Howard sociologist judged that overall the report was one of great force and timeliness. It would make, he assured Myrdal, the so-called "disinterested" social scientists rethink their position.' Southern, *Gunnar Myrdal*, 41.

98 Jackson, *Gunnar Myrdal*, 111.

99 'The black sociologist Horace Cayton of Chicago, who also worked for the WPA and had a Rosenwald Fellowship, lobbied Myrdal constantly for a full-time job at $5,000. When Myrdal learned about Cayton's other duties and income, he offered the Chicago scholar a modest stipend for a small research project. He accepted.' Southern, *Gunnar Myrdal*, 23.

100 'W.E.B. Du Bois was kept at a discrete [sic] distance from the effort at the insistence of Frederick Keppel, the Carnegie Commission organizer of the project, whose racial politics were hardly progressive.' Howard Winant, 'Dark Side,' 559.

101 Myrdal, *American Dilemma*, 96.

102 W.E.B. Du Bois, 'Review.'

103 Pierre Bourdieu, *Les usages*, 14.

104 Ibid., 15.

105 Shortly before Myrdal's death, W.A. Jackson asked him why he had hired a large number of radical young African Americans. He replied, 'It's not my choice. It's history's choice that the Negroes in the situation they were in, if they were intellectually advanced people, they were of course radical.' Jackson, *Gunnar Myrdal*, 111.

106 Oliver C. Cox, '*An American Dilemma*.'

107 John H. Franklin, 'Dilemma,' 75–6. Franklin's reference here is to Ralph Ellison's great novel *Invisible Man* (1952).

108 Burkart Holzner, *Reality Construction*, 69.

109 Academic racism was obviously not the only factor responsible for this situation, but its existence undoubtedly exacerbated and fed into other factors (funding shortages, personal animosities, etc.). Nor, obviously, is it my intention to suggest that the marginalization of Frazier, Cox, and the others was a deliberate, diabolical plot carried out by any specific Anglo-American scholars. It should be clear that it was a structural obstacle resulting from the pervasiveness of racist practices and attitudes in the northern university circuit.

110 'The Jazz Age can also be called the age of *recorded* blues and jazz because it was in the twenties that the great masses of jazz and blues material began to be recorded, and not only were the race records sold in great numbers but Americans began to realize for the first time that there was a *native* American music [that was] traditionally wild, happy, disenchanted, and unfettered ...' LeRoi Jones, *Blues People*, 100.

111 Michel Fabre, *Unfinished Quest*, 178–9.

112 His biographer describes him as follows at this stage of his life: 'By 1953, Wright was a novelist with an international audience, an "established writer" and what could be called a Parisian intellectual ... Wright also had a well-established group of friends, admirers and literary acquaintances, and enjoyed somewhat of a reputation as a *maître* to whom younger writers came for advice on their manuscripts ... He was more than ever at the center of the international exchange of ideas, with the comings and goings of compatriots such as Elmer Carter, Dorothy Norman, Nelson Algren, E. Franklin Frazier, Louis Wirth and Dorothy Maynor [and] of the Africans Léopold Senghor and Alioune Diop ...' Ibid., 382–3.

113 The treatment that follows is modeled on the one used in my *Park, Dos Passos, metropolis.*

114 Richard Wright, 'Blueprint,' 42.

115 Ibid., 43.

116 Ibid., 44.

117 Ibid.

118 Fabre, *Unfinished Quest*, 232.

119 '[T]his party provided a chance for Wright to become better acquainted with Professor Louis Wirth, who obliged him by providing a program of readings in sociology that Wright consciously followed.' Ibid.

120 Richard Wright, *Twelve Million Black Voices*, xx.

121 A wealth of critical work has been devoted to Richard Wright; see Henry L. Gates, Jr, and Kwame A. Appiah, eds, *Richard Wright*, particularly the papers by Carla Cappetti, 'Sociology of an Existence: Wright and the Chicago School' (255–71), and John M. Reilly, 'Richard Wright and the Art of Non-Fiction: Stepping Out on the Stage of the World' (409–23).

122 'After reading "I Have Seen Black Hands" and "Between the World and Me," he asked Langston Hughes to put him in touch with Wright. They met almost as soon as Wright reached New York and began a literary friendship that lasted for years. Surprised by Ellison's intellectual curiosity and talents, Wright was only too happy to act as mentor to this slightly younger man so predisposed to admire him.' Fabre, *Unfinished Quest*, 145.

123 For intellectuals of Ellison's generation, the U.S. Communist Party 'offered a program, an organization, and a sphere of action for the politically aware; it provided an apparatus in which minority groups could form social and cultural units and feel themselves proud parts of a larger struggle. It provided also what was a major opportunity for the African-American intellectual to write and publish and also to move in a literary world.' Edith Schor, *Visible Ellison*, 4.

124 See, on this point, Ellison's introduction to his *Shadow and Act*.

125 Schor, *Visible Ellison*, 54.

126 Ralph Ellison, *Invisible Man*, 15, quoting Booker T. Washington, *Up from Slavery*, 107.

127 'I had undergone, not too many months before taking the path which led to writing, the humiliation of being taught in a class in sociology at a Negro college (from Park and Burgess, the leading textbook in the field) that Negroes represented the "lady of the races." This contention the Negro instructor passed blandly along to us without even bothering to wash his hands, much less his teeth. Well, I had no intention of being bound by any such humiliating definition of my relationship to American literature. Not even to those works which depicted Negroes negatively.' Ralph Ellison, *Shadow and Act*, xx.

128 Ibid., 303–17. The novelist argued rather subtly that the sociology of

knowledge is a promising approach to research on the genesis and content of black intellectual production; see Hall, 'E. Franklin Frazier,' 48.

129 For more insight into Ellison's work, see Ralph Ellison, *Conversations.*

130 Dumont, *Genèse*, 347.

Postface: Imagining a Different History

1 From a speech given in London to the Pan-African Congress, reproduced in W.E.B. Du Bois, *Souls*, 10.

2 Lawrence A. Young and Lynn J. England, 'One Hundred Years,' 134; see also Aldon D. Morris, 'Sociology of Race.'

3 On these sources of Du Bois's thought, see Shamoon Zamir, *Dark Voices*, 68–112, and David L. Lewis, *W.E.B. Du Bois: Biography*, 140–7.

4 Max Weber understood this, and upon publication of *The Souls of Black Folk*, he 'contacted Du Bois, insisting that his "splendid work ... ought *to be translated into German*" (Weber's emphasis). Weber proposed a suitable translator for the task, and then offered "to write a short introduction about the Negro question and literature and should be much obligated to you for some information about your life, viz: age, birthplace, descent, positions held by you – of course only *if you give* your authorization" (Weber's emphasis).' Manning Marable, *Living Black History*, 95, quoting Weber to Du Bois, 30 March 1905, *Correspondence of W.E.B. Du Bois*, 106–7.

5 Judith R. Blau and Eric S. Brown, 'Du Bois and Diasporic Identity,' 220. Marable, too, stresses the continuing topicality of *Souls:* 'It is no exaggeration to say that *The Souls of Black Folk* has remained the most influential text about the African-American experience for a century ... Few books make history, and fewer still become foundational texts for the movements and struggles of an entire people. *The Souls of Black Folk* occupies this rare position. It helped to create the intellectual argument for the Black freedom struggle in the twentieth century. *Souls* justified the pursuit of higher education for Negroes and thus contributed to the rise of the Black middle class.' Marable, *Living Black History*, 79, 96.

6 The publication in 1902 of Charles Cooley's *Human Nature and the Social Order* had already given a clear indication that sociological science was in the process of constructively absorbing the rewarding pragmatic and subjectivist insights of the philosophers Charles S. Peirce (1839–1914), William James (1842–1910), and John Dewey (1859–1952), who were all profoundly influenced by German idealism even as they critiqued various aspects of it. See Donald N. Levine, *Visions*, 251–68, and J. David Lewis and Richard L. Smith, *American Sociology.*

Bibliography

I. Archival Sources

The University of Massachusetts Amherst has the largest collection of unpublished work by W.E.B. Du Bois. The Special Collections and University Archives Department of the university's W.E.B. Du Bois Library houses the Du Bois Papers, which are divided into twenty sections covering the years 1877 to 1963, the most voluminous of them being the 100,000-plus items of correspondence. In addition there are speeches, pamphlets, book reviews, newspaper columns, audiovisuals, and photographs. Also available is a digital resource with a selection of Du Bois's public-domain writings and an image gallery. Atlanta University has an analogous but much smaller collection of documents covering the period 1897 to 1910, when Du Bois left his imprint on the university as a professor of history and sociology, a field researcher, and a conference organizer and editor. Three other institutions have limited numbers of Du Bois-related documents: Yale University, Fisk University, and the Schomburg Center for Research in Black Culture of the New York Public Library. Also of note are three university research centers named after Du Bois: the W.E.B. Du Bois Department of Afro-American Studies at the University of Massachusetts Amherst (founded 1969); the W.E.B. Du Bois Institute for African and African American Research at Harvard University (1975), named in honor of the institution's first black PhD; and the W.E.B. Du Bois Collective Research Institute at the University of Pennsylvania (1998), a multidisciplinary academic enterprise whose mission is to 'continue the tradition of "engaged scholarship" in the pursuit of urban issues and themes raised by W.E.B. Du Bois in his landmark study, *The Philadelphia Negro.*'

The E. Franklin Frazier Papers are housed in the Manuscript Division of Howard University's Moorland-Spingarn Research Center, one of the country's oldest centers for research on African American history and culture; the University of Chicago has a smaller number of archival documents related to Frazier. The Charles Spurgeon Johnson Collection at Fisk University Library, created shortly after Johnson's death in 1956, covers the years 1935 to 1956 and documents both his administrative and scholarly career at Fisk; additional archival material relating to him is housed in others of the university's collections. To my knowledge, there are no special collections or archives in the country relating to Horace R. Cayton, J.G. St Clair Drake, or Oliver C. Cox. Of interest to Cox researchers are a few archival documents kept by Lincoln University (Pennsylvania) and Wayne State University, where Cox spent much of his career.

II. Books and Articles

Abbott, Andrew. *Department and Discipline: Chicago Sociology at One Hundred.* Chicago: University of Chicago Press, 1999.

Adorno, Theodor W., et al. *The Authoritarian Personality.* New York: Harper, 1950.

An American Dilemma *Revisited.* Special issue, *Daedalus* 124, no. 1 (Winter 1995).

American Journal of Sociology, Editorial Board. "What Is Americanism?" *American Journal of Sociology* 20, no. 4 (January 1915): 433–86.

Bacharan, Nicole. *Histoire des Noirs americains au XXe siecle.* Brussels: Éditions Complexe, 1994.

Bailey, Thomas P. *Race Orthodoxy in the South.* New York: Neale Publishing Co., 1914.

Bannister, Robert C. *Social Darwinism: Science and Myth in Anglo-American Social Thought.* Philadelphia: Temple University Press, 1979.

– *Sociology and Scientism: The American Quest for Objectivity, 1880–1940.* Chapel Hill: University of North Carolina Press, 1987.

Barkan, Elazar. *The Retreat of Scientific Racism: Changing Concepts of Race in Britain and the United States between the World Wars.* Cambridge: Cambridge University Press, 1992.

Bash, Harry H. *Sociology, Race and Ethnicity: A Critique of American Ideological Intrusions upon Sociological Theory.* New York: Gordon and Breach, 1979.

Bassett, John S. "Discussion of the Paper by Alfred H. Stone, "Is Race Friction between Blacks and Whites in the United States Growing and Inevitable?"' *American Journal of Sociology* 13, no. 6 (May 1908): 828–31.

Bay, Mia. "'The World Was Thinking Wrong about Race": *The Philadelphia Negro* and Nineteenth Century Science.' In Michael B. Katz and Thomas J. Sugrue, eds, *W.E.B. Du Bois, Race, and the City,* 41–52.

Belin, H.E. 'The Civil War as Seen through Southern Glasses.' *American Journal of Sociology* 9, no. 2 (September 1903): 259–67.

– 'Is Race Friction between Blacks and Whites in the United States Growing and Inevitable?' *American Journal of Sociology* 13, no. 5 (March 1908): 676–97.

– 'A Southern View of Slavery.' *American Journal of Sociology* 13, no. 4 (January 1908): 517–20.

Ben-David, Joseph. *Scientific Growth: Essays on the Social Organization and Ethos of Science.* Ed. Gad Freudenthal. Berkeley: University of California Press, c1991.

Berger, Peter, and Thomas Luckman. *The Social Construction of Reality.* Garden City, NY: Doubleday, 1966.

Bernard, L.L. 'The Teaching of Sociology in the United States.' *American Journal of Sociology* 15, no. 2 (September 1909): 164–213.

Berthelot, Jean-Michel. *Épistémologie des sciences sociales.* Paris: Presses Universitaires de France, 2001.

– *Sociologie: Épistémologie d'une discipline. Textes fondamentaux.* Brussels: De Boeck Université, 2000.

Blackwell, James, and Morris Janowitz, eds. *Black Sociologists: Historical and Contemporary Perspectives.* Chicago: University of Chicago Press, 1974.

Blasi, Anthony, ed. *Diverse Histories of American Sociology.* Leiden: Brill, 2005.

Blau, Judith R., and Eric S. Brown. 'Du Bois and Diasporic Identity: The Veil and the Unveiling Project.' *Sociological Theory* 19, no. 2 (July 2001): 219–33.

Bledstein, Burton J. *The Culture of Professionalism: The Middle Class and the Development of Higher Education in America.* New York: Norton, 1976.

Blumer, Herbert. 'Industrialisation and Race Relations.' In Guy Hunter, ed., *Industrialisation and Race Relations: A Symposium*, 220–53.

– 'Recent Research on Racial Relations: United States of America.' *International Social Science Bulletin* 10, no. 3 (1958): 403–47.

– 'Reflections on the Theory of Race Relations.' In Lind, ed., *Race Relations in World Perspective*, 3–21.

– 'Social Science and the Desegregation Process.' *Annals of the American Academy of Political and Social Science* 304 (March 1956): 137–43.

Boas, Franz. 'Human Faculty as Determined by Race.' *Proceedings of the American Association for the Advancement of Science* 43 (August 1894): 301–27.

– *The Mind of Primitive Man.* New York: Macmillan, 1911.

Bogardus, Emery S. 'A Race-Relations Cycle.' *American Journal of Sociology* 35, no. 4 (January 1930): 612–17.

Booth, Charles. *Labour and Life of the People in London.* London: Williams and Norgate, 1889–1991.

Boudon, Raymond, 'Les deux sociologies de la connaissance scientifique.' In R. Boudon and M. Clavelin, eds, *Le relativisme est-il résistible?*, 17–43.

Boudon, Raymond, and Maurice Clavelin, eds. *Le relativisme est-il résistible? Regards sur la sociologie des sciences.* Paris: Presses Universitaires de France, 1994.

Bourdieu, Pierre. *Homo Academicus.* Trans. Peter Collier. Cambridge: Polity Press in association with Basil Blackwell, 1990, c1988.

– *Pascalian Meditations.* Trans. Richard Nice. Cambridge: Polity Press, 2000.

– *Science of Science and Reflexivity.* Trans. Richard Nice. Chicago: University of Chicago Press, 2004.

– *Les usages sociaux de la science: Pour une sociologie clinique du champ scientifique.* Paris: Institut national de la recherche agronimique, 1997.

Bracey, John, August Meier, and Elliott M. Rudwick, eds. *The Black Sociologists: The First Half Century.* Belmont, CA: Wadsworth Publishing Co., 1971.

Bramson, Leon. *The Political Context of Sociology.* Princeton, NJ: Princeton University Press, 1961.

Breslau, Daniel. 'The American Spencerians: Theorizing a New Science.' In Craig Calhoun, ed., *Sociology in America: A History*, 39–62. Chicago: University of Chicago Press, 2007.

Brinton, Crane. *English Political Thought in the Nineteenth Century.* London: E. Benn, 1933.

Bruce, Philip Alexander. *Economic History of Virginia in the Seventeenth Century: An Inquiry into the Material Condition of the People, Based upon Original and Contemporaneous Records.* New York and London: Macmillan and Co., 1895.

Bulmer, Martin. *The Chicago School of Sociology: Institutionalization, Diversity and the Rise of Sociological Research.* Chicago: University of Chicago Press, 1984.

Burgess, Ernest W. 'Charles S. Johnson: Social Scientist and Race Relations.' *Phylon* 17, no. 4 (1956): 317–21.

– 'The Growth of the City: An Introduction to a Research Project.' In Robert E. Park and Ernest W. Burgess, eds, *The City*, 47–62.

Burnet, Jean. 'Robert E. Park and the Chicago School of Sociology: A Centennial Tribute.' *Canadian Review of Sociology and Anthropology* 1, no. 3 (August 1964): 156–64.

Calhoun, Craig. 'Sociology in America: An Introduction.' In Craig Calhoun, ed., *Sociology in America: A History*, 1–38. Chicago: University of Chicago Press, 2007.

Cappetti, Carla. 'Sociology of an Existence: Wright and the Chicago School.' In Henry L. Gates, Jr, and Kwame A. Appiah, eds, *Richard Wright: Critical Perspectives Past and Present*, 255–71.

Carey, Henry C. *The Slave Trade, Domestic and Foreign*. Philadelphia: H.C. Baird, 1867.

Carey, James T. *Sociology and Public Affairs: The Chicago School*. Beverly Hills, CA: Sage Publications, 1975.

Caute, David. *The Great Fear: The Anti-Communist Purge under Truman and Eisenhower.* New York: Simon and Schuster, 1979.

Cayton, Horace R. *Long Old Road.* New York: Trident Press, 1965.

– 'Robert Park: A Great Man Died, but Leaves Keen Observation on Our Democracy.' *Pittsburgh Courier*, 26 February 1944, 8.

Cayton, Horace R., and J.G. St Clair Drake. *Black Metropolis: A Study of Negro Life in a Northern City.* Chicago: University of Chicago Press, 1993.

Cayton, Horace R., and George S. Mitchell. *Black Workers and the New Unions.* Chapel Hill: University of North Carolina Press, 1939.

Chapoulie, Jean-Michel. 'E.C. Hughes et la tradition de Chicago.' Introduction to Everett C. Hughes, *Le regard sociologique: Essais choisis*, 13–57. Ed. and trans. Jean-Michel Chapoulie. Paris: École des hautes études en sciences sociales, 1996.

– *La tradition sociologique de Chicago, 1892–1961*. Paris: Seuil, 2001.

Chicago Commission on Race Relations. *The Negro in Chicago: A Study of Race Relations and a Race Riot in 1919.* Chicago: University of Chicago Press, 1922.

Cole, Stephen, ed. *What's Wrong with Sociology?* New Brunswick, NJ: Transaction Publishers, 2001.

Collins, Randall, and Michael Makowski. *The Discovery of Society.* New York: McGraw-Hill, 1997.

Converse, Jean M. *Survey Research in the United States: Roots and Emergence 1890–1960*. Berkeley: University of California Press, 1987.

Cooley, Charles. 'Genius, Fame and the Comparison of Races.' *Annals of the American Academy of Political and Social Science* 9 (May 1897): 1–42.

– *Human Nature and the Social Order.* New York: Scribners, 1902.

– *Social Organization.* New York: Scribners, 1909.

– *Social Process.* New York: Scribners, 1918.

Coser, Lewis. *Continuities in the Study of Social Conflict.* New York: The Free Press, 1967.

Cox, Oliver C. '*An American Dilemma:* A Mystical Approach to the Study of Race Relations.' *Journal of Negro Education* 14, no. 2 (Spring 1945): 132–48.

– *Capitalism and American Leadership.* New York: Philosophical Library, 1962.

– *Capitalism as a System.* New York: Monthly Review Press, 1964.

– *Caste, Class and Race: A Study in Social Dynamics.* New York: Doubleday and Co., 1948.

– *The Foundations of Capitalism.* New York: Philosophical Library, 1959.

– 'The Modern Caste School of Race Relations.' *Social Forces* 21, no. 2 (December 1942): 218–26.

– *Race Relations: Elements and Social Dynamics.* Detroit: Wayne State University Press, 1976.

Cromwell, Adelaide M. 'Frazier's Background and an Overview.' In James E. Teele, ed., *E. Franklin Frazier and* Black Bourgeoisie, 30–43.

Cruse, Harold. *The Crisis of the Negro Intellectual: A Historical Analysis of the Failure of Black Leadership.* 1st Quill ed. New York: Quill, 1984, c1967.

Cunard, Nancy, ed. *Negro.* London: Nancy Cunard at Wishart and Co., 1934. Reprint, New York: Negro Universities Press, 1969.

Daniels, John. *In Freedom's Birthplace: A Study of the Boston Negroes.* Boston: Houghton Mifflin, 1914.

Davis, Allison, Burleigh Gardner, and Mary Gardner. *Deep South: A Social Anthropological Study of Caste and Class.* Chicago: University of Chicago Press, 1941.

Davis, David B. *Inhuman Bondage: The Rise and Fall of Slavery in the New World.* New York: Oxford University Press, 2006.

Deegan, Mary Jo. 'Oliver C. Cox and the Chicago School of Race Relations, 1892–1960.' In Herbert Hunter, ed., *The Sociology of Oliver C. Cox: New Perspectives*, 271–88.

– *Race, Hull-House, and the University of Chicago: A New Conscience against Ancient Evils.* Westport, CT: Praeger, 2002.

Degler, Carl N. *In Search of Human Nature: The Decline and Revival of Darwinism in American Social Thought.* New York: Oxford University Press, 1991.

Dollard, John. *Caste and Class in a Southern Town.* New Haven, CT: Yale University Press, 1937.

Dowd, Jerome. *The Negro Races.* New York: Macmillan, 1907.

Doyle, Bertram. *The Etiquette of Race Relations in the South: A Study in Social Control.* Chicago: University of Chicago Press, 1937.

Drake, J.G. St Clair. *Black Folk Here and There: An Essay in History and Anthropology.* 2 vols. Los Angeles: Center for Afro-American Studies, University of California, c1987–c1990.

– *The Redemption of Africa and Black Religion.* Chicago: Third World Press, 1970.

Draper, Theodore. *American Communism and Soviet Russia: The Formative Period.* New York: Random House, 1986.

Dubofsky, Melvyn. *Hard Work: The Making of Labor History.* Urbana: University of Illinois Press, 2000.

Du Bois, W.E.B. 'The Atlanta Conferences.' *Voice of the Negro* 1 (March 1904): 85–9.

– *The Autobiography of W.E.B. Du Bois: A Soliloquy on Viewing My Life from the Last Decade of Its First Century.* [New York]: International Publishers, c1968.
– *Black Reconstruction in America, 1860–1880.* New York: Russell and Russell, 1935.
– 'The Conservation of Races.' American Negro Academy Occasional Paper no. 2 (1897): 5–15. Reprinted in W.E.B. Du Bois, *W.E.B. Du Bois on Sociology and the Black Community,* ed. Green and Driver, 238–49.
– *The Correspondence of W.E.B. Du Bois.* Ed. Herbert Aptheker. [Amherst]: University of Massachusetts Press, 1973–8.
– 'The Development of a People.' *International Journal of Ethics* 14 (April 1904): 292–311.
– *Dusk of Dawn: An Essay toward an Autobiography of a Race Concept.* New York: Harcourt Brace, 1940.
– 'The Economic Aspects of Race Prejudice.' *Editorial Review* 2 (May 1910): 488–93.
– 'The Laboratory in Sociology at Atlanta University.' *Annals of the American Academy of Political and Social Science* 21 (May 1903): 502–5.
– 'Die Negerfrage in den Vereinigten Staaten (The Negro Question in the United States, 1906).' Trans. Joseph Fracchia. *New Centennial Review* 6, no. 3 (Winter 2006): 241–90.
– 'The Negro Farmer.' In U.S. Department of Commerce and Labor, Bureau of the Census, *Negroes in the United States*, 69–98. Washington, DC: Government Printing Office, 1904.
– 'The Negroes of Farmville, Virginia: A Social Study.' *U.S. Department of Labor Bulletin* 14 (January 1898): 1–38.
– *The Philadelphia Negro: A Social Study.* Philadelphia: University of Pennsylvania Press, 1899.
– 'Post Graduate Work in Sociology at Atlanta University.' W.E.B. Du Bois Papers, 1803–1999. University of Massachusetts at Amherst, W.E.B. Du Bois Library, Special Collections and Archives, 1900.
– 'A Program for a Sociological Society.' W.E.B. Du Bois Papers. University of Massachusetts at Amherst, W.E.B. Du Bois Library, Special Collections and Archives, 1897, reel 80: 61.
– 'Race Friction between Black and White.' *American Journal of Sociology* 13 (May 1908): 834–8.
– 'Review of *An American Dilemma.*' *Phylon* 5, no. 2 (1944): 118–24.
– 'Sociology Hesitant.' *Boundary 2* 27, no. 3 (Fall 2000): 37–44.
– *The Souls of Black Folk: Essays and Sketches.* Chicago: A.C. McClurg, 1903.
– 'The Study of the Negro Problems.' *Annals of the American Academy of Political and Social Science* 11 (January 1898): 1–23.

– *The Suppression of the African Slave Trade to the United States of America, 1638–1870.* New York: Longmans, 1896.
– 'The Talented Tenth.' In Booker T. Washington, ed., *The Negro Problem*, 31–75. New York: Pott, 1903.
– 'The Twelfth Census and the Negro Problems.' *Southern Workman* 29 (May 1900): 305–9.
– *W.E.B. Du Bois: A Reader.* Ed. David L. Lewis. New York: H. Holt and Co., 1995.
– *W.E.B. Du Bois on Sociology and the Black Community.* Ed. Dan S. Green and Edwin D. Driver. Chicago: University of Chicago Press, 1980.
W.E.B. Du Bois, ed. *The Negro American Family: Report of a Racial Study Made Principally by the College Classes of 1909 and 1910 of Atlanta University, under the Patronage of the Trustees of the John F. Slater Fund; Together with the Proceedings of the 13th Annual Conference for the Study of the Negro Problems, Held at Atlanta University, on Tuesday, May the 26th, 1908.* Atlanta: Atlanta University Press, 1908.
– *The Negro Artisan: Report of a Social Study Made under the Direction of Atlanta University; Together with the Proceedings of the Seventh Conference for the Study of the Negro Problems, Held at Atlanta University on May 27th, 1902.* Atlanta: Atlanta University Press, 1902.
Dumont, Fernand. *L'avenir de la mémoire.* Quebec: Nuit Blanche, 1995.
– *Genèse de la société québécoise.* Montreal: Éditions du Boréal, 1993.
– *Les idéologies.* Paris: Presses Universitaires de France, 1974.
– *Récit d'une émigration: Mémoires.* Montreal: Éditions du Boréal, 1997.
Edwards, G. Franklin. 'E. Franklin Frazier.' In James Blackwell and Morris Janowitz, eds, *Black Sociologists: Historical and Contemporary Perspectives*, 85–117.
– 'E. Franklin Frazier: Race, Education, and Community.' In Robert K. Merton and Matilda Riley, eds, *Sociological Traditions from Generation to Generation: Glimpses of the American Experience*, 109–29. Norwood, NJ: Ablex Publishing, 1980.
Ellison, Ralph. *Conversations with Ralph Ellison.* Ed. Maryemma Graham and Amritjit Singh. Jackson: University Press of Mississippi, c1995.
– *Going to the Territory.* New York: Random House, 1986.
– *The Invisible Man.* New York: New American Library, 1952.
– *Shadow and Act.* New York: Vintage Books, [1964]. See especially '*An American Dilemma:* A Review,' 303–17.
Essed, Philomena, and David T. Goldberg, eds. *Race Critical Theories: Text and Context.* Malden, MA: Blackwell, 2002.
Eubank, Earle E. A *Treatise Presenting a Suggested Organization of Sociological Theory in Terms of Its Major Concepts.* Boston: Heath and Co., 1932.

Fabre, Michel. *The Unfinished Quest of Richard Wright.* Chicago: University of Illinois Press, 1993.

Fairclough, Adam. *Better Day Coming: Blacks and Equality, 1890–2000.* New York: Penguin Putnam, 2001.

Farber, Naomi. 'Charles S. Johnson's *The Negro in Chicago.*' In Ken Plummer, ed., *The Chicago School: Critical Assessments*, vol. 3, *Substantive Concerns: Race, Crime and the City*, 209–20. London and New York: Routledge, 1997.

Faris, Ellsworth. 'The Mental Capacity of Savages.' *American Journal of Sociology* 23, no. 5 (February 1918): 603–19.

Faulkner, Harold U. *American Economic History.* 6th ed. New York: Harper, 1949.

Fitzhugh, George. *Sociology for the South; Or, the Failure of a Free Society.* Richmond, VA: A. Morris, 1854.

Fleming, Walter L. 'Reorganization of the Industrial System in Alabama after the Civil War.' *American Journal of Sociology* 10, no. 4 (January 1905): 473–500.

Fourez, Gérard. *La construction des sciences*. Brussels: De Boeck-Westmael, 1988.

Franklin, John H. 'The Dilemma of the American Negro Scholar.' In Herbert Hill, ed., *Soon One Morning: New Writings by American Negroes, 1940–1962,* 60–76.

– *From Slavery to Freedom: A History of Negro Americans.* New York: Knopf, [1974].

Frazier, E. Franklin. *Black Bourgeoisie.* New York: The Free Press, 1957.

– 'La Bourgeoisie Noire.' *Modern Quarterly* 5, no. 1 (November 1928): 78–84. Reprinted in David L. Lewis, ed., *The Portable Harlem Renaissance Reader*, 173–81.

– 'Desegregation as an Object of Sociological Study.' In Arnold Rose, ed., *Human Behavior and Sociological Processes: An Interactionist Approach*, 608–24. Boston: Houghton Mifflin Co., 1961.

– 'The Du Bois Program in the Present Crisis.' *Race* 1 (Winter 1935–6): 11–13.

– 'Durham: Capital of the Black Middle Class.' In Alain Locke, ed., *The New Negro*, 1st Touchstone ed., 333–40.

– 'The Failure of the Negro Intellectual.' *Negro Digest* 11 (February 1962): 26–36. Reprinted in Joyce A. Ladner, ed., *The Death of White Sociology: Essays on Race and Culture,* 52–66.

– *The Free Negro Family.* Nashville, TN: Fisk University Press, 1932.

– 'Group Tactics and Ideals.' *Messenger* 9 (January 1927): 31.

– 'Human, All Too Human: The Negro's Vested Interest in Segregation.' *Survey Graphic* 36, no. 1 (January 1947): 74–5, 99–100. Reprinted in E. Franklin Frazier, *On Race Relations: Selected Writings*, 283–91.

– 'The Impact of Urban Civilization upon Negro Family Life.' *American Sociological Review* 2 (1937): 609–18. Reprinted in E. Franklin Frazier, *On Race Relations: Selected Writings*, 161–74.
– 'Letter to Reverend J.B. Adams, 22 January 1930.' Edward Franklin Frazier Papers, 1908–72. Moorland-Spingarn Research Center, Howard University, Washington, DC.
– 'The Negro and Non-Resistance.' *Crisis* 27 (March 1924): 213–14.
– *The Negro Family in Chicago.* Chicago: University of Chicago Press, 1932.
– *The Negro Family in the United States.* Chicago: University of Chicago Press, 1939.
– *The Negro in the United States.* Chicago: University of Chicago Press, 1949.
– 'The Negro in the United States.' In Andrew Lind, ed., *Race Relations in World Perspective: Papers Read at the Conference on Race Relations in World Perspective, Honolulu, 1954*, 339–70.
– 'A Negro Looks at the Soviet Union.' In *Proceedings of the Nationalities Panel. The Soviet Union: A Family of Nations in the War.* New York: National Council of American-Soviet Friendship, 1943.
– 'The Negro Slave Family.' *Journal of Negro History* 15, no. 2 (April 1930): 198–206.
– *Negro Youth at the Crossways: Their Personality Development in the Middle States.* Washington, DC: American Council on Education, 1940.
– 'New Currents of Thought among the Colored People of America.' MA thesis, Clark University, Worcester, MA, 1920.
– 'The New Negro Middle Class.' In Rayford W. Logan, ed., *The New Negro Thirty Years Afterward*, 25–32. Washington, DC: Howard University Press, 1955.
– 'Occupational Classes among Negroes in Cities.' *American Journal of Sociology* 35, no. 5 (March 1930): 718–38.
– *On Race Relations: Selected Writings.* Ed. G. Franklin Edwards. Chicago: University of Chicago Press, [c1968].
– 'The Pathology of Race Prejudice.' *Forum* 27 (June 1927): 856–62.
– 'The Present State of Sociological Knowledge Concerning Race Relations.' *Transactions of the Fourth World Congress of Sociology* 5 (1959): 73–80.
– 'Quo Vadis?' *Journal of Negro Education* 4, no. 1 (January 1935): 129–31.
– 'Race: An American Dilemma.' *Crisis* 41 (April 1944): 105–6.
– *Race and Culture Contacts in the Modern World.* New York: Knopf, 1957.
– 'Race Contacts and the Social Structure.' *American Sociological Review* 14, no. 1 (February 1949): 1–11. Reprinted in E. Franklin Frazier, *On Race Relations: Selected Writings*, 43–60.

– 'Racial Self-Expression.' In Charles S. Johnson, ed., *Ebony and Topaz: A Collectanea*, 119–21. New York: National Urban League, 1927.
– 'Rejoinder to "Social Determination in the Writing of Negro Scholars," by William T. Fontaine.' *American Journal of Sociology* 49, no. 4 (1944): 313–15.
– 'Review of *An American Dilemma*.' *American Journal of Sociology* 50, no. 6 (May 1945): 557–8.
– 'Sociological Theory and Race Relations.' *American Sociological Review* 12, no. 3 (June 1947): 265–71. Reprinted in E. Franklin Frazier, *On Race Relations: Selected Writings*, 30–42.
– 'Some Effects of the Depression on the Negro in the Northern Cities.' *Science and Society* 2 (Fall 1938): 496–7.
– 'The Status of the Negro in the American Social Order.' *Journal of Negro Education* 4, no. 3 (July 1935): 293–307.
– 'Theoretical Structure of Sociology and Sociological Research.' *British Journal of Sociology* 4, no. 4 (December 1953): 293–311. Reprinted in E. Franklin Frazier, *On Race Relations: Selected Writings*, 3–29.
– 'What Can the American Negro Contribute to the Social and Economic Life of Africa?' In John Davis, ed., *Africa: Seen by American Negroes*, 263–78. Paris: Présence Africaine, 1959.
Frazier, E. Franklin, et al. 'Editorial.' *Race*, 1 (Winter 1935–6): 1–10.
Fredrickson, George M. *The Black Image in the White Mind: The Debate on Afro-American Character and Destiny, 1817–1914*. Middletown, CT: Wesleyan University Press, 1987.
– *Racism: A Short History*. Princeton, NJ, and Oxford: Princeton University Press, 2002.
Fried, Richard M. *Nightmare in Red: The McCarthy Era in Perspective*. New York: Oxford University Press, 1990.
Gabbidon, Shaun L. 1999. 'W.E.B. Du Bois and the "Atlanta School" of Social Scientific Research, 1897–1913.' *Journal of Criminal Justice Education* 10, no. 1 (March): 21–38.
Gaines, Kevin K. *Uplifting the Race: Black Leadership, Politics, and Culture in the Twentieth Century*. Chapel Hill: University of North Carolina Press, 1996.
Garner, James W. 'Discussion of the Paper by Alfred H. Stone, "Is Race Friction Between Blacks and Whites in the United States Growing and Inevitable?"' *American Journal of Sociology* 13, no. 6 (May 1908): 825–8.
Gates, Henry Louis, Jr. Introduction to W.E.B. Du Bois, *The Souls of Black Folk*, vii–xxix. New York: Bantam Classic, 1989.
Gates, Henry Louis, Jr, and Cornel West. *The Future of the Race*. New York: Vintage Books, 1996.

Gates, Henry Louis, Jr, and Kwame Anthony Appiah, eds. *Richard Wright: Critical Perspectives Past and Present*. New York: Amistad, 1993.

Gerstle, Gary. *American Crucible: Race and Nation in the Twentieth Century*. Princeton, NJ: Princeton University Press, 2001.

Giddings, Franklin H. *The Elements of Sociology*. New York: Macmillan, c1898.

– *The Principles of Sociology: An Analysis of the Phenomena of Association and of Social Organization*. New York: Macmillan, 1896.

Gilbert, Dennis, and Joseph Kahl. *The American Class Structure: A New Synthesis*. Belmont, CA: Wadsworth, 1993.

Gitlin, Todd. *The Twilight of Common Dreams*. New York: Holt, 1995.

Gordon, Lewis R. *Bad Faith and Antiblack Racism*. Atlantic Highlands, NJ: Humanities Press, 1995.

Gordon, Milton M. *Assimilation in American Life: The Role of Race, Religion, and National Origins*. New York: Oxford University Press, 1964.

Gosset, Thomas F. *Race: The History of an Idea in America*. New York: Schocken, 1963.

Gottlieb, Robert, ed. *Reading Jazz: A Gathering of Autobiography, Reportage and Criticism from 1919 to Now*. New York: Pantheon Books, 1996.

Green, Dan S., and Edwin D. Driver. 'W.E.B. Du Bois: A Case Study in the Sociology of Sociological Negation.' *Phylon* 37, no. 4 (1976): 308–33.

Hacker, Andrew. *Two Nations: Black and White, Separate, Hostile, Unequal*. Expanded and updated ed. New York: Ballantine Books, 1995.

Hagstrom, Warren O. *The Scientific Community*. New York: Basic Books, 1965.

Hall, Robert L. 'E. Franklin Frazier and the Chicago School of Sociology: A Study in the Sociology of Knowledge.' In James E. Teele, ed., *E. Franklin Frazier and* Black Bourgeoisie, 47–67.

Haller, John S. *Outcasts from Evolution: Scientific Attitudes of Racial Inferiority, 1859–1900*. Urbana: University of Illinois Press, 1971.

Hare, Nathan. *The Black Anglo-Saxons*. New York: Collier Books, 1970.

Harlan, Louis. *Booker T. Washington: The Wizard of Tuskegee, 1901–1915*. New York: Oxford University Press, 1983.

Haskell, Thomas L. *The Emergence of Professional Social Science: The American Social Science Association and the Nineteenth-Century Crisis of Authority*. Urbana: University of Illinois Press, 1977.

Hayes, Edward C. 'Some Social Relations Restated.' *American Journal of Sociology* 31, no. 3 (Nov. 25): 333–46.

Haynes, George E. *The Negro at Work in New York City: A Study in Economic Progress*. New York: Longmans, Green and Co., 1912.

Herskovits, Melville. *The Myth of the Negro Past*. Boston: Beacon Press, 1927.

Hill, Herbert, ed. *Soon One Morning: New Writings by American Negroes, 1940–1962.* New York: Knopf, 1963.

Hinkle, Roscoe C. *Developments in American Sociological Theory, 1915–1950.* Albany: State University of New York Press, 1994.

– *Founding Theory of American Sociology, 1881–1915.* Boston: Routledge and Kegan Paul, 1980.

Hofstadter, Richard. *Social Darwinism in American Thought.* Boston: Beacon Press, 1944.

Holt, Thomas C. 'W.E.B. Du Bois's Archaeology of Race.' In Michael B. Katz and Thomas J. Sugrue, eds, *W.E.B. Du Bois, Race, and the City,* 61–76.

Holzner, Burkart. *Reality Construction in Society.* Cambridge: Schenkman, 1968.

Horkheimer, Max. 'Traditional and Critical Theory.' In Max Horkheimer, *Critical Theory: Selected Essays,* 244–52. Trans. Matthew J. O'Connell et al. New York: Herder and Herder [1972].

House, Floyd N. 'Social Relations and Social Interaction.' *American Journal of Sociology* 31, no. 5 (Mar. 1926): 617–33.

Hughes, Everett C. *French Canada in Transition.* Chicago: University of Chicago Press; Toronto: Gage, c1943.

– 'Race Relations and the Sociological Imagination.' *American Sociological Review* 28, no. 6 (December 1963): 879–90.

Hughes, Everett C., and Helen MacGill Hughes. *Where Peoples Meet: Racial and Ethnic Frontiers.* Glencoe, IL: The Free Press, 1952.

Hughes, Henry. *Treatise on Sociology, Theoretical and Practical.* Philadelphia: Lippincott, 1854.

Hunter, Guy, ed. *Industrialisation and Race Relations: A Symposium.* London: Oxford University Press, 1965.

Hunter, Herbert. M., ed. *The Sociology of Oliver C. Cox: New Perspectives.* Stamford, CT: JAI Press, 2000.

Hunter, Herbert M., and Sameer Y. Abraham, eds. *Race, Class, and the World System: The Sociology of Oliver C. Cox.* New York: Monthly Review Press, 1987.

Jackson, Walter A. *Gunnar Myrdal and America's Conscience: Social Engineering and Racial Liberalism, 1938–1987.* Chapel Hill: University of North Carolina Press, 1990.

Johnson, Charles S. *Bitter Canaan: The Story of the Negro Republic.* New Brunswick, NJ, and Oxford: Transaction Books, 1987.

– *Education and the Cultural Crisis.* New York: Macmillan, 1951.

– *Growing Up in the Black Belt: Negro Youth in the Rural South.* New York: Schocken Books, 1941.

– *Into the Main Stream: A Survey of Best Practices in Race Relations in the South.* Chapel Hill: University of North Carolina Press, 1947.

– *Patterns of Negro Segregation.* New York: Harper, 1943.

– *Shadow of the Plantation.* Chicago: University of Chicago Press, 1934.

– *To Stem This Tide: A Survey of Racial Tension Areas in the United States.* Boston and Chicago: Pilgrim Press, 1943.

Johnson, Charles S., Edwin Embree, and Will Alexander. *The Collapse of Cotton Tenancy.* Chapel Hill: University of North Carolina Press, 1935.

Johnson, Charles S., et al. *The Negro in American Civilization: A Study of Negro Life and Race Relations in the Light of Social Research.* New York: Holt, 1930.

Jones, LeRoi. *Blues People: Negro Music in White America.* New York: W. Morrow, 1963.

Katz, Michael B., and Thomas J. Sugrue, eds. *W.E.B. Du Bois, Race, and the City:* The Philadelphia Negro *and Its Legacy.* Philadelphia: University of Pennsylvania Press, 1998.

Keen, Mike Forrest. *Stalking the Sociological Imagination: J. Edgar Hoover's FBI Surveillance of American Sociology.* Westport, CT: Greenwood Press, 1999.

Kelley, Robin. *Freedom Dreams: The Black Radical Imagination.* Boston: Beacon, 2002.

Kelsey, Carl. 'The Evolution of Negro Labor.' *Annals of the American Academy of Political and Social Science* 21 (January 1903): 56–75.

Kerbo, Harold R. *Social Stratification and Inequality: Class Conflict in Historical and Comparative Perspective.* New York: McGraw-Hill, 1991.

Kuhn, Thomas S. *The Essential Tension: Selected Studies in Scientific Tradition and Change.* Chicago: University of Chicago Press, 1977.

Ladner, Joyce A., ed. *The Death of White Sociology: Essays on Race and Culture.* Baltimore, MD: Black Classic Press, 1998.

Lakatos, Imre. 'Falsification and the Methodology of Scientific Research Programmes.' In Imre Lakatos and Allan Musgrave, eds, *Criticism and the Growth of Knowledge,* 91–195. Cambridge: Cambridge University Press, 1970.

Lal, Barbara B. 'Black and Blue in Chicago: Robert E. Park's Perspective on Race Relations in Urban America, 1914–44.' In Ken Plummer, ed., *The Chicago School: Critical Assessments,* vol. 3, *Substantive Concerns: Race, Crime and the City,* 231–51. London and New York: Routledge, 1997.

– *The Romance of Culture in an Urban Civilization: Robert E. Park on Race and Ethnic Relations in Cities.* London and New York: Routledge, 1990.

Landry, Bart. 'A Reinterpretation of the Writings of Frazier on the Black Middle Class.' *Social Problems* 26 (December 1978): 211–22.

Levine, Donald N. *Visions of the Sociological Tradition.* Chicago: University of Chicago Press, 1995.

Levine, Rhonda F., ed. *Enriching the Sociological Imagination: How Radical Sociology Changed the Discipline.* Leiden: Brill, 2004.

Lewis, David L. *W.E.B. Du Bois: Biography of a Race, 1868–1919.* New York: Holt, 1993.

– *W.E.B. Du Bois: The Fight for Equality and the American Century, 1919–1963.* New York: Holt, 2000.

– *When Harlem Was in Vogue.* New York: Oxford University Press, 1989.

Lewis, David L., ed. *The Portable Harlem Renaissance Reader.* New York: Penguin Books, 1994. See especially editor's introduction, xiii–xli.

Lewis, J. David, and Richard L. Smith. *American Sociology and Pragmatism: Mead, Chicago Sociology, and Symbolic Interaction.* Chicago: University of Chicago Press, 1980.

Lind, Andrew, ed. *Race Relations in World Perspective: Papers Read at the Conference on Race Relations in World Perspective, Honolulu, 1954.* Honolulu: University of Hawaii Press, 1955.

Lipset, Seymour Martin. *American Exceptionalism: A Double-Edged Sword.* New York: Norton, 1997.

Locke, Alain, ed. *The New Negro.* 1st Touchstone ed. New York: Simon and Schuster, 1997.

– *The New Negro.* Special issue of *Survey Graphic* 6, no. 6 (March 1925).

Logan, Rayford W., ed. *The New Negro: Thirty Years Afterward.* Washington, DC: Howard University Press, 1955.

Lyman, Stanford M. *The Black American in Sociological Thought.* New York: G.P. Putnam's Sons, 1972.

– *Color, Culture, Civilization: Race and Minority Issues in American Society.* Urbana and Chicago: University of Illinois Press, 1994.

– 'The Race Relations Cycle of Robert E. Park.' In Ken Plummer, ed., *The Chicago School: Critical Assessments,* vol. 3, *Substantive Concerns: Race, Crime and the City,* 221–30. London and New York: Routledge, 1997.

Lyman, Stanford M., ed. *Selected Writings of Henry Hughes: Antebellum Southerner, Slavocrat, Sociologist.* Jackson: University Press of Mississippi, 1985.

Lynd, Robert S. *Knowledge for What? The Place of Social Science in American Culture.* Princeton, NJ: Princeton University Press, 1939.

Lynd, Robert S., and Helen M. Lynd. *Middletown:* A *Study in Modern American Culture.* New York: Harcourt Brace, 1929.

– *Middletown in Transition: A Study in Cultural Conflicts.* New York: Harcourt Brace, 1937.

MacIver, Robert, ed. *Discrimination and the National Welfare.* New York: Harper, 1949.

– *The More Perfect Union: A Program for the Control of Inter-Group Discrimination in the United States.* New York: Macmillan, 1948.

Marable, Manning. 'Black Studies: Marxism and the Black Intellectual Tradition.' In Bertell Ollman and Edward Vernoff, eds, *The Left Academy: Marxist Scholarship on American Campuses*, vol. 3, 35–66. New York: Praeger Publishers, 1986.

– *The Great Wells of Democracy: The Meaning of Race in American Life*. New York: Basic Civitas Books, 2002.

– *Living Black History: How Reimagining the African-American Past Can Remake America's Racial Future*. New York: Basic Civitas, c2005.

– *Race, Reform and Rebellion: The Second Reconstruction in Black America, 1945–1982*. London: Macmillan Press, 1984.

– *W.E.B. Du Bois, Black Radical Democrat*. Boston: Twayne Publishers, 1986.

Marks, Jonathan. *Human Biodiversity: Genes, Race and History*. New York: Aldine de Gruyter, 1995.

Martin, Elmer P. 'The Sociology of Oliver C. Cox.' MA thesis, Atlanta University, 1971.

Masuoka, Jitsuichi, and Preston Valien, eds. *Race Relations, Problems and Theory: Essays in Honor of Robert E. Park*. Chapel Hill: University of North Carolina Press, 1961.

Matalon, Benjamin. *La construction de la science: De l'épistémologie à la sociologie de la connaissance scientifique*. Lausanne and Paris: Delachaux and Niestlé, 1996.

Mathews, Fred H. *Quest for an American Sociology: Robert E. Park and the Chicago School*. Montreal: McGill Queen's University Press, 1977.

McAuley, Christopher A. *The Mind of Oliver C. Cox*. Notre Dame, IN: University of Notre Dame Press, c2004.

McKee, James B. *Sociology and the Race Problem: The Failure of a Perspective*. Urbana: University of Illinois Press, c1993.

McNeil, Elaine O., and Horace R. Cayton. 'Research on the Urban Negro.' *American Journal of Sociology* 47, no. 2 (September 1941): 176–83.

Meier, August, and Elliott M. Rudwick. *From Plantation to Ghetto: An Interpretive History of American Negroes*. 3rd ed. New York: Hill and Wang, 1976.

Mélandri, Pierre. *Histoire des États-Unis depuis 1865*. Paris: Nathan, 1984.

Metzger, Walter P. *Academic Freedom in the Age of the University*. New York: Columbia University Press, 1969.

Miller, Zane L., and Patricia M. Melvin. *The Urbanization of Modern America: A Brief History*. 2nd ed. San Diego: Harcourt Brace Jovanovich, c1987.

Mohl, Raymond, ed. *The Making of Urban America*. Wilmington, DE: Scholarly Resources Inc., 1997.

Montagu, M.F. Ashley. *Man's Most Dangerous Myth: The Fallacy of Race*. New York: Columbia University Press, 1942.

Morgan, J. Graham. 'Contextual Factors in the Rise of Academic Sociology in the United States.' *Canadian Review of Sociology and Anthropology* 7, no. 3 (1970): 159–71.

Morris, Aldon D. 'Sociology of Race and W.E.B. Du Bois: The Path Not Taken.' In Craig Calhoun, ed., *Sociology in America: A History*, 503–34. Chicago: University of Chicago Press, 2007.

Mulkay, Michael. *Sociology of Science: A Sociological Pilgrimage*. Bloomington: Indiana University Press, 1991.

Myrdal, Gunnar, et al. *An American Dilemma: The Negro Problem and Modern Democracy*. New York and London: Harper, 1944.

Nairn, Allan. 'An Exclusive Report on the U.S. Role in El Salvador's Official Terror: Behind the Death Squads.' *The Progressive*, May 1984, 20–9.

Oberschall, Anthony. 'The Institutionalization of American Sociology.' In *The Establishment of Empirical Sociology: Studies in Continuity, Discontinuity and Institutionalization*. New York: Harper and Row, 1972.

Odum, Howard. *American Sociology: The Story of Sociology in the United States through 1950*. New York: Longmans, Green and Co., 1951.

– *Social and Mental Traits of the Negro*. New York: Columbia University Press, 1910.

Ogburn, William. *Social Change with Respect to Cultural and Original Nature*. New York: Huebsch, 1922.

Ovington, Mary. *Half a Man: The Status of the Negro in New York*. New York: Longmans, Green, and Co, 1911. Reprint, New York: Hill and Wang, 1969.

Park, Robert E. 'An Autobiographical Note.' Reprinted in Robert E. Park, *Race and Culture*, vii–viii.

– 'Assimilation, Social.' In Edwin R.A. Selignay and Alvin Johnson, eds, *Encyclopedia of the Social Sciences*, vol. 2, 281–3. New York: Macmillan, 1930.

– 'The Bases of Race Prejudice.' *Annals of the American Academy of Political and Social Science* 140 (November 1928): 11–20. Reprinted in Robert E. Park, *Race and Culture*, 230–43.

– 'Behind Our Masks.' *Survey Graphic* 56 (May 1926): 135–9. Reprinted in Robert E. Park, *Race and Culture*, 244–55.

– 'The City: Suggestions for the Investigation of Human Behavior in the Urban Environment.' *American Journal of Sociology* 20, no. 5 (March 1915): 577–612.

– 'The Concept of Social Distance.' *Journal of Applied Sociology* 8 (1924): 339–44. Reprinted in Robert E. Park, *Race and Culture*, 256–60.

– 'Education in Its Relation to the Conflict and Fusion of Cultures.' *Publications of the American Sociological Society* 13 (December 1918): 38–63. Reprinted in Robert E. Park, *Race and Culture*, 261–83.

– *Human Communities: The City and Human Ecology.* Vol. 2 of *The Collected Papers of Robert Ezra Park.* Glencoe, IL: The Free Press, c1952.
– 'Human Ecology.' *American Journal of Sociology* 42, no. 1 (1936): 1–15. Reprinted in Robert E. Park, *Human Communities: The City and Human Ecology,* 145–64.
– 'Human Migration and the Marginal Man.' *American Journal of Sociology* 33, no. 6 (May 1928): 881–93. Reprinted in Robert E. Park, *Race and Culture,* 345–56.
– 'Mentality of Racial Hybrids.' *American Journal of Sociology* 36, no. 4 (January 1931): 534–51. Reprinted in Robert E. Park, *Race and Culture,* 377–92.
– 'Modern Society.' *Biological Symposia* 8 (1942): 217–40. Reprinted in Robert E. Park, *Society: Collective Behavior, News and Opinion, Sociology and Modern Society,* 322–41.
– 'The Nature of Race Relations.' In Edgar T. Thompson, ed., *Race Relations and the Race Problem,* 3–45. Durham, NC: Duke University Press, 1939. Reprinted in Robert E. Park, *Race and Culture,* 81–116.
– 'Negro Home Life and Standards of Living.' *Annals of the American Academy of Political and Social Science* 49 (September 1913): 147–63.
– 'Negro Race Consciousness as Reflected in Race Literature.' *American Review* 1 (September-October 1923): 505–16. Reprinted in Robert E. Park, *Race and Culture,* 284–300.
– 'Our Racial Frontier on the Pacific.' *Survey Graphic* 56 (May 1926): 192–6. Reprinted in Robert E. Park, *Race and Culture,* 138–51.
– *Race and Culture.* Vol. 1 of *The Collected Papers of Robert Ezra Park.* Glencoe, IL: The Free Press, 1950.
– 'Race Ideologies.' In William Ogburn, ed., *American Society in Wartime,* 165–83. Chicago: University of Chicago Press, 1943. Reprinted in Robert E. Park, *Race and Culture,* 301–15.
– 'Race Prejudice and Japanese-American Relations.' Introduction to Jesse Steiner, *The Japanese Invasion.* Chicago: A.C. McClurg, 1917. Reprinted in Robert E. Park, *Race and Culture,* 223–9.
– 'The Race Relations Cycle in Hawaii.' In Robert E. Park, *Race and Culture,* 189–95.
– 'Racial Assimilation in Secondary Groups with Particular Reference to the Negro.' *Publications of the American Sociological Society* 8 (1913): 66–83. Reprinted in Robert E. Park, *Race and Culture,* 204–20.
– *Society: Collective Behavior, News and Opinion, Sociology and Modern Society.* Vol. 3 of *The Collected Papers of Robert Ezra Park.* Glencoe, IL: The Free Press, [1955].
– 'The Urban Community as a Spatial Pattern and a Moral Order.' *Publications*

of the American Sociological Society 20 (1925): 1–14. Reprinted in Robert E. Park, *Human Communities: The City and Human Ecology*, 165–77.

Park, Robert E., and Ernest W. Burgess. *Introduction to the Science of Sociology*. Chicago: University of Chicago Press, 1921.

Park, Robert E., and Ernest W. Burgess, eds. *The City*. Chicago: University of Chicago Press, 1925.

Parsons, Talcott. 'The Present Position and Prospects of Systematic Theory in Sociology.' In Georges Gurvitch and Wilbert Moore, eds, *Twentieth Century Sociology*, 42–69. New York: Philosophical Library, 1945.

– *The Structure of Social Action*. Glencoe, IL: The Free Press, 1937.

Patterson, Orlando. *Slavery and Social Death: A Comparative Study*. Cambridge, MA: Harvard University Press, 1982.

Pells, Richard. *Radical Visions and American Dreams: Culture and Social Thought in the Depression Years*. Middletown, CT: Wesleyan University Press, 1984.

Persons, Stow. 'E. Franklin Frazier.' In Ken Plummer, ed., *The Chicago School: Critical Assessments*, vol. 3, *Substantive Concerns: Race, Crime and the City*, 252–70. London and New York: Routledge, 1997.

– *Ethnic Studies at Chicago, 1905–45*. Urbana and Chicago: University of Illinois Press, 1987.

Phillips, Ulrich B. *American Negro Slavery*. 2nd paperback ed. Baton Rouge: Louisiana State University Press, 1968.

– 'The Decadence of the Plantation System.' *Annals of the American Academy of Political and Social Science* 35, no. 1 (January 1910): 37–41.

Platt, Anthony M. 'Between Scorn and Longing: Frazier's Black Bourgeoisie.' In James E. Teele, ed., *E. Franklin Frazier and* Black Bourgeoisie, 71–84.

– *E. Franklin Frazier Reconsidered*. New Brunswick, NJ, and London: Rutgers University Press, 1991.

Platt, Jennifer. 'Chicago Methods: Reputations and Realities.' In Luigi Tomasi, ed., *The Tradition of the Chicago School of Sociology*, 89–103.

Popper, Karl. *The Logic of Scientific Discovery*. Toronto: University of Toronto Press, 1959.

Rabaka, Reiland. *W.E.B. Du Bois and the Problems of the Twenty-first Century: An Essay on Africana Critical Theory*. Lanham, MD: Lexington Books, c2007.

Raushenbush, Winifred. *Robert E. Park: Biography of a Sociologist*. Durham, NC: Duke University Press, 1979.

Reed, John S. *One South: An Ethnic Approach to Regional Culture*. Baton Rouge: Louisiana State University Press, c1982.

Reilly, John M. 'Richard Wright and the Art of Non-Fiction: Stepping Out on the Stage of the World.' In Henry L. Gates, Jr, and Kwame A. Appiah, eds, *Richard Wright: Critical Perspectives Past and Present*, 409–23.

Residents of Hull-House. *Hull-House Maps and Papers: A Presentation of Nationalities and Wages in a Congested District of Chicago, Together with Comments and Essays on Problems Growing out of the Social Conditions.* New York: T.Y. Crowell and Company, [c1895].

Ricoeur, Paul. *Lectures on Ideology and Utopia.* Ed. George H. Taylor. New York: Columbia University Press, 1986.

– *Memory, History, Forgetting.* Trans. Kathleen Blamey and David Pellauer. Chicago: University of Chicago Press, 2004.

Robbins, Richard. 'Charles S. Johnson.' In James Blackwell and Morris Janowitz, eds, *Black Sociologists: Historical and Contemporary Perspectives*, 56–84.

– *Sidelines Activist: Charles S. Johnson and the Struggle for Civil Rights*. Jackson: University Press of Mississippi, 1996.

Robinson, Cedric J. *Black Marxism: The Making of the Black Radical Tradition*. Chapel Hill: University of North Carolina Press, 2000.

– *Black Movements in America*. New York and London: Routledge, 1997.

Rose, Arnold, ed. *Studies in Reduction of Prejudice.* New York: Harper, 1947.

Ross, Edward. *Foundations of Sociology.* New York: Macmillan, 1905.

– *Social Control: A Survey of the Foundations of Social Order.* New York: Macmillan, 1901.

Rudwick, Elliott M. 'Note on a Forgotten Black Sociologist: W.E.B. Du Bois and the Sociological Profession.' *American Sociologist* 4, no. 4 (November 1969): 303–6.

– 'W.E.B. Du Bois as Sociologist.' In James Blackwell and Morris Janowitz, eds, *Black Sociologists: Historical and Contemporary Perspectives*, 25–55.

Saint-Arnaud, Pierre. *Park, Dos Passos, metropolis: Regards croisés sur la modernité urbaine aux États-Unis.* [Sainte-Foy, QC]: Presses de l'Université Laval, 1997.

– 'Sur le concept de "classe sociale" dans la sociologie américaine des deux premières générations.' In Simon Langlois and Yves Martin, eds, *L'horizon de la culture: Hommage à Fernand Dumont*, 345–59. Sainte-Foy, QC: Presses de l'Université Laval, 1995.

– *William Graham Sumner et les débuts de la sociologie américaine*. Quebec: Presses de l'Université Laval, 1984.

Scheiber, Harry N., Harold G. Vatter, and Harold U. Faulkner. *American Economic History: A Comprehensive Revision of the Earlier Work by Harold Underwood Faulkner.* [9th ed.] New York: Harper and Row, c1976.

Schor, Edith. *Visible Ellison: A Study of Ralph Ellison's Fiction*. Westport, CT: Greenwood Press, 1993.

Schrecker, Ellen. *Many Are the Crimes: McCarthyism in America*. Princeton, NJ: Princeton University Press, 1998.

– *No Ivory Tower: McCarthyism and the Universities.* New York: Oxford University Press, 1986.

Schwendinger, Hermann, and Julia R. Schwendinger. *The Sociologists of the Chair: A Radical Analysis of the Formative Years of North American Sociology, 1883–1922.* New York: Basic Books, 1974.

Seidman, Steven. *Contested Knowledge: Social Theory in the Postmodern Era.* 2nd ed. Malden, MA, and Oxford: Blackwell, 1998.

Shapin, Steven. *The Scientific Revolution.* Chicago: University of Chicago Press, 1996.

Shils, Edward. *The Calling of Sociology and Other Essays on the Pursuit of Learning.* Chicago: University of Chicago Press, 1980.

– *Center and Periphery: Essays in Macrosociology.* Chicago: University of Chicago Press, 1975.

– 'Color, the Universal Intellectual Community, and the Afro-Asian Intellectual.' *Daedalus* 96, no. 2 (Spring 1967): 279–95.

– *The Order of Learning: Essays on the Contemporary University.* Ed. Philip G. Altbach. New Brunswick, NJ: Transaction Publishers, c1997.

– 'Tradition, Ecology and Institution in the History of Sociology.' *Daedalus* 99, no. 4 (1970): 760–825. Reprinted in Edward Shils, *The Constitution of Society,* 275–383. Chicago: University of Chicago Press, 1982.

Simpson, George E., and J. Milton Yinger. *Racial and Cultural Minorities: An Analysis of Prejudice and Discrimination.* New York: Harper, 1954.

Small, Albion. 'Fifty Years of Sociology in the United States.' *American Journal of Sociology* 21 (May 1916): 721–864.

– *General Sociology: An Exposition of the Main Development in Sociological Theory from Spencer to Ratzenhofer.* Chicago: University of Chicago Press, 1905.

– *Seminar Notes: The Methodology of the Social Problem.* Chicago: University of Chicago Press, 1898.

Smedley, Audrey. *Race in North America: Origin and Evolution of a Worldview.* Boulder, CO: Westview Press, 1999.

Sombart, Werner. *Socialism and the Social Movement in the Nineteenth Century.* Trans. Anson P. Atterbury. New York: G.P. Putnam's Sons, 1898.

Sorokin, Pitirim A. *Contemporary Sociological Theories.* New York and London: Harper, 1928.

– *Social and Cultural Dynamics.* 4 vols. Boston: American Book Co., 1937–41.

Southern, David W. *Gunnar Myrdal and Black-White Relations: The Use and Abuse of* An American Dilemma, *1944–1969.* Baton Rouge: Louisiana State University Press, 1987.

Springer, Robert. *Fonctions sociales du blues.* Marseille: Éditions Parenthèses, 1999.

Stanfield, John H. 'The "Negro Problem" within and beyond the Institutional Nexus of Pre-World War I Sociology.' *Phylon* 43, no. 3 (Fall 1982): 187–201.

Staples, Robert. 'What Is Black Sociology? Toward a Sociology of Black Liberation.' In Joyce A. Ladner, ed., *The Death of White Sociology: Essays on Race and Culture,* 161–72.

Stepan, Nancy L., and Sander L. Gilman. 'Appropriating the Idioms of Science: The Rejection of Scientific Racism.' In Dominick La Capra, ed., *The Bounds of Race: Perspectives on Hegemony and Resistance,* 72–103. Ithaca, NY: Cornell University Press, 1991.

Stone, Alfred H. 'Is Race Friction between Blacks and Whites in the United States Growing and Inevitable?' *American Journal of Sociology* 13, no. 5 (March 1908): 676–9.

Stone, John, and Dennis Rutledge, eds. *Race and Ethnicity: Comparative and Theoretical Approaches.* Malden, MA: Blackwell, 2003.

Strasser, Hermann. *The Normative Structure of Sociology: Conservative and Emancipatory Themes in Social Thought.* London: Routledge and Kegan Paul, 1976.

Sumner, William Graham. *Folkways: A Study of the Sociological Importance of Usages, Manners, Customs, Mores and Morals.* Boston: Ginn and Co., 1906.

Taylor, Charles. *Multiculturalism and the Politics of Recognition.* Ed. Amy Gutmann. Princeton, NJ: Princeton University Press, 1992.

Teele, James E., ed. *E. Franklin Frazier and* Black Bourgeoisie. Columbia, MO, and London: University of Missouri Press, 2002.

Thomas, William I. 'The Mind of Woman and the Lower Races.' *American Journal of Sociology* 12, no. 4 (January 1907): 435–69.

– 'The Psychology of Race Prejudice.' *American Journal of Sociology* 9, no. 5 (March 1904): 593–611.

– 'Race Psychology: Standpoint and Questionnaire, with Particular Reference to the Immigrant and the Negro.' *American Journal of Sociology* 17, no. 6 (May 1912): 725–75.

Thomas, William I., and Florian Znaniecki. *The Polish Peasant in Europe and America.* Chicago: University of Chicago Press, 1918.

Thomas, William I., Herbert A. Miller, and Robert E. Park. *Old World Traits Transplanted.* Montclair, NJ: Patterson Smith, 1971 [c1921].

Tillinghast, Joseph. *The Negro in Africa and America.* New York: Macmillan, 1902.

Tiryakian, Edward. 'The Significance of Schools in the Development of Sociology.' In William E. Snizek, Ellsworth R. Fuhrman, and Robert K. Miller, eds, *Contemporary Issues in Theory and Research: A Metasociological Perspective,* 211–33. Westport, CT: Greenwood Press, 1979.

Tolman, Frank L. 'The Study of Sociology in Institutions of Learning in the

United States, Part II.' *American Journal of Sociology* 8, no. 1 (July 1902): 85–121.

Tomasi, Luigi, ed. *The Tradition of the Chicago School of Sociology.* Aldershot, Hants, and Brookfield, VT: Ashgate, 1998.

Touraine, Alain. *Université et société aux États-Unis.* Paris: Seuil, 1972.

Turner, Stephen P., and Jonathan H. Turner. *The Impossible Science: An Institutional Analysis of American Sociology.* Newbury Park, CA: Sage Publications, c1990.

United States. Bureau of the Census. *Negro Population in the United States, 1790–1915.* New York: Arno Press, 1968.

United States. Bureau of the Census. *Historical Statistics of the United States, Colonial Times to 1970.* 2 vols. White Plains, NY: Kraus International Publications, c1989.

Van Deburg, William L., ed. *Modern Black Nationalism: From Marcus Garvey to Louis Farrakhan.* New York: New York University Press, 1997.

Van den Berghe, Pierre. *Race and Racism.* New York: John Wiley, 1967.

Veysey, Laurence. *The Emergence of the American University, 1865–1910: A Study in Relations between Ideals and Institutions.* Chicago: University of Chicago Press, 1965.

Vlasek, Dale R. 'E. Franklin Frazier and the Problem of Assimilation.' In Hamilton Cravens, ed., *Ideas in America's Cultures: From Republic to Mass Society,* 141–79. Iowa City: Iowa State University Press, 1982.

Wacker, R. Fred. *Ethnicity, Pluralism and Race: Race Relations Theory in America before Myrdal.* Westport, CT, and London: Greenwood Press, 1983.

– 'The Sociology of Race and Ethnicity in the Second Chicago School.' In Gary Alan Fine, ed., *A Second Chicago School? The Development of a Postwar American Sociology,* 136–63. Chicago: University of Chicago Press, 1995.

Wacquant, Loic J.D. 'De la "Terre Promise" au ghetto: La grande migration noire américaine, 1916–1930.' *Actes de la recherche en sciences sociales* 99 (September 1993): 43–51.

Wallerstein, Immanuel. 'Oliver C. Cox as World-Systems Analyst.' In Herbert P. Hunter, ed., *The Sociology of Oliver C. Cox: New Perspectives,* 173–83.

Walton, Gary M., and Ross M. Robertson. *History of the American Economy.* 5th ed. New York: Harcourt Brace Jovanovich, c1983.

Ward, Lester F. *Applied Sociology: A Treatise on the Conscious Improvement of Society by Society.* Boston: Ginn and Co, 1906.

– 'Evolution of Social Structures.' *American Journal of Sociology* 10, no. 5 (March 1905): 589–605.

– *Pure Sociology: A Treatise on the Origin and Spontaneous Development of Society.* New York: Macmillan Co., 1903.

Warner, W. Lloyd. 'American Caste and Class.' *American Journal of Sociology* 42, no. 2 (September 1936): 234–7.
– Methodological Note to J.G. St Clair Drake and Horace R. Cayton, *Black Metropolis, A Study of Negro Life in a Northern City*, 769–82.
Washington, Booker T. *Up from Slavery: An Autobiography*. New York: Doubleday, 1901.
Washington, Robert E., and Donald Cunnigen, eds. *Confronting the American Dilemma of Race: The Second Generation Black Sociologists*. Lanham, MD: University Press of America, 2002.
Weatherly, Ulysses G. 'Discussion of the Paper by Alfred H. Stone, "Is Race Friction between Blacks and Whites in the United States Growing and Inevitable?"' *American Journal of Sociology* 13, no. 6 (May 1908): 823–5.
Weber, Max. *Essais sur la théorie de la science*. Paris: Plon, [c1965].
Wieviorka, Michel. *The Arena of Racism*. Trans. Chris Turner. London: Thousand Oaks, 1995.
Willcox, Walter F. 'Discussion of the Paper by Alfred H. Stone, "Is Race Friction between Blacks and Whites in the United States Growing and Inevitable?"' *American Journal of Sociology* 13, no. 6 (May 1908): 820–3.
Willer, Judith. *The Social Determination of Knowledge*. Englewood Cliffs, NJ: Prentice-Hall, 1971.
Williams, Robin. *The Reduction of Intergroup Tensions: A Survey of Research on Problems of Ethnic, Racial, and Religious Group Relations*. Prepared under the direction of the Committee on Techniques for Reducing Group Hostility. New York: Social Science Research Council, 1947.
Williams, Vernon J. *From a Caste to a Minority: Changing Attitudes of American Sociologists toward Afro-Americans, 1896–1945*. New York: Greenwood Press, 1989.
– *Rethinking Race: Franz Boas and His Contemporaries*. Lexington: University Press of Kentucky, 1996.
Wilson, William J. *The Bridge over the Racial Divide: Rising Inequality and Coalition Politics*. Berkeley: University of California Press, 1999.
– *The Declining Significance of Race: Blacks and Changing American Institutions*. Chicago: University of Chicago Press, 1979.
– *Power, Racism and Privilege: Race Relations in Theoretical and Sociohistorical Perspectives*. New York: The Free Press, 1973.
Winant, Howard. 'The Dark Side of the Force: One Hundred Years of the Sociology of Race.' In Craig Calhoun, ed., *Sociology in America: A History*, 535–71. Chicago: University of Chicago Press, 2007.
Winston, Michael R. 'Through the Back Door: Academic Racism and the Negro Scholar in Historical Perspective.' *Daedalus* 100, no. 3 (Summer 1971): 678–94.

Wirth, Louis. 'The Problem of Minority Groups.' In Ralph Linton, ed., *The Science of Man in the World Crisis*, 347–72. New York: Columbia University Press, 1945.

Wolters, Raymond. *The New Negro on Campus: Black College Rebellion of the 1920s*. Princeton, NJ: Princeton University Press, 1975.

Wright II, Earl. 'Deferred Legacy! The Continued Marginalization of the Atlanta Sociological Laboratory.' *Sociology Compass* 2, no. 1 (January 2008): 195–207.

– 'Using the Master's Tools: The Atlanta Sociological Laboratory and American Sociology, 1896–1924.' *Sociological Spectrum* 22, no. 1 (January 2002): 15–39.

Wright, Richard. *Black Boy*. New York: Harper and Brothers, 1945.

– 'Blueprint for Negro Writing.' *New Challenge* 2 (Fall 1937): 53–65. Reprinted in Richard Wright, *The Richard Wright Reader*, ed. Ellen Wright and Michel Fabre, 36–49. New York: Da Capo Press, 1997.

– *The Long Dream*. New York: Doubleday, 1958.

– *Native Son*. New York: Harper and Brothers, 1940.

– *The Outsider*. New York: Harper and Row, 1953.

– *Twelve Million Black Voices: A Folk History of the Negro in the U.S.* New York: Viking Press, 1941.

– *White Man Listen!* New York: Doubleday, 1957.

Wright, Thomas C. *Latin America in the Era of the Cuban Revolution*. Westport, CT, and London: Praeger, 2001.

Wright, William D. *Black Intellectuals, Black Cognition, and a Black Aesthetic*. Westport, CT: Praeger, 1997.

Young, James O. *Black Writers of the Thirties*. Baton Rouge: Louisiana State University Press, 1973.

Young, Lawrence A., and Lynn England. 'One Hundred Years of Methodological Research.' In Luigi Tomasi, ed., *The Tradition of the Chicago School of Sociology*, 129–46.

Zamir, Shamoon. *Dark Voices: W.E.B. Du Bois and American Thought, 1888–1903*. Chicago: University of Chicago Press, 1995.

Zangwill, Israel. *The Melting-Pot: [A] Drama in Four Acts*. New York: Arno Press, 1975, c1914.

Zinn, Howard. *A People's History of the United States*. New York: Harper Perennial, 1995.

Zuberi, Tukufu. *Thicker Than Blood: How Racial Statistics Lie*. Minneapolis: University of Minnesota Press, 2001.

Zuckerman, Phil, ed. *The Social Theory of W.E.B. Du Bois*. Thousand Oaks, CA: Pine Forge Press, c2004.

Index